Self-Efficacy

SELF-EFFICACY:
THOUGHT CONTROL
OF ACTION

Edited by

Ralf Schwarzer

Freie Universität Berlin

●HEMISPHERE PUBLISHING CORPORATION
A member of the Taylor & Francis Group

Washington   Philadelphia   London

SELF—EFFICACY: Thought Control of Action

1 2 3 4 5 6 7 8 9 0   B R B R   9 8 7 6 5 4 3 2

Cover design by Michelle Fleitz.
Cover design by Michelle Fleitz.
A CIP catalog record for this book is available from the British Library.

∞ The paper in this publication meets the requirements of the ANSI Standard Z39.48-1984 (Permanence of Paper)

Library of Congress Cataloging-in-Publication Data

Self-efficacy : thought control of action / edited by Ralf Schwarzer.
    p. cm.
   Includes bibliographical references and indexes.

   1. Control (Psychology) 2. Self-perception. 3. Action theory.
4. Medicine and psychology. I. Schwarzer, Ralf.
   [DNLM: 1. Adaptation, Psychological. 2. Internal-External Control. 3. Self Concept. BF 697 S4653]
BF611.S43   1992
153.8—dc20
DNLM/DLC
for Library of Congress   92-1465
ISBN 1-56032-269-1   CIP

CONTENTS

CONTRIBUTORS

Albert Bandura, Department of Psychology, Stanford University, Building 420, Jordan Hall, Stanford, CA 94305, USA

Jochen Brandtstädter, Fachbereich I—Psychologie, Universität Trier, Postfach 3825, W-5500 Trier, Germany

Martin V. Covington, Psychology Department, University of California at Berkeley, 3210 Tolman Hall, Berkeley, CA 94720, USA

Dirk-Jan Den Boer, Rijksuniversiteit Limburg, Department of Health Education, P.O. Box 616, 6200 MD Maastricht, The Netherlands

Hein De Vries, Rijksuniversiteit Limburg, Department of Health Education, P.O. Box 616, 6200 MD Maastricht, The Netherlands

Christine Dunkel-Schetter, Department of Psychology, University of California at Los Angeles, Los Angeles, CA 90024-1563, USA

Craig K. Ewart, The Johns Hopkins University, Department of Behavioral Sciences & Health Education, School of Hygiene and Public Health, 624 N. Broadway, Baltimore, MD 21205, USA

Frans Gerards, Rijksuniversiteit Limburg, Department of Health Education, P.O. Box 616, 6200 MD Maastricht, The Netherlands

Jutta Heckhausen, Max-Planck-Institut für Bildungsforschung, Lentzeallee 94, W-1000 Berlin 33, Germany

Halsted R. Holman, Stanford University Medical Center, Division of Immunology and Rheumatology, 1000 Welch Road, Suite 203, Palo Alto, CA 94304, USA

Harm J. Hospers, Rijksuniversiteit Limburg, Department of Health Education, P.O. Box 616, 6200 MD Maastricht, The Netherlands

Matthias Jerusalem, Institut für Psychologie (WE 7), Freie Universität Berlin, Habelschwerdter Allee 45, W-1000 Berlin 33, Germany

Robert M. Kaplan, Department of Community and Family Medicine, School of Medicine, University of California at San Diego, 9500 Gilman Drive, La Jolla, CA 92093-0622, USA

David Kavanagh, Department of Psychology, University of Sydney, Sydney, NSW 2006, Australia

Gerjo Kok, Rijksuniversiteit Limburg, Department of Health Education, P.O. Box 616, 6200 MD Maastricht, The Netherlands

Kate Lorig, Department of Medicine, Stanford University, 1000 Welch Road, Suite 320, Palo Alto, CA 94304-1808, USA

William J. McCarthy, Department of Cancer Control, 1100 Glendon Avenue, Suite 711, Los Angeles, CA 90024-1563, USA

Aart N. Mudde, Rijksuniversiteit Limburg, Department of Health Education, P.O. Box 616, 6200 MD Maastricht, The Netherlands

Michael D. Newcomb, Division of Counseling and Educational Psychology, WPH 500, University of Southern California, Los Angeles, CA 90089-0031, USA

Carol L. Omelich, Psychology Department, University of California at Berkeley, 3210 Tolman Hall, Berkeley, CA 94720, USA

Andrew L. Ries, Department of Community and Family Medicine, School of Medicine, University of California at San Diego, La Jolla, CA 92093-0622, USA

Ralf Schwarzer, Institut für Psychologie (WE 7), Freie Universität Berlin, Habelschwerdter Allee 45, W-1000 Berlin 33, Germany

Ellen Skinner, Graduate School of Education and Human Development, University of Rochester, Rochester, NY 14627, USA

Michelle Toshima, Department of Rehabilitation Medicine, School of Medicine, University of Washington, Seattle, WA 98109, USA

Bernard Weiner, Department of Psychology, University of California at Los Angeles, Los Angeles, CA 90024-1563, USA

S. Lloyd Williams, Department of Psychology, Lehigh University, Chandler-Ullmann Hall #17, Bethlehem, PA 18015, USA

Grace Woo, Department of Psychology, University of California at Los Angeles, Los Angeles, CA 90024-1563, USA

PREFACE

Human functioning is facilitated by a personal sense of control. If people believe that they can take action to solve a problem instrumentally, they become more inclined to do so and feel more committed to this decision.

While outcome expectancies refer to the perception of the possible consequences of one's action, self-efficacy expectancies refer to personal action control or agency. A person who believes in being able to cause an event can conduct a more active and self-determined life course. This "can do"-cognition mirrors a sense of control over one's environment. It reflects the belief of being able to control challenging environmental demands by means of taking adaptive action. It can be regarded as a self-confident view of one's capability to deal with certain life stressors.

Self-efficacy makes a difference in how people feel, think and act. In terms of feeling, a low sense of self-efficacy is associated with depression, anxiety, and helplessness. Such individuals also have low self-esteem and harbor pessimistic thoughts about their accomplishments and personal development. In terms of thinking, a strong sense of competence facilitates cognitive processes and academic performance. When it comes to preparing action, self-related cognitions are a major ingredient of the motivation process. Self-efficacy levels can enhance or impede motivation. People with high self-efficacy choose to perform more challenging tasks. They set themselves higher goals and stick to them. Actions are preshaped in thought, and people anticipate either optimistic or pessimistic scenarios in line with their level of self-efficacy. Once an action has been taken, high self-efficacious persons invest more effort and persist longer than those low in self-efficacy. When setbacks occur, they recover more quickly and maintain the commitment to their goals. Self-efficacy also allows people to select challenging settings, explore their environments, or create new environments.

Self-efficacy is considered to be specific, that is, one can have more or less firm beliefs in different domains of functioning. A sense of competence can be acquired by mastery experience, vicarious experience, verbal persuasion, or physiological feedback. Self-efficacy, however, is not the same as positive illusions or unrealistic optimism. Since it is based on experience and does not lead to unreasonable risk taking. Instead, it leads to venturesome behavior that is within reach of one's capabilities.

Self-referent thought has become an issue that pervades psychological research in many domains. It has been found that a strong sense of personal efficacy is related to better health, higher achievement, and better social integration. This concept has been applied to such diverse areas as school achievement, emotional disorders, mental and physical health, career choice, and sociopolitical change. It has become a key variable in clinical, educational, social, developmental, health, and personality psychology.

The present volume, organized in five sections, covers a broad range of studies that deal with self-efficacy. The first section refers to self-efficacy and human functioning.

In his introductory chapter, Albert Bandura outlines the role of self-efficacy as part of his Social Cognitive Theory. Self-efficacy does not simply reflect the perception of accomplishments; instead, it is based on subjective inferences from different sources of information. Perceived self-efficacy has been shown to exert an effect on performance, independent of actual ability levels. For example, self-beliefs that were induced experimentally led to subsequent behavioral change. A sense of efficacy is considered to influence different processes of human functioning: cognitive processes, motivation, affect, and selection of environments.

William McCarthy and Michael Newcomb focus their chapter on the distinction of perceived self-efficacy either in terms of thought control or in terms of actual performance. This parallels the common distinction between cognitive coping ability and behavioral coping ability. In some situations, people may feel competent to regulate themselves by reappraising the demands or by controlling their emotions, whereas in other situations they may feel competent to change the stressful encounters instrumentally. The authors studied the perceptions of a large sample of young adults and found that issues such as purpose in life or loss of control were only related to the cognitive control dimension, whereas social stress issues such as assertiveness, leadership, and dating were only related to the behavioral control dimension. These results may stimulate further research on one's beliefs about self-regulation in cases where no explicit action is desired.

Social support has been found to buffer stress under certain circumstances. Ralf Schwarzer, Christine Dunkel-Schetter, Bernard Weiner, and Grace Woo have experimentally investigated conditions under which social support is extended. Victims who suffer from uncontrollable life events and invest high coping efforts are more likely to receive support, in contrast to those who experience controllable events and do not cope well. Outcome expectancies and self-efficacy expectancies emerged as mediators in the cognition—emotion—behavior process. If the victim's condition was judged as changeable, and if the provider felt competent to extend support, then the intent to help was most likely. This research points to the possibility that people often do not behave in a supportive way because they believe they are not capable of taking appropriate action.

The following three chapters add a developmental perspective in the second section. Ellen Skinner reviews research on competence motivation and perceived control in children and establishes a connection to the self-efficacy construct. Self-efficacy expectancies are labeled "capacity beliefs" in her theoretical model, as opposed to "strategy beliefs" or outcome expectancies, which are perceptions of the behavioral causes of success or failure. Human beings are supposed to strive for mastery and control over their environments and to attempt to generate desired events. A need for competence, that may be innate and pervasive, motivates behavior across the life span. Loss of perceived control can lead to coping deficits and helplessness, particularly if this is due to self-efficacy impairment.

However, this is not so much the case if it is due to the interference of powerful others.

Jutta Heckhausen explores the psychological mechanisms that alter and maintain self-efficacy, particularly the role of information from social comparison processes. Self-efficacy expectancies have to be realistic in order to translate into successful actions and to avoid high risk-taking. On the other hand, positive illusions set the stage for venturesome behavior and for an optimistic approach toward life's challenges. The self-serving bias in beliefs about one's capabilities and coping skills conveys motivational benefits but can be counterproductive when the appropriate action either fails or is not available. Strategic social comparison can balance these conflicting demands. Age groups provide a frame of reference for such comparisons. Goals that are congruent with those of one's reference group can be seen as realistic, whereas those that transcend this norm can be considered as self-enhancing.

Jochen Brandtstädter states that individuals contribute actively to shaping their personal development and circumstances of living. This chapter focusses on developmental implications of self-efficacy by using a large cohort study to examine perceived control and coping preferences across the life-span. Specifically, Brandtstädter studies how people deal with their perceived gains and losses over the life span and how these are actively constructed. Personal self-regulation changes with increasing age, reflected by a decline in tenacious goal pursuit and an increase in flexible adjustment of developmental goals. This is in line with a shift from a more instrumental or active-assimilative coping mode to a more accomodative mode of coping.

Self-efficacy expectancy is inversely related to anxiety and depression and can represent a powerful stress resource factor. This resource factor also allows one to deal better with uncertainty, distress, and conflict. The third section of this volume gathers articles that deal with stress and emotions and the way self-efficacy interacts with them. S. Lloyd Williams reviews the literature on self-beliefs as causal factors in phobia and finds that self-efficacy judgments are the best predictors of therapeutic change. No other available theory provides such strong evidence. He presents empirical research on severely phobic patients who underwent psychological treatment. Those who were trained to master threatening situations and, by this, to build up a sense of competence, were more successful than those exposed to other psychotherapeutic procedures.

David Kavanagh extends the scope of self-efficacy theory to the development of depression and explores the predictive and causal influence that self-beliefs have on the occurrence of depressive episodes. There appears to be a reciprocal relationship between emotions and self-related cognitions. Depressive mood is triggered by cognitions; emotions represent one source of information, among others, to shape self-efficacy. On the other hand, low self-efficacy deepens sadness and increases vulnerability toward depressive episodes. This issue has been examined by manipulating emotions experimentally. People in an induced sad mood were reporting lower self-efficacy than those in a happy mood. In addition, performance is related to both emotions and self-related cognitions. All three constructs exert a direct effect on each other but also serve as mediators between one another.

Matthias Jerusalem and Ralf Schwarzer attempt to integrate transactional stress theory with social cognitive theory. They regard generalized self-efficacy as one of the personal resource factors that counterbalance taxing environmental demands in the stress appraisal process. Stress can be cognitively appraised as either a challenge, threat, or harm/loss. In a laboratory experiment, subjects who were confronted with difficult tasks under time pressure received fictitious performance feedback. Those with high trait self-efficacy made more favorable interpretations of the stressors compared to their low self-efficacy counterparts. The authors conclude that dispositional self-efficacy not only facilitates coping with stress but is already operating at an earlier phase of the stress process, namely at the cognitive appraisal stage.

The fourth section relates self-beliefs to health behaviors. The intention to adopt a specific health behavior such as exercise, dieting, or condom use depends on, among other things, the perception of one's ability to acquire the necessary skills to change one's habits. Ralf Schwarzer discusses health behavior theories that explain and predict behavior change and maintenance. In recent years, the major theories have been revised by including a self-efficacy factor in the set of predictor variables because, in many studies, self-efficacy has emerged as the single best determinant for adopting precaution strategies, abandoning detrimental health habits, and preventing relapse. It is not yet clear, however, how this dimension interacts with perceived risks, outcome expectancies, previous experience, situational constraints, and other interfering variables. A new model is presented that may stimulate further inquiry.

Gerjo Kok and his co-workers provide a good example of advanced research in this field. They studied people's attitudes, perceived social norms, and self-efficacy toward risk behaviors. They also measured the intention to abstain from these risk behaviors in the future. It turned out that all three factors predicted intentions, and that the model would be much less powerful without the self-efficacy factor. In addition, self-efficacy succeeded in directly influencing actual behavior. This suggests that low self-efficacy should be conceived as a personal barrier to the process of adopting appropriate health behaviors. If the individual has good intentions but feels incompetent to perform the desired action, health promotion efforts should aim at skill improvement and guided mastery experience to boost a sense of self-efficacy.

Martin Covington and Carol Omelich have studied the relationship between the temptation to smoke and the intention to smoke in several thousand high-school students. They looked at potential mediators that might influence this relationship. Although a strong direct effect of temptations on intentions emerged, there were also a number of mediating effects by outcome expectancies and self-efficacy expectancies. The outcome expectancies were differentiated into affective consequences and needs consequences, while self-efficacy expectancies were distinguished as decision-making strategies, interpersonal strategies, and self-peer strategies. These cognitions altered the levels of temptation for the students. Smoking decisions in teenagers, therefore, may be seen as dependent on their perceived problem-solving capabilities.

The last section deals with applications of self-efficacy theory to physical symptoms, coping with illness, and rehabilitation of chronic disease. It is assumed that self-related cognitions exert an effect on illness controllability and on biological systems that mediate health and illness. The first three chapters of this section focus on psychological mechanisms in rehabilitation of coronary heart disease, arthritis, and pulmonary disease.

Craig Ewart investigates the role of self-appraisals in the rehabilitation of myocardial infarction patients. Convalescence can be prolonged far longer than desirable by unwarranted fears of a reinfarct when resuming one's normal activities. An improvement of self-efficacy accelerates progress in exercise and enhances mood and well-being. Self-efficacy responses to treadmill exercise testing predict activity levels better than medical data. Pretraining self-efficacy levels predict posttraining gains in terms of perseverance in demanding exercise regimens. It is also of interest that spouses tend to overprotect the patients, but spouse participation in exercise programs leads to more realistic assessments of the patients' capabilities.

Halsted Holman and Kate Lorig have launched an arthritis self-management program to teach patients how to cope with the consequences of their chronic disease. They found that patients' perceived self-efficacy to cope with their ailment was mediating the outcomes of this program. This was particularly true for pain and depression. The more self-efficacious the patients had become during the training, the better they were able to tolerate pain and the less depression was reported. Beneficial effects were maintained even at a four-year follow-up.

Michelle Toshima, Robert Kaplan and Andrew Ries apply self-efficacy theory to the rehabilitation of chronic obstructive pulmonary disease and examine changes in self-appraisals from different sources such as mastery experience and physiological feedback. The patients reported their self-efficacy expectancies while undergoing an exercise regimen. Physiological feedback from pulmonary tests and from treadmill endurance walk tests had a strong influence on self-efficacy, but mastery experience did not. It is argued that, under certain circumstances, information from one source can attenuate information from another. This may stimulate further research on the joint effects of multiple-source information on changes in self-beliefs.

In conclusion, Albert Bandura provides an overview of self-efficacy mechanisms in psychobiological functioning and points to empirical evidence for biochemical effects of self-efficacy in coping with stress, such as autonomous, catecholamine, and opioid activation. Research on pain control as well as on immunocompetence demonstrates that people with optimistic self-beliefs are better off and cope well. They are also at an advantage in the self-management of chronic disease and in the rehabilitation process. Self-efficacy improves changes in health behaviors and thus helps to minimize health risks.

The idea to publish this book this arose when the Freie Universität Berlin bestowed upon Albert Bandura an honary doctorate in 1990, at which time a scientific workshop was organized. The speakers agreed to write up their presentations, and these papers were supplemented by some invited chapters. I would like to thank the authors for their excellent contributions. The entire technical composition of this volume was skillfully accomplished by Mary Wegner. Her meticulous copy editing and proficient desktop publishing are gratefully acknowledged.

This book was compiled and edited while I was a visiting scholar at the University of California at Los Angeles. I appreciate the generous travel grant from the Volkswagen Foundation that has made my sojourn possible.

Los Angeles, September 1991   Ralf Schwarzer

I

SELF-EFFICACY AND HUMAN FUNCTIONING

EXERCISE OF PERSONAL AGENCY THROUGH THE SELF-EFFICACY MECHANISM

Albert Bandura

The present chapter analyzes the influential role of perceived self-efficacy in agent causality. The construction of a sense of personal efficacy involves a complex process of self-persuasion that relies on cognitive processing of diverse sources of efficacy information conveyed enactively, vicariously, socially, and physiologically. Convergent evidence from diverse lines of research reveals that self-beliefs of efficacy function as important proximal determinants of human motivation, affect, thought and action. Self-beliefs of efficacy exert their affects on human functioning through motivational, cognitive and affective intervening processes. Some of these processes, such as affective states and thinking patterns, are of considerable interest in their own right, as well as serve as intervening influencers of action. Self-efficacy beliefs also shape developmental trajectories by influencing choice of pursuits and selection of environments. Self-efficacy theory adopts a nondualistic but nonreductional conception of human agency that operates within a model of triadic reciprocal causation.

The recent years have witnessed a resurgence of interest in self-referent phenomena. One can point to several reasons why self processes have come to pervade the research in many areas of psychology. Self-generated activities lie at the very heart of causal processes. They not only give meaning and valence to most external influences, but they function as important proximal determinants of motivation and action. People make causal contributions to their own psychosocial functioning through mechanisms of personal agency. Among the mechanisms of agency, the most focal and pervading one involves people's beliefs about their capabilities to exercise control over events that affect their lives. Self-beliefs of efficacy influence how people feel, think, and act. This chapter analyzes the causal function of self-efficacy beliefs and the different psychological processes through which they exert their effects.

SELF-EFFICACY CAUSALITY

A central question in any theory of cognitive regulation of motivation, affect and action concerns the issue of causality. Do self-efficacy beliefs operate as causal factors in human functioning? This issue has been investigated by a variety of experimental strategies. Each approach tests the dual-causal link in which instating conditions affect efficacy beliefs, and efficacy beliefs, in turn, affect motivation and action. In one strategy, perceived self-efficacy is raised in phobics from virtually non-existent levels to preselected low, moderate, or high levels by providing them with mastery experiences or simply by modeling coping strategies for them until the desired level of efficacy was attained (Bandura, Reese, & Adams, 1982).

As shown in Figure 1, higher levels of perceived self-efficacy are accompanied by higher performance attainments. The efficacy-action relationship is replicated across different dysfunctions and in both intergroup and intrasubject comparisons, regardless of whether perceived self-efficacy was raised by mastery experiences or solely by vicarious influence. The vicarious mode of self-efficacy induction is especially well-suited for demonstrating the causal contribution of perceived self-efficacy to performance. Individuals simply observe models' performances without executing any actions, make inferences from the modeled information about their own coping efficacy, and later behave in accordance with their self-judged efficacy. Microanalysis of efficacy-action congruences reveals a close fit between perceived self-efficacy and performance on individual tasks.

Another approach to the test of causality is to control, by selection, level of ability but to vary perceived self-efficacy within each ability level. Collins (1982) selected children who judged themselves to be of high or low mathematical efficacy at each of three levels of mathematical ability. They were then given difficult problems to solve. Within each level of mathematical ability, children who regarded themselves as efficacious were quicker to discard faulty strategies, solved more problems (Figure 2), chose to rework more of those they failed, and did so more accurately than those of equal ability who doubted their efficacy. Perceived self-efficacy thus exerted a substantial independent effect on performance. Positive attitude toward mathematics was better predicted by perceived self-efficacy than by actual ability. As this study shows, people may perform poorly because they lack the ability, or they have the ability but they lack the perceived self-efficacy to make optimal use of their skills.

A third approach to causality is to introduce a trivial factor devoid of information to affect competency, but that can bias self-efficacy judgment. The impact of the altered perceived self-efficacy on level of motivation is then measured. Studies of anchoring influences show that arbitrary reference points from which judgments are adjusted either upward or downward can bias the judgments because the adjustments are usually insufficient. Cervone and Peake (1986) used arbitrary anchor values to influence self-appraisals of efficacy. Self-appraisals made from an arbitrary high starting point biased students' perceived self-efficacy in the positive direction, whereas an arbitrary low starting point lowered students' appraisals of their efficacy (Figure 3). The initial reference points in a sequence of performance descriptors similarly biased self-efficacy appraisal (Peake & Cervone, 1989). In a further study, Cervone (1989) biased self-efficacy appraisal

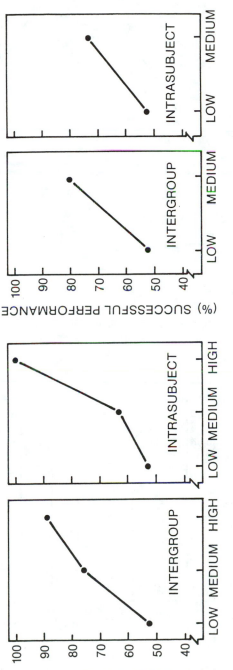

Figure 1 Mean performance attainments as a function of differential levels of perceived self-efficacy. The two left panels present the relationship for perceived self-efficacy raised by mastery experiences; the two right panels present the relationship for perceived self-efficacy raised by vicarious experiences. The intergroup panels show the performance attainments of groups of subjects whose self-percepts of efficacy were raised to different levels; the intrasubject panels show the performance attainments for the same subjects after their self-percepts of efficacy were successively raised to different levels (Bandura, Reese, & Adams, 1982).

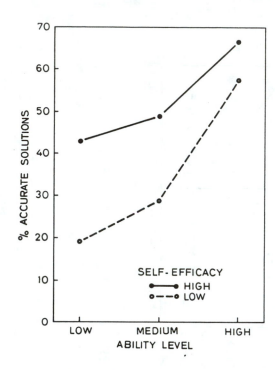

Figure 2 Mean levels of mathematical solutions achieved by students as a function of mathematical ability and perceived mathematical self-efficacy. Plotted from data of Collins, 1982.

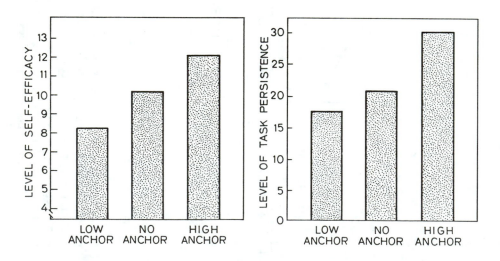

Figure 3 Mean changes induced in perceived self-efficacy by anchoring influences and the corresponding effects on level of subsequent perseverant effort (Cervone & Peake, 1986).

by differential cognitive focus on things about the task that might make it troublesome or tractable. Dwelling on formidable aspects weakened people's belief in their efficacy, but focusing on doable aspects raised self-judgment of capabilities. In all of these experiments, the higher the instated perceived self-efficacy, the longer individuals persevere on difficult and unsolvable problems before they quit. Mediational analyses reveal that neither anchoring influences nor cognitive focus has any effect on motivation when perceived self-efficacy is partialed out. The effect of the external influences on performance motivation is thus completely mediated by changes in perceived self-efficacy.

A number of experiments have been conducted in which self-efficacy beliefs are altered by bogus feedback unrelated to one's actual performance. People partly judge their capabilities through social comparison. Using this type of efficacy induction procedure, Weinberg, Gould, and Jackson (1979) showed that physical stamina in competitive situations is mediated by perceived self-efficacy. They raised the self-efficacy beliefs of one group by telling them that they had triumphed in a competition of muscular strength. They lowered the self-efficacy beliefs of another group by telling them that they were outperformed by their competitor. The higher the illusory beliefs of physical strength, the more physical endurance subjects displayed during competition on a new task measuring physical stamina (Figure 4). Failure in a subsequent competition spurred those with a high sense of self-efficacy to even greater physical effort, whereas failure further impaired the performance of those whose perceived self-efficacy had been undermined. Self-beliefs of physical efficacy illusorily heightened in females and illusorily weakened in males obliterated large preexisting sex differences in physical strength.

Another variant of social self-appraisal that has also been used to raise or weaken beliefs of self-efficacy relies on bogus normative comparison. Individuals are led to believe that they performed at the highest or lowest percentile ranks of the reference group, regardless of their actual performance (Jacobs, Prentice-Dunn, & Rogers, 1984). Perceived self-efficacy heightened by this means produced stronger perseverant effort (Figure 5). The regulatory role of self-belief of efficacy instated by unauthentic normative comparison is replicated in a markedly different domain of functioning, namely pain tolerance (Litt, 1988). Self-efficacy beliefs were altered by having individuals appear as strong or weak pain tolerators compared to the capabilities of an ostensibly normative group. The higher the instated belief in one's capabilities, the greater the pain tolerance.

Still another approach to the verification of causality employs a contravening experimental design in which a procedure that can impair functioning is applied, but in ways that raise perceived self-efficacy. The changes accompanying psychological ministrations may result as much, if not more, from instilling beliefs of personal efficacy as from the particular skills imparted. If people's beliefs in their coping efficacy are strengthened, they approach situations more assuredly and make better use of the skills they have. Holroyd and his colleagues (Holroyd

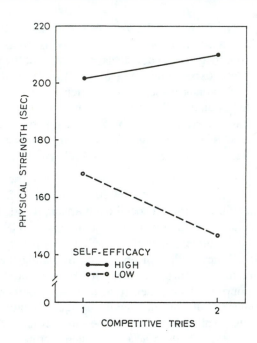

Figure 4 Mean level of physical stamina mobilized in competitive situations as a function of illusorily instated high or low self-percepts of physical efficacy (Weinberg, Gould, & Jackson, 1979).

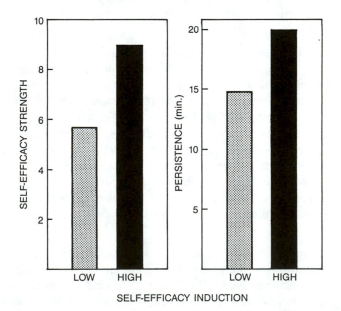

Figure 5 Mean changes in perceived self-efficacy induced by arbitrary normative comparison and the corresponding effects on level of subsequent perseverant effort (Jacobs, Prentice-Dunn, & Rogers, 1984).

et al., 1984), demonstrated with sufferers of tension headaches that the benefits of biofeedback training may stem more from enhancement of perceived coping efficacy than from the muscular exercises themselves. In biofeedback sessions, they trained one group to become good relaxers. Unbeknownst to another group, they received feedback signals that they were relaxing whenever they tensed their muscles. They became good tensers of facial muscles, which, if anything, would aggravate tension headaches. Regardless of whether people were tensing or relaxing their musculator, bogus feedback that they were exercising good control over muscular tension instilled a strong sense of efficacy that they could prevent the occurrence of headaches in different stressful situations. The higher their perceived self-efficacy, the fewer headaches they experienced. The actual amount of change in muscular activity achieved in treatment was unrelated to the incidence of subsequent headaches.

The findings of the preceding experiments should not be taken to mean that arbitrary persuasory information is a good way of enhancing self-efficacy beliefs for the pursuits of everyday life. Rather, these studies have special bearing on the issue of causality because self-efficacy beliefs are altered independently of a performance modality and, therefore, cannot be discounted as epiphenomenal byproducts of performance. They demonstrate that changes in self-beliefs of efficacy affect motivation and action. In actual social practice, personal empowerment through mastery experiences is the most powerful means of creating a strong, resilient sense of efficacy (Bandura, 1986, 1988). This is achieved by equipping people with knowledge, subskills and the strong self-belief of efficacy needed to use one's skills effectively.

The final way of verifying the causal contribution of self-efficacy beliefs to human functioning is to test the multivariate relations between relevant determinants and the predicted variable in the theoretical causal model by hierarchical regression analysis or path analysis. These analytic tools for theory testing indicate how much of the variation in the predicted variable is explained by perceived self-efficacy when the influence of other determinants is controlled.

The multivariate investigations involve panel designs in which self-efficacy and the predicted variable are measured on two or more occasions to determine what effect either factor may have on the other. In some of these studies, perceived self-efficacy is altered by naturally occurring influences during the intervening period. More often, self-efficacy beliefs are altered by experimentally varied influences. The temporal ordering and systematic variation of perceived self-efficacy antecedently to the predicted outcome helps to remove ambiguities about the source and direction of causality. In addition to systematic variation and temporal priority of the self-efficacy beliefs, controls are applied for potential confounding variables. The results of such studies reveal that self-efficacy beliefs usually make substantial contribution to variations in motivation and performance accomplishments (Bandura & Jourden, 1991; Dzewaltowski, 1989; Locke, Frederick, Lee, & Bobko, 1984; Ozer & Bandura, 1990; Wood & Bandura, 1989a). The causal contribution of self-efficacy beliefs to sociocognitive functioning is further documented in comparative tests of the predictive power of social cognitive theory and alternative conceptual models (Dzewaltowski, Noble, & Shaw, 1991; Lent, Brown, & Larkin, 1987; McCaul, O'Neill, & Glasgow, 1988; Siegel, Galassi, & Ware, 1985; Wheeler, 1983).

These diverse causal tests were conducted with different modes of efficacy induction, diverse populations, both interindividual and intraindividual verification, and all sorts of domains of functioning, and with microlevel and macrolevel relations. The evidence is consistent in showing that perceived self-efficacy contributes significantly to level of motivation and performance accomplishments. Evidence that divergent procedures produce convergent results adds to the explanatory and predictive generality of the self-efficacy mediator.

EFFICACY-ACTIVATED PROCESSES

Self-efficacy beliefs regulate human functioning through four major processes. They include cognitive, motivational, affective and selection processes. Some of these efficacy-activated events are of interest in their own right rather than merely intervening influencers of action. These processes are analyzed in some detail in the sections that follow.

Cognitive Processes

Self-beliefs of efficacy affect thought patterns that can enhance or undermine performance. These cognitive effects take various forms. Much human behavior, being purposive, is regulated by forethought embodying cognized goals. Personal goal setting is influenced by self-appraisal of capabilities. The stronger the perceived self-efficacy, the higher the goals people set for themselves and the firmer their commitment to them (Bandura & Wood, 1989; Locke et al., 1984; Taylor, Locke, Lee, & Gist, 1984). Challenging goals raise the level of motivation and performance attainments (Locke & Latham, 1990).

Most courses of behavior are initially shaped in thought (Bandura, 1986). People's beliefs about their efficacy influences the types of anticipatory scenarios they construct and rehearse. Those who have a high sense of efficacy visualize success scenarios that provide positive guides for performance. Those who judge themselves as inefficacious are more inclined to visualize failure scenarios which undermine performance by dwelling on how things will go wrong. Numerous studies have shown that cognitive simulations in which individuals visualize themselves executing activities skillfully enhance subsequent performance (Bandura, 1986; Corbin, 1972; Feltz & Landers, 1983; Kazdin, 1978). Perceived self-efficacy and cognitive simulation affect each other bidirectionally. A high sense of efficacy fosters cognitive constructions of effective actions and cognitive reiteration of efficacious courses of action strengthens self-beliefs of efficacy (Bandura & Adams, 1977; Kazdin, 1979).

A major function of thought is to enable people to predict the occurrence of events and to create the means for exercising control over those that affect their daily lives. Many activities involve inferential judgments about conditional relations between events. Discovery of such predictive rules requires effective cognitive processing of multidimensional information that contains ambiguities and uncertainties. The fact that the same predictor may contribute to different effects and the same effect may have multiple predictors creates uncertainty as to what is likely to lead to what in probabilistic environments.

In ferreting out predictive rules people must draw on their preexisting knowledge to construct options, to weigh and integrate predictive factors into composite rules, to test and revise their judgments against the immediate and distal results of their actions, and to remember which factors they had tested and how well they had worked. It requires a strong sense of efficacy to remain task oriented in the face of pressing situational demands and judgment failures that can have important social repercussions.

The powerful influence of self-efficacy beliefs on self-regulatory cognitive processes is revealed in a program of research on complex organizational decision-making (Wood & Bandura, 1989b). Much of the research on human decision-making involves discrete judgments in static environments under non-taxing conditions (Beach, Barnes, & Christensen-Szalanski, 1986; Hogarth, 1981). Judgments under such circumstances may not provide a sufficient basis for developing either descriptive or normative models of decision making in dynamic naturalistic environments which involve repeated judgments in the face of a wide array of information within a continuing flow of activity under time constraints and social and self-evaluative consequences. To complicate matters further, organizational decision making requires working through others and coordinating, monitoring and managing collective efforts.

The mechanisms and outcomes of organizational decision making do not lend themselves readily to experimental analysis in actual organizational settings. Advances in this complex field can be achieved by experimental analyses of decision making in simulated organizational environments. A simulated environment permits systematic variation of theoretically relevant factors and precise assessment of their impact on organizational performance and the psychological mechanisms through which they achieve their effects.

In this research, executives managed a computer-simulated organization in which they had to match their supervisees to subfunctions based on their talents and to learn and implement managerial rules to achieve organizational levels of performance that were difficult to fulfill. At periodic intervals we measured the managers' perceived self-efficacy, the goals of group performance they sought to achieve, the adequacy of their analytic thinking for discovering managerial rules, and the level of organizational performance they realized.

Social cognitive theory explains psychosocial functioning in terms of triadic reciprocal causation (Bandura, 1986). In this model of reciprocal determinism,

(1) cognitive, biological and other personal factors, (2) behavior, and (3) environmental events all operate as interacting determinants that influence each other bidirectionally. Each of the major interactants in the triadic causal structure —cognitive, behavioral, and environmental—functions as an important constituent in the dynamic environment. The cognitive determinant is indexed by self-beliefs of efficacy, personal goal setting, and quality of analytic thinking. The managerial choices that are actually executed constitute the behavioral determinant. The properties of the organizational environment, the level of challenge it prescribes, and its responsiveness to managerial interventions represent the environmental determinant. Analyses of ongoing processes clarify how the interactional causal structure operates and changes over time.

The interactional causal structure was tested in conjunction with experimentally varied organizational properties and belief systems that can enhance or undermine the operation of self-regulatory determinants. One important belief system is concerned with the conception of ability (M. M. Bandura & Dweck, 1988; Dweck & Leggett, 1988; Nicholls, 1984). Some people regard ability as an acquirable skill that can be increased by gaining knowledge and perfecting competencies. They adopt a functional learning goal. They seek challenges that provide opportunities to expand their knowledge and competencies. They regard errors as a natural part of an acquisition process. One learns from mistakes. They judge their capabilities more in terms of personal improvement than by comparison against the achievement of others. For people who view ability as a more or less fixed capacity, performance level is regarded as diagnostic of inherent cognitive capacities. Errors and deficient performances carry high evaluative threat. Therefore, they prefer tasks that minimize errors and permit ready display of intellectual proficiency at the expense of expanding their knowledge and competencies. High effort is also threatening because it presumably reveals low ability. The successes of others belittle their own perceived ability.

We instilled these different conceptions of ability and then examined their effects on the self-regulatory mechanisms governing the utilization of skills and performance accomplishments (Wood & Bandura, 1989a). Managers who viewed decision-making ability as reflecting basic cognitive aptitude were beset by increasing self-doubts about their managerial efficacy as they encountered problems (Figure 6). They became more and more erratic in their analytic thinking, they lowered their organizational aspirations, and they achieved progressively less with the organization they were managing. In contrast, construal of ability as an acquirable skill fostered a highly resilient sense of personal efficacy. Under this belief system, the managers remained steadfast in their perceived managerial self-efficacy even when performance standards were difficult to fulfill, they continued to set themselves challenging organizational goals, and they used analytic strategies in efficient ways that aided discovery of optimal managerial decision rules. Such a self-efficacious orientation paid off in high organizational attainments. Viewing ability as an inherent capacity similarly lowers

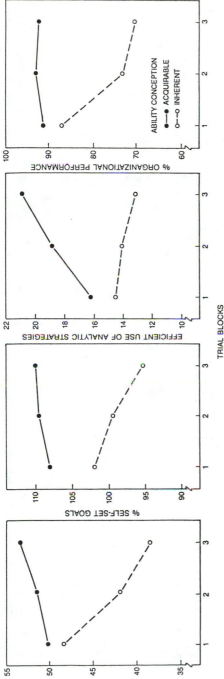

Figure 6 Changes in perceived managerial for the organization relative to the preset standard, effective use of analytic strategies, and achieved level of organizational performance across blocks of production trials under conceptions of ability as an acquirable skill or as an inherent aptitude. Each trial block comprises six different production orders (Wood & Bandura, 1989a).

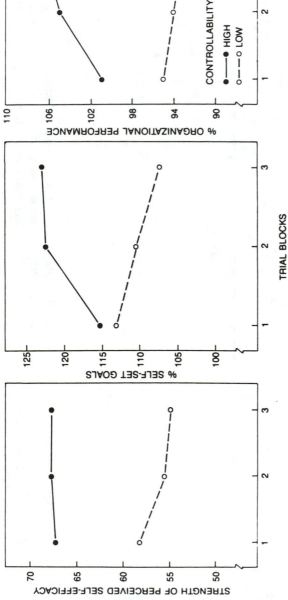
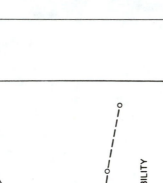

Figure 7 Changes in strength of perceived managerial self-efficacy, the performance goals set for the organization, and level of organizational performance for managers who operated under a cognitive set that organizations are controllable or difficult to control. Each trial block comprises six different production orders (Bandura & Wood, 1989).

perceived self-efficacy, retards physical skill development and diminishes interest in the activity (Jourden, Bandura, & Banfield, 1991).

Another important belief system that affects how efficacy-relevant information is cognitively processed is concerned with people's beliefs about the extent to which their environment is influenceable or controllable. This aspect to the exercise of control represents the level of system constraints, the opportunity structures to exercise personal efficacy, and the ease of access to those opportunity structures. Our organizational simulation research underscores the strong impact of perceived controllability on the self-regulatory factors governing decision making that can enhance or impede performance (Bandura & Wood, 1989). People who managed the simulated organization under a cognitive set that organizations are not easily changeable quickly lost faith in their decision-making capabilities even when performance standards were within easy reach (Figure 7). They lowered their aspirations. Those who operated under a cognitive set that organizations are controllable displayed a strong sense of managerial efficacy. They set themselves increasingly challenging goals and used good analytic thinking for discovering effective managerial rules. They exhibited high resiliency of self-efficacy even in the face of numerous difficulties. The divergent changes in the self-regulatory factors are accompanied by large differences in organizational attainments.

Path analyses confirm the postulated causal ordering of self-regulatory determinants. When initially faced with managing a complex unfamiliar environment, people relied heavily on their past performance in judging their efficacy and setting their personal goals. But as they began to form a self-schema concerning their efficacy through further experience, the performance system is powered more strongly and intricately by self-perceptions of efficacy (Figure 8). Perceived self-efficacy influences performance both directly and through its strong effects on personal goal setting and proficient analytic thinking. Personal goals, in turn, enhance performance attainments through the mediation of analytic strategies.

As previously noted, people judge their capabilities partly through comparison with the performances of others. A further experiment in this series examined how different forms of social comparison affect the mediating self-regulatory mechanisms and organizational attainments (Bandura & Jourden, 1991). Different patterns of performance disparities were conveyed but the findings summarized here are concerned with two that are of special psychological interest. A progressive mastery pattern showed the managers performing below the comparison group at the outset but they gradually closed the gap and eventually surpassed their counterparts. A contrasting pattern of progressive decline showed the managers performing as well as their counterparts at the outset, but then they began to fall behind and ended well below the comparison group. Figure 9 summarizes the the substantial impact of comparative appraisal on self-regulatory mechanisms and organizational attainment.

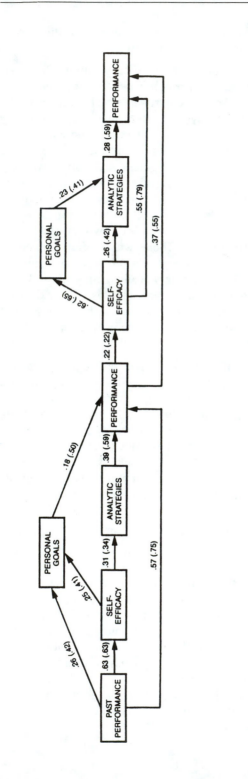
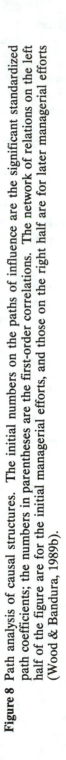

Figure 8 Path analysis of causal structures. The initial numbers on the paths of influence are the significant standardized path coefficients; the numbers in parentheses are the first-order correlations. The network of relations on the left half of the figure are for the initial managerial efforts, and those on the right half are for later managerial efforts (Wood & Bandura, 1989b).

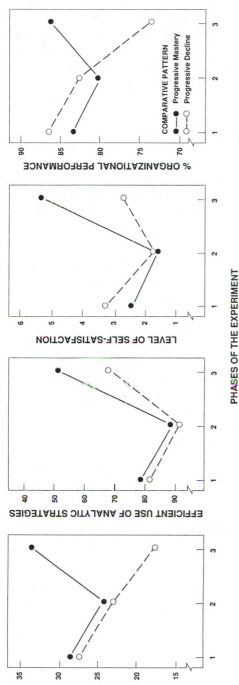

Figure 9 Changes in perceived managerial self-efficacy, quality of analytic thinking, and achieved level of organizational performance across blocks of production orders under comparative appraisal suggesting progressive mastery or progressive decline relative to a similar comparison group (Bandura & Jourden, 1991).

Seeing oneself surpassed by similar social referents undermined perceived self-efficacy, disrupted analytic thinking, created unremitting self-discontent and increasingly impaired organizational attainments. By contrast, seeing oneself gain progressive mastery strengthened a sense of personal efficacy, fostered efficient analytic thinking, transformed self-evaluation from self-discontent to self-satisfaction with accelerating progress and enhanced organizational attainments. Path analysis confirms that the different performance trajectories are mediated by changes in self-regulatory factors.

Motivational Processes

Self-beliefs of efficacy play a central role in the self-regulation of motivation. Most human motivation is cognitively generated. In cognitive motivation, people motivate themselves and guide their actions anticipatorily through the exercise of forethought. They form beliefs about what they can do, they anticipate likely outcomes of prospective actions, they set goals for themselves and plan courses of action designed to realize valued futures.

One can distinguish three different forms of cognitive motivators around which different theories have been built. These include causal attributions, outcome expectancies, and cognized goals. The corresponding theories are attribution theory, expectancy-value theory, and goal theory, respectively. Figure 10 summarizes schematically these alternative conceptions of cognitive motivation. Outcome and goal motivators clearly operate through the anticipation mechanism. Causal reasons conceived retrospectively for prior attainments can also affect future actions anticipatorily by altering self-appraisal of capability and perception of task demands.

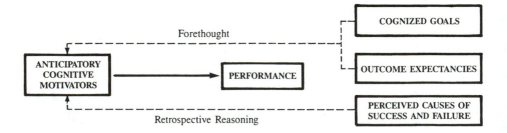

Figure 10 Schematic representation of conceptions of cognitive motivation based on cognized goals, outcome expectancies and causal attributions.

The self-efficacy mechanism of personal agency operates in all of these variant forms of cognitive motivation. Causal attributions and self-efficacy appraisals involve bidirectional causation. Self-beliefs of efficacy bias causal attribution (Alden, 1986; Collins, 1982; Silver, Mitchell, & Gist, 1989). The relative weight given to information regarding adeptness, effort, task complexity, and situational circumstances affects self-efficacy appraisal. Causal analyses indicate that the effects of causal attributions on performance attainments are mediated through self-efficacy beliefs rather than operate directly on performance (Relich, Debus, & Walker, 1986; Schunk & Cox, 1986; Schunk & Gunn, 1986; Schunk & Rice, 1986). The stronger the self-efficacy belief, the higher the subsequent performance attainments.

In expectancy-value theory, strength of motivation is governed jointly by the expectation that particular actions will produce specified outcomes and the value placed on those outcomes (Ajzen & Fishbein, 1980; Atkinson, 1964; Feather, 1982; Rotter, 1954). However, people act on their beliefs about what they can do, as well as their beliefs about the likely outcomes of various actions. The effects of outcome expectancies on performance motivation are partly governed by self-beliefs of efficacy. There are many activities which, if done well, guarantee valued outcomes, but they are not pursued by people who doubt they can do what it takes to succeed (Beck & Lund, 1981; Betz & Hackett, 1986). The predictiveness of expectancy-value theory can be enhanced by including the self-efficacy determinant (Ajzen & Madden, 1986; De Vries, Dijkstra, & Kuhlman, 1988; McCaul et al., 1988; Schwarzer, 1992; Wheeler, 1983).

The degree to which outcome expectations contribute independently to performance motivation varies depending on how tightly contingencies between actions and outcomes are structured, either inherently or socially, in a given domain of functioning. For many activities, outcomes are determined by level of accomplishment. Hence, the types of outcomes people anticipate depend largely on how well they believe they will be able to perform in given situations. In most social, intellectual, and physical pursuits, those who judge themselves highly efficacious will expect favorable outcomes, whereas those who expect poor performances of themselves will conjure up negative outcomes. Thus, in activities in which outcomes are highly contingent on quality of performance, self-judged efficacy accounts for most of the variance in expected outcomes. When variations in perceived self-efficacy are partialed out, the outcomes expected for given performances do not have much of an independent effect on behavior (Barling & Abel, 1983; Barling & Beattie, 1983; Godding & Glasgow, 1985; Lee, 1984a, 1984b; Williams & Watson, 1985).

Self-efficacy beliefs account for only part of the variance in expected outcomes when outcomes are not completely controlled by quality of performance. This occurs when extraneous factors also affect outcomes, or outcomes are socially tied to a minimum level of performance so that some variations in quality of performance above and below the standard do not produce differential outcomes. And finally, expected outcomes are independent of perceived self-efficacy when contingencies are discriminatively structured so that no level of competence can produce desired outcomes. This occurs in pursuits that are rigidly segregated by sex, race, age or some other factor. Under such circumstances, people in disfavored groups expect poor outcomes however efficacious they judge themselves to be.

The capacity to exercise self-influence by personal challenge and evaluative reaction to one's own attainments provides a major cognitive mechanism of motivation and self-directedness (Bandura, 1991). A large body of evidence is consistent in showing that explicit challenging goals enhance and sustain motivation (Locke & Latham, 1990). Goals operate largely through self-referent processes rather than regulate motivation and action directly. Motivation based on aspirational standards involves a cognitive comparison process. By making self-satisfaction conditional on matching adopted goals, people give direction to their actions and create self incentives to persist in their efforts until their performances match their goals. They seek self-satisfactions from fulfilling valued goals and are prompted to intensify their efforts by discontent with substandard performances.

Activation of self-evaluation processes through cognitive comparison requires both comparative factors—a personal standard and knowledge of one's performance level. Simply adopting a goal, without knowing how one is doing, or knowing how one is doing in the absence of a goal, has no lasting motivational impact (Bandura & Cervone, 1983; Becker, 1978; Strang, Lawrence, & Fowler, 1978). But the combined influence of goals with performance feedback heightens motivation substantially.

Cognitive motivation based on goal intentions is mediated by three types of self-influences: affective self-evaluative reactions to one's performance, perceived self-efficacy for goal attainment, and adjustment of personal standards in light of one's attainments. Perceived self-efficacy contributes to motivation in several ways. It is partly on the basis of self-beliefs of efficacy that people choose what challenges to undertake, how much effort to expend in the endeavor, and how long to persevere in the face of difficulties (Bandura, 1986, 1991). When faced with obstacles and failures, people who have self-doubts about their capabilities slacken their efforts or abort their attempts prematurely and settle for mediocre solutions, whereas those who have a strong belief in their capabilities exert greater effort to master the challenge (Bandura & Cervone, 1983; Cervone & Peake, 1986; Jacobs et al., 1984; Peake & Cervone, 1989; Weinberg et al., 1979). Strong perseverance usually pays off in performance accomplishments.

As previously noted, affective self-reactions provide a dual source of incentive motivation—the anticipated self-satisfaction for personal accomplishment operates as a positive motivator and discontent with deficient performance functions as a negative motivator. The more self-dissatisfied people are with substandard attainments, the more they heighten their efforts. These two forms of self-motivators contribute differentially to performance accomplishments depending on the complexity of the activity. On tasks where success is attainable solely by increased level of effort, self-discontent with substandard attainments is the major regulator of performance accomplishments (Bandura & Cervone, 1983, 1986). In contrast, on tasks that make heavy attentional and cognitive demands, self-satisfaction with personal progress toward challenging standards provides a positive motivational orientation for performance accomplishments. Strong self-critical reactions can detract from the intricate task of generating and testing alternative organizational strategies (Bandura & Jourden, 1991; Cervone, Jiwani, & Wood, 1991). As people approach or surpass the adopted standard, they set new goals for themselves that serve as additional motivators. The higher the self-set challenges, the more effort invested in the endeavor. Thus, notable attainments bring temporary satisfaction, but people who are assured of their capabilities enlist new challenges as personal motivators for further accomplishment.

The contribution of these self-reactive influences to motivation is strikingly revealed in a study that systematically varied the direction and magnitude of discrepancy between performance and a difficult assigned standard (Bandura & Cervone, 1986). Inspection of Figure 11 shows that the more sources of self-influence individuals brought to bear on themselves, the higher the effort they exerted and sustained to attain what they seek. Taken together this set of self-reactive influences accounts for the major share of variation in motivation.

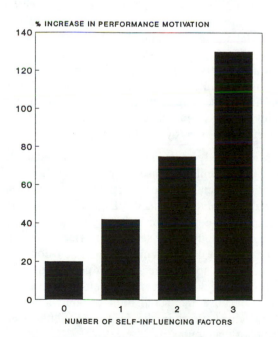

Figure 11 Mean percent change in motivational level as a function of the number of self-reactive influences operating in given individuals. The three self-reactive factors included strong perceived self-efficacy for goal attainment; self-dissatisfaction with substandard performance; and adoption of challenging standards. Plotted from data of Bandura & Cervone, 1986.

Many theories of motivation and self-regulation are founded on a negative feedback control model (Carver & Scheier, 1981; Lord & Hanges, 1987; Miller, Galanter, & Pribram, 1960). This type of system functions as a motivator and regulator of action through a discrepancy reduction mechanism. Perceived discrepancy between performance and a reference standard motivates action to reduce the incongruity. Discrepancy reduction clearly plays a central role in any system of self-regulation. However, in the negative feedback control system, if performance matches the standard the person does nothing. Such a feedback control system would produce circular action that leads nowhere. Nor could people be stirred to action until they received feedback that their performance is negatively discrepant from the standard.

Self-regulation by negative discrepancy tells only half the story and not necessarily the more interesting half. People are proactive, aspiring organisms. Their capacity for forethought enables them to organize and regulate their lives proactively. Human self-motivation relies on both discrepancy production and discrepancy reduction (Bandura, 1991). It requires proactive control as well as reactive control. People motivate and guide their actions through proactive control by setting themselves valued challenging standards that create a state of disequilibrium and then mobilizing their effort on the basis of anticipatory estimation of what it would take to reach them. Reactive feedback control comes into play in subsequent adjustments of effort to attain desired results. As previously shown, after people attain the standard they have been pursuing, those with a strong sense of efficacy set a higher standard for themselves. Adopting further challenges creates new motivating discrepancies to be mastered. Similarly, surpassing a standard is more likely to raise aspiration than to lower subsequent performance to conform to the surpassed standard. Self-regulation of motivation and action thus involves a hierarchical dual control process of disequilibrating discrepancy production followed by equilibrating discrepancy reduction.

There is a growing body of evidence that human attainments and positive well-being require an optimistic sense of personal efficacy (Bandura, 1986). This is because ordinary social realities are strewn with difficulties. They are full of impediments, failures, adversities, setbacks, frustrations, and inequities. People must have a robust sense of personal efficacy to sustain the perseverant effort needed to succeed. Self-doubts can set in fast after some failures or reverses. The important matter is not that difficulties arouse self-doubt, which is a natural immediate reaction, but the speed of recovery of perceived self-efficacy from difficulties. Some people quickly recover their self-assurance, others lose faith in their capabilities. Because the acquisition of knowledge and competencies usually requires sustained effort in the face of difficulties and setbacks, it is resiliency of self-belief that counts.

In his informative book, titled Rejection, John White (1982) provides vivid testimony that the striking characteristic of people who have achieved eminence in their fields is an inextinguishable sense of efficacy and a firm belief in the worth of what they are doing. This resilient self-belief system enabled them to override repeated early rejections of their work.

Many of our literary classics brought their authors repeated rejections. The novelist, Saroyan, accumulated several thousand rejections before he had his first literary piece published. James Joyce's, the Dubliners, was rejected by 22 publishers. Gertrude Stein continued to submit poems to editors for about 20 years before one was finally accepted. Now that's invincible self-efficacy. Over a dozen publishers rejected a manuscript by e. e. cummings. When he finally got it published by his mother the dedication, printed in upper case, read: With no thanks to... followed by the list of 16 publishers who had rejected his offering.

Early rejection is the rule, rather than the exception, in other creative endeavors. The Impressionists had to arrange their own art exhibitions because their works were routinely rejected by the Paris Salon. Van Gogh sold only one painting during his life. Rodin was rejected repeatedly by the Ecole des Beaux-Arts. The musical works of most renowned composers were initially greeted with derision. Stravinsky was run out of town by an enraged audience and critics when he first served them the Rite of Spring. Many other composers suffered the same fate, especially in the early phases of their career. The brilliant architect, Frank Lloyd Wright, was one of the more widely rejected architects during much of his career.

To turn to more familiar examples, Hollywood initially rejected the incomparable Fred Astaire for being only "a balding, skinny actor who can dance a little." Decca Records turned down a recording contract with the Beatles with the nonprophetic evaluation, "We don't like their sound. Groups of guitars are on their way out." Whoever issued that rejective pronouncement must cringe at each sight of a guitar. After Decca Records got through rejecting the Beatles, Columbia Records followed suit with a prompt rejection.

It is not uncommon for authors of scientific classics to experience repeated initial rejection of their work, often with hostile embellishments if it is too discordant with what is in vogue at the time. For example, John Garcia, who eventually won well-deserved recognition for his fundamental psychological discoveries, was once told by a reviewer of his oft rejected manuscripts that one is no more likely to find the phenomenon he discovered than bird droppings in a cuckoo clock. Verbal droppings of this type demand tenacious self-belief to continue the tortuous search for new Muses. Scientists often reject theories and technologies that are ahead of their time. Because of the cold reception given to most innovations, the time between conception and technical realization typically spans several decades.

The findings of laboratory investigations are in accord with these records of human triumphs regarding the centrality of the motivational effects of self-beliefs of efficacy in human attainments. It takes a resilient sense of efficacy to override the numerous dissuading impediments to significant accomplishments.

It is widely believed that misjudgment breeds dysfunction. The functional value of veridical self-appraisal depends on the nature of the endeavor. In activities where the margins of error are narrow and missteps can produce costly or injurious consequences, personal well-being is best served by highly accurate self-appraisal. It is a different matter when difficult accomplishments can produce substantial personal or social benefits and where the personal costs involve time, effort and expendable resources. Individuals have to decide for themselves which creative abilities to cultivate, whether to invest their efforts and resources in endeavors that are difficult to fulfill, and how much hardship they are willing to endure for pursuits strewn with obstacles.

In most endeavors, optimistic self-appraisals of capability that are not unduly disparate from what is possible can be advantageous, whereas veridical judgments can be self-limiting. When people err in their self-appraisal they tend to overestimate their capabilities. This is a benefit rather than a cognitive failing to be eradicated. If self-efficacy beliefs always reflected only what people can do routinely, they would rarely fail but they would not mount the extra effort needed to surpass their ordinary performances. The emerging evidence indicates that the successful, the innovative, the sociable, the nonanxious, the nondespondent, and the social reformers take an optimistic view of their personal efficacy to exercise influence over events that affect their lives (Bandura, 1986). If not unrealistically exaggerated, such self-beliefs enhance and sustain the level of motivation needed for personal and social accomplishments. Societies enjoy considerable benefits from the eventual accomplishments of its persisters.

Affective Processes

The self-efficacy mechanism also plays a pivotal role in the self-regulation of affective states. One can distinguish three principal ways in which self-efficacy beliefs affect the nature and intensity of emotional experiences. Such beliefs create attentional biases and influence how emotive life events are construed and cognitively represented; they operate in the exercise of control over perturbing thought patterns; and they sponsor courses of action that transform environments in ways that alter their emotive potential. These alternative paths of affective influence are amply documented in the self-regulation of anxiety arousal and depressive mood.

In social cognitive theory (Bandura, 1986), perceived self-efficacy to exercise control over potentially threatening events plays a central role in anxiety arousal. Threat is not a fixed property of situational events. Nor does appraisal of the likelihood of aversive happenings rely solely on reading external signs of danger or safety. Rather, threat is a relational property concerning the match between perceived coping capabilities and potentially hurtful aspects of the environment. Therefore, to understand people's appraisals of external threats and their affective reactions to them it is necessary to analyze their judgments of their coping capabilities which, in large part, determine the subjective perilousness of environmental events.

People who believe they can exercise control over potential threats do not conjure up apprehensive cognitions and, hence, are not perturbed by them. But those who believe they cannot manage potential threats experience high levels of anxiety arousal. They dwell on their coping deficiencies, view many aspects of their environment as fraught with danger, magnify the severity of possible threats and worry about perils that rarely, if ever, happen. Through such inefficacious thought they distress themselves and constrain and impair their level of functioning (Beck, Emery, & Greenberg, 1985; Lazarus & Folkman, 1984; Meichenbaum, 1977; Sarason, 1975).

That perceived coping efficacy operates as a cognitive mediator of anxiety and stress reactions has been tested by creating different levels of perceived self-efficacy and relating them at a microlevel to different manifestations of anxiety. People display little affective arousal while coping with potential threats they regard with high efficacy. But as they cope with threats for which they distrust their coping efficacy, their stress mounts, their heart rate accelerates, their blood pressure rises, and they display increased catecholamine secretion (Bandura et al., 1982; Bandura, Taylor, Williams, Mefford, & Barchas, 1985). After perceived efficacy is strengthened to the maximal level by guided mastery, previously intimidating tasks no longer elicit differential autonomic or catecholamine reactions.

The foregoing discussion documents how perceived coping self-efficacy affects the neurobiological aspects of emotional states. The types of biochemical reactions that have been shown to accompany a weak sense of coping efficacy, such as autonomic and catecholamine activation, are involved in the regulation of immune systems. Perceived self-inefficacy in exercising control over stressors also activates endogenous opioid systems (Bandura, Cioffi, Taylor, & Brouillard, 1988). Some of the immunosuppressive effects of inefficacy in controlling stressors are mediated by release of endogenous opioids (Shavit & Martin, 1987) When opioid mechanisms are blocked by an opiate antagonist, the stress of uncontrollability loses its immunosuppressive power. These combined findings identify some of the neurobiological paths through which perceived self-efficacy can affect immunoregulatory processes.

Several converging lines of evidence show that exposure to stressors without the ability to control them impairs the immune system (Coe & Levine, 1991; Maier, Laudenslager, & Ryan, 1985). However, stress activated in the process of acquiring controlling mastery may have very different effects than stress in aversive situations with no prospect in sight of ever gaining any self-protective efficacy. This view receives some support from examination of immunological changes accompanying self-efficacy enhancement through guided mastery experiences (Wiedenfeld et al., 1990). The rate with which people acquired a sense of controlling efficacy was a good predictor of whether exposure to acute stressors enhanced or suppressed various components of the immune system.

Development of a strong sense of efficacy to control phobic stressors had an immunoenhancing effect. A slow growth of perceived self-efficacy attenuated components of the immune system.

Anxiety arousal in situations involving some risks is affected not only by perceived coping efficacy, but also by perceived efficacy to control distressing cognitions. The exercise of control over one's own consciousness is summed up well in the proverb: "You cannot prevent the birds of worry and care from flying over your head. But you can stop them from building a nest in your head." Perceived self-efficacy in thought control is a key factor in the regulation of cognitively-generated arousal. It is not the sheer frequency of disturbing cognitions, but the perceived inability to turn them off that is the major source of distress (Churchill, 1990; Churchill & McMurray, 1990; Kent, 1987; Salkovskis & Harrison, 1984). Thus, the incidence of aversive cognitions is unrelated to anxiety level when variations in perceived thought control efficacy are controlled for, whereas perceived thought control efficacy is strongly related to anxiety level when extent of frightful cognitions is controlled (Kent & Gibbons, 1987).

The dual regulation of anxiety arousal and behavior by perceived coping efficacy and thought control efficacy is revealed in a study of the mechanisms governing personal empowerment over pervasive social threats (Ozer & Bandura, 1990). Sexual violence toward women is a prevalent problem. Because any woman may be a victim, the lives of many women are distressed and constricted by a sense of inefficacy to cope with the threat of sexual assault. Such concerns often preoccupy their thinking in situations posing potential risks. To address this problem at a self-protective level, women participated in a mastery modeling program in which they perfected the physical skills to defend themselves successfully against sexual assailants. Mastery modeling enhanced perceived coping efficacy and cognitive control efficacy, decreased perceived vulnerability to assault and reduced the incidence of intrusive aversive thoughts and anxiety arousal. These changes were accompanied by increased freedom of action and decreased avoidant social behavior. Path analysis of the causal structure revealed a dual path of regulation of behavior by perceived self-efficacy: One path was mediated through the effects of perceived coping self-efficacy on perceived vulnerability and risk discernment, and the other through the impact of perceived cognitive control self-efficacy on intrusive aversive thoughts (Figure 12). A strong sense of coping efficacy rooted in performance capabilities has substantial impact on perceived self-efficacy to abort the escalation or perseveration of perturbing cognitions.

Perceived coping efficacy regulates avoidance behavior in risky situations, as well as anxiety arousal. The stronger the perceived coping self-efficacy the more venturesome the behavior, regardless of whether self-beliefs of efficacy are strengthened by mastery experiences, modeling influences, or cognitive simulations (Bandura, 1988). The role of perceived self-efficacy and anxiety arousal in the causal structure of avoidant behavior has been examined in a number of studies. The results show that people base their actions on self-beliefs of efficacy

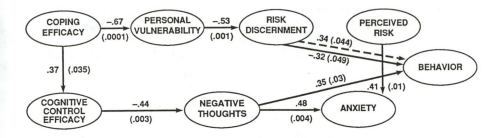

Figure 12 Path analysis of the causal structure. The numbers on the paths of influence are the significant standardized path coefficients; the numbers in parentheses are the significance levels. The solid line to behavior represents different activities pursued outside the home, the hatch line represents avoided activities because of concern over personal safety (Ozer & Bandura, 1990).

in situations they regard as risky. Williams and his colleagues (Williams, Dooseman, & Kleifield, 1984; Williams, Kinney, & Falbo, 1989; Williams & Rappoport, 1983; Williams, Turner, & Peer, 1985) have analyzed by partial correlation numerous data sets from studies in which perceived self-efficacy, anticipated anxiety, and phobic behavior were measured. Perceived self-efficacy accounts for a substantial amount of variance in phobic behavior when anticipated anxiety is partialed out, whereas the relationship between anticipated anxiety and phobic behavior essentially disappears when perceived self-efficacy is partialed out (Table 1). Studies of other threatening activities similarly demonstrate the predictive superiority of perceived self-efficacy over perceived dangerous outcomes in level of anxiety arousal (Hackett & Betz, 1984; Leland, 1983; McAuley, 1985; Williams & Watson, 1985).

The data taken as a whole indicate that anxiety arousal and avoidant behavior are largely coeffects of perceived coping inefficacy rather than causally linked. People avoid potentially threatening situations and activities, not because they experience anxiety arousal or anticipate they will be anxious, but because they believe they will be unable to cope successfully with situations they regard as risky. They take self-protective action regardless of whether or not they happen to be anxious at the moment. They do not have to conjure up an anxious state before they can take action. They commonly perform risky activities at lower strengths of perceived self-efficacy despite high anxiety arousal (Bandura, 1988).

Perceived self-efficacy to exercise control can give rise to despondency as well as anxiety. The nature of the outcomes over which personal control is sought operates as an important differentiating factor. People experience anxiety when they perceive themselves ill equipped to control potentially injurious events. Attenuation or control of aversive outcomes is central to anxiety. People are saddened and depressed by their perceived inefficacy in gaining highly valued outcomes. Irreparable loss or failure to gain valued outcomes figures

Table 1

*Comparison of the Relation Between Perceived Self-Efficacy and Coping Behavior
When Anticipated Anxiety is Controlled, and the Relation Between Anticipated Anxiety
and Coping Behavior When Perceived Self-Efficacy is Controlled*

	Coping Behavior	
	Anticipated Anxiety With Self-Efficacy Controlled	Perceived Self-Efficacy With Anticipated Anxiety Controlled
Williams & Rappoport (1983)		
Pretreatment 1 [a]	-.12	.40*
Pretreatment 2	-.28	.59**
Posttreatment	.13	.45*
Follow-up	.06	.45*
Williams et al. (1984)		
Pretreatment	-.36*	.22
Posttreatment	-.21	.59***
Williams et al. (1985)		
Pretreatment	-.35*	.28*
Posttreatment	.05	.72***
Follow-up	-.12	.66***
Telch et al. (1985)		
Pretreatment	-.56***	-.28
Posttreatment	.15	.48**
Follow-up	-.05	.42*
Kirsch et al. (1983)		
Pretreatment	-.34*	.54***
Posttreatment	-.48**	.48**
Arnow et al. (1985)		
Pretreatment	.17	.77***
Posttreatment	-.08	.43*
Follow-up	-.06	.88**
Williams et al. (1989)		
Midtreatment	-.15	.65***
Posttreatment	.02	.47**
Follow-up	-.03	.71***

Notes. [a] The pretreatment phases of some of these experiments include only subjects
selected for severe phobic behavior. They have a uniformly low sense of coping
efficacy. In such instances, the highly restricted range of self-efficacy scores
tends to lower the correlation coefficients in pretreatment phases.
$*p < .05, **p < .01, ***p < .001$.

prominently in despondency. When the valued outcomes one seeks also protect against future aversive circumstances, as when failure to secure a job jeopardizes one's livelihood, perceived self-inefficacy is both distressing and depressing. Because of the interdependence of outcomes, both anxiety and despair often accompany perceived personal efficacy.

Several lines of evidence support the role of perceived self-inefficacy in depression. A sense of fulfillment and self-worth can have different sources, each of which is linked to an aspect of self-efficacy. Perceived self-inefficacy to attain valued goals that contribute to self-esteem and to secure things that bring satisfaction to one's life can give rise to bouts of depression (Bandura, 1991; Davis & Yates, 1982; Kanfer & Zeiss, 1983). A low sense of efficacy to fulfill role demands that reflect on personal adequacy also contributes to depression (Cutrona & Troutman, 1986; Olioff & Aboud, 1991).

Self-regulatory theories of motivation and of depression make seemingly contradictory predictions regarding the effects of negative discrepancies between attainments and standards invested with self-evaluative significance. Standards that exceed attainments are said to enhance motivation through goal challenges, but negative discrepancies are also invoked as activators of despondent mood. Moreover, when negative discrepancies do have adverse effects, they may give rise to apathy rather than to despondency. A conceptual scheme is needed that differentiates the conditions under which negative discrepancies will be motivating, depressing, or induce apathy.

In accord with social cognitive theory, the directional effects of negative goal discrepancies are predictable from the relationship between perceived self-efficacy for goal attainment and level of personal goal setting (Bandura & Abrams, 1986). Whether negative discrepancies are motivating or depressing depends on beliefs on one's efficacy to attain them. Negative disparities give rise to high motivation and low despondency when people believe they have the efficacy to fulfill difficult standards and continue to strive for them. Negative disparities diminish motivation and generate despondency for people who judge themselves as inefficacious to attain difficult standards but continue to demand them of themselves as the basis for self-satisfaction. People who view difficult goals as beyond their capabilities and abandon them as unrealistic for themselves become apathetic rather than despondent.

Supportive interpersonal relations can reduce the aversiveness of negative life events that give rise to stress and depression. However, social support does more than simply operate as a buffer against stressors. In addition to its protective function, social support serves a positive proactive function in fostering coping competencies that alter the threat value of potential stressors. Analyses of causal structures reveal that perceived interpersonal self-efficacy and social support contribute bidirectionally to depression. Social support is not a fixed entity cushioning people against stressors. Rather people have to seek out, cultivate and maintain social networks. Indeed, the Holahans have shown that people with a high sense of social efficacy create social supports for themselves. Perceived social self-efficacy reduces vulnerability to depression both directly and through the cultivation of socially supportive networks (Holahan & Holahan, 1987a, 1987b). Acquaintances model coping attitudes and strategies, provide incentives for beneficial courses of behavior, and motivate others by showing that difficulties are surmountable by perseverant effort. Social support enhances perceived self-efficacy which, in turn, fosters successful adaptation and reduces stress and depression (Cutrona & Troutman, 1986; Major et al., 1990). A strong sense of social efficacy thus facilitates development of socially supportive relationships and social support, in turn, enhances perceived self-efficacy for rendering adversities less depressogenic.

Much human depression is cognitively generated by dejecting thought patterns. Therefore, perceived self-efficacy to exercise control over ruminative thought figures prominently in the occurrence, duration, and recurrence of depressive episodes. Kavanagh and Wilson (1989) found that the weaker the perceived efficacy to terminate ruminative thoughts the higher the depression ($r = -.51$), and the stronger the perceived thought control efficacy instilled by treatment the greater the decline in depression ($r = .71$) and the lower the vulnerability to recurrence of depressive episodes ($r = -.48$). Perceived self-efficacy retains its predictiveness of improvement and reduced vulnerability to depressive relapse when level of prior depression is controlled.

The preceding analysis centers on the path of influence from perceived self-inefficacy to depression. Mood states bias the way in which events are interpreted, cognitively organized, and retrieved from memory (Bower, 1983; Isen, 1987). Mood and self-efficacy influence each other bidirectionally. Perceived self-inefficacy breeds depression. Despondent mood diminishes perceived self-efficacy, positive mood enhances it (Kavanagh & Bower, 1985). People then act in accordance with their mood altered efficacy beliefs, choosing more challenging activities in a self-efficacious frame of mind than if they doubt their efficacy (Kavanagh, 1983). Despondency can thus lower self-efficacy beliefs, which undermine motivation and spawn deficient performances, causing even deeper despondency. In contrast, by raising perceived self-efficacy that facilitates motivation, aidful cognitive self-guidance and accomplishments, positive mood can set in motion an affirmative reciprocal process.

Selection Processes

People can exert some influence over their life paths by the environments they select and the environments they create. Thus far, the discussion has centered on efficacy-related processes that enable people to create beneficial environments and to exercise control over them. Judgments of personal efficacy also shape developmental trajectories by influencing selection of activities and environments. People tend to avoid activities and situations they believe exceed their coping capabilities, but they readily undertake challenging activities and pick social environments they judge themselves capable of handling. Any factor that influences choice behavior can profoundly affect the direction of personal development. This is because the social influences operating in selected environments continue to promote certain competencies, values, and interests long after the decisional determinant has rendered its inaugurating effect (Bandura, 1986; Snyder, 1987). Thus, seemingly inconsequential efficacy determinants of choices can initiate selective associations that produce major and enduring personal changes. Selection processes are differentiated from cognitive, motivational and affective processes because, in prompt dismissal of certain courses of action on grounds of perceived personal inefficacy, the latter regulative processes never come into play. It is only after people choose to engage in an activity that they mobilize their effort, generate possible solutions and strategies of action and become elated, anxious, or depressed over how they are doing.

The power of self-efficacy beliefs to affect the course of life paths through choice-related processes is most clearly revealed in studies of career decision-making and career development (Betz & Hackett, 1986; Lent & Hackett, 1987). The stronger people's self-belief in their capabilities, the more career options they consider possible, the greater the interest they show in them, the better they prepare themselves educationally for different pursuits and the more successful they are at them. A high sense of decisional self-efficacy is also accompanied by a high level of exploratory activity designed to aid selection of pursuits (Blustein, 1989).

Biased cultural practices, stereotypic modeling of gender roles, and dissuading opportunity structures eventually leave their mark on women's beliefs about their occupational efficacy (Hackett & Betz, 1981). Women are especially prone to limit their interests and range of career options by self-beliefs that they lack the necessary capabilities for occupations traditionally dominated by men, even though they do not differ from men in actual ability. The self-limitation of career development arises from perceived inefficacy, rather than from actual inability. By constricting choice behavior that can cultivate interests and competencies, self-disbeliefs create their own behavioral validation and protection from corrective influence. However, changes in cultural attitudes and practices may be weakening self-efficacy barriers. Students currently coming through the school ranks reveal a much smaller disparity between males and females in their beliefs about their efficacy to pursue successfully different types of careers (Post-Kammer & Smith, 1985).

Self-efficacy beliefs contribute to the course of social development as well as occupational pursuits (Perry, Perry & Rasmussen, 1986). The developmental processes undoubtedly involve bidirectional causation. Beliefs of personal capabilities determine choice of associates and activities, and affiliation patterns, in turn, affect the direction of self-efficacy development.

Construction of Self-Efficacy as a Self-Persuasion Process

The multiple benefits of a sense of personal efficacy do not arise simply from the incantation of capability. Saying something should not be confused with believing it to be so. Simply saying that one is capable is not necessarily self-convincing, especially when it contradicts preexisting beliefs. For example, no amount of reiteration that I can fly, will persuade me that I have the efficacy to get myself airborne. Self-efficacy beliefs are the product of a complex process of self-persuasion that relies on cognitive processing of diverse sources of efficacy information conveyed enactively, vicariously, socially, and physiologically (Bandura, 1986). People cannot persuade themselves of their efficacy if they regard the information from which they construct their self-beliefs as unrepresentative, tainted or erroneous.

The cognitive processing of efficacy information involves two separable functions: The first concerns the types of information people attend to and use as indicators of personal efficacy. Each of the four modes of conveying information about personal capabilities has its distinctive set of efficacy indicators. The second function concerns the combination rules or heuristics people use to weight and integrate efficacy information from different sources in forming their self-efficacy beliefs. Self processes govern the construction of such belief systems at the level of selection, interpretation, and integration of efficacy-relevant information.

Converging lines of evidence indicate that the self-efficacy mechanism plays a central role in the exercise of personal agency. The value of a psychological theory is judged not only by its explanatory and predictive power, but also by its operative power to enhance the quality of human functioning. Social cognitive theory provides prescriptive specificity on how to empower people with the competencies, self-regulatory capabilities and resilient self-belief of efficacy that enables them to enhance their psychological well-being and accomplishments.

REFERENCES

Ajzen, I., & Fishbein, M. (1980). *Understanding attitudes and predicting social behavior*. Englewood Cliffs, NJ: Prentice-Hall.

Ajzen, I., & Madden, T. J. (1986). Prediction of goal-directed behavior: Attitudes, intentions, and perceived behavioral control. *Journal of Experimental Social Psychology, 22*, 453-474.

Alden, L. (1986). Self-efficacy and causal attributions for social feedback. *Journal of Research in Personality, 20*, 460-473.

Atkinson, J. W. (1964). *An introduction to motivation*. Princeton, NJ: Van Nostrand.

Bandura, A. (1986). *Social foundations of thought and action: A social cognitive theory*. Englewood Cliffs, NJ: Prentice-Hall.

Bandura, A. (1988). Perceived self-efficacy: Exercise of control through self-belief. In J. P. Dauwalder, M. Perrez, & V. Hobi (Eds.), *Annual series of European research in behavior therapy* (Vol. 2, pp. 27-59). Lisse, The Netherlands: Swets & Zeitlinger.

Bandura, A. (1991). Self-regulation of motivation through anticipatory and self-regulatory mechanisms. In R. A. Dienstbier (Ed.), *Perspectives on motivation: Nebraska symposium on motivation* (Vol. 38, pp. 69-164). Lincoln: University of Nebraska Press.

Bandura, A., & Abrams, K. (1986). *Self-regulatory mechanisms in motivating, apathetic, and despondent reactions to unfulfilled standards.* Unpublished manuscript, Stanford University, Stanford.

Bandura, A., & Adams, N. E. (1977). Analysis of self-efficacy theory of behavioral change. *Cognitive Therapy and Research, 1,* 287-308.

Bandura, A., & Cervone, D. (1983). Self-evaluative and self-efficacy mechanisms governing the motivational effects of goal systems. *Journal of Personality and Social Psychology, 45,* 1017-1028.

Bandura, A., & Cervone, D. (1986). Differential engagement of self-reactive influences in cognitive motivation. *Organizational Behavior and Human Decision Processes, 38,* 92-113.

Bandura, A., Cioffi, D., Taylor, C. B., & Brouillard, M. E. (1988). Perceived self-efficacy in coping with cognitive stressors and opioid activation. *Journal of Personality and Social Psychology, 55,* 479-488.

Bandura, A., & Jourden, F. J. (1991). Self-regulatory mechanisms governing the impact of social-comparison on complex decision making. *Journal of Personality and Social Psychology, 60,* 941-951.

Bandura, A., Reese, L., & Adams, N. E. (1982). Microanalysis of action and fear arousal as a function of differential levels of perceived self-efficacy. *Journal of Personality and Social Psychology, 43,* 5-21.

Bandura, A., Taylor, C. B., Williams, S. L, Mefford, I. N., & Barchas, J. D. (1985). Catecholamine secretion as a function of perceived coping self-efficacy. *Journal of Consulting and Clinical Psychology, 53,* 406-414.

Bandura, A., & Wood, R. E. (1989). Effect of perceived controllability and performance standards on self-regulation of complex decision-making. *Journal of Personality and Social Psychology, 56,* 805-814.

Bandura, M. M., & Dweck, C. S. (1988). *The relationship of conceptions of intelligence and achievement goals to achievement-related cognition, affect and behavior.* Unpublished manuscript.

Barling, J., & Abel, M. (1983). Self-efficacy beliefs and tennis performance. *Cognitive Therapy and Research, 7,* 265-272.

Barling, J., & Beattie, R. (1983). Self-efficacy beliefs and sales performance. *Journal of Organizational Behavior Management, 5,* 41-51.

Beach, L. R., Barnes, V. E., & Christensen-Szalanski, J. J. J. (1986). Beyond heuristics and biases: A contingency model of judgmental forecasting. *Journal of Forecasting, 5,* 143-157.

Beck, A. T., Emery, G., & Greenberg, R. L. (1985). *Anxiety disorders and phobias.* New York: Basic Books.

Beck, K. H., & Lund, A. K. (1981). The effects of health threat seriousness and personal efficacy upon intentions and behavior. *Journal of Applied Social Psychology, 11,* 401-415.

Becker, L. J. (1978). Joint effect of feedback and goal setting on performance: A field study of residential energy conservation. *Journal of Applied Psychology, 63,* 428-433.

Betz, N. E., & Hackett, G. (1986). Applications of self-efficacy theory to understanding career choice behavior. *Journal of Social and Clinical Psychology, 4,* 279-289.

Blustein, D. L. (1989). The role of goal instability and career self-efficacy in the career exploration process. *Journal of Vocational Behavior, 35,* 194-203.

Bower, G. H., (1983). Affect and cognition. *Philosophical Transactions of the Royal Society of London (Series B), 302,* 387-402.

Carver, C. S., & Scheier, M. F. (1981). *Attention and self-regulation: A control-theory approach to human behavior.* New York: Springer-Verlag.

Cervone, D. (1989). Effects of envisioning future activities on self-efficacy judgments and motivation: An availability heuristic interpretation. *Cognitive Therapy and Research, 13,* 247-261.

Cervone, D., Jiwani, N., & Wood, R. (1991). Goal-setting and the differential influence of self-regulatory processes on complex decision-making performance. *Journal of Personality and Social Psychology, 61,* 257-266.

Cervone, D., & Peake, P. K. (1986). Anchoring, efficacy, and action: The influence of judgmental heuristics on self-efficacy judgments and behavior. *Journal of Personality and Social Psychology, 50,* 492-501.

Churchill, A. C. (1990). *Metacognitive self-efficacy and intrusive thought.* Unpublished doctoral dissertation. University of Melbourne, Australia.

Churchill, A. C., & McMurray, N. E. (1990). *Self-efficacy and unpleasant intrusive thought.* Submitted for publication.

Coe, C. L., & Levine, S. (1991, in press). Psychoimmunology: An old idea whose time has come. In P. R. Barchas (Ed.), *Social physiology of social relations.* Oxford: Oxford University Press.

Collins, J. L. (1982, March). *Self-efficacy and ability in achievement behavior.* Paper presented at the annual meeting of the American Educational Research Association, N.Y.

Corbin, C. (1972). Mental practice. In W. Morgan (Ed.), *Ergogenic aids and muscular performance* (pp. 93-118). New York: Academic Press.

Cutrona, C. E., & Troutman, B. R. (1986). Social support, infant temperament, and parenting self-efficacy: A mediational model of postpartum depression. *Child Development, 57,* 1507-1518.

Davis, F. W., & Yates, B. T. (1982). Self-efficacy expectancies versus outcome expectancies as determinants of performance deficits and depressive affect. *Cognitive Therapy and Research, 6,* 23-35.

De Vries, H., Dijkstra, M., & Kuhlman, P. (1988). Self-efficacy: The third factor besides attitude and subjective norm as a predictor of behavioural intentions. *Health Education Research, 3,* 273-282.

Dweck, C. S., & Leggett, E. L. (1988). A social-cognitive approach to motivation and personality. *Psychological Review, 95,* 256-273.

Dzewaltowski, D. A. (1989). Towards a model of exercise motivation. *Journal of Sport and Exercise Psychology, 11,* 251-269.

Dzewaltowski, D. A., Noble, J. M., & Shaw, J. M. (1991). Physical activity participation: Social cognitive theory versus the theories of reasoned action and planned behavior. *Journal of Sport and Exercise Psychology, 12,* 388-405.

Feather, N. T. (Ed.) (1982). *Expectations and actions: Expectancy-value models in psychology.* Hillsdale, NJ: Erlbaum.

Feltz, D. L., & Landers, D. M. (1983). Effects of mental practice on motor skill learning and performance: A meta-analysis. *Journal of Sport Psychology, 5,* 25-57.

Godding, P. R., & Glasgow, R. E. (1985). Self-efficacy and outcome expectations as predictors of controlled smoking status. *Cognitive Therapy and Research, 9,* 583-590.

Hackett, G., & Betz, N. E. (1981). A self-efficacy approach to the career development of women. *Journal of Vocational Behavior, 18,* 326-339.

Hackett, G., & Betz, N. E. (1984). *Mathematics performance, mathematics self-efficacy, and the prediction of science-based college majors.* Unpublished manuscript, University of California, Santa Barbara.

Hogarth, R. (1981). Beyond discrete biases: Functional and dysfunctional aspects of judgmental heuristics. *Psychological Bulletin, 90,* 197-217.

Holahan, C. K., & Holahan, C. J. (1987a). Self-efficacy, social support, and depression in aging: A longitudinal analysis. *Journal of Gerontology, 42,* 65-68.

Holahan, C. K., & Holahan, C. J. (1987b). Life stress, hassles, and self-efficacy in aging: A replication and extension. *Journal of Applied Social Psychology, 17,* 574-592.

Holroyd, K. A., Penzien, D. B., Hursey, K. G., Tobin, D. L., Rogers, L., Holm, J. E., Marcille, P. J., Hall, J. R., & Chila, A. G. (1984). Change mechanisms in EMG biofeedback training: Cognitive changes underlying improvements in tension headache. *Journal of Consulting and Clinical Psychology, 52,* 1039-1053.

Isen, A. M. (1987). Positive affect, cognitive processes, and social behavior. In L. Berkowitz (Ed.), *Advances in experimental social psychology* (Vol. 20, pp. 203-253). New York: Academic Press.

Jacobs, B., Prentice-Dunn, S., & Rogers, R. W. (1984). Understanding persistence: An interface of control theory and self-efficacy theory. *Basic and Applied Social Psychology, 5,* 333-347.

Jourden, F. J., Bandura, A., & Banfield, J. T. (1991, in press). Impact of conceptions of ability on self-regulatory mechanisms and skill development. *Journal of Sport and Exercise Psychology.*

Kanfer, R., & Zeiss, A. M. (1983). Depression, interpersonal standard-setting, and judgments of self-efficacy. *Journal of Abnormal Psychology, 92,* 319-329.

Kavanagh, D. J. (1983). *Mood and self-efficacy.* Unpublished doctoral dissertation, Stanford University, Stanford, CA.

Kavanagh, D. J., & Bower, G. H. (1985). Mood and self-efficacy: Impact of joy and sadness on perceived capabilities. *Cognitive Therapy and Research, 9,* 507-525.

Kavanagh, D. J., & Wilson, P. H. (1989). Prediction of outcome with a group version of cognitive therapy for depression. *Behaviour Research and Therapy, 27,* 333-343.

Kazdin, A. E. (1978). Covert modeling—Therapeutic application of imagined rehearsal. In J. L. Singer & K. S. Pope (Eds.) *The power of human imagination: New methods in psychotherapy. Emotions, personality, and psychotherapy* (pp. 255-278). New York: Plenum.

Kazdin, A. E. (1979). Imagery elaboration and self-efficacy in the covert modeling treatment of unassertive behavior. *Journal of Consulting and Clinical Psychology, 47,* 725-733.

Kent, G. (1987). Self-efficacious control over reported physiological, cognitive and behavioural symptoms of dental anxiety. *Behaviour Research and Therapy, 25,* 341-347.

Kent, G., & Gibbons, R. (1987). Self-efficacy and the control of anxious cognitions. *Journal of Behavior Therapy & Experimental Psychiatry, 18,* 33-40.

Lazarus, R. S., & Folkman, S. (1984). *Stress, appraisal, and coping.* New York: Springer.

Lee, C. (1984a). Accuracy of efficacy and outcome expectations in predicting performance in a simulated assertiveness task. *Cognitive Therapy and Research, 8,* 37-48.

Lee, C. (1984b). Efficacy expectations and outcome expectations as predictors of performance in a snake-handling task. *Cognitive Therapy and Research, 8,* 509-516.

Leland, E. I. (1983). Self-efficacy and other variables as they relate to precompetitive anxiety among male interscholastic basketball players. (Doctoral dissertation, Stanford University, 1983). *Dissertation Abstracts International, 44*, 1376A.

Lent, R. W., Brown, S. D., & Larkin, K. C. (1987). Comparison of three theoretically derived variables in predicting career and academic behavior: Self-efficacy, interest congruence, and consequence thinking. *Journal of Counseling Psychology, 34*, 293-298.

Lent, R. W., & Hackett, G. (1987). Career self-efficacy: Empirical status and future directions. *Journal of Vocational Behavior, 30*, 347-382.

Litt, M. D. (1988). Self-efficacy and perceived control: Cognitive mediators of pain tolerance. *Journal of Personality and Social Psychology, 54*, 149-160.

Locke, E. A., Frederick, E., Lee, C., & Bobko, P. (1984). Effect of self-efficacy, goals, and task strategies on task performance. *Journal of Applied Psychology, 69*, 241-251.

Locke, E. A., & Latham, G. P. (1990). *A theory of goal setting and task performance.* Englewood Cliffs, NJ: Prentice-Hall.

Lord, R. G., & Hanges, P. J. (1987). A control system model of organizational motivation: Theoretical development and applied implications. *Behavioral Science, 32*, 161-178.

Maier, S. F., Laudenslager, M. L., & Ryan, S. M. (1985). Stressor controllability, immune function, and endogenous opiates. In F. R. Brush & J. B. Overmier (Eds.), *Affect, conditioning, and cognition: Essays on the determinants of behavior* (pp. 183-201). Hillsdale, NJ: Erlbaum.

Major, B., Cozzarelli, C., Sciacchitano, A. M., Cooper, M. L., Testa, M., & Mueller, P. M. (1990). Perceived social support, self-efficacy, and adjustment to abortion. *Journal of Personality and Social Psychology, 59*, 452-463.

McAuley, E. (1985). Modeling and self-efficacy: A test of Bandura's model. *Journal of Sport Psychology, 7*, 283-295.

McCaul, K. D., O'Neill, K., & Glasgow, R. E. (1988). Predicting the performance of dental hygiene behaviors: An examination of the Fishbein and Ajzen model and self-efficacy expectations. *Journal of Applied Social Psychology, 18*, 114-128.

Meichenbaum, D. H. (1977). *Cognitive-behavior modification: An integrative approach.* New York: Plenum Press.

Miller, G. A., Galanter, E., & Pribram, K. H. (1960). *Plans and the structure of behavior.* New York: Holt.

Nicholls, J. G. (1984). Achievement motivation: Conceptions of ability, subjective experience, task choice, and performance. *Psychological Review*, 91, 328-346.

Olioff, M., & Aboud, F. E. (1991). Predicting postpartum dysphoria in primiparous mothers: Roles of perceived parenting self-efficacy and self-esteem. *Journal of Cognitive Psychotherapy, 5*, 3-14.

Ozer, E., & Bandura, A. (1990). Mechanisms governing empowerment effects: A self-efficacy analysis. *Journal of Personality and Social Psychology, 58*, 472-486.

Peake, P. K., & Cervone, D. (1989). Sequence anchoring and self-efficacy: Primacy effects in the consideration of possibilities. *Social Cognition, 7*, 31-50.

Perry, D. G., Perry, L. C., & Rasmussen, P. (1986). Cognitive social learning mediators of aggression. *Child Development, 57*, 700-711.

Post-Kammer, P., & Smith, P. (1985). Sex differences in career self-efficacy, consideration, and interests of eighth and ninth graders. *Journal of Counseling Psychology, 32*, 551-559.

Relich, J. D., Debus, R. L., & Walker, R. (1986). The mediation role of attribution and self-efficacy variables for treatment effects on achievement outcomes. *Contemporary Educational Psychology, 11*, 195-216.

Rotter, J. B. (1954). *Social learning and clinical psychology.* Englewood Cliffs, NJ: Prentice-Hall.

Salkovskis, P. M., & Harrison, J. (1984). Abnormal and normal obsessions—a replication. *Behaviour Research and Therapy, 22*, 549-552.

Sarason, I. G. (1975). Anxiety and self-preoccupation. In I. G. Sarason & C. D. Spielberger (Eds.), *Stress and anxiety* (Vol. 2, pp. 27-44). Washington, DC: Hemisphere.

Schunk, D. H., & Cox, P. D. (1986). Strategy training and attributional feedback with learning disabled students. *Journal of Educational Psychology, 78*, 201-209.

Schunk, D. H., & Gunn, T. P. (1986). Self-efficacy and skill development: Influence of task strategies and attributions. *Journal of Educational Research, 79*, 238-244.

Schunk, D. H., & Rice, J. M. (1986). Extended attributional feedback: Sequence effects during remedial reading instruction. *Journal of Early Adolescence, 6*, 55-66.

Schwarzer, R. (1992). Self-efficacy in the adoption and maintenance of health behaviors: A critical analysis of theoretical approaches and a new model. In Schwarzer, R. (Ed.), *Self-efficacy: Thought control of action.* New York: Hemisphere (this volume).

Shavit, Y., & Martin, F. C. (1987). Opiates, stress, and immunity: Animal studies. *Annals of Behavioral Medicine, 9*, 11-20.

Siegel, R. G., Galassi, J. P., & Ware, W. B. (1985). A comparison of two models for predicting mathematics performance: Social learning versus math aptitude-anxiety. *Journal of Counseling Psychology, 32*, 531-538.

Silver, W. S., Mitchell, T. R., & Gist, M. E. (1989). *The impact of self-efficacy on causal attributions for successful and unsuccessful performance.* Unpublished manuscript, University of Washington, Seattle, Washington.

Snyder, M. (1987). *Public appearances, private realities: The psychology of self-monitoring.* New York: W. H. Freeman.

Strang, H. R., Lawrence, E. C., & Fowler, P. C. (1978). Effects of assigned goal level and knowledge of results on arithmetic computation: Laboratory study. *Journal of Applied Psychology, 63*, 446-450.

Taylor, M. S., Locke, E. A., Lee, C., & Gist, M. E. (1984). Type A behavior and faculty research productivity: What are the mechanisms? *Organizational Behavior and Human Performance, 34*, 402-418.

Weinberg, R. S., Gould, D., & Jackson, A. (1979). Expectations and performance: An empirical test of Bandura's self-efficacy theory. *Journal of Sport Psychology, 1*, 320-331.

Wheeler, K. G. (1983). Comparisons of self-efficacy and expectancy models of occupational preferences for college males and females. *Journal of Occupational Psychology, 56*, 73-78.

White, J. (1982). Rejection. Reading, MA: Addison-Wesley.

Wiedenfeld, S. A., O'Leary, A., Bandura, A., Brown, S., Levine, S., & Raska, K. (1990). Impact of perceived self-efficacy in coping with stressors on components of the immune system. *Journal of Personality and Social Psychology, 59*, 1082-1094.

Williams, S. L., Dooseman, G., & Kleifield, E. (1984). Comparative power of guided mastery and exposure treatments for intractable phobias. *Journal of Consulting and Clinical Psychology, 52*, 505-518.

Williams, S. L., Kinney, P. J., & Falbo, J. (1989). Generalization of therapeutic changes in agoraphobia: The role of perceived self-efficacy. *Journal of Consulting and Clinical Psychology, 57*, 436-442.

Williams, S. L., & Rappoport, A. (1983). Cognitive treatment in the natural environment for agoraphobics. *Behavior Therapy, 14*, 299-313.

Williams, S. L., Turner, S. M., & Peer, D. F. (1985). Guided mastery and performance desensitization treatments for severe acrophobia. *Journal of Consulting and Clinical Psychology, 53*, 237-247.

Williams, S. L., & Watson, N. (1985). Perceived danger and perceived self-efficacy as cognitive mediators of acrophobic behavior. *Behavior Therapy, 16*, 136-146.

Wood, R. E., & Bandura, A. (1989a). Impact of conceptions of ability on self-regulatory mechanisms and complex decision making. *Journal of Personality and Social Psychology, 56*, 407-415.

Wood, R. E., & Bandura, A. (1989b). Social cognitive theory of organizational management. *Academy of Management Review, 14*, 361-384.

Author Notes

This chapter includes revised and expanded material from an article published in *The Psychologist* as an invited address at the annual meeting of the British Psychological Society, St. Andrews, Scotland, April 1989.

TWO DIMENSIONS OF PERCEIVED SELF-EFFICACY: COGNITIVE CONTROL AND BEHAVIORAL COPING ABILITY

William J. McCarthy
and Michael D. Newcomb

Confirmatory factor analyses were conducted to test the empirical justification for distinguishing between perceptions of behavioral coping ability and perceptions of cognitive control coping ability for handling environmental challenges. Twenty-four measures of perceived personal effectiveness were collected from 739 young adults, including measures of perceived ability to have a social impact, assertiveness, leadership style, and dating competence. These items were submitted to a hierarchical confirmatory factor analysis in a random half of the sample. As expected, two empirically well-justified second order factors were obtained reflecting perceived cognitive control and behavioral coping strategies. This factor structure was cross-validated in the other half of the sample, and separately for males and females, with all hypothesized features confirmed. Literature on coping strategies, on sex role differences and on self-efficacy predictors is cited as support for distinguishing between perceived cognitive control and perceived behavioral coping abilities. Implications of this distinction for elucidating developmental patterns of drug use and for improving understanding of relapse in lifestyle change programs are discussed.

Why do individuals rely primarily on intrapsychic coping in some contexts and behavioral coping in other contexts? Suppose that a middle-aged woman whose children have grown and left home is distressed to find that her husband pays her inadequate attention, responding perfunctorily to her comments and showing more enthusiasm for newspaper reading and TV watching than for talking with her. Her perceived ability to cope *cognitively* with this situation may be high or low. If it is high, then by merely reframing her thoughts, she can palliate or eliminate her distress, perhaps by thinking of evidence that she is indeed an interesting person and that her husband pays her no attention because he is preoccupied by his work. If it is low, then the distressful observation that her husband finds her boring will intrude on her thoughts unless the situation changes.

Similarly, her perceived ability to cope behaviorally with the situation may be high or low. If it is high, she may elect to leave him or feel confident that she can alter his behavior. If it is low, she will feel that the situation is inescapable and that all of her alternatives are less attractive than the status quo.

Perceptions of personal coping ability have been related to a wide range of health-related outcomes, including smoking cessation, weight control, alcohol abuse, exercise, and contraceptive behavior (e.g., Strecher, DeVellis, Becker, & Rosenstock, 1986, and O'Leary, 1985). As individuals' self-percepts of coping ability increase, so does the probability of their achieving self-set health goals.

Between the identification of an important self-relevant goal and the ultimate achievement of the goal are interposed challenges with which the individual must cope. These challenges may be primarily cognitive or primarily behavioral in nature. The coping behaviors appropriate for dealing with these challenges have been termed emotion-focused or problem-focused (e.g., Folkman & Lazarus, 1980). Emotion-focused coping includes such behaviors as avoidance, intellectualization, isolation, suppression, and magical thinking. Problem-focused coping includes such behaviors as information-seeking, cognitive problem-solving, inhibition of action and direct action. The perception that one can effectively implement emotion-focused or problem-focused coping can be termed perceived cognitive control ability and perceived behavioral coping ability, respectively.

Other literature on coping has promoted a distinction between behavioral and cognitive ways of coping. For example, Pearlin and Schooler (1978) discussed three major categories of coping responses, two of which involved cognitive strategies to reduce or eliminate stress, whereas the third concerned the active manipulation of the environment. In her review, Taylor (1986) identified four types of control that mediated the effects of coping with stressors, but concluded that these four types of control could be reduced to two: (a) changing thoughts with respect to the stressor, and (b) taking some action with respect to the stressor. If people differ in whether they rely primarily on cognitive or behavioral means of coping with a challenge, they also probably differ in their perceived ability to use either cognitive control or behavioral strategies for coping with the challenges. The following report seeks to confirm the validity and usefulness of distinguishing between perceived cognitive control and behavioral coping ability through confirmatory factor analysis of young adult data on coping strategies and through example.

Although we find it useful to distinguish between perceived cognitive control ability and perceived behavioral coping ability, we note that efficacious behavior is rarely a function exclusively of only one of these. Characteristics of the context (such as the amount of freedom individuals have to change the environment) and characteristics of the individual (such as age) determine which type of perceived coping ability is the more important contributor to self-perceived ability to perform the desired behavior.

In their study of adult responses to 1,332 stress episodes, Folkman and Lazarus (1980) noted that both problem-focused and emotion-focused coping were used to cope with 98% of the episodes. They also noted that the *importance* of the type of coping varied, however, with context and according to the characteristics of the individuals. Cognitive strategies were employed most frequently in situations where the individual was relatively helpless to bring about the desired behavior by themselves, such as when recovering from an illness. Problem-focused strategies were employed more frequently in work situations. Folkman and Lazarus found that the importance of type of coping varied with gender, with men relying more heavily than women on problem-focused coping even when the context permitted only emotion-focused coping. It should be noted, again, that distinguishing conceptually between perceived cognitive control and perceived behavioral coping ability should not imply that we view these concepts as independent. Folkman and Lazarus (1980), in fact, observed a mean correlation of .44 between emotion-focused and problem-focused coping across three different samples.

This study was designed to confirm the reasonableness of distinguishing generically between perceived cognitive coping ability and perceived behavioral coping ability as separate components of self-efficacy. The importance of this distinction, if accepted, is that it would be likely to stimulate more careful examination of the contextual, temporal, and individual influences on percepts of self-efficacy. Individuals may have similar perceptions concerning their respective abilities to accomplish their jobs or to effect major lifestyle changes, but nevertheless vary greatly in their perceived ability to cope with the behavioral or cognitive challenges associated with accomplishing the desired behavior. Moreover, within individuals the relative importance of perceived cognitive control and behavioral coping ability may vary with time, age and the individual's experience with coping with the specific challenge.

In settings such as prisons, where inmates would find that a problem-focused coping strategy is often inappropriate, individuals can still vary in their ability to cope with environmental stressors, depending on their perceived ability to regulate their thoughts. In the same vein, children's responses to environmental challenges often are limited to cognitive coping strategies because their dependency on adults and their immaturity are such as to obviate the use of behavioral coping strategies. A child who is sexually abused by an adult relative, for instance, typically relies on cognitive strategies to cope with the situation, especially disassociation, and later, amnesia (Courtois, 1988).

Contrariwise, the theoretical necessity for the separate concept of a perceived ability to cope behaviorally seems justified by attempts to relate the use of coping strategies to spontaneous major lifestyle change. Spontaneous major lifestyle changes, such as taking up jogging, reducing the percentage of calories in one's diet derived from fat, and adopting a child, put a premium on behavioral coping relative to cognitive control coping, because there are simply too many changes in day-to-day behaviors resulting from the major lifestyle change in question to be anticipated cognitively. It is reasonable to assume that persons with strong beliefs in their general ability to change their social and physical environment will be more likely to embark on major voluntary lifestyle changes than are persons who perceive themselves as generally having weak behavioral coping strategies. When discussing the influences on adoption of major lifestyle change one has to speak of "general" ability because many of the specific challenges that follow the major life style change are unanticipated at the time of the decision. Successful voluntary lifestyle change is often accompanied by multiple changes in how the individual interacts with her/his social and physical environment. A successful change in diet, for instance, will typically be accompanied by changes in shopping habits, changes in cooking habits, and changes in where, when and with whom to dine out. For predicting the success of major lifestyle change efforts, one's ability to cope intrapsychically with specific challenges seems less relevant than one's general ability to have a behavioral impact on one's environment. This focus on "general" ability might seem inappropriate for a discussion of self-efficacy as it is classically defined (Bandura, 1977). This focus is consistent, however, with recent demonstrations that global judgments about a subject's ability to train employees or to influence organizational performance can influence their perception of their own organizational ability (Bandura & Wood, 1989; Wood & Bandura, 1989) and subsequent organizational performance.

Description of Proposed Study

For this study, we followed the strategy of Ryckman, Thornton, and Cantrell (1982). A comprehensive range of 24 measures of personal effectiveness was administered to a community sample of young adults being followed in a longitudinal study of growth and development. These measures were submitted to a hierarchical, confirmatory factor analysis in a random half of the sample and cross-validated in the other half. Based on the literature discussed above, we hypothesized finding two second order factors of perceived behavioral ability (Perceived Behavioral Coping Ability) and perceived cognitive control ability to cope with environmental challenges (Perceived Cognitive Control Ability). Multiple assessments of personal effectiveness included measures of perceived ability to have a social impact, general assertiveness, dating competence, social support, depression, perceived loss of control, purpose in life, and leadership style. These were selected to provide a comprehensive range of measures of the subjects' cognitive and behavioral skills and emotional states related to interpersonal relations. We expected that Perceived Behavioral Coping Ability would be reflected in first-order factors of social impact efficacy (perceived ability to have a social impact), general assertiveness, social resources, dating competence, and leadership style because these represent ways of behaviorally operating on the environment. On the other hand, we expected that Cognitive Control Coping Ability would be reflected in constructs of social impact efficacy, depression, purpose in life, and perceived loss of control because these involve internal coping or cognitive qualities. Expected social impact efficacy was expected to load on both second-order factors because this measure included cognitive and behavioral coping items (Blatt, Quinlan, Chevron, McDonald, & Zuroff, 1982).

Table 1

Description of Sample

Characteristic	N	%
Sex		
Male	221	30
Female	518	70
Age		
Mean		21.93
Range		19 - 24
Ethnicity		
Black	111	15
Hispanic	72	10
White	490	66
Asian	66	9
High School Graduate		
Yes	684	93
No	55	7
Living Situation		
Alone	28	4
Parents	343	46
Spouse	77	10
Spouse and Child	56	8
Cohabitation	67	9
Dormitory	40	5
Roommates	96	13
Other	32	4
Number of Children		
None	619	84
One	106	14
Two or more	14	2
Current Life Activity		
Military	23	3
Junior College	87	12
Four-year college	153	21
Part-time job	102	14
Full-time job	343	46
Other	31	4
Income for Past Year		
None	71	10
Under $5,000	242	33
$5,001 to $15,000	334	45
Over $15,001	92	12

The analyses proceeded in steps, first testing for sex differences on the measures. Then the adequacy of the hypothesized latent measurement model was tested followed by testing the second-order factor model of the primary-order latent variables. These analyses were conducted in the derivation sample, and then the second-order factor results were confirmed in the cross-validation sample, and in separate samples of men and women.

METHOD

Subjects

Participants in this study were 739 young adults who completed an eight-year (fifth wave data assessment point) longitudinal study of adolescent and young adult development. Data were collected initially from 1,634 students in the seventh, eighth, and ninth grades at 11 randomly-selected Los Angeles County schools. At this young adult follow-up, each participant was paid $12.50 to complete the questionnaire and all subjects were apprised of a grant of confidentiality given by the U.S. Department of Justice. Forty-five percent of the original sample participated as young adults. The loss of subjects due to attrition over the eight years has been shown not likely to bias the results adversely (Newcomb, 1986; Newcomb & Bentler, 1988a).

Table 1 presents a description of the sample. As evident, 30% were men and 70% were women, which parallels the sex distribution in the initial sample and does not reflect differential attrition by sex. Most were employed full-time and represented varied ethnic backgrounds. Additional information is provided about their current living arrangements, income, and current life pursuits. When these sample characteristics are compared with national samples of young adults (e.g., Bachman, O'Malley, & Johnston, 1984; Miller et al., 1983) or other studies of young adult populations (e.g., Donovan, Jessor, & Jessor, 1983; Kandel, 1984) very similar patterns emerged. Consequently, we consider this sample to be reasonably representative of young adults in general.

Measures

Table 2 presents a listing of the 24 variables used in this study. They are organized according to the latent construct they are hypothesized to reflect. For instance, the latent construct of Social Impact Efficacy is assumed to generate the variation in three observed indicators called inner resources, independence, and others' respect. For factors which tend to be unidimensional in nature, three measured-variable indicators were constructed from the items to reflect the latent factor or construct. This was done, since, as a rule, it is recommended to have at least three, highly correlated indicators to identify a latent construct (e.g., Bentler & Newcomb, 1986). This was done on the self-efficacy, dating competence, general assertiveness, and purpose of life factors. Standard univariate statistics for each variable are also given in the table. Below we describe how each variable was assessed in regard to the latent construct it represents.

Social impact efficacy. Three scales are used to reflect the Social Impact Efficacy construct. These were derived from the five-item scale of efficacy developed by Blatt et al. (1982). Responses to these five items were given on a five-point anchored rating scale that ranged from *strongly disagree* (1) to *strongly agree* (5). The items were factor analyzed and found to reflect a unitary construct (only one eigenvalue greater than 1.00 and all factor loadings were greater than .4 on the first unrotated factor). As a result, these five items were combined into three scales based on content. Inner resources was assessed with a single item—"I have many inner resources." Independence was the average of two items—"I am a very independent person" and "I set my personal goals as high as possible." Others' respect was the average of two items—"Others have high expectations of me" and "What I do and say has a great impact on those around me."

General assertiveness and dating competence. Dating Competence was assessed by three scales (dating 1, dating 2, and dating 3) derived from a nine-item scale of social competence in dating situations. General Assertiveness was assessed by three scales (assertive 1, assertive 2, and assertive 3) obtained from a nine-item social assertiveness scale. The total Dating Competence and Social Assertiveness scales were developed by Levenson and Gottman (1978), and in several studies had quite good discriminant validity in both normal and clinic samples. In the derivation study the entire Dating Competence scale had an internal consistency reliability alpha of .92, while for the General Assertiveness scale the alpha was .85. Latent constructs derived from these scales have also been used in a study of sexual behavior and responsiveness (Newcomb, 1984).

Social resources. Three questions were asked to determine the quantity or amount of social supports as perceived in three life contexts. The first item asked "How many clubs, groups, or organizations do you belong to (including church groups)?" The second item asked "How many friends do you really feel close to?" And the third item asked "How many family members or relatives can you talk to about things personal to you?" Responses were given on a rating scale that ranged from none to nine or more. These items were specifically developed for this research project, but are similar to standard measures of social support that focus on amount of social resources and correlate quite highly with satisfaction with social support from various types of social networks (Newcomb & Bentler, 1988b).

Depression. The 20-item depression scale from the Center for Epidemiologic Study of Depression (CES-D) was completed by all subjects. The development, validities, and reliabilities of the measure have been reported elsewhere (Husaini, Neff, Harrington, Hughes, & Stone, 1980; Radloff, 1977; Weissman, Sholomskas, Pottenger, Prusoff, & Locke, 1977). Participants were asked to rate their frequency of occurrence for each of the 20 symptom items during the past week on a scale from *none* (0) to *5 -7 days* (3). The 20 items were factor analyzed in this sample and found to contain four distinct factors, which is consistent with previous attempts to determine the factor structure of the CES-D (e.g., Clark, Aneshensel, Frerichs, & Morgan, 1981; Radloff, 1977; Roberts, 1980). The four factors included positive affect, negative affect, impaired motivation, and impaired relationships. Items were averaged into the respective four factors and were used as indicators of a general latent construct of Depression.

Perceived loss of control. Three single-item variables are hypothesized to reflect the construct of Perceived Loss of Control. Subjects were asked to rate their degree of agreement with three statements: (1) "I feel I am not in control of my life," (2) "I feel that whether or not I am successful is just a matter of luck and chance, rather than my own doing," and (3) "I feel that others are running my life for me." Responses were given on a seven-point anchored rating scale that ranged from *strongly disagree* (1) to *strongly agree* (7). Cronbach's alpha for these three items was .65. This construct assesses a general lack of control over life events, and has been validated in other samples and studies (Newcomb, 1986; Newcomb & Harlow, 1986).

Purpose in life. The Purpose in Life test (Crumbaugh, 1968; Crumbaugh & Maholic, 1964, 1969) consists of 20 items designed to assess one's level of or purpose in life. Each item was rated on a seven-point anchored rating scale ranging from *strongly disagree* (1) to *strongly agree* (7). Previous research on the Purpose in Life test indicated that it contains several small primary factors and one large general factor (Harlow, Newcomb, & Bentler, 1987). For purposes of this study, the 20 items were randomly assigned into three scales (PIL 1, PIL 2, and PIL 3) which were used as manifest indicators of a latent construct of Purpose in Life.

Leadership style. Two personality scales, ambition and leadership, were used to reflect the construct of Leadership Style. These traits were assessed using a self-rating test modified for this research program, but based on the Bentler Psychological Inventory (BPI; Bentler & Newcomb, 1978; Huba & Bentler, 1982). Although the BPI was developed with multivariate methods, the items have a high degree of face validity. Half of the items for each trait are reverse-scored to minimize response bias or acquiescence. Four items were used to assess each trait and each item was rated on a 5-point bipolar scale. Thus, each scale had a range of 4 to 20. The BPI has proved useful in studies of marital success and failure (Bentler & Newcomb, 1978), criminal behavior (Huba & Bentler, 1983), and adolescent substance use (Huba & Bentler, 1982). The period-free test-retest reliability for ambition was .72 and the reliability for leadership was .71 (Stein, Newcomb, & Bentler, 1986).

Analyses

Our first set of analyses use point-biserial correlations to test for mean differences between men and women on each of the 24 variables. We next use a confirmatory factor analysis with latent variables to evaluate the adequacy of the hypothesized factor structure (e.g., Bentler, 1980; Bentler & Newcomb, 1986), in a random half of the sample, which we call the derivation sample. An inspection of the skew and kurtosis estimates for the 24 observed measures indicates that they are relatively normally distributed. As a result we will use the maximum likelihood structural model estimator, which requires multivariately normal data (e.g., Bentler, 1983, 1986). If the initial hypothesized model does not adequately reflect the data (which is common in models with many variables and many subjects), we will modify the model until an acceptable fit is achieved, in a manner which will not disturb the critical features of the model. These empirical model modifications will be guided by the multivariate Lagrangian Multiplier test for adding parameters and the multivariate Wald test for deleting parameters (Bentler & Chou, 1986). Once this is accomplished, we will attempt to confirm our two hypothesized second-order constructs in this model, making modifications where necessary. This final model will be tested separately in the other random half of our sample (called the cross-validation sample), as well as the samples of men and women to determine whether the second-order factor structure is an accurate representation in these samples. The final model will also be tested in the original derivation sample, but without the empirical modifications to establish whether the model modifications may have distorted or biased the final results.

RESULTS

Sex Differences

Mean differences between men and women on the 24 variables were tested using point-biserial correlations. Males were coded 1 and females were coded 2, so that a positive correlation indicates that the women had the larger value and a negative correlation indicates that the men had the larger value. These mean difference correlations are presented in the right-hand column of Table 2.

Of the 24 variables, significant mean differences were found on 14 of them. These differences indicate that the women, compared to the men, felt that they had fewer inner resources, less independence, less respect from others, less assertiveness (on all three scales), a smaller number of friends they could rely on, less positive affect, more negative affect, more impaired motivation, others controlled her life more, slightly less dating competence (only one scale significantly different), less ambition, and fewer leadership qualities. Although there were many mean differences between the men and women, the magnitude of these differences was quite small. For instance, the largest difference accounted for only four percent of the variance between groups (on ambition). Based on these rather small in magnitude mean differences between men and women, and previous results indicating that there were not different factor structures for men and women on social support and loneliness variables (Newcomb & Bentler, 1986) and on physical health status indicators (Newcomb & Bentler, 1987), we will collapse across sex for the bulk of the remaining analyses. However, we will test our final

model in the separate samples of men and women to determine whether we may
have obscured any important findings by combining the men with the women.

Table 2
Summary of Variable Characteristics and Sex Mean Difference Tests

Factor/Variable	Mean	Range	SD	Skew	Kurtosis	Sex Difference r_{pb}^{a}
Social Impact Efficacy						
Inner resources	3.87	1-5	.75	-.55	.61	-.18***
Independence	3.86	1-5	.76	-.76	.41	-.11**
Others respect	3.64	1-5	.62	-.39	.56	-.08*
General Assertiveness						
Assertive 1	8.89	4-13	1.84	-.13	-.38	-.13**
Assertive 2	9.07	4-14	1.90	.03	-.32	-.18***
Assertive 3	8.74	4-14	1.87	.05	-.24	-.09*
Social Resources						
Number of family members	3.48	0-9	2.44	.91	.12	.02
Number of friends	4.04	0-9	2.34	.71	-.10	-.14***
Number of organizations	1.34	0-9	1.36	1.21	2.54	-.06
Depression (CES-D)						
Positive affect	2.34	0-3	.64	-.96	.32	-.10**
Negative affect	.63	0-3	.64	1.20	1.20	.15***
Impaired motivation	.71	0-2.75	.46	.79	.79	.08*
Impaired relationships	.34	0-3	.47	1.72	3.30	.00
Purpose in Life						
PIL 1	5.57	2-7	1.80	-.81	.22	-.04
PIL 2	5.30	2.4-7	1.80	-.58	.06	-.06
PIL 3	5.41	2-7	1.77	-.57	.13	-.05
Perceived Loss of Control						
Not in control	2.26	1-7	1.51	1.31	1.05	-.02
Powerless	2.28	1-7	1.45	1.20	.82	.03
Others control life	2.73	1-7	1.50	.87	.01	.11**
Dating Competence						
Dating 1	8.84	4-13	1.75	-.06	-.28	-.08*
Dating 2	9.25	3-13	1.82	-.19	-.23	-.03
Dating 3	9.96	4-14	1.87	-.14	-.17	-.05
Leadership Style						
Ambition	14.52	4-20	3.53	-.41	-.49	-.20***
Leadership	14.29	5-20	2.83	-.13	-.30	-.16***

Note. [a] Males were coded 1 and females were coded 2, so that a positive point-biserial correlation indicates that the females had the larger value.
*p < .05; **p < .01; ***p < .001.

First-Order Latent Factor Model

This first sequence of models are tested on a random half (n = 370) of our total sample, which we call our derivation sample. In the initial confirmatory factor model, the eight latent constructs were hypothesized to "cause" or generate the variation in the 24 observed variables. The factor structure of this first model was "pure" in that each observed variable was allowed to load on only one latent construct. For instance, inner resources was assumed to be an indicator only of Social Impact Efficacy. This assumption of mutual exclusivity may be an overly constrained imposition on the model, since many of the variables are conceptually similar and may in fact reflect more than one underlying quality.

To identify the model all factor loadings were freed, the variances of the constructs were fixed at unity, and all factor intercorrelations were allowed to be freely estimated. This initial confirmatory factor model did not fit the data to an acceptable degree, chi^2 (df = 224, N = 370) = 480.17, p < .001, NFI (normed fit index: Bentler & Bonett, 1980) = .86. Latent-factor intercorrelations for this model are presented in the upper triangle of Table 3. All hypothesized factor loadings were highly significant, p < .001. The NFI was sufficiently large to suggest that an acceptable model could be achieved by adding several small empirically determined parameters that were not hypothesized in the initial model.

Based on an examination of selected modification indices for additional factor loadings and correlated uniquenesses (Bentler & Chou, 1986), five non-hypothesized factor loadings and 22 correlations among manifest variable residuals were added to the model. With these additions the model adequately fit the data, chi^2 (df = 196, N = 370) = 181.97, p = .76, NFI = .95. This new model was a significant improvement over the initial model (p < .001). A summary of all model fit statistics and difference chi^2 tests are given in Table 4. To test whether the addition of these empirically-determined parameters distorted the substantive interpretation of the model, the latent-factor intercorrelations from the initial model were correlated with those obtained in the final, modified model. These parameters were correlated greater than .99. As a result, the final model was not considered biased due to the model modifications.

Standardized factor loadings and residual variances for the final first-order confirmatory factor model are given in Figure 1. The rectangles represent the observed variables, the large circles indicate the latent constructs, and the small circles reflect residual variances of the observed variables. These five non-hypothesized factor loadings tend to be small in magnitude (only one is over .40) and all are in interpretable directions. For instance, general assertiveness also negatively influenced the perception that others control your life. The latent-factor intercorrelations for this model are given in the lower triangle of Table 3. The absolute value of the correlations ranged from a low of .06 to a high of .88, and 11 were higher than .5. In other words, many of the constructs appear to be highly correlated and may reflect higher-order factors, as originally hypothesized.

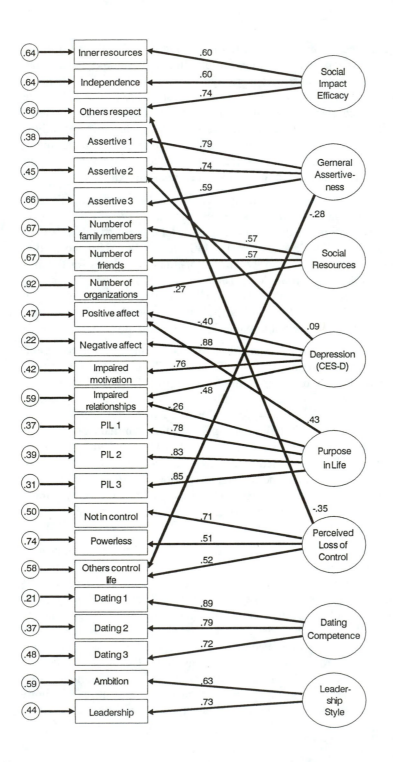

Figure 1 Final confirmatory factor analysis model for the derivation sample. Large circles represent latent factors, rectangles observed variables, and small circles residuals. Not depicted in the figure for reasons of clarity are two-headed arrows (correlations) joining all possible pairs of latent factors. Parameter estimates are standardized and residual variables are variances. Significance levels were determined by critical ratios (**$p < .01$; ***$p < .001$).

Table 3

Factor Intercorrelations Between the Initial (Upper Triangle) and Final (Lower Triangle) First-Order Confirmatory Factor Models

Factor	I	II	III	IV	V	VI	VII	VIII
I Social Impact Efficacy	1.00	.65	.44	-.44	.71	-.59	.51	.62
II General Assertiveness	.60	1.00	.30	-.31	.50	-.40	.58	.67
III Social Resources	.40	.31	1.00	-.37	.50	-.30	.48	.20
IV Depression (CES-D)	-.44	-.34	-.29	1.00	-.59	.73	-.35	-.22
V Purpose in Life	.78	.46	.50	-.53	1.00	-.88	.54	.30
VI Perceived Loss of Control	-.61	-.39	-.25	.61	-.84	1.00	-.48	-.32
VII Dating Competence	.56	.61	.49	-.32	.52	-.4	1.00	.48
VIII Leadership Style	.61	.56	.12	-.06	.27	-.25	.41	1.00

Note. r between initial and final correlations > .99. All correlations are significant at $p < .01$.

Second-Order Confirmatory Factor Models

Based upon our theoretical position, which hypothesized that two second-order factors should underlie the construct of self-efficacy, two second-order factors were introduced into the confirmatory factor analysis. One second-order factor represented Perceived Behavioral Coping Ability and was reflected in loadings allowed on social impact efficacy, general assertiveness, social resources, dating competence, and leadership style. The other second-order factor reflected Perceived Cognitive Control Coping Ability with hypothesized factor indicators of social impact efficacy (the only first-order construct to load on both second-order factors), a lack of depression, purpose in life, and a lack of perceived loss of control.

A model was tested which included the two second-order factors as defined above. Perceived Behavioral Coping Ability and Perceived Cognitive Control Coping Ability were allowed to correlate freely. Three additional empirically-determined correlations were included between pairs of first-order factor residuals: Depression and leadership style, social impact efficacy and leadership style, and depression and perceived loss of control. The factor residual of purpose in life was fixed at zero in order to prevent it from being estimated as negative.

This model adequately fit the data and was not significantly different from the first-order confirmatory factor models, even though 16 fewer parameters were necessary to represent the first-order latent factor intercorrelations (see summary of fit indices in Table 4). This model is graphically depicted in

Figure 2 omitting the observed variables for clarity. Parameter estimates are standardized and residual variables are variances.

Table 4
Summary of Fit Statistics

Model	chi^2	Degrees of Freedom	p Value	Normed Fit Index
		Derivation Sample (N = 370)		
1. Initial CFA[a]	480.17	224	<.001	.86
2. Final CFA[b]	191.97	196	.76	.95
Model 1-2 difference	288.20	28	<.001	
3. Two second-order factors on Model 2	211.13	212	.50	.94
Model 3-2 difference	19.16	16	.26	
4. Two second-order factors on Model 1	501.04	240	<.001	.87
Model 4-1 difference	20.87	16	.18	
5. Second-order factors correlated at unity	278.89	213	.001	.92
Model 5-3 difference	67.76	1	<.001	
		Cross-Validation Samples		
6. Separate cross-validation sample-Model 3	358.54	212	<.001	.89
7. Males only, Model 3	219.29	212	.35	.90
8. Females only, Model 3	352.51	212	<.001	.92

Note. [a] CFA = Confirmatory factor analysis. [b] Modified by adding 22 correlated residuals and 5 nonhypothesized factor loadings.

Perceived Behavioral Coping Ability and Perceived Cognitive Control Coping Ability were correlated .66, indicating a moderate association between them (44% common variance), while retaining their own uniqueness. This correlation resembled the correlation of .44 that Folkman and Lazarus (1980) observed between emotion-focused and problem-focused coping and the range of correlations (.48-.37) between perceived coping and cognitive control efficacy that Ozer and Bandura (1990) recently reported. (These studies measured variables rather than latent constructs, which might account for the smaller size). The largest additional correlation was between the residuals of Social Impact

Efficacy and Leadership Style, indicating that the two second-order factors did not account for the entire association between these two constructs. This association may reflect an additional second-order factor for these two constructs, over-and-above the relationship accounted for by the Perceived Behavioral Coping Ability factor. A similar possibility may exist for Depression and Perceived Loss of Control. These were not tested because two-indicator factors tend to be very unstable, and the fit and interpretability of the model seem to be quite good as it stands.

In order to determine whether the two second-order factors of self-efficacy that we have identified are in fact separate constructs, an additional more restricted model was tested. In this model the correlation between the two second-order factors was fixed at 1.0, operationalizing the hypothesis that they are assessing the same quality. This model did not accurately reflect the data and was significantly worse when compared to the previous model which allowed the two second-order constructs to be unique (see summary of fit statistics in Table 4).

Finally, we tested the second-order factor model in the initial confirmatory model that did not include the additional five factor loadings nor the 22 correlated uniquenesses. All significant relationships were retained and the resultant model was not significantly different from the initial model. Thus, we conclude that the model depicted in Figure 2 is an accurate portrayal of the data that is not biased or distorted due to model modifications.

Cross-Validation of the Second-Order Factor Model

This final model was tested in the separate, untouched random half of the total sample, as well as the separate samples of men and women. Fit indices for these runs are given in Table 4 (Models 6, 7, and 8). In each of these three samples, all hypothesized factor loadings and second-order factor results were significant.

Although only the male sample fit the model according to the p-value criterion, all three models had NFIs greater than .89, indicating that each fit the data reasonably well. Similarly, the ratio of chi^2 to degrees of freedom was consistently under 2.0, also reflecting an excellent degree of fit. All hypothesized factor loadings on the first-order factors were significant in each of the three sample partitions. Table 5 presents the standardized parameter estimates for the second-order factors for the derivation sample, as well as the cross-validation, female, and male samples. Although the magnitude of the factor loadings varied somewhat, the general patterns of association were remarkably similar. The correlation between the two second-order factors was consistently in the .64 to .66 range. Using the cross-validation method suggested by Cudeck and Browne (1983), the specific model developed in the derivation sample was used in the cross-validation sample (by imposing identical parameterization and parameter estimates) and accounted for 86% of the variance of their new data. Although the fit was worse in this second sample, the decrement was not substantial, and more important, the substantive conclusions (i.e., interpretation of parameter estimates) was virtually identical in the derivation and cross-validation sample, when parameters were estimated freely (Table 5). As a result, we conclude that the factor model presented in Figure 2 is equally representative of men and women, and thus does not differ by sex of the subject, and has been cross-validated in a separate sample.

Table 5
Summary of Second-Order Factor Parameters for Several Sample Partitions

Parameter	Derivation Sample	Cross-Validation Sample	Female Sample	Male Sample
	Second-Order Factor Loadings			
Behavioral Coping Efficacy				
Social impact efficacy	.40	.28	.32	.31
General assertiveness	.73	.74	.74	.66
Social resources	.57	.49	.60	.47
Dating competence	.81	.64	.69	.81
Leadership style	.50	.50	.56	.46
Cognitive/Emotional Coping Efficacy				
Social impact efficacy	.51	.59	.55	.59
Depression	-.53	-.47	-.47	-.56
Purpose in life	1.00	.97	1.00	1.00
Perceived loss of control	-.85	-.93	-.91	-.85
	Factor Correlations			
Perceived Behavioral Coping Ability with Perceived Cognitive/Emotional Ability	.66	.64	.66	.66
Depression (R)[a] with perceived loss of control (R)	.41	.25	.35	.32
Social impact efficacy, (R) with leadership style (R)	.48	.49	.52	.31
Depression (R) with leadership style (R)	-.20	-.12	-.15	-.17

Note. [a] (R) denotes factor residual.

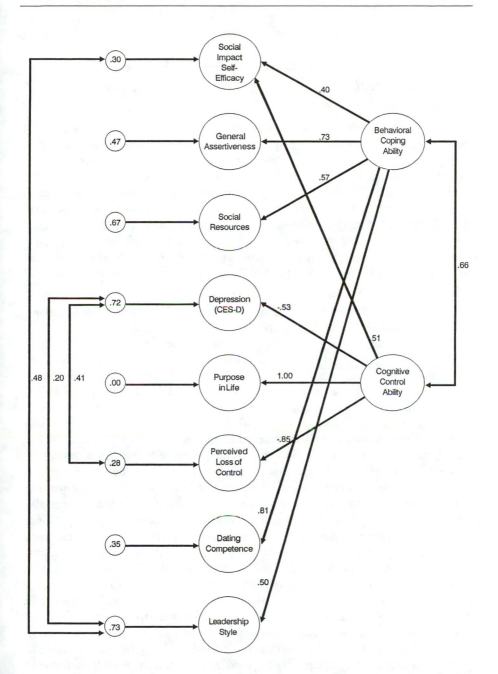

Figure 2 Final second-order factor model for the derivation sample. The large circles are latent constructs (the two on the right-hand side are second-order factors); the small circles represent factor residuals. Two-headed arrows are correlations. Parameter estimates are standardized and residual variables are variances. Significance levels were determined by critical ratios (**$p < .01$; ***$p < .001$).

DISCUSSION

Affirmation of the Distinction Between Perceived Ability to
Self-Regulate Cognitively and Perceived Ability to Cope Behaviorally
With Environmental Challenges

Our results confirm the validity of distinguishing between beliefs about one's ability to regulate cognitions in response to challenges associated with accomplishing desired goals and beliefs about one's ability to have an impact on the environment to accomplish desired goals. Those constructs that are primarily intrapsychic, such as depression, purpose in life, and perceived loss of control loaded heavily on the Perceived Cognitive Control Ability factor, but did not load on the Perceived Behavioral Coping Ability factor. Those constructs that concern active involvement with one's social environment, such as general assertiveness, leadership, and dating competence, on the other hand, loaded heavily on the Perceived Behavioral Coping Ability factor, but not on the Perceived Cognitive Control factor.

The empirical results obtained in this study confirm the usefulness of a theoretical distinction that is already current and frequently applied in the literature on coping with stress. This report, of course, goes beyond the literature on coping to justify elaborating the self-efficacy construct to include the distinction between perceived cognitive control and perceived behavioral abilities. The findings from a recent prospective study involving these two distinguishable percepts of ability (Ozer & Bandura, 1990) further affirm the importance of distinguishing between cognitive control and behavioral coping ability. Ozer and Bandura noted in this study of women mastering self-defense skills that perceived [behavioral] coping self-efficacy developed more rapidly during the period of training than did cognitive control self-efficacy. One explanation for this finding is that the behavioral and attitudinal changes engendered by 22 contact hours of training in thwarting simulated physical assaults were too many, too disparate, and too emotionally disturbing to be fully apprehended and integrated at the time of skill acquisition. The resulting dissociation of perceived cognitive control and perceived [behavioral] coping self-efficacy during the skill acquisition phase was temporary. By the 6-month follow-up the positive correlation between cognitive control efficacy and [behavioral] coping self-efficacy was restored ($r = .37$), despite sustained increases in self-defense efficacy and sustained decreases in perceived vulnerability and anxiety. It is as if time and effort were required to alter existing patterns of cognitive control following sudden major changes in perceived behavioral coping self-efficacy. If these findings are generalizable to other efforts at mastering complex behaviors, they suggest the need to examine in more detail the nature and sequencing of self-efficacy beliefs prior to, during, and following the acquisition of mastery.

Health Consequences of High Intrapsychic Efficacy
Relative to Problem-Focused Efficacy

Individuals high in Perceived Cognitive Control Coping Ability, relative to Perceived Behavioral Coping Ability, may end up merely palliating problems that could be resolved behaviorally. For example, a woman suffering from an unhappy marriage may successfully reduce that unhappiness via psychotherapy that boosts her self-esteem, thereby increasing her ability to avoid intrusive, self-denigrating thoughts, without doing anything about increasing her perceived ability to influence her husband's insensitivity to her needs.

Individuals who perceive that they have little control over their environment can nevertheless increase their probability of achieving a healthful lifestyle change by maximizing their Perceived Cognitive Control. An example would be an individual working in a tobacco processing plant who would like to quit smoking. Such an individual would find few opportunities for changing the social and physical environment to make it more conducive to quitting smoking, but might nevertheless embark on a plan to become an exsmoker by relying on primarily cognitive control strategies for coping with temptations to smoke. Cognitive strategies such as thought management, self-reward, and distractive thoughts for reducing urges to smoke could be employed to accomplish a successful transition to being a nonsmoker even though the individual's Perceived Behavioral Coping Ability was low.

Conversely, smokers who feel that they have little "willpower" and who are hostile to conventional intrapsychic approaches to behavior change can nevertheless be successfully counseled to effect a successful change to being a non-smoker by being encouraged to adopt behaviors seriatim that cumulatively are antithetical to the smoking habit. A program of steadily increasing physical activity, for instance, is likely to improve one's chances of becoming a long-term nonsmoker because aerobic exercise is inherently inconsistent or incompatible with the cigarette smoking lifestyle (e.g., Koplan, Powell, Sikes, Shirley, & Campbell, 1982). Successful adoption of behaviors that are inconsistent with smoking should lead to increased access to images of the self as a nonsmoker, with an attendant increase in perceived ability to abstain from smoking (Kazdin, 1979).

Implications of the Distinction for Interventions Designed to Change
Perceptions of Self-Efficacy

Interventions designed to influence individuals' self-efficacy with respect to a desirable health-related lifestyle change have not distinguished between Perceived Behavioral Coping Ability and Perceived Cognitive Control Ability. In the few instances where distinctions have been made between the use of cognitive or behavioral coping strategies, there have been notable differences in the contribution of behavioral and cognitive coping to explaining the behavior change. The literature on the behavior change involved in drug use cessation, to take one example, includes reports of contrasts between behavioral and cognitive methods of coping with temptations to return to drug use. One such applied study found that recidivists among would-be exsmokers reported relying more heavily on behavioral coping than did the more successful exsmokers who continued to abstain from smoking (Shiffman, Reed, Maltese, Rapkin, & Jarvik, 1985). Another study investigated the determinants of cessation of heroin use and found a similar advantage for cognitive coping relative to behavioral coping strategies (Chaney & Roszell, 1985).

The findings reported above could be an artifact of the intervention model used, namely the Relapse Prevention model (Marlatt & Gordon, 1985). Much of the work on relapse prevention has focused on how to equip individuals with self-efficacy percepts that would help them cope in situations that pose a high risk of recidivism. The focus however, has not been on increasing the individual's perceived ability to *reduce* exposure to high-risk situations, but rather on the individual's perceived ability to reduce the experience of stress in high-risk situations. In other words, the focus has been such as to exaggerate the importance of perceived cognitive control for coping with high-risk situations relative to the importance of perceived ability to respond behaviorally for avoiding or escaping from high-risk situations.

The superiority of enhancing percepts of Behavioral Coping Ability rather than enhancing percepts of Cognitive Control Coping Ability in lifestyle change programs is suggested by some multi-year follow-ups of heroin addicts. In their 12-year follow-up of the effects of treatment of 405 black and white male opiate addicts, Simpson, Joe, Lehman, and Sells (1986) concluded that the most predictive determinants of long-term continued abstinence were primarily behavioral: Avoiding old drug-using friends and old hangouts, developing new friendships with nonusers, and establishing new family ties and new work habits. In their review of the determinants of spontaneous remission from substance use, Stall and Biernacki (1986) arrived at similar conclusions. These results suggest that would-be ex-addicts with strong beliefs about their ability to cope behaviorally will experience higher rates of long-term abstinence than would-be ex-addicts who may have strong beliefs in their ability to cope cognitively but weak beliefs about their ability to cope behaviorally.

Percepts of ability have been shown to be important determinants of effort and achievement (Bandura, 1986). Failure to distinguish between perceptions of cognitive control ability and perceptions of behavioral coping ability, however, could mask important information about the processes by which actions, beliefs and perceptions of ability influence each other. Two examples are given below where potentially important applications of social cognitive theory may be limited by the failure to make this distinction.

Conjecture Relating to Adolescent Maturation and Risk of Drug Abuse

An important, unexplained phenomenon in the literature on drug abuse onset is the "window of vulnerability," namely, the relatively few teenage and young adult years when individuals are at risk of adopting a drug abusing lifestyle (Abelson, Fishburne, & Cisin, 1980; Johnston, O'Malley, & Eveland, 1978; Kandel & Logan, 1984). Lifestyle drug abuse rarely begins earnestly before adolescence and almost never manifests de novo after age 25. The "Just Say No" drug prevention program is premised on the belief that success in dissuading teenagers from starting drug abuse during the teenage years will prevent drug abuse at any age.

Why, over a lifespan of 72-78 years, should the average American only be at risk of lifestyle drug abuse between the ages of 13 and 25, with peak onset during the high school years? Part of the answer may be facilitated by distinguishing between cognitive control and behavioral coping ability. The behavioral coping ability of children is generally limited to secondary control (e.g., Rothbaum & Weisz, 1989) because of their societally-mandated dependency on their parents and because of their lack of life skills. Children's maturation is marked more by increases in their cognitive control ability (e.g., distractive thoughts) than in their behavioral coping skills (e.g., progressive goal-setting to achieve mastery over challenge; Altshuler & Ruble, 1989).

The transition from childhood to adulthood is almost inevitably accompanied by increases in behavioral coping ability. The life skills that are acquired include decision-making skills, communication skills, dating skills, and employment skills. At the beginning of the transition, these behavioral skills are uniformly absent but young adolescents become increasingly aware of the need to acquire them (Katz & Zigler, 1967). There is considerable distress and anxiety that accompanies adolescents' increasing realization of the need for life skills in the immediate absence of their acquisition. This distress and anxiety are palliated in teenagers performing well in school by societally-administered reassurances that their career trajectory is favorable and that, by implication, the teenagers need not fear a characterological inability to acquire the necessary life skills. For these success-bound teenagers, positive self-statements are easily accessible as antidotes to the inevitable anxiety that their immaturity occasions. For many teenagers not performing well in school and otherwise not receiving societal reassurances concerning future expectations of success, however, only the actual acquisition of life skills will permanently reduce the fear that they will never be fully accepted as autonomous, responsible adults. The literature, shows, in fact, that drug abuse-prone teenagers are characterized by a syndrome of "accelerated maturity," (Gritz, 1977), which manifests in precocious sexual behavior, marriage, cessation of schooling, and employment. Despite the uniform absence of life skills at the beginning of adolescence, only a minority go on to adopt a lifestyle habit of drug abuse. The at-risk teenagers who successfully avoid drug abuse are those who can through cognitive control alone reduce their immaturity-associated anxiety to acceptable levels. At-risk teenagers who successfully avoid drug abuse tend to come from intact families, suggesting that family social support can strengthen self-percepts of ability to control immaturity-associated anxiety. For at-risk teenagers without the requisite cognitive control skills, their immaturity-associated anxiety is functionally (but only intermittently) palliated by regular administration of psychoactive drugs, especially nicotine and alcohol. Kaplan, Martin, and Robbins (1982) demonstrated prospectively that non-drug abusing teenagers with low self-esteem were significantly more likely in future years to become drug abusers than their non-drug abusing agemates with high self-esteem. Drug abuse, therefore, can be viewed as a functional way to medicate for intrapsychic discomfort. By the time of onset of adulthood, most individuals have demonstrated successful mastery of at least the rudiments of the most important life skills. With the ebbing of immaturity-associated anxiety, there is decreased need for psychoactive agents to provide functional relief. By the time of young adulthood, unfortunately, many individuals have become physiologically dependent on their chosen drugs and cannot, therefore, stop using the drug just because the original need for the drug has disappeared.

A Conjecture Concerning Self-Efficacy Gender Differences in Sex-Role Socialization

The distinction between perceived cognitive control ability and perceived behavioral coping ability may similarly shed light on the origins of observed differences between men and women in mastery of a variety of life's challenges, including occupational achievement (Austin & Hanisch, 1990) and weight control (Jeffery, French, & Schmid, 1990). Women's continuing preference for teaching, nursing, and childcare, and men's continuing preference for construction, community safety (policy, fire, paramedics), and surgery, are consistent with women relying more on cognitive control coping and men relying more on behavioral coping. Similarly, women's relative reluctance to adopt increased physical activity and their preference for relying on willpower relative to men as a strategy for maintaining desirable weight is also consistent with women relying on cognitive control and men relying on behavioral coping. This difference between men and women may help to explain why women to view weight as less controllable than men (Jeffery et al., 1990), given the clear long-term advantage that exercise represents as a weight loss strategy (King, Frey-Hewitt, Dreon, & Wood, 1989; Koplan et al., 1982).

In her review of the literature on sex role socialization, Weitz (1977) cited studies of adult communication patterns in same-sex groups in which it was observed that women tended to be socioemotional whereas men tended to be task-oriented. Although similar communication patterns were not observed in children, Weitz noted a consistent association of activity and aggression in boys and not in girls. Her evidence suggested that boys were encouraged to combat their frustrations behaviorally and that girls were more encouraged to palliate their frustrations through cognitive control strategies. Consistent gender differences in adult performance could well have roots in the different coping strategies that boys and girls are encouraged to develop.

CONCLUSION

Further research on how perceived cognitive control ability and perceived behavioral coping ability vary among individuals, among situations, and within individuals over time seems warranted. Investigating the relative importance of perceived cognitive control and perceived behavioral coping ability in therapy-mediated lifestyle change and spontaneous, unaided lifestyle change would seem especially worthwhile. This distinction would also seem useful in illuminating more clearly why there exist differences in mastery between men and women, and in better understanding what contributes to the youthful decision to adopt a drug abusing lifestyle.

REFERENCES

Abelson, H., Fishburne, P., & Cisin, I. (1980). The national survey on drug abuse: Main findings 1979. Rockville, MD: National Institute on Drug Abuse.

Altshuler, J. L., & Ruble, D. N. (1989). Developmental changes in children's awareness of strategies for coping with uncontrollable stress. *Child Development, 60*, 1337-1349.

Austin, J. T., & Hanisch, K. A. (1990). Occupational attainment as a function of abilities and interets: A longitudinal analysis using project TALENT data. *Journal of Applied Psychology, 75*, 77-86.

Bachman, J. G., O'Malley, P. M., & Johnston, L. D. (1984). Drug use among young adults: The impacts of role status and social environment. *Journal of Personality and Social Psychology, 47*, 629-645.

Bandura, A. (1977). Self-efficacy: Toward a unifying theory of behavioral change. *Psychological Review, 84*, 191-215.

Bandura, A. (1986). *Social foundations of thought and action: A social cognitive theory.* Englewood Cliffs, NJ: Prentice-Hall.

Bandura, A., & Wood, R. (1989). Effect of perceived controllability and performance standards on self-regulation of complex decision making. *Journal of Personality and Social Psychology, 56*, 805-814.

Bentler, P. M. (1980). Multivariate analysis with latent variables: Causal modeling. *Annual Review of Psychology, 31*, 419-456.

Bentler, P. M. (1983). Some contributions to efficient statistics in structural models: Specification and estimation of moment structures. *Psychometrika, 48*, 493-517.

Bentler, P. M. (1986). Structural modeling and Psychometrika: An historical perspective on growth and achievements. *Psychometrika, 51*, 35-51.

Bentler, P. M., & Bonett, D. G. (1980). Significance tests and goodness of fit in the analysis of covariance structures. *Psychological Bulletin, 88*, 588-606.

Bentler, P. M., & Chou, C. P. (1986, April). *Statistics for parameter expansion and construction in structural models.* Paper presented at the American Educational Research Association meeting, San Francisco.

Bentler, P. M., & Newcomb, M. D. (1978). Longitudinal study of marital success and failure. *Journal of Consulting and Clinical Psychology, 46*, 1053-1070.

Bentler, P. M., & Newcomb, M. D. (1986). Personality, sexual behavior, and drug use revealed through latent variable methods. *Clinical Psychology Review, 6*, 363-385.

Blatt, S. J., Quinlan, D. M., Chevron, E. S., McDonald, C., & Zuroff, D. (1982). Dependency and self-criticism: Psychological dimensions of depression. *Journal of Consulting and Clinical Psychology, 50,* 113-124.

Chaney, E. F., & Roszell, D. K. (1985). Coping in opiate addicts maintained on methadone. In S. Shiffman & T. A. Wills (Eds.), Coping and substance use (pp. 267-291). Orlando, FL: Academic Press.

Clark, V. A., Aneshensel, C. S., Frerichs, R. R., & Morgan, T. M. (1981). Analysis of effects of sex and age in response to items on the CES-D scale. *Psychiatry Research, 5,* 171-181.

Courtois, C. A. (1988). *Healing the incest wound.* New York: Norton.

Crumbaugh, J. C. (1968). Cross-validation of purpose in life test based on Frankl's concepts. *Journal of Individual Psychology, 24,* 74-81.

Crumbaugh, J. C., & Maholick, L. T. (1964). An experimental study in existentialism: The psychometric approach to Frankl's concept of neogenic neurosis. *Journal of Clinical Psychology, 20,* 200-207.

Crumbaugh, J. C., & Maholick, L. T. (1969). *Manual of instructions for the purpose in life test.* Munster, IN: Psychometric Affiliates.

Cudeck, R., & Browne, M. W. (1983). Cross-validation of covariance structures. *Multivariate Behavioral Research, 18,* 147-167.

Donovan, J. E., Jessor, R., & Jessor, L. (1983). Problem drinking in adolescence and young adulthood: A follow-up study. *Journal of Studies on Alcohol, 44,* 109-137.

Folkman, S., & Lazarus, R. S. (1980). An analysis of coping in a middle-aged community sample. *Journal of Health and Social Behavior, 21,* 219-239.

Gritz, E. R. (1977). Smoking: The prevention of onset. In Jarvik, M. E. et al. *Research on smoking behavior* (pp. 290-307). NIDA Research Monograph #17, DHEW Pub. No. (ADM) 78-581.

Harlow, L. L., Newcomb, M. D., & Bentler, P. M. (1987). Purpose in life test assessment using latent variable methods. *British Journal of Clinical Psychology, 26,* 235-236.

Huba, G. J., & Bentler, P. M. (1982). A developmental theory of drug use: Derivation and assessment of a causal modeling approach. In B. P. Baltes, & O. G. Brim, Jr. (Eds.), *Life-span development and behavior, Volume 4* (pp. 147-203). New York: Academic Press.

Huba, G. J., & Bentler, P. M. (1983). Causal models of the development of law abidance and its relationship to psychosocial factors and drug use. In W. S. Laufer & J. M. Day (Eds.), *Personality theory, moral development, and criminal behavior* (pp. 165-215). Lexington, MA: Heath.

Husaini, B. A., Neff, J. A., Harrington, J. B., Hughes, M. D., & Stone, R. H. (1980). Depression in rural communities: Validating the CES-D scale. *Journal of Community Psychology, 7,* 137-146.

Jeffery, R. W., French, S. A., & Schmid, T. O. (1990). Attributions for dietary failures: Problems reported by participants in the Hypertension Prevention Trial. *Health Psychology, 9,* 315-329.

Johnston, L., O'Malley, P., & Eveland, L. (1978). Drugs and delinquency: A search for causal connections. In D. B. Kandel (Ed.), *Longitudinal research on drug use: Empirical findings and methodological issues* (pp. 137-156). Washington, DC: Hemisphere-Wiley.

Kandel, D. B. (1984). Marijuana users in young adulthood. *Archives of General Psychiatry, 41,* 200-209.

Kandel, D. B., & Logan, J. A. (1984). Patterns of drug use from adolescence to young adulthood: I. Periods of risk for initiation, continued use, and discontinuation. *American Journal of Public Health, 74*, 660-666.

Kaplan, H. B., Martin, S. S., & Robbins, C. (1982). Applications of a general theory of deviant behavior: Self-derogation and adolescent drug use. *Journal of Health and Social Behavior, 23*, 274-294.

Katz, P., & Zigler, E. (1967). Self-image disparity: A developmental approach. *Journal of Personality and Social Psychology, 5*, 186-195.

Kazdin, A. E. (1979). Imagery elaboration and self-efficacy in the covert modeling treatment of unassertive behavior. *Journal of Consulting and Clinical Psychology, 47*, 725-733.

King, A. C., Frey-Hewitt, B., Dreon, D. M., & Wood, P. D. (1989). Diet vs. exercise in weight maintenance. The effects of minimal intervention strategies on long-term outcomes in men. *Archives of Internal Medicine, 149*, 2741-2746.

Koplan, J. P., Powell, K. E., Sikes, R. K., Shirley, R. W., Campbell, C. C. (1982). An epidemiologic study of the benefits and risks of running. *Journal of the American Medical Association, 248*, 3118-3121.

Levenson, R. W., & Gottman, J. M. (1978). Toward the assessment of social competence. *Journal of Consulting and Clinical Psychology, 46*, 453-462.

Marlatt, G. A., & Gordon, J. (1985). *Relapse prevention: Maintenance strategies in addictive behavior change.* New York: Guilford.

Miller, J. D., Cisin, I. H., Gardner-Keaton, H., Harrell, A. V., Wirtz, P. W., Abelson, H. I., & Fishburne, P. M. (1983). *National survey on drug abuse: Main findings 1982.* PHS, NIDA, DHHS Pub. No. (ADM) 83-1263. Washington, DC: U. S. Government Printing Office.

Newcomb, M. D. (1984). Sexual behavior, responsiveness, and attitudes among women: A test of two theories. *Journal of Sex & Marital Therapy, 10*, 272-286.

Newcomb, M. D. (1986). Nuclear attitudes and reactions: Associations with depression, drug use, and quality of life. *Journal of Personality and Social Psychology, 50*, 906-920.

Newcomb, M. D., & Bentler, P. M. (1986). Loneliness and social support: A confirmatory hierarchical analysis. *Personality and Social Psychology Bulletin, 12*, 520-535.

Newcomb, M. D., & Bentler, P. M. (1987). Self-report methods of assessing health status and health service utilization: A hierarchical confirmatory analysis. *Multivariate Behavioral Research, 22*, 415-436.

Newcomb, M. D., & Bentler, P. M. (1988a). *Consequences of adolescent drug use: Impact on the lives of young adults.* Newbury Park, CA: Sage.

Newcomb, M. D., & Bentler, P. M. (1988b). Impact of adolescent drug use and social support on problems of young adults: A longitudinal study. *Journal of Abnormal Psychology, 97*, 64-75.

Newcomb, M. D., & Harlow, L. L. (1986). Life events and substance use among adolescents: Mediating effects of perceived loss of control and meaninglessness in life. *Journal of Personality and Social Psychology, 51*, 564-577.

O'Leary, A. (1985). Self-efficacy and health. *Behavior Research and Therapy, 23*, 437-451.

Ozer, E. M., & Bandura, A. (1990). Mechanisms governing empowerment effects: A self-efficacy analysis. *Journal of Personality and Social Psychology, 58*, 472-486.

Pearlin, L., & Schooler, C. (1978). The structure of coping. *Journal of Health and Social Behavior, 19*, 2-21.

Radloff, L. S. (1977). The CES-D scale: A self-report depression scale for research in the general population. *Applied Psychological Measurement, 1*, 385-401.

Roberts, R. E. (1980). Reliability of the CES-D scale in different ethnic contexts. *Psychiatry Research, 2*, 125-134.

Rothbaum, F., & Weisz, J. R. (1989). *Child psychopathology and the quest for control.* Newbury Park, CA: Sage.

Ryckman, R. M., Robbins, M. A., Thornton, B., & Cantrell, P. (1982). Development and validation of a physical self-efficacy scale. *Journal of Personality and Social Psychology, 42*, 891-900.

Shiffman, S., Read, L., Maltese, J., Rapkin, D., & Jarvik, M. E. (1985). Preventing relapse in ex-smokers: A self-management approach. In A. Marlatt & J. Gordon (Eds.), *Relapse prevention* (Chapter 8, pp. 472-520). New York: The Guilford Press.

Simpson, D. D., Joe, G. W., Lehman, W. E., & Sells, S. B. (1986). Addiction careers: Etiology, treatment, and 12-year follow-up outcomes. *Journal of Drug Issues, 16*, 107-121.

Stall, R., & Biernacki, P. (1986). Spontaneous remission from the problematic use of substances: An inductive model derived from a comparative analysis of the alcohol, opiate, tobacco, and food/obesity literatures. *International Journal of the Addictions, 21*, 1-23.

Stein, J. A., Newcomb, M. D., & Bentler, P. M. (1986). Stability and change in personality: A longitudinal study from early adolescence to young adulthood. *Journal of Research in Personality, 20*, 276-291.

Strecher, V. J., DeVellis, B. M., Becker, M. H., & Rosenstock, I. M. (1986). The role of self-efficacy in achieving health behavior change. *Health Education Quarterly, 13*, 73-91.

Taylor, S. E. (1986). *Health psychology.* New York: Random House.

Weissman, M. M., Shokomskas, D., Pottenger, M., Prusoff, B. A., & Locke, B. Z. (1977). Assessing depressive symptoms in five psychiatric populations: A validation study. *American Journal of Epidemiology, 106*, 203-214.

Weitz, S. (1977). *Sex roles.* New York: Oxford University Press.

Wood, R., & Bandura, A. (1989). Impact of conceptions of ability on self-regulatory mechanisms and complex decision making. *Journal of Personality and Social Psychology, 56*, 407-415.

Author Notes

This research was supported by grant DA01070 from the National Institute on Drug Abuse. The computer assistance of Sandy Yu and production assistance of Julie Speckart are gratefully acknowledged.

EXPECTANCIES AS MEDIATORS BETWEEN RECIPIENT CHARACTERISTICS AND SOCIAL SUPPORT INTENTIONS

Ralf Schwarzer, Christine Dunkel-Schetter,
Bernard Weiner, and Grace Woo

It is assumed that the motivation to extend social support is governed by specific emotions and cognitions, among them outcome expectancies and self-efficacy expectancies. Two experiments were conducted to explore this assumption, Study I dealing with outcome expectancy and Study II dealing with self-efficacy expectancy. In Study I, outcome expectancies toward eight disease-related stigmas and the intention to extend social support were examined with two experimental conditions. The onset of the stigmas was varied as being either controllable or uncontrollable. In addition, the target person was described either as actively coping with the stigma or as not actively coping. Examined were the effects of onset controllability and coping on pity, outcome expectancy, and willingness to support the target person. In a within-groups design, 84 subjects were confronted with all eight stigmas under four different conditions. Both experimental factors influenced the reported reactions. The coping variable appeared to be stronger than the controllability variable and, in addition, outcome expectancy was a somewhat more important mediator of helping than pity. However, the pattern of data was context-specific, i.e., different sets of predictors emerged for different stigmas. Study II was a similar experiment pursuing the notion that the motivation to help is affected by the belief that one can be effective as a helper (self-efficacy expectancy). It examined whether self-efficacy expectancy for helping a rape victim served as a mediator of the relationship between recipient characteristics and support intentions. The recipient characteristics assessed were victim coping and controllability of the assault. Both pity and self-efficacy expectancy emerged as good predictors of support, whereas controllability and coping were of lesser influence.

According to Bandura's cognitive-social theory, human behaviors are partly governed by expectancies, in particular by outcome expectancies and self-efficacy expectancies (Bandura, 1977, 1986, 1991). Many studies, some of them presented in this volume, have applied this assumption to specific behaviors in various domains of human functioning such as achievement, organizational management, or health. There seems to be, however, no application to studies on social support. The willingness to help others depends partly on one's emotions at the time, but helping also depends on judgments about the specific situation, characteristics of the recipient, and one's self. Among such cognitions are expectancies about the likelihood that the situation can be changed and regarding one's ability to provide the necessary social support. Expecting a condition to improve under certain circumstances represents an outcome expectancy. Belief in oneself as an effective support provider in a particular situation represents a self-efficacy expectancy. These cognitions are hypothesized to serve as causal mediators of the relationships between antecedent recipient characteristics and consequent intentions to extend social support. In addition, a number of other factors outlined below are considered important in the study of social support.

The present chapter reports two studies. The first one deals with the mediating role of outcome expectancy, the second one with the mediating role of self-efficacy expectancy. In the following sections, we describe in more detail the constructs involved in this research, in particular perceived controllability, perceived coping, expectancies, and social support.

Perceived Controllability

Attribution theory has recently been extended to the study of social stigmas and reactions to the stigmatized (Weiner, Perry, & Magnusson, 1988). By social stigma we mean a discrediting condition or mark that defines a person as "deviant, flawed, limited, spoiled, or generally undesirable" (Jones et al., 1984, p. 6). Among others, physical deformities, behavioral problems such as excessive eating and drinking, and diseases can be regarded as stigmas. Attribution theory is relevant to the study of stigmas because individuals typically search for the cause(s) of a negative state or condition existing in others. That is, observers confronted with a "markable" target initiate an attributional search to determine the origin of the stigma.

Researchers have identified *controllability* as one of the basic dimensions of perceived causality (Weiner, 1985, 1986). Controllable causes are those which an actor can volitionally change, whereas uncontrollable causes are not subject to personal mastery or management. The onset of a drug problem, for example, is seen as controllable if a person has been experimenting with drugs out of curiosity, whereas it is perceived as comparatively uncontrollable if a person has had medical treatment with drugs and thereby developed a dependency (Weiner et al., 1988). In a similar manner, the onset of a heart disease is construed as controllable if the person has led an unhealthy life-style, including smoking and a poor diet, whereas it is considered relatively uncontrollable if hereditary factors have played a major role in the illness.

Affective and Behavioral Reactions

It has been documented that the perceived controllability of a social stigma determines disparate *affective reactions* toward the target person and different *behavioral responses* as well (e.g., DeJong, 1980; Weiner et al., 1988). More specifically, uncontrollable origins of stigmas tend to elicit pity and offers of help, whereas controllable origins tend to elicit anger and no help (see Reisenzein, 1986; Schmidt & Weiner, 1988; Weiner et al., 1988). Hence, it has been shown that experimentation with drugs and an unhealthy life-style as causes of stigmas yield much anger, little pity, and relative neglect, whereas drug problems due to medical treatment, and heart disease derived from genetic factors, give rise to little anger, much pity, and prosocial responses.

Perhaps more than in any other area within the field of social motivation, investigators of helping behavior have assumed that emotions play an important motivational role (see review in Carlson & Miller, 1987). These emotions have included discomfort (e.g., Cialdini, Darby, & Vincent, 1973), distress (e.g., Batson, O'Quinn, Fultz, Vanderplas, & Isen, 1983), empathy (e.g., Batson, 1990; Hoffman, 1975), gratitude (e.g., Goranson & Berkowitz, 1966), guilt (e.g., Hoffman, 1982), as well as pity and anger (Schwarzer & Weiner, 1990, 1991). While there is strong support for an attribution—emotion—helping link, there are also studies that have failed to demonstrate this effect. Capitalizing on a real-life event, Amato, Ho, and Partidge (1984) sent survey questionnaires to residents living near the setting of a major bushfire which killed 46 people and destroyed over 2,000 homes. The questionnaire addressed perceptions of causality and responsibility, affective reactions, and helping behavior. Most people reported donating to the victims regardless of the amount of responsibility attributed to them. The obvious high degree of need in this context seemed to have over-powered the attribution of control effects.

Jung (1988) presented subjects with vignettes depicting a close friend experiencing a variety of common problems, with manipulations of the responsibility for the problem. For each vignette, subjects rated the target person's deservedness of fate, perception of how helpful social support would be for the problem, and their likelihood of providing social support. Perceived deservedness of fate was greater for those viewed as having high responsibility. Perceived benefits of social support were also higher in this case. However, neither factor affected the likelihood of social support provision.

Skokan (1990) examined the affective responses and support behaviors extended towards a roommate who is dealing with either cancer or the death of her father. Subjects were presented with scenarios which depicted the roommate as either responsible or as not responsible for the onset of the critical event. In her initial within-subjects analysis, controllability was associated with more anger, less sympathy and less social support; however, when reanalyzed as a between-subjects design because of order effects, the impact of controllability on sympathy and support disappeared.

Perceived Coping

It remains unclear whether stigma onset, which is a distant event, is the sole or main determinant of affective and behavioral reactions toward the stigmatized or whether subsequent events, controllable or uncontrollable, alter the causal sequence. Drug experimentation and poor life-style, for example, might be weak predictors of the emotions and behaviors of observers when compared with the present *efforts* of the target person to cope with the consequences of the stigma. In the achievement domain, it is obvious that even after failure due to lack of effort, present expenditure of effort to compensate or recover generates positive affect and rewards for the failed student (Karasawa, 1991; Weiner, 1985). When generalized to the health domain, this finding suggests that positive *coping attempts* with a serious health condition could play an important role in determining the affective and behavioral reactions of others.

Skokan (1990) distinguished in her scenario experiment between adaptive coping and maladaptive coping. In the adaptive condition, the target person who either had cancer or was bereaved, tried to stay optimistic and to look for ways to go on with her life and to grow from the experience. In the maladaptive condition, she dwelled on the negative aspects of the situation and did not try to overcome the crisis instrumentally. Adaptive coping of the target was related to less anger in subjects but had mixed effects on their willingness to offer social support. In the bereavement condition, poor coping elicited less support, but in the cancer condition, unexpectedly, poor coping elicited even more support.

Silver, Wortman, and Crofton (1990) studied subject reactions to a cancer patient who was portrayed either as a "good coper," a "bad coper" or a "balanced coper." In the good coping condition, the target person expressed an optimistic view of her illness and appeared to be coping well. In the balanced coping condition, she conveyed distress about what was happening, but also indicated that she was trying her best. In the poor coping condition, she displayed distress about what was happening and appeared to have difficulty coping. In nine out of ten comparisons, the responses to confederates who were portrayed as having positive or balanced coping styles were significantly more favorable than were responses to poor copers.

In sum, both the origin of a problem and its solution are hypothesized to be important when examining reactions of others toward the stigmatized person (Brickman et al., 1982). That is, the responsibility for causing a problem should be separated from the responsibility for maintaining or not alleviating it. This important distinction has been ignored in prior research on attributions (see also Karasawa, 1991; Schwarzer & Weiner, 1991). The present studies compare the effects of perceived onset controllability with those of perceived coping efforts on pity, outcome expectancy, and social support towards the stigmatized and examines the mediating role of pity and expectancy.

Expectancies

The focus of the present paper is on the role of mediating factors that link attributions and affect regarding a social stigma to behavioral intentions or to actual support behavior. Bandura (1977, 1986, 1991) has convincingly demonstrated that expectancies are very important social-cognitive mediators of action. There are two major cognitions of this kind, outcome expectancies and self-efficacy expectancies. In the first experiment, we deal with *outcome expectancies* that refer to the possibility of improvement of a condition. The subjects were asked how likely it is that a target person's condition would improve under particular circumstances. It is hypothesized that an individual's active coping with an ailment will trigger positive outcome expectancies in the observer. Coping behavior implicitly refers to the stability of a stigma. If the victim is not actively involved in alleviating the distress, maintaining functioning and moving on with daily life, one would have little reason to expect an improvement; support may be seen as wasted labor. If, however, a great deal of effort is expended by the victim in solving the problem, one can expect that changes are more likely and that supplementary contributions would be a worthwhile investment. This reasoning does not apply to situations that require acceptance; that is, we are likely to help people who behave passively when passivity is required in the situation.

In the second experiment, the focus is on *self-efficacy expectancy* in terms of one's helping capabilities. Empathy, perspective taking, comforting skills and so on, not only facilitate social support in an objective sense (Batson, 1990; Clary & Orenstein, 1991); these abilities also have to be perceived by the help provider in order to establish a motivation to help. Help-specific self-efficacy deals with cognitions about one's capability to support others and to make a difference with this support; it refers to one's perceived personal resources to provide competent assistance and to achieve relief for a sufferer.

Social Support

Social support has been defined as an exchange of resources "perceived by the provider or the recipient to be intended to enhance the well-being of the recipient" (Shumaker & Brownell, 1984, p. 13). This definition requires that either the provider or the recipient must perceive that the provider has a positive intent. Intentions have also been claimed as being the best predictors of a variety of behaviors; this is well-documented in research based upon the Theory of Reasoned Action (Fishbein & Ajzen, 1975) and the Theory of Planned Behavior (Ajzen, 1988). Evidence of the influence of help intentions on actual helping behavior has been found by Borgida, Simmons, Conner, and Lombard (1990) and Dalbert, Montada, and Schmitt (1988). Whether intentions to help are accurately perceived by the provider or by the recipient is a related but different question (Dunkel-Schetter & Bennett, 1990; Dunkel-Schetter, Blasband, Feinstein, & Bennett, 1991).

Several factors determine the likelihood that a supportive exchange actually takes place. Stress factors, relationship factors, recipient factors, and provider factors have been discussed and somewhat studied (Dunkel-Schetter & Skokan, 1990). We will deal here with the latter two exclusively. *Recipient factors* are critical determinants of support. Victims who are not only distressed, but are also not responsible for the event, and who invest a great deal of effort to manage their condition, are apt to elicit more help than those who are responsible themselves for their misfortune and who do not take action to solve their issue (Bennett-Herbert & Dunkel-Schetter, in press; Brickman et al., 1982). Creating frustration and helplessness in the potential provider leads to a lesser likelihood of support (Dunkel-Schetter & Wortman, 1981, 1982). The expression of too much distress strains the social network, evokes negative reactions, and turns those away who would have been supportive if the distress level had only been moderate. Another reason why the network may not be mobilized is if a victim is not coping adaptively. Passive, depressive and ungrateful victims or patients are seen as socially unattractive and, therefore, receive less support in the long run (Barbee, 1990; Gurtman, 1986; Notarius & Herrick, 1988). Paradoxically, those subjects who have valuable personal resources such as competence, high self-esteem, locus of control, and optimism and who make use of their resources seem to elicit a stronger tendency in others to extend support.

Provider factors have been intensively studied in social psychology research on helping (Batson, 1990; Berkowitz, 1987; Dovidio, 1984; Eisenberg & Miller, 1987; Jung, 1988). It makes a difference how the cause of the problem is attributed. If it is seen as controllable then the victim is blamed and negative emotional reactions are aroused such as anger, leading to neglect of the sufferer. If, on the other hand, the cause is seen as uncontrollable and the person does not seem to be responsible for the problem, then positive emotions such as pity emerge, which make help more likely (Weiner, 1985). Thus, emotions are mediators of attributions and behavioral intentions. According to Batson (1990), empathy predicts altruistic motivation to help, whereas a provider's distress tends to elicit egoistic motivation, which does not induce help. These two theories by Weiner and Batson are closely related in terms of emotional mediators of motivation. Pity can be matched to empathy as a predictor of help, and anger parallels distress in predicting neglect. Betancourt (1990) has attempted to integrate both views by manipulating experimentally the controllability of onset of a problem as well as inducing different perspectives in the potential support provider. He found that both experimental factors influenced perceived controllability and empathic emotions that, in turn, influenced helping.

In the present chapter, the focus is on experimentally manipulated recipient factors, but it is kept in mind that these do not operate in an isolated manner. Rather, they interact with on-going responses by the provider during a specific social encounter. It is only of secondary importance whether the victim is actually responsible for the problem and whether active coping is executed. Moreover, the degree to which the provider makes these attributions, is considered to be critical. The perception in the beholder may be more relevant than the actual cause of the onset of the stigma or the actual coping behavior.

The present experiments were designed to examine the effects of perceived controllability and perceived coping on pity as an affective reaction and on expectancies that, in turn, were hypothesized to exert an influence on support intent. The studies differ in terms of the scenarios used and in terms of the expectancy variables. While Study I deals with outcome expectancy, Study II deals with self-efficacy expectancy.

STUDY I

Method

Sample. The subjects were 84 male and female students at the University of California, Los Angeles, who received credit in an introductory psychology course for their participation. They were randomly assigned to one of four groups (see below) and given questionnaires in small group sessions with anonymity assured.[1]

Design. Eight health-related stigmas were selected, each of which was manipulated with respect to onset controllability and coping effort. Each subject received four of the eight stigmas paired uniquely with one of the four controllability conditions (2 Levels of Onset Responsibility x 2 Levels of Coping). Subjects were divided into four groups that received different combinations of stigmas and conditions (see Table 1).

Table 1
Experimental Design

	Onset Responsible		Onset Irresponsible	
	No Coping	Coping	No Coping	Coping
Group 1	Aids	Cancer	Drug abuse	Heart disease
Group 2	Cancer	Drug abuse	Heart disease	Aids
Group 3	Drug abuse	Heart disease	Aids	Cancer
Group 4	Heart disease	Aids	Cancer	Drug abuse
Group 1	Anorexia	Child abuse	Depression	Obesity
Group 2	Child abuse	Depression	Obesity	Anorexia
Group 3	Depression	Obesity	Anorexia	Child abuse
Group 4	Obesity	Anorexia	Child abuse	Depression

---

[1] Study I was conducted by Ralf Schwarzer and Bernard Weiner.

As shown in Table 1, one part of the design included four stigmas (AIDS, cancer, drug abuse, and heart disease) paired with the four conditions, while a second part replicated the first but used another four stigmas (anorexia, depression, obesity, and child abuse). Thus, there were two within-group factors (onset controllability and coping) and one between-group factor (stigma set). This design allowed for an overall analysis as well as for stigma-specific subanalyses.

Four vignettes were created for each stigma consisting of: (a) onset responsibility and low coping; (b) onset responsibility and high coping; (c) no onset responsibility and low coping; and (d) no onset responsibility and high coping. As an example, the obesity vignettes are given:

1. *Maladaptive coping, controllable.* Your roommate has become excessively over-weight, and is experiencing severe problems in social- and work-related activities. Excessive eating and lack of exercise have been the primary contributors to the obesity. This roommate does not take any steps to lose weight, either by dieting, exercising or by following a medical regimen.

2. *Adaptive coping, controllable.* Your roommate has become excessively overweight, and is experiencing severe problems in social- and work-related activities. Excessive eating and lack of exercise have been the primary contributors to the obesity. Recently this roommate has commenced a new diet prescribed by a physician, and is regularly exercising.

3. *Maladaptive coping, uncontrollable.* Your roommate has become excessively over-weight, and is experiencing severe problems in social- and work-related activities. Glandular dysfunction has been identified as the reason for the obesity. This roommate does not take any steps to lose weight, either by dieting, exercising or by following a medical regimen.

4. *Adaptive coping, uncontrollable.* Your roommate has become excessively over-weight, and is experiencing severe problems in social- and work-related activities. Glandular dysfunction has been identified as the reason for the obesity. Recently this roommate has commenced a new diet prescribed by a physician, and is regularly exercising.

Measures. The dependent variables were the following 9-point rating scales, anchored with extremes such as *not at all* and *very much so*. Pity was assessed by the single item "How much pity would you feel?"

Typically, *outcome expectancies* are worded in an "if-then manner." In the present experiment, however, the if-component was given by the four experimental conditions such as: "If the stigma is uncontrollable and if the victim is actively coping with it, then..." Because of these implicit assumptions, the measurement of the outcome expectancy was restricted to the then-component and simply worded: "How likely is it that the condition will improve?"

Social support intention was measured by seven items representing different kinds of social support. However, this was a homogeneous scale (Cronbach's alpha for the seven social support items was .91), and, therefore, the aggregated score was used as an indicator of support intentions. The items were:

1. How much would you like to extend support to your roommate?
2. How much time would you be willing to spend talking and listening?
3. How much money would you be willing to donate in order to provide the best possible treatment?
4. How much would you like to go on a holiday trip with your roommate?
5. How much would you be willing to give advice and information?
6. How much would you be willing to console and reassure your roommate when being upset?
7. How willing would you be to assist with a small problem?

Other dependent variables were analyzed previously within the framework of analysis of variance, and some of the results are published elsewhere. However, we have only reported about the stigmas of heart disease (Schwarzer & Weiner, 1990), AIDS and cancer (Schwarzer & Weiner, 1991).

Results

To examine the role of pity and outcome expectancy as mediators of the relationship between victim characteristics and provider support intentions, a structural equation model was specified with controllability and coping as exogenous variables and pity, expectancy, and support as endogenous variables. This is a straightforward single indicator model with manifest variables. The two orthogonal experimental factors were believed to influence emotions and cognitions, whereas emotions and cognitions were specified to influence the behavioral intention directly. Controllability and coping, therefore, could exert indirect effects on support intent through pity and expectancy but were constrained not to exert direct effects, because this would not be in line with theory or past research. The two alternative mediating factors were pity and expectancy, and for both of them the size of their mediating effect was computed in addition to their direct impact on support intent (see Figures 2 to 9). This procedure was repeated eight times, for each stigma individually. Eight path analyses were carried out with the LISREL VII program (Jöreskog & Sörbom, 1988).

First, the degree to which the experimental data fitted the structural equation model was examined. Several indices of fit have been suggested in the literature (cf. Bentler, 1980). We have used five of them in this study, (a) the chi-square test which, if significant, indicates that the data deviate from the model, (b) the chi-square /df ratio which takes the degrees of freedom into account (df = 3) and which should be as low as possible; ratios above 3.0 are usually seen as unsatisfactory, (c) Jöreskog's Goodness of Fit Index (GFI) which should be close to unity, (d) his Adjusted Goodness of Fit Index (AGFI) that makes an adjustment to the degrees of freedom and also should be as high as possible, and (e) the Root Mean Square Residual (RMSR) which is an index derived from the deviations of the original correlation matrix from the reproduced correlation matrix on the basis of the estimated parameters; this index should not exceed .05.

Table 2 summarizes the results of all eight path analyses. In six of eight cases, an excellent fit emerged, whereas the stigmas "Cancer" and "Child Abuse" turned out to be associated with a less appropriate fit. Overall, these satisfactory results indicate that the model specification is in line with the experimental data, but also that the specific stigma context makes a difference.

Table 2
Goodness of Fit for the Eight Path Models

Stigma	chi^2	p	chi^2/df	GFI	AGFI	RMSR
AIDS	4.36	.23	1.45	.98	.90	.05
Cancer	9.49	.02	3.16	.96	.79	.07
Drug abuse	1.46	.69	0.49	.99	.97	.03
Heart disease	2.44	.49	0.81	.99	.94	.04
Anorexia	0.92	.82	0.31	.99	.98	.02
Child abuse	15.18	.002	5.06	.94	.69	.08
Depression	1.50	.68	0.50	.99	.97	.03
Obesity	4.65	.20	1.55	.98	.90	.05

Note. GFI = goodness of fit, AGFI = adjusted GFI, RMSR = root mean square residual.

Table 3
Percent of Explained Variance

	Endogenous Factor		
Stigma	Pity	Expectancy	Support
AIDS	22	1	31
Cancer	6	29	21
Drug abuse	9	51	15
Heart disease	1	31	11
Anorexia	4	51	6
Child abuse	9	36	29
Depression	1	16	14
Obesity	1	38	11

This is corroborated by the explained variance for the three endogenous variables pity, expectancy and support (Table 3). The model succeeded in explaining a great deal of the variance of expectancy and support but much less so of pity. This shows that the emotion of pity is not sufficiently predicted by controllability and coping. Other factors, not under scrutiny here, must be responsible for the variation in pity.

The stigma-specific path coefficients are displayed in Figures 1-8; Table 4 contains the decomposition of total effects into direct and indirect effects. Results for each stigma will be described briefly. Coefficients above .21 are significant.

Table 4

Decomposition of Effects on Social Support Intention

Stigma	Predictor	Direct	Indirect	Total Effect
AIDS	Control	0	21	21
	Coping	0	14	14
	Pity	55	0	55
	Expectancy	7	0	7
Cancer	Control	0	6	6
	Coping	0	13	13
	Pity	43	0	43
	Expectancy	7	0	7
Drug abuse	Control	0	6	6
	Coping	0	29	29
	Pity	14	0	14
	Expectancy	40	0	40
Heart disease	Control	0	3	3
	Coping	0	16	16
	Pity	19	0	19
	Expectancy	26	0	26
Anorexia	Control	0	0	0
	Coping	0	17	17
	Pity	14	0	14
	Expectancy	24	0	24
Child abuse	Control	0	12	12
	Coping	0	25	25
	Pity	37	0	37
	Expectancy	31	0	31
Depression	Control	0	4	4
	Coping	0	14	14
	Pity	14	0	14
	Expectancy	34	0	34
Obesity	Control	0	4	4
	Coping	0	18	18
	Pity	14	0	14
	Expectancy	30	0	30

In the case of *AIDS*, a substantial causal path leads from controllability to pity ($p = -.39$) and another from pity to support ($p = .55$). Coping has a somewhat lower impact on pity ($p = .25$). Expectancy does not play a role: it is predicted neither by controllability nor by coping, and it does not predict support. Since AIDS is a terminal disease, it is not surprising not to find a large variation in outcome expectancy. Pity appears to be the appropriate emotional reaction which facilitates the likelihood to extend support (see Figure 1 and Table 4).

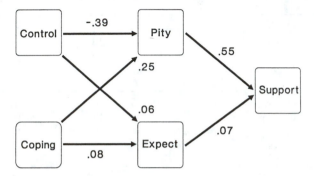

Figure 1 Pity and expectancy as mediators between controllability and coping and social support in the AIDS scenario.

For *cancer*, pity was again the best predictor of support ($p = .43$), whereas expectancy failed to contribute anything ($p = .07$). But the antecedents were different; controllability had no significant impact on pity or expectancy, whereas coping had a strong path to expectancy ($p = .52$) and a moderate one to pity ($p = .22$). Although cancer can be a terminal disease in many cases, there are better survival chances for those who comply with treatment. This explains the association between coping and expectancy, but, surprisingly, there was little effect on support intentions that were based more on pity (see Figure 2 and Table 4).

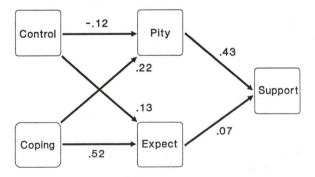

Figure 2 Pity and expectancy as mediators between controllability and coping and social support in the cancer scenario.

In case of *drug abuse*, variations in controllability elicited no effects reactions but coping did. A strong path from coping to expectancy emerged ($p = .70$), accompanied by another strong path from expectancy to support ($p = .40$) making this the major pathway to help intentions. A minor pathway was added from coping through pity ($p = .25$, $p = .13$). Drug abuse is a rather unstable condition and appears to be modifiable. Whether one is ready to support a drug user mainly depends on the likelihood of perceived change based on his or her coping efforts, no matter how the problem was originally caused (see Figure 3 and Table 4).

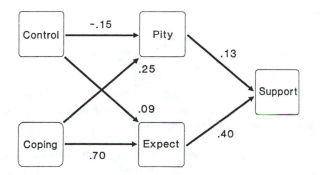

Figure 3 Pity and expectancy as mediators between controllability and coping and social support in the drug abuse scenario.

In case of *heart disease*, there was no effect of controllability, and pity also had no significant relationships (see Figure 4 and Table 4. The only pathway to support led from coping via expectancy ($p = .56$, $p = .26$). Heart disease is interpreted as a modifiable condition that varies with one's health behavior such as nutrition, exercise, and relaxation. The origin of this condition seems to be unimportant for a decision to help the patient.

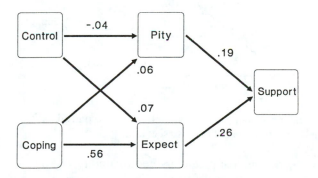

Figure 4 Pity and expectancy as mediators between controllability and coping and social support in the heart disease scenario.

Anorexia nervosa can also be regarded as an unstable condition where active coping makes a difference. Controllability had no influence but coping determined expectancy ($p = .70$) and pity ($p = .20$) (see Figure 5 and Table 4).

Anorexia is considered a highly modifiable condition. If a patient copes well it will vanish, no matter how controllable the origin was.

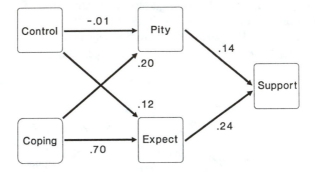

Figure 5 Pity and expectancy as mediators between controllability and coping and social support in the anorexia scenario.

A different picture emerged for *child abuse*. Both direct effects on support were almost equal, with pity (e = .37) and expectancy (e = .31) accounting for a similar amount of variation in support. The key antecedent factor, however, was coping which was closely related to expectancy ($p = .60$). Compared to drug abuse, child abuse is not a health-compromising behavior but more a socially deviant act that elicits emotions such as either outrage or pity towards the actor, the latter emotion only if there was not much control over the behavior (see Figure 6 and Table 4).

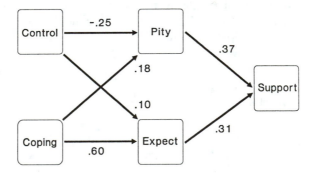

Figure 6 Pity and expectancy as mediators between controllability and coping and social support in the child abuse scenario.

In case of *depression*, the predictors controllability and pity turned out to be irrelevant, whereas expectancy had an influence on support ($p = .34$), based on the coping efforts of the target person ($p = .38$). This clearly documents that an active contribution on behalf of the mental health patient is required in order to make the condition look changeable, so that support would not be in vain. Only expectancy had an effect on support (see Figure 7 and Table 4).

Finally, in case of *obesity*, an almost identical result emerged. Again, controllability and pity were negligible factors but expectancy ($p = .30$), based on coping ($p = .61$), made the difference. Obesity is an unstable condition, and those who do not counteract their problem cannot count on help from others. Only active coping efforts elicit expectancy which in turn trigger readiness for social support (see Figure 8 and Table 4).

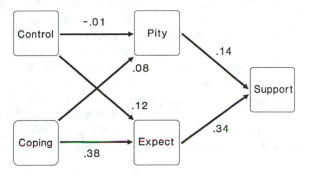

Figure 7 Pity and expectancy as mediators between controllability and coping and social support in the depression scenario.

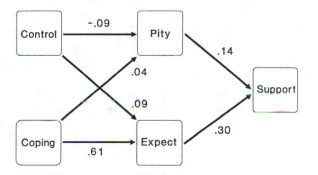

Figure 8 Pity and expectancy as mediators between controllability and coping and social support in the obesity scenario.

In sum, in five of the eight stigmas, *outcome expectancy* was the main predictor of support intention. These five were drug abuse, heart disease, anorexia, depression, and obesity. The two terminal diseases, AIDS and cancer, differed from the majority by their conspicuous pathway from pity to support intent. In these two cases, one's intention to help was almost exclusively based on pity. For child abuse, a balanced influence of pity and expectancy emerged. *Coping* was a stronger antecedent than *controllability* in seven out of eight cases. The exception was AIDS. The overall picture corroborates the assumption that outcome expectancy is a critical mediator between target coping and social support intention. From these results, whether one extends help or not is primarily dependent on the expectancies aroused by the victim characteristics, and particularly the person's way of coping.

Discussion

Each of the eight stigmas was examined in separate path analyses with respect to the two experimental factors, controllability and coping as antecedents, and pity and expectancy as mediators. The model fit the data and expectancies were a major direct source of support variation. Pity was a direct predictor of social support only in three specific contexts. It is noteworthy that there was a high degree of variation between the eight stigmas, indicating that the specific circumstances decide whether the willingness to help is primarily based on either pity or expectancy. In terminal diseases such as AIDS or cancer, pity appeared to be more influential than expectancy, whereas for unstable health conditions such as drug abuse, anorexia or obesity the coping-expectancy-support link was obvious. It might be, therefore, that the perceived stability of a condition is a critical underlying dimension that affects judgments of help. Controllability was less influential compared to coping which, in turn, partly determined expectancy. The most conspicuous pathway led from coping via expectancy to support intent.

STUDY II

In the first experiment, the expected improvement of the target's condition was one of the mediators under investigation. In the second experiment, the attention was shifted to a support provider characteristic to address the question of whether the perception of one's ability to help would make it more likely that a support intention occurs. In other words, self-efficacy expectancy, one's perceived personal capability of extending effective support, was the focus. It was hypothesized that self-efficacy expectancy played the same role as a mediator that outcome expectancy did in the first experiment.[2]

Method

Design. The path-analytic model was the same as in the first study but there were some differences in the experimental manipulations and in the measures involved. Only one problem situation was selected, a sexual assault scenario, that was varied with respect to controllability and coping. A rape victim in the *uncontrollable* condition was described as a student who studied one night at the library and was raped on the way to her car by a stranger. In the condition designed to seem slightly more *controllable* she was described as someone who attended a party where she drank too much and flirted with the males; when she was taken home by one of them, she invited him up to her apartment and was raped. The *adaptively coping* victim was characterized as one who was trying hard to go on with her life after the assault, having joined a support group and seeing a counselor each week. The *maladaptively coping* victim did not try to

---

[2] Study II was conducted by Grace Woo, Christine Dunkel-Schetter, and Ralf Schwarzer.

overcome her problem situation. She had withdrawn from friends and did not eat; she also refused to attend a support group meeting and to see a counselor.

The experiment was arranged as a 2 x 2 between-subjects design; 70 under-graduate students responded to the vignette randomly assigned to one of four conditions. There were 55 males and only 15 females, but their distribution over the four cells was about equal, with cell sizes of 19, 17, 18 and 16.

Measures. Pity, self-efficacy expectancy and support intentions were the dependent variables used in this report. All were rated on a 5-point scale. *Pity* was assessed by four adjectives as part of a checklist, namely empathy, sym-pathy, pity, and compassion. *Emotional support intent* was measured by four items such as "Would you be willing to try to console and reassure your friend when she is upset?" and "Would you spend time listening to her emotional reac-tions to the assault?" *Tangible support intent* was measured by six items such as "Would you be willing to offer her help with her school work if she needed it?" and "Would you lend her money to see a therapist?" *Self-efficacy expectancy* was measured by a newly developed 10-item scale that was employed for the first time. Its psychometric properties were satisfactory with an average item-total correlation of .55 and an internal consistency of Cronbach's alpha = .85. The items were worded in the following way:

1. I possess the necessary social skills to alleviate the distress of a sexual assault victim.
2. It is easy for me to comfort someone in distress.
3. I am capable of providing the appropriate resources for a rape victim.
4. It is difficult for me to communicate empathic understanding. (-)
5. I could make someone feel better no matter how depressed she is.
6. When it comes to comforting someone, I feel awkward. (-)
7. I am not sensitive enough to meet the support needs of a sufferer. (-)
8. I do not trust my skills to communicate in a beneficial way with a sexual assault victim. (-)
9. I am not the kind of person who can meet the emotional needs of others who are in a crisis. (-)
10. I have sufficient communication skills to cheer up someone who is experiencing stress.

Results

A structural model was specified with the two experimental factors as ante-cedents, and with pity, self-efficacy expectancy, and support as the dependent variables. In contrast to the previous study, this is a *multiple* indicator model. The three endogenous variables were specified with two indicators each. The four pity items were divided into two sets (each pity indicator had two items); support was specified by the emotional support scale as well as the tangible support scale, and the two self-efficacy indicators were two 5-item subsets of the instrument described above. The results of the LISREL analysis are depicted in Figure 9.

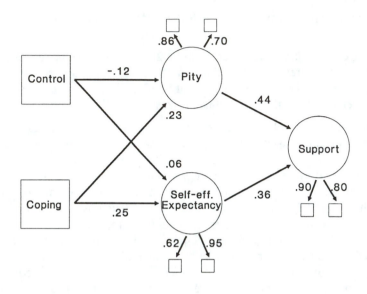

Figure 9 Pity and expectancy as mediators between controllability and coping and social support in the rape scenario.

The fit of the model was chi-square = 17.4 (15 df, $p = .295$) with a chi-square/df ratio of 1.16. Goodness of fit was GFI = .94 and adjusted goodness of fit AGFI = .87. The root mean square residual was RMSR = .09. Although the latter two indices fall short of the usual requirement, the overall fit can be regarded as satisfactory, based on the other indices. The explained variance for social support was 34%, which is quite good, whereas those for pity and for self-efficacy expectancy were low (7% each). Decomposing the effects on support led to substantial direct effects for pity (e = .44) and for self-efficacy expectancy (e = .36), and to smaller indirect effects for controllability (e = .03), and for coping (e = .17). Pity and expectancy were very good predictors of support intent, but the underlying experimental factors (control, coping) were of lesser influence.

Discussion

The second experiment has replicated the general causal model leading from victim characteristics to support provider emotional reactions or cognitions, resulting in an intention formation. Pity emerged here as the strongest predictor of support, but self-efficacy expectancy also contributed substantially. Controllability turned out to be negligible, whereas coping exerted a weak, but statistically significant, influence on pity and self-efficacy.

However, it is difficult to construe a sexual assault as controllable, and the two conditions differed in ratings of controllability only by one point, although significantly. In addition, the rape scenario is quite different from the eight stigma scenarios described in Study I. There is no disease or bodily condition involved but a single violent act caused by an external agent. An assault is likely to be viewed generally as less controllable than other social stigmas such as obesity or drug abuse. The degree of controllability only varied in the study from *uncontrollable* to *somewhat controllable*; there was not really a "controllable" experimental condition. Adverse chance events seem especially likely to trigger pity, whereupon the victim is not blamed.

GENERAL DISCUSSION

The present findings from Studies I and II are based on hypothetical scenarios with students. Therefore, the results can be generalized neither to actual helping situations nor to other populations. This procedure also has some inherent limitations in that respondents may be unable to judge accurately their affective reactions and whether they would or would not offer help to particular individuals. In addition, some key variables that affect emotion and social support certainly are excluded from the manipulated factors. However, as noted by Cooper (1976), "when looked at from the point of view of generating hypotheses, finding new leads, and initiating models of behavior, [role playing] may be the [best] method" (p. 605). In addition, in the investigations presented here and by Weiner et al. (1988), the stimulus configurations examined could not be found without overwhelming difficulty in field research, with the consequences that variables would be confounded. Finally, prior research has suggested that role-enactment strategies in the study of help-giving have yielded data comparable with observations of actual behavior (see review in Weiner, 1986). For these reasons, and particularly in light of the relatively recent growth of the study of social support, we used a hypothetical scenario method. Research must extend theoretical and experimental analyses within the current framework before applying these research questions to real-life situations.

The present studies have underscored the notion of emotional and cognitive mediators in the process of forming behavioral intentions. When dealing with victims of life events including medical patients, the likelihood of mobilizing help is dependent on a number of recipient and provider characteristics (Dunkel-Schetter & Skokan, 1990). The controllability of the cause of the problem appears to play a role in the determination of help. Moreover, the changeability or instability of the problem as reflected in coping efforts seems to elicit positive expectancies in the observer and motivation to help. Such efforts may create both a sense that the situation can be improved and a belief that one can effectively assist the victim. Thus, outcome expectancy as well as self-efficacy expectancy are useful cognitive mediators. They are part of a mechanism that governs the translation of thought into action. Both studies have dealt with one of these cognitions exclusively, and it would be worthwhile to integrate both concepts into one empirical framework in a subsequent study.

One conclusion of the first experiment concerns the specificity of the result pattern to individual situations. To what degree pity or expectancy mediate recipient characteristics and support intent depended on the particular circumstances, i.e., the stigma chosen and, probably, the unique wording of the vignettes. In the second experiment, there was only one context provided, namely the rape scenario. Therefore, it remains unclear, as to whether these circumstances have affected the results. It could be, for example, that for a divorce or an accident, completely different path coefficients would emerge. The evidence for self-efficacy expectancy as a mediator is limited to the context chosen, and further research should make use of a number of different problem domains.

There are underlying similarities, however, between the selected problems that may suggest a common pattern of reactions to victims. For AIDS, cancer, and rape, the emotion of pity appears to be a stronger mediator than expectancy. These problems are loss/harm situations, whereas contexts such as anorexia, obesity, drug abuse, child abuse, depression and heart disease are more like threats (see Dunkel-Schetter et al., 1991; Hobfoll, 1988; Lazarus, 1990; Lazarus & Folkman, 1984). Different stress appraisals may determine the amount of pity and specific expectancies in potential support providers. If a victim is severely harmed or if the physical integrity of a victim is lost, then pity prevails; if, however, an on-going risky or threatening behavior is the topic, it is seen as more unstable and modifiable and, therefore, gives rise to a greater role for expectancies.

Expectancies can be pessimistic or optimistic. Pessimism undermines the motivation to help because the investment of further support efforts appears to be wasted; optimism, however, assumes that the victim will be responsive to future support attempts and thereby render them worthwhile. Optimism, as a psychological construct, has been defined as "generalized outcome expectancies" (Scheier & Carver, 1985, 1987). This construct has recently become one of the key issues in research on stress, coping, and mental health as well as physical health (Scheier et al., 1989; Seligman, 1991). The present studies have underscored the role of situation-specific outcome expectancies and self-efficacy expectancies after Bandura (1977, 1991). Further research should address the notion of specificity versus generality of expectancy, with dispositional optimism being one example of a more general construct. Jerusalem and Schwarzer (this volume) have developed a global self-efficacy scale that has demonstrated high predictive and construct validity in several field studies. Although specific measures are preferred in clinical intervention studies of behavioral change, there might be an advantage to global measures in other research domains.

Although the present studies have provided preliminary evidence for the role of expectancies as mediators in the helping process, it remains undetermined how outcome expectancy and self-efficacy expectancy are interrelated. Each experiment has dealt with only one of these cognitions but failed to account for their joint influence. It would be premature to conclude from the above findings that outcome expectancy exerts a stronger influence on support intent than self-efficacy expectancy. There might be a causal order among the two. For example, it might be that a support provider does not scrutinize her helping capability unless being faced with a target's condition that is improving or one that is, at least, modifiable. A third variable could be critical here, namely one's personal experience with (a) crisis situations that require support, and with (b) the effectiveness of one's previous helping attempts (Dunkel-Schetter & Skokan, 1990). Self-efficacy expectancy is shaped by context-specific mastery experiences, among others, and therefore it would be necessary to investigate expectancies jointly with an assessment of previous help experience.

REFERENCES

Ajzen, I. (1988). *Attitudes, personality, and behavior*. Milton Keynes: Open University Press.

Amato, P. R, Ho, R., & Partidge, S. (1984). Responsibility attribution and helping behavior in the Ash Wednesday bushfires. *Australian Journal of Psychology, 36*, 191-203.

Bandura, A. (1977). Self-efficacy: Toward a unifying theory of behavioral change. *Psychological Review, 84*, 191-215.

Bandura, A. (1986). *Social foundations of thought and action*. Englewood Cliffs, NJ: Prentice-Hall.

Bandura, A. (1991). Self-efficacy conception of anxiety. In R. Schwarzer & R. Wicklund (Eds.), *Anxiety and self-focused attention* (pp. 89-110). London: Harwood.

Barbee, A. P. (1990). Interactive coping: The cheering-up process in close relationships. In S. Duck with R. Silver (Ed.), *Social support and personal relationships* (pp. 46-65). London: Sage.

Batson, C. D. (1990). How social an animal? *American Psychologist, 45*, 336-346.

Batson, C. D., O'Quinn, K., Fultz, J., Vanderplas, M., & Isen, A. (1983). Influence of self-report distress and empathy on egoistic versus altruistic motivation to help. *Journal of Personality and Social Psychology, 45*, 706-718.

Bennett-Herbert, T., & Dunkel-Schetter, C. (in press). Negative social reactions to victims: An overview of responses and their determinants. In L. Montada, S. H. Filipp, & M. J. Lerner (Eds.), *Life crises and experiences of loss in adulthood*. Hillsdale, NJ: Erlbaum.

Bentler, P. M. (1980). Multivariate analysis with latent variables: Causal modeling. *Annual Review of Psychology, 31*, 419-456.

Berkowitz, L. (1987). Mood, self-awareness, and willingness to help. *Journal of Personality and Social Psychology, 52*, 721-729.

Betancourt, H. (1990). An attribution-empathy model of helping behavior: Behavioral intentions and judgments of help-giving. *Personality and Social Psychology Bulletin, 16*, 573-591.

Borgida, E., Simmons, R. G., Conner, C., & Lombard, K. (1990). The Minnesota Living Donor Studies: Implications for organ procurement. In J. Shanteau & R. Harris (Eds.), *Psychological research on organ donation* (pp. 108-121). Washington, DC: American Psychological Association.

Brickman, P., Rabinowitz, P. C., Karuza, J. Jr., Coates, D., Cohn, E., & Kidder, L. (1982). Models of helping and coping. *American Psychologist, 37*, 368-384.

Carlson, M., & Miller, N. (1987). Explanation of the relation between negative mood and helping. *Psychological Bulletin, 102*, 72-90.

Cialdini, R., Darby, B., & Vincent, J. (1973). Transgression and altruism: A case for hedonism. *Journal of Experimental Social Psychology, 9*, 502-516.

Clary, E. G., & Orenstein, L. (1991). The amount and effectiveness of help: The relationship of motives and abilities to helping behavior. *Personality and Social Psychology Bulletin, 17*, 58-64.

. Cooper, J. (1976). Deception and role playing. *American Psychologist, 31*, 605-610.

Dalbert, C., Montada, L., & Schmitt, M. (1988). Intention and ability as predictors of change in adult daughters' prosocial behavior towards their mothers. *Verantwortung, Gerechtigkeit, Moral, 46*, 1-17.

DeJong, W. (1980). The stigma of obesity: The consequences of naive assumptions concerning the causes of physical deviance. *Journal of Health and Social Behavior, 21*, 75-87.

Dovidio, J. F. (1984). Helping behavior and altruism: An empirical and conceptual overview. In L. Berkowitz (Ed.), *Advances in experimental social psychology* (Vol. 17, pp. 362-428). New York: Academic Press.

Dunkel-Schetter, C., & Bennett, T. L. (1990). Differentiating the cognitive and behavioral aspects of social support. In I. G. Sarason, B. R. Sarason, & G. R. Pierce (Eds.), *Social support: An interactional view* (pp. 267-296). New York: Wiley.

Dunkel-Schetter, C., Blasband, D. E., Feinstein, L. G., & Bennett, T. L. (1991). Elements of supportive social interactions: When are support attempts effective? In S. Spacapan & S. Oskamp (Eds.), *Helping and being helped in the real world* (pp. 83-114). Newbury Park, CA: Sage.

Dunkel-Schetter, C., Folkman, S., & Lazarus, R. S. (1987). Correlates of social support receipt. *Journal of Personality and Social Psychology, 53*, 71-80.

Dunkel-Schetter, C., & Skokan, L. A. (1990). Determinants of social support provision in personal relationships. *Journal of Social and Personal Relationships, 7*, 437-450.

Dunkel-Schetter, C., & Wortman, C. B. (1981). Dilemmas of social support: Parallels between victimization and aging. In I. B. Kiesler, J. N. Morgan, & V. K. Oppenheimer (Eds.), *Aging: Social change* (pp. 349- 381). New York: Academic Press.

Dunkel-Schetter, C., & Wortman, C. B. (1982). The interpersonal dynamics of cancer: Problems in social relationships and their impact on the patient. In H. S. Friedman & M. R. DiMatteo (Eds.), *Interpersonal issues in health care* (pp. 69-100). New York: Academic Press.

Eisenberg, N., & Miller, P. A. (1987). The relation of empathy to prosocial and related behaviors. *Psychological Bulletin, 101*, 91-119.

Fishbein, M., & Ajzen, I. (1975). *Belief, attitude, intention, and behavior: An introduction to theory and research*. Reading, MA: Addison-Wesley.

Goranson, R. E., & Berkowitz, L. (1966). Reciprocity and responsibility reactions to prior help. *Journal of Personality and Social Psychology, 3*, 227-232.

Gurtman, M. B. (1986). Depression and the response of others: Re-evaluating the evaluation. *Journal of Abnormal Psychology, 95*, 99-101.

Hobfoll, S. E. (1988). *The ecology of stress*. Washington, DC: Hemisphere.

Hoffman, M. L. (1975). Developmental synthesis of affect and cognition and its implications for altruistic motivation. *Developmental Psychology, 11*, 607-622.

Hoffman, M. L. (1982). Development of prosocial motivation: Empathy and guilt. In N. Eisenberg (Ed.), *Development of prosocial behavior* (pp. 281-313). New York: Academic Press.

Jöreskog, K., & Sörbom, D. (1988). *LISREL VII: A guide to the program and applications*. Mooresville, IN: Scientific Software.

Jones, E. E., Farina, A., Hastorf, A. H., Markus, H., Miller, D., & Scott, R. A. (1984). *Social stigma. The psychology of marked relationships*. New York: Freeman.

Jung, J. (1988). Social support providers: Why do they help? *Basic and Applied Psychology, 9*, 231-240.

Karasawa, K. (1991). The effects of onset and offset responsibility on affects and helping judgments. *Journal of Applied Social Psychology, 21*, 482-499.

Lazarus, R. S. (1990). Theory-based stress measurement. *Psychological Inquiry, 1*, 3-13.

Lazarus, R. S., & Folkman, S. (1984). *Stress, appraisal, and coping*. New York: Springer.

Notarius, C. I., & Herrick, L. R. (1988). Listener response strategies to a distressed other. *Journal of Social and Personal Relationships, 5*, 97-108.

Reisenzein, R. (1986). A structural equation analysis of Weiner's attribution-affect model of helping behavior. *Journal of Personality and Social Psychology, 50*, 1123-1133.

Scheier, M. F., & Carver, C. S. (1985). Optimism, coping, and health: Assessment and implications of generalized outcome expectancies. *Health Psychology, 4*, 219-247.

Scheier, M. F., & Carver, C. S. (1987). Dispositional optimism and physical well-being: The influence of generalized outcome expectancies on health. *Journal of Personality, 55*, 169-210.

Scheier, M. F., Matthews, K. A., Owens, J., Magovern, G. J. Sr., Lefebre, R. C., Abbott, R. A., & Carver, C. S. (1989). Dispositional optimism and recovery from coronary artery bypass surgery: The beneficial effects on physical and psychological well-being. *Journal of Personality and Social Psychology*.

Schmidt, G., & Weiner, B. (1988). An attribution-affect-action theory of motivated behavior: Replications examining judgments of help-giving. *Personality and Social Psychology Bulletin, 14*, 610-621.

Schwarzer, R., & Leppin, A. (1991). Social support and health: A theoretical and empirical overview. *Journal of Social and Personal Relationships, 8*, 99-127.

Schwarzer, R., & Weiner, B. (1990). Die Wirkung von Kontrollierbarkeit und Bewältigungsverhalten auf Emotionen und soziale Unterstützung [The effect of controllability and coping on emotions and social support]. *Zeitschrift für Sozialpsychologie, 21*, 118-125.

Schwarzer, R., & Weiner, B. (1991). Stigma controllability and coping as predictors of emotions and social support. *Journal of Social and Personal Relationships, 8*, 133-140.

Seligman, M. E. P. (1991). *Learned optimism*. New York: Knopf.

Shumaker, S. A., & Brownell, A. (1984). Toward a theory of social support: Closing conceptual gaps. *Journal of Social Issues, 40*, 11-36.

Silver, R. C., Wortman, C. B., & Crofton, C. (1990). The role of coping in support provision: The self-presentational dilemma of victims of life crises. In I. G. Sarason, B. R. Sarason, & G. R. Pierce (Eds.), *Social support: An interactional view* (pp. 397-426). New York: Wiley.

Skokan, L. A. (1990). *Motivational determinants of social support provision*. Unpublished doctoral dissertation. University of California: Los Angeles.

Weiner, B. (1985). An attributional theory of achievement motivation and emotion. *Psychological Review, 92*, 548-573.

Weiner, B. (1986). *An attributional theory of motivation and emotion*. Berlin: Springer.

Weiner, B., Perry, R. P., & Magnusson, J. (1988). An attributional analysis of reactions to stigmas. *Journal of Personality and Social Psychology, 55*(5) 738-748.

II

SELF-EFFICACY AND
HUMAN DEVELOPMENT

PERCEIVED CONTROL: MOTIVATION, COPING, AND DEVELOPMENT

Ellen A. Skinner

All individuals need to feel that they are capable of producing desired and avoiding undesired events. This need gives perceived control its power to regulate behavior, emotion, and motivation under conditions of challenge. Based on this assumption, we formulated an integrative conceptualization of perceived control which distinguishes between individuals' beliefs about the causes of success and failure, or strategy beliefs, and beliefs about their own abilities to enact those strategies, or capacity beliefs. We examine the aspects of strategy and capacity beliefs which influence children's behavior and emotion, especially in stressful situations. Special emphasis is placed on development. We explore systematic changes in the mean level and organization of children's beliefs, as well as changes in the beliefs which influence motivation and coping at different ages and changes in the mechanisms through which these influences operate.

Why are individuals' beliefs about how much control they can exert over important events in their lives such a powerful force in human motivation and development? Why is self-efficacy one of the best predictors of effort exertion, persistence, and coping from infancy to old age (Bandura, 1977; Baltes & Baltes, 1986)? Why should robbing individuals of control result in helplessness, apathy, and even death (Seligman, 1975)? Why should children with low perceived control become unhappy, anxious, and eventually depressed (Nolen-Hoeksema, Girgus, & Seligman, 1986)? Why is uncontrollability one of the few experiences that researchers can agree upon as a category of major psychological stress (Weinberg & Levine, 1980)? These questions may explain the fascination which the study of perceived control has held for social scientists from a broad range of disciplines. One answer was offered by White in his seminal paper on effectance motivation (1959) and has been elaborated by motivational theorists (Connell & Wellborn, 1990; Deci & Ryan, 1985): Humans have a basic psychological need to be effective in their interactions with the world. This desire has been labelled the need for effectance or for competence.

According to motivational needs theorists, from birth all people are intrinsically motivated to produce desired events and to prevent undesired events from occurring (Connell & Wellborn, 1990; Deci & Ryan, 1985). In support of this assertion, needs theories can muster evolutionary, empirical, and logical arguments. The evolutionary value of such motivation can be imagined. If individuals innately desire to interact effectively with their environments, then they will continue attempting to manipulate physical and social events until they figure out how to reliably produce and reproduce desired outcomes. Learning of great adaptive value would accrue: about contingencies in the environment and about repertoires of one's own effective behaviors.

Empirical arguments in support of the need for competence as innate can be found in research with newborns. Researchers point out that the capacity to detect contingencies is present in the youngest ages we are able to tap empirically, and that infants express joy and satisfaction when their behaviors are followed contingently by effects (Watson, 1979). As one account of the mechanism by which the need for competence is "hardwired" at birth, a feedback system could be suggested in which experiences of effectance trigger positive emotions. White's (1959) article summarizes research from a wide variety of perspectives which supports the occurrence of such behaviors. Finally, as empirical evidence for the need for competence, theorists point to research documenting the devastating effects of loss of control on people from infancy to adulthood. Forms of loss of control include non-contingency, unpredictability, normlessness (unclear expectations), and inconsistency. The former two conditions have been studied as major forms of psychological (and immunological) stress and the latter two have been studied as developmentally detrimental aspects of parenting. A needs theory can explain why helplessness is so distressing: It represents a state in which a basic psychological need is violated.

The logical argument is that if the experience of control is a basic psychological need, then its study should represent a major theme in psychological theories and research. This is indeed the case. At least three major theories of perceived control have proved to be extremely useful in charting research in this area: Bandura's theory of self-efficacy (1977), Seligman's reformulated model of learned helplessness (Abramson, Seligman, & Teasdale, 1978), and Weiner's summary of his attribution theory (1979). These theories and the research they generate have enriched an already voluminous literature on locus of control, the most prominent childhood theory of which was proposed by the Crandalls (Connell, 1985; Crandall, Katkovsky, & Crandall, 1965). Perceived control constructs enjoy empirical success at predicting a wide range of behavior, emotion, and performance variables. Although most personality and attitude assessments have difficulty establishing any links whatsoever to behavior, in contrast, hundreds of studies per year have been published documenting the power of perceived control to predict performance in many domains.

The Need for Competence and Motivation

A needs theory of motivation has been proposed (Connell & Wellborn, 1990; Deci & Ryan, 1985) which posits competence among its basic psychological needs (along with the need for self-determination and relatedness). According to this model, individuals appraise the extent to which the context is meeting each of their psychological needs. These appraisals, called self-system processes, have been conceptualized and studied for the competence need under the rubric of perceived control. (The need for self-determination has been studied under the rubric of autonomy orientation and for relatedness under the rubric of internal working models for attachment figures.) Hence, individual differences in perceived control are thought to reflect variations in the extent to which individuals have experienced themselves as competent to produce desired and prevent undesired outcomes, based on their history of interactions with the environment.

Social context. According to this theory, the role of the social context is crucial in creating experiences of control (Connell & Wellborn, 1990; Skinner, 1990b). Important others in individuals' lives either directly provide or arrange for the amount and quality of *structure* in their environments. Structure refers to the amount of information in the environment available to individuals about the best strategies for reaching desired and preventing undesired outcomes, and about the self's capacity to enact those strategies. A context high in structure provides high contingencies between actions and outcomes, is consistent and predictable; it also encourages the development of actual capacities through the provision of opportunities for practice, help, support, and advice (Skinner, 1990b). The opposite of structure is *chaos*, in which contexts are non-contingent, inconsistent, or unpredictable, and at the same time provide challenges which are either under-stimulating or overwhelming. The effects of chaotic environments have been well-documented empirically. According to this theory, their consequences are played out through their impact on an individuals' perceived control.

Engagement versus disaffection. This motivational theory posits that when an individuals' basic psychological needs have been fulfilled, they will be energized to be enthusiastically involved with ongoing activities (Connell & Wellborn, 1990). The motivational construct that is the proximal outcome of having one's needs met is engagement versus disaffection. *Engagement* includes three components: behavior (e.g., initiation, effort, concentrated attention, persistence, and continued attempts in the face of difficulty or failure), emotion (enthusiasm, happiness, curiosity, interest), and orientation (toward the goal of understanding how to be effective). Likewise, *disaffection* includes behavior (e.g., avoidance, passivity, resistance, giving up, fleeing), emotion (boredom, anger, anxiety, fear), and orientation (away from the goal of understanding how to be effective, for example, toward trying to *appear* effective). The idea, central to many theories, is that individuals who believe they have more control will be more likely to engage actively, whereas those who feel powerless are more likely to be disaffected. In turn, an individual's engagement versus disaffection can influence long-term outcomes, such as level of performance, learning, and even development. According to motivational theories, the links established between perceived control and higher levels of performance and psychological functioning are largely mediated by engagement and disaffection.

In sum, perceived control can be seen as part of a larger system which, by motivating individuals to meet the need for competence, has the function of regulating an individual's interactions with the environment. The system is activated when the individual attempts to produce a desired effect. When the social context presents minor resistance, the individual will experience it as a challenge and will produce active behaviors and enthusiastic emotions in energized pursuit of the outcome (engagement). If these behaviors are ineffective or if the context mounts major obstacles, the system may show one last angry burst of energy (reactance) and then it will shut down, as evidenced in passivity and disinterest (disengagement). Disengagement is, of course, an adaptive reaction to excessive environmental challenge. It protects the individual from exhaustion in pursuit of impossible tasks; and it is the basis for learning effective strategies (and discarding ineffective ones) as well as calibrating one's own developing capacities and limitations. With prolonged exposure to ineffectiveness and chaos, however, the competence system may be severely impaired, as evidenced by its failure to reactivate under conditions of manageable challenge (disaffection). Different theories of perceived control have focused on different aspects of the competence system. For example, self-efficacy judgments function primarily to regulate engagement, whereas learned helplessness attributions influence disaffection.

Conceptualization of Perceived Control

If all individuals desire competence or control, and all individuals eventually construct appraisals of the self in relation to this need, then it follows that the variety of theories depicting the components of perceived control are all addressing the same psychological phenomenon: the self-system process associated with the need for competence or control. If this is indeed the case, then it should be possible to integrate theories as diverse as locus of control, self-efficacy, learned helplessness, and attribution theories. In fact, a new conceptualization of perceived control, aimed to do just that, was constructed at the crossroads of these theories.

Even if one does not share motivational assumptions, it may still be useful to distinguish and integrate key constructs from these multiple theoretical perspectives. It would allow the components to be assessed separately and then compared for their unique contributions and interactions in predicting behavior. The distinction, offered by Bandura, between response-outcome judgments and efficacy judgments seems pivotal in this regard. Whereas most theories focus on beliefs about "whether my responses produce outcomes," Bandura pointed out that this belief is irrelevant unless one also believes that "I can myself produce the required responses." This distinction, which can also be found in the sociological work of the Gurins (Gurin, Gurin, & Morrison, 1978), in learned helplessness research (Abramson et al., 1978), and in the developmental theories of Weisz (Weisz & Stipek, 1982), was the cornerstone for a new conceptualization and measure of perceived control.

On expanding the scope of the conceptualization to include multiple internal and external causal categories (based on the locus of control construct), three aspects of perceived control are distinguished : (a) *strategy beliefs* or generalized expectancies about the extent to which certain categories of potential causes are effective in producing desired outcomes (originally refered to as means-ends beliefs); (b) *capacity beliefs* or generalized expectancies about the extent to which the self possesses or has access to those potential means (originally referred to as agency beliefs); and (c) *control beliefs* or generalized expectancies about the extent to which the self can produce desired outcomes irrespective of the means involved (Skinner, Chapman, & Baltes, 1988a).

In a series of five studies completed at the Max Planck Institute with Michael Chapman and Paul Baltes, a questionnaire was developed which tapped these beliefs for children in the domain of school performance. For this domain and age group, five categories of means were considered: effort, ability, powerful others, luck, and unknown factors (Skinner et al., 1988a). The measurement studies showed that the factor structure of children's responses to the questionnaire reflected the theoretical distinctions between beliefs, and that different aspects of beliefs could be mapped onto other constructs. The "final" version of the measure was refined using the creativity and measurement expertise of James Connell and James Wellborn (Student Perceptions of Control Questionnaire, SPOCQ; Wellborn, Connell, & Skinner, 1989) (see Appendix I). Like other psychologists interested in perceived control, we began by examining the connections between the construct and aspects of performance. Because the domain was *school* performance, the natural dependent variables were academic achievement, intelligence, and school grades. Not surprisingly, like so many generations of expectancy constructs before them, multiple robust relations with control, strategy, and capacity beliefs have been found (e.g., Chapman, Skinner, & Baltes, 1990; Skinner, Wellborn, & Connell, 1990).

Motivation and Perceived Control

According to the motivational perspective, the effects of perceived control on level of performance are mediated by the individual's engagement versus disaffection with learning activities. A brief description of the results of a cross-sectional study (Skinner et al., 1990) and a recently completed short-term longitudinal study will be used in order to illustrate two issues about the links between beliefs and motivation: first, the importance of examining the unique and interactive effects of *both* strategy and capacity beliefs; and second, the importance of examining sets of beliefs which both promote *and* undermine motivation.

The cross-sectional and longitudinal studies involved 220 and 365 third to sixth graders, respectively, and their 12 and 14 teachers. Both school districts were suburban/rural with about 10% minority students. *Engagement versus disaffection* was assessed using 20-item teacher-reports of individual children's active behavioral involvement and emotional tone in the classroom (Wellborn &

Connell, 1986). These scores were internally consistent (alpha = .82) and could range from -3 to +3, with higher scores indicating more engagement. As expected, level of engagement was a strong predictor of subsequent academic performance. For example, the cross-time correlations with grades was .40. *Perceived control* was measured using our new scale (Skinner et. al., 1988a; Wellborn et al., 1989). Internal consistencies were satisfactory (Cronbach alphas ranged from .75 to .85 and averaged .79); most importantly, reliability did not differ appreciably across scales.

The basic question was whether the new conceptualization could provide a more differentiated picture of the aspects of children's beliefs which predicted to their engagement. As would be predicted from other theories: engagement was *promoted* by control beliefs as well as capacity beliefs for effort and ability. Engagement was *undermined* by beliefs in the effectiveness of non-action means, including powerful others, luck, and unknown factors. Of greatest interest was the issue of the effects of *both* strategy and capacity beliefs in predicting to motivation. When considering matched pairs for each cause, unique contributions were made by both strategy (negative) and capacity (positive) beliefs for ability, powerful others, and luck. The *interaction* between strategy and capacity beliefs also provided new information. *Highest* levels of engagement were found for children who reported that effort was an effective means *and* that they had the capacity to exert effort (as would be predicted by self-efficacy theory). *Lowest* levels of engagement were found for children who endorsed high strategy beliefs for non-action causes (ability, powerful others and luck) *and* who at the same time reported that they did not have the capacity to enact those strategies. For example, lowest levels of engagement were found for children who said that luck is required for success in school *and* that they are unlucky (as would be predicted by attribution theories).

Finally, scores were constructed summarizing profiles of beliefs which would be predicted to *promote* and *undermine* motivation. Children who were high on the "Promote Profile" believed that they could control school success and failure, that effort was important and that they could exert it, that ability was not an important strategy but that they themselves nevertheless were smart, that they could influence powerful others, and that they were lucky. In contrast, children who scored high on the "Undermine Profile" saw themselves as unable to exert effort and not very smart, believed that although powerful others and luck are the keys to school performance, they could not get teachers to like them and were unlucky; finally, they did not know the strategies to achieve success and avoid failure. (Note that each score included strategy and capacity beliefs from each cause.) When these two profiles were pitted against each other in a path analysis, both accounted for significant unique variance in teacher-rated engagement. However, more of the variance was accounted for by beliefs which *undermine* motivation than by those which promote it (Skinner et al., 1990).

Taken together, these findings may have implications for major theories of perceived control. First, they indicate that *internal* locus of control may *not* be a powerful positive predictor of motivation. Strategy beliefs about effort were uncorrelated with engagement and strategy beliefs about ability were negatively correlated. Instead, the predictive power seems to emanate from the external pole; strategy beliefs about non-action causes undermine motivation. Second, with respect to attribution theories such as the reformulated learned helplessness model, these findings suggest that attributions can be "unpacked" for their implications for both the effectiveness of causes and for one's own capacities. For example, an attribution of failure to ability is detrimental to motivation because it implies both a belief about causes (ability is required to succeed) *and* about the self's capacity (low ability). Third, for self-efficacy theory, these results point out the importance of other causes in addition to behavior (or responses). For this age group and in this domain, the most powerful predictors of engagement and performance involved ability, powerful others, luck, and unknown means.

Development of Perceived Control

The assumption that the self-system processes associated with the need for competence and control develop out of initially "hardwired" appraisals of the extent to which this need is challenged or threatened, implies that cognitive constructions of perceived control may change with age. Because perceived control is considered within an individual differences perspective, it is usually assumed that the key developmental questions in this area center on differential trajectories of change as antecedents of current differences in level. Indeed, research in this area has provided some interesting insights into the issue of age-graded changes in mean level of perceived control. However, other aspects of perceived control may develop as well, such as the organization or structure of perceived control, the aspects of perceived control which predict to motivation and performance, and the mechanisms which mediate between experiences of chaos/non-contingency and individuals' actions (Skinner & Connell, 1986).

Development of mean level of perceived control. Assessments of perceived control have been conducted across the life-span, from the earliest ages at which children can reliably report their beliefs (about age 4) to research with the "old old" (age 85). A fairly consistent picture emerges (see Skinner & Connell, 1986, for a review). Very young children report extremely high potential control, which decreases sharply until about age 7 or 8, at which time it first correlates with actual performance levels. From middle childhood until early adulthood, perceived control increases gradually. It remains fairly stable across adulthood, decreasing slightly as old age is encountered. These general trends are products of differential trajectories of different kinds of control beliefs. For example, beliefs about the effectiveness of the *self* remain stable into old age; the net decrease in perceived control is accounted for by the fact that older adults increasingly believe that powerful others and chance play a bigger role as causal factors.

Of most interest to theorists of perceived control has been the *process* by which trajectories of control are constructed. Research which indicates that perceived control influences behavior and that performance outcomes influence perceived control suggest that a cyclic process may be at work (Seligman, 1975; Skinner, 1990b). Children who believe that they can exert control may initiate more attempts and sustain more effort, leading to more successful outcomes, and thereby boosting perceptions of control. In contrast, children who believe that they have no control may subsequently approach the world in ways (passive, apathetic, depressed) which forfeit any chance for exerting control. If these cycles continue unabated, individual differences in perceived control will be consolidated and then magnified over time. The result would be relative stability of mean levels in the context of increasingly divergent individual developmental trajectories (Skinner, 1990b).

Development of the organization of perceived control. According to our research, children's beliefs about the effectiveness of causes (strategy beliefs) become more differentiated from each other in terms of mean level across middle childhood. (This pattern has been replicated in German and American samples; Skinner, Chapman, & Baltes, 1988b.) Following this lead, we investigated age differences in the factor structure of children's causal beliefs (Skinner, 1990a). From these findings (also replicated), it appears that the dimensionalization of perceived control in the academic domain *does* change with age: At age 7 to 8, the key dimensions are known versus unknown causes; at ages 9 to 10, three dimensions are present: "internal," "external," and unknown factors; and at ages 11 to 12, four dimensions emerge: effort, ability, "external," and unknown means.

Development of the functions of perceived control. Corresponding to age differences in the dimensionalization of perceived control, the primary predictors of school performance change with age. Although at all ages unknown source of control is a significant (negative) predictor, it is the only predictor at ages 7 to 8; at ages 9 to 10, "external" causes are added; and by ages 11 to 12, strategy beliefs for ability are the central (again negative) correlate (Skinner, 1990a). A review of the few studies in which age differences in the correlations between aspects of perceived control and engagement or performance were calculated reveals convergent evidence for this position (Skinner, 1990b). Correlations between behavior or performance and locus of control (Findley & Cooper, 1983) and classical learned helplessness (Fincham, Hokoda, & Sanders, 1989; Rholes, Blackwell, Jordan, & Walters, 1980) emerge at ages 9 to 10; correlations with attributions of failure to ability (Miller, 1985) and capacity for ability are strongest at ages 11 to 12 (Chapman et al., 1990).

It is tempting to conclude that different theories of perceived control are most useful at different ages. Perhaps, the *known versus unknown* distinction as proposed by Connell portrays the critical dimension when children first begin school. In contrast, for children a bit older, the distinction between *internal versus external* causes begins to play a role as proposed by locus of control theorists, with the external pole playing the bigger part, as predicted by classical learned helplessness theory. Only after age 11 do beliefs suggested by self-efficacy and attributional theorists begin to regulate performance, namely, organized around *ability causes*. Some recent research indicates that changes in the dimensionalization of perceived control can be accounted for by progressive differentiation of children's concepts of effort, noncontingency, luck, and ability (Miller, 1985; Nicholls & Miller, 1984). It may be that these changes "activate" individual differences in beliefs to begin regulating and interpreting behavior and performance (Chapman & Skinner, 1989). A recently completed longitudinal study will allow us to follow up on these issues empirically.

Development of the mechanisms of perceived control. Taken together, these age changes imply that the mechanisms by which the competence system functions change with development. In other words, although people (like infra-human species) react to uncontrollability from birth to death, the mediators of these reactions change with age. At some ages (e.g., infancy), mechanisms may not even include beliefs about control. At other ages, simpler forms of perceived control, such as expectations, may operate. At all ages, multiple potential mediators are likely to be the rule rather than the exception. Although the issue of mechanisms is at the heart of any discussion of perceived control, the issue of multiple and changing mechanisms has received little empirical attention.

During infancy, activation of motivation (behavior, emotion, and orientation) in the face of challenge, as well as de-activation of motivation when the system is overwhelmed, is probably accomplished by neuro-endocrine mechanisms (Gunnar, 1980). The concurrent generalization of the effects of exposure to non-contingency, although empirically demonstrated (e.g., Watson, 1979), follows very specific time- and modality-limited parameters. The competence system appears to be relatively plastic during infancy, in that the motivational effects of exposure to uncontrollability seem to be easily reversible. However, these early experiences may leave neurological traces which could have cumulative effects when the competence system is challenged in the future.

With the onset of representational capacities, an additional mechanism seems to be added, namely, performance expectations. These expectations are usually very task- and context-specific and take the general form of "I can produce outcome X." These are the rudiments of generalized beliefs about control and have been studied extensively during the preschool years by the Crandalls (Crandall et al., 1965). These performance expectations provide anticipatory regulation of action (Crandall & Linn, 1989). When operating adaptively, they lead children to engage in optimally challenging activities.

When problem-solving and strategy-testing skills emerge, an additional mechanism can be suggested: "mental exhaustion" (Kofta & Sedek, 1989). According to this perspective, exposure to non-contingency results in prolonged activation of problem-solving activity, resulting in a depletion of mental resources. This theory can explain two interesting phenomena which are puzzling to reformulated learned helplessness theory. First, it explains why non-contingency leads to greater subsequent helplessness deficits than failure. Failure deactivates the system sooner and so does not exhaust it. Second, it explains the effects of positive non-contingency, in which subjects show helplessness deficits even when they are told (non-contingently) that they are succeeding. Despite reported high levels of perceived control, exhaustion would undermine subsequent motivation.

All of these mechanisms are probably still operating when full-blown belief systems emerge at about age 7 or 8 (at least in the academic domain). As described in the previous section, the mechanisms by which perceived control regulates motivation and interprets performance continue to develop across middle childhood, perhaps from beliefs about unknown control, to an understanding of "conceptual" (as opposed to empirical) non-contingency, to the development of beliefs about the stable and unchangable self. These developments are of both conceptual and pragmatic interest. As these systems of perceived control become organized, they also become less plastic and less open to disconfirming information from interactions with the context (Skinner, 1990b). Taken together with the notion that levels of perceived control may also be responsible for producing actual confirming experiences, either positive or negative (e.g., Skinner, 1985), the importance of thoroughly understanding the development of mechanisms of perceived control is highlighted.

Coping and Perceived Control

From a motivational perspective, perceived control should support children's active engagement both in ongoing activities and under conditions of challenge. Conceptualizations of how children's perceived control makes them more vulnerable or resistant to the effects of stressful encounters typically fall under the study of stress and coping (Garmezy & Rutter, 1983). The motivational perspective described above can be used to set the stage for questions about the mechanisms through which perceived control ameliorates or exacerbates the effects of stress (Skinner & Wellborn, in press). For the psychological need competence, the objective psychological stress involved would be loss of control, in all its variations. Hence, the stresses against which perceived control should offer protection can be subsumed under the label chaos. Any encounters with non-contingency, inconsistency, unpredictability, failure, and ineffectiveness would qualify as objectively impinging on the need for competence. Children who have high perceived control should be able to maintain their functioning under these conditions and children with low perceived control should not. Of course, the study of childhood helplessness is prototypic in its research of just this phenomenon (Dweck & Wortman, 1982). The objective stressor is failure or non-contingency; the aspect of perceived control is beliefs about the efficacy of effort versus ability; and the stress-related outcomes are mastery (strategizing, persistence, and effort) versus helplessness (passivity, anxiety, and self-derogation).

A recently developed theory of coping attempts to unpack the components of stressful encounters and to discover the mechanisms by which loss of control can have an impact on motivation and performance. This framework posits four conceptually distinct aspects of the coping process. First, appraisal: Following an encounter with an event involving loss of control (e.g., failure), the child appraises whether this event has implications for his/her experience of competence. This appraisal is intuitive, non-rational, and almost instantaneous. Second, a distress reaction follows. If the child experiences the failure as threatening his/her competence, he/she will react with psychological distress, which includes anxiety and a desire to withdraw from the situation. If on the other hand, the event is experienced as a challenge to competence, the child will react with energy and a desire for behavioral involvement.

Third, the child copes with the event and his/her distress reaction to it. Coping refers to how children regulate their engagement, specifically, their behavior, emotion, and orientation under conditions of psychological distress, or how they fail to do so. A number of regulatory processes can be energized by perceived threats to the competence need and directed by the specific self-system processes of perceived control. Finally, coping responses produce their effects on engagement versus disaffection, resulting in behavior that is either active or passive, emotion that is either positive or negative, and an orientation that is either toward or away from the activity. These hypotheses were used as the basis for a recently completed study of children's coping and perceived control (Skinner & Wellborn, 1991). High strategy and capacity beliefs about effort were hypothesized to result in coping characterized by strategizing and persistence; beliefs organized around ability should produce avoidance when ability capacity beliefs are low; beliefs organized around powerful others should lead to delegation if children believe they can influence those others and to projection if they believe that they cannot; and finally, the higher children's unknown control, the less children will regulate their behavior and emotion, resulting in impulsivity and confusion.

These constructs were assessed in the academic domain in a sample of 246 children, ages 8 to 15. A description of the coping categories, sample items, and their internal consistencies are reported in Appendix II. As can be seen, several of the scales with only four items had reliabilities that were less than .65. Hence, the results of the study should be viewed as exploratory. Examination of mean levels revealed the extent to which the categories were endorsed in this sample. The coping responses most likely to be used were the more adaptive ones, namely, strategizing and perseverance. Of the less adaptive coping responses, avoidance was the most often endorsed, followed by confusion and impulsivity; delegation and projection were least often used. The correlations between children's coping responses and the emotional and behavioral components of their engagement in the classroom revealed that coping responses predicted to both emotion (especially anxiety) and to behavioral engagement (both ongoing and following failure). Projection and confusion seemed to have the most negative implications for emotion, predicting to anger and anxiety respectively. And, strategizing and impulsivity seemed to be the strongest positive and negative predictors of behavioral involvement, both ongoing and in response to failure.

Coping responses showed multiple robust relations to perceived control, but not always in the predicted pattern. Consistent with predictions, strategizing and perseverance coping responses were most closely related to beliefs about the efficacy of effort; and confusion was closely related to unknown control. For delegation and projection, the close relations predicted to beliefs about powerful others were found for strategy beliefs only. Contrary to predictions, avoidance was *not* most closely related to beliefs about ability. Instead, avoidance was predicted most strongly by unknown strategy beliefs.

In order to examine the unique effects of the five categories of means on coping, a series of multiple regressions were performed. Using the coping categories as dependent variables, the independent variables were "interaction" scores calculated for each cause by multiplying the respective strategy beliefs by its capacity beliefs (e.g., the effort interaction score was the effort strategy beliefs score multiplied times the effort capacity beliefs score). As hypothesized, effort beliefs were the highest unique predictors for both strategizing and perseverance. Contrary to predictions, effort (not ability) beliefs also made the highest unique contribution to avoidance (unknown strategy beliefs also predicted uniquely to avoidance). Ability beliefs contributed uniquely to delegation coping. As predicted, powerful others made unique contributions to both delegation and projection coping. Finally, the highest unique predictors of confusion were luck and unknown beliefs; and the only unique predictor of impulsivity was luck beliefs.

In sum, children with high effort and ability beliefs were more likely, in the face of challenges, to strategize and persevere, and less likely to attempt to get others to solve their problems for them (delegation). On the other hand, children who endorsed powerful others, luck, and unknown strategy beliefs were more likely to react to challenges impulsively and with confusion, to blame others (projection), and to avoid the situation. These results provide encouragement for the continued study of coping and control in children.

Summary

Far from closing the book on research on perceived control, a motivational perspective opens up new directions for this line of research. First, it points out the importance of examining more closely different profiles of beliefs. Loss of control due to lack of self-efficacy may have different emotional and behavioral consequences than loss of control due to interference by powerful others. In this regard, it may be important to note the relatively greater power of beliefs to undermine as opposed to promote motivation. It is possible that lack of control (whatever its source) may be sufficient to put a *halt* to action, but that full sustained engagement my require additional self-system supports, such as perceived autonomy or feelings of connectedness to important others in the social context. The motivational model should be helpful in guiding an exploration of these issues (Connell & Wellborn, 1990; Deci & Ryan, 1985).

Second, it may be interesting to follow some of the leads uncovered in the developmental research. Answers to the question: "Which control-related beliefs are good news and which are bad news?" may be different depending on the age of the target population. More research is needed to determine whether developmental differentiation of children's causal concepts "activate" individual differences in the power of beliefs about the effectiveness of those causes to regulate and interpret performance. If they do, then such findings would have implications for the developmental appropriateness of the targets and methods for interventions designed to optimize children's perceived control.

Third, if the need for competence is innate and pervasive, then its presence should be felt in domains outside academics. The domains of parent-child relations and friendships seem to be arenas in which children may be likely to develop self-system processes about control. To follow up on these questions will require a discovery of the important causal categories in these domains as well as research about their developmental course. If these beliefs predict children's engagement in friendships and how they cope with challenges and setbacks in their social relationships, then perhaps the investment will be worthwhile.

Finally, it seems important to use some of these theories and research to rethink intervention attempts. Because research links perceived control to so many aspects of psychological functioning, many intervention efforts have been aimed at strengthening children's perceptions of control. The current program of research highlights the notion that interventions should be developmentally appropriate as well as taking into consideration how the context creates experiences for children which undermine or promote their perceived control. Assessing the effects of changes in beliefs on subsequent coping, behavior, emotion, and motivation may provide a more complete picture of the effectiveness of these important intervention efforts.

REFERENCES

Abramson, L. Y., Seligman, M. E. P., & Teasdale, J. D. (1978). Learned helplessness in humans: Critique and reformulation. *Journal of Abnormal Psychology, 87,* 49-74.

Baltes, M. M., & Baltes, P. B. (Eds.) (1986). *Aging and the psychology of control.* Hillsdale, NJ: Erlbaum.

Bandura, A. (1977). Self-efficacy: Toward a unified theory of behavioral change. *Psychological Review, 84,* 191-215.

Chapman, M., & Skinner, E. A. (1989). Children's agency beliefs, cognitive performance and conceptions of effort and ability: Interaction of individual and developmental differences. *Child Development, 60,* 1229-1238.

Chapman, M., Skinner, E. A., & Baltes, P. B. (1990). Interpreting correlations between children's perceived control and cognitive performance: Control, agency, or means-ends beliefs? *Developmental Psychology, 23,* 246-253.

Connell, J. P. (1985). A new multidimensional measure of children's perceptions of control. *Child Development, 56,* 1018-1041.

Connell, J. P., & Wellborn, J. G. (1990). Competence, autonomy, and relatedness: A motivational analysis of self-system processes. In M. Gunnar & L. A. Sroufe (Eds.), *Minnesota symposium on child psychology* (Vol. 22, pp. 43-77). Minneapolis: University of Minnesota Press.

Crandall, V. C., Katkovsky, W., & Crandall, V. J. (1965). Children's beliefs in their control of reinforcement in intellectual academic achievement behaviors. *Child Development, 36*, 91-109.

Crandall, V. C., & Linn, P. L. (1989, April). Children's achievement orientation: Sex differences, developmental trends, and emergence of motivational functions. In J. G. Nicholls (Chair), *Achievement strivings, expectations, and values in the toddler to first grade years.* Symposium at the Biennial Meetings of the Society for Research in Child Development, Kansas City, MO.

Deci, E. L., & Ryan, R. M. (1985). *Intrinsic motivation and self-determination in human behavior.* New York: Plenum.

Dweck, C. S., & Wortman, C. B. (1982). Learned helplessness, anxiety, and achievement motivation: Neglected parallels in cognitive, affective, and coping responses. In H. W. Krohne & L. Laux (Eds.), *Achievement, stress, and anxiety* (pp. 93-125). Washington, DC: Hemisphere.

Fincham, F., Hokoda, A., & Sanders, R., Jr. (1989). Learned helplessness, test anxiety, and academic achievement: A longitudinal analysis. *Child Development, 60*, 138-145.

Findley, M. J., & Cooper, H. M. (1983). Locus of control and academic achievement: A literature review. *Journal of Personality and Social Psychology, 44*, 419-427.

Garmezy, N., & Rutter, M. (Eds.) (1983). *Stress, coping, and development in children.* New York: McGraw-Hill.

Gurin, P., Gurin, G., & Morrison, B. M. (1978). Personal and ideological aspects of internal-external locus of control. *Social Psychology, 41*, 275-296.

Gunnar, M. R. (1980). Contingent stimulation: A review of its role in early development. In S. Levine & H. Ursin (Eds.), *Coping and health* (pp. 101-119). New York: Plenum.

Miller, A. (1985). A developmental study of the cognitive basis of performance impairment after failure. *Journal of Personality and Social Psychology, 49*, 529-538.

Nicholls, J. G., & Miller, A. T. (1984). Development and its discontents: The differentiation of the concept of ability. In J. G. Nicholls (Ed.), *The development of achievement motivation* (pp. 185-218). Greenwich, CT: JAI Press.

Nolen-Hoeksema, S., Girgus, J. S., & Seligman, M. E. P. (1986). Learned helplessness in children: A longitudinal study of depression, achievement, and explanatory style. *Journal of Personality and Social Psychology, 52*, 435-442.

Rholes, W. S., Blackwell, J., Jordan, C., & Walters, C. (1980). A developmental study of learned helplessness. *Developmental Psychology, 16*, 616-624.

Seligman, M. E. P. (1975). *Helplessness: On depression, development, and death.* San Francisco: Freeman Press.

Skinner, E. A. (1985). Action, control judgments, and the structure of control experience. *Psychological Review, 92*, 39-58.

Skinner, E. A. (1990a). Age differences in the structure of perceived control during middle childhood: Implications for developmental conceptualizations and research. *Child Development, 61*, 1882-1890.

Skinner, E. A. (1990b). Development and perceived control: A dynamic model of action in context. In M. Gunnar & L. A. Sroufe (Eds.), *Minnesota symposium on child psychology, Vol. XXII* (pp. 167-216). Minneapolis: University of Minnesota Press.

Skinner, E. A., Chapman, M., & Baltes, P. B. (1988a). Beliefs about control, means-ends, and agency: A new conceptualization and its measurement during childhood. *Journal of Personality and Social Psychology, 54*, 117-133.

Skinner, E. A., Chapman, M., & Baltes, P. B. (1988b). Children's beliefs about control, means-ends, and agency: Developmental differences during middle childhood. *International Journal of Behavioral Development, 11*, 369-388.

Skinner, E. A., & Connell, J. P. (1986). Development and the understanding of control. In M. M. Baltes & P. B. Baltes (Eds.), *Aging and the psychology of control* (pp. 35-63). Hillsdale, NJ: Erlbaum.

Skinner, E. A., & Wellborn, J. G. (1991, April). *Coping and perceived control.* Paper presented at the Biennial Meetings of the Society for Research in Child Development, Seattle, WA.

Skinner, E. A., & Wellborn J. G. (in press). Coping across the life span: A motivational perspective. In M. Perlmutter, D. Featherman, & R. Lerner (Eds.), *Life-span development and behavior, Vol. 12.* New York: Academic Press.

Skinner, E. A., Wellborn, J. G., & Connell, J. P. (1990). What it takes to do well in school and whether I've got it: The role of perceived control in children's engagement and school achievement. *Journal of Educational Psychology, 82*, 22-32.

Watson, J. S. (1979). Perception of contingency as a determinant of social responsiveness. In E. B. Truman (Ed.), *Origins of the infant's social responsiveness* (pp. 33-64). Hillsdale, NJ: Erlbaum.

Weinberg, J., & Levine, S. (1980). Psychobiology of coping in animals: The effects of unpredictability. In S. Levine & H. Ursin (Eds.), *Coping and health.* New York: Plenum.

Weiner, B. (1979). A theory of motivation for some classroom experiences. *Journal of Educational Psychology, 71*, 3-25.

Weisz, J. R., & Stipek, D. J. (1982). Competence, contingency, and the development of perceived control. *Human Development, 25*, 250-281.

Wellborn, J. G., & Connell, J. P. (1986). *Manual for the Rochester Assessment Package for Schools.* University of Rochester, Rochester, NY.

Wellborn, J. G., Connell, J. P., & Skinner, E. A. (1989). *The Student Perceptions of Control Questionnaire (SPOCQ).* Technical Report, University of Rochester, Rochester, NY.

White, R. W. (1959). Motivation reconsidered: The concept of competence. *Psychological Review, 66*, 297-333.

Author Notes

The contributions of collaborators are gratefully acknowledged, both those in Berlin, Paul Baltes and Michael Chapman; and in Rochester, James Connell, Edward Deci, Richard Ryan, and James Wellborn. This paper was completed with the generous support of the Max Planck Institute for Human Development and Education and a Faculty Scholar's Grant from the William T. Grant Foundation.

APPENDIX I

SAMPLE ITEMS FROM THE STUDENT PERCEPTIONS OF CONTROL
QUESTIONNAIRE (SPOCQ, Wellborn, Connell, & Skinner, 1989)

Control Beliefs   If I decide to learn something hard, I can. (+)
                           I can't get good grades, no matter what I do. (-)

Strategy Beliefs

Effort:	For me to do well in school, all I have to do is work hard.
	If I get bad grades, it's because I don't work hard enough.
Ability:	I have to be smart to get good grades in school.
	If I'm not smart, I can't get good grades.
Powerful:	If I want to get good grades, I have to get along with my teacher.
Others:	If my teacher doesn't like me, I won't do well in that class.
Luck:	For me, getting good grades is a matter of luck.
	If I get bad grades, it's because I'm unlucky.
Unknown:	When I do well in school, I usually can't figure out why.
	I don't know how to keep myself from getting bad grades.

Capacity Beliefs

Effort:	When I'm in class, I can work hard. (+)
	I can't seem to try very hard in school. (−)
Ability:	I think I'm pretty smart in school. (+)
	I don't have the brains to do well in school. (−)
Powerful:	I can get my teacher to like me. (+)
Others:	I just can't get along with my teacher. (−)
Luck:	I am lucky in school. (+)
	When it comes to grades, I'm unlucky. (−)

APPENDIX II

SAMPLE ITEMS AND PSYCHOMETRIC PROPERTIES FOR THE COPING CATEGORIES (From Skinner & Wellborn, 1991)

When something bad happens to me in school (like not doing well on a test or not being able to answer an important question in class)...

Strategizing (5 items, alpha = .68):	I try to see what I did wrong.
	I slow down and think carefully.
Perseverance (5 items, alpha = .73):	I go over the problem again and again.
	I can't go on until I've solved it.
Avoidance (5 items, alpha = .62):	I try not to think about it.
	I put it out of my mind.
Delegation (5 items, alpha = .63):	I get the teacher to solve the problem.
	I want the teacher to tell me the answer.
Projection (5 items, alpha = .66):	I get real mad at other people.
	I say the teacher didn't cover the things on the test.
Confusion (5 items, alpha = .60):	my mind goes blank.
	I get all confused.
Impulsivity (6 items, alpha = .68):	I just say the first thing that comes into my head.
	I just do anything.

ADULTS' EXPECTANCIES ABOUT DEVELOPMENT AND ITS CONTROLLABILITY: ENHANCING SELF-EFFICACY BY SOCIAL COMPARISON

Jutta Heckhausen

The human life span with its radical changes and structured constraints in control potential confronts the individual with a highly taxing coping task. If developmental tasks and everyday challenges are to be tackled successfully, not only at one point in the life span, but across shifting developmental ecologies, the individual has to maintain and balance two requirements. On the one hand, expectations, plans, and evaluations have to reflect reality, so as to allow appropriate action planning. On the other hand, conceptions about life-span change need to be biased so as to protect self-efficacy, and thus maintain motivational prerequisites of action. One way to balance both these apparently contradictory requirements is strategic social comparison. Social comparison in terms of age-graded phenomena is based on normative conceptions about life-span development. Such normative conceptions help generate age-graded social reference groups, which provide both, a realistically tailored and a self-enhancing framework for personal evaluations and aspirations. Recent research is presented, which demonstrates the structure and consensual nature of normative conceptions about adult development. Moreover, development-related expectations for the self entail substantial congruence with those ascribed to "most other people," thus exemplifying a focus on validity, rather than on excessive self-serving illusion. However, differences between normative and self-related expectations reflect a self-enhancement strategy, particularly with regard to old age, which is regarded a more threatening period of the life span.

The present chapter addresses adults' expectancies about age trajectories and controllability of adult development. Conceptions about one's own personal development are contrasted with conceptions about "most other people's" development. Accordingly, beliefs about self-efficacy (i.e., controllability for self) are juxtaposed to beliefs about general controllability (i.e., for "most other people") of developmental processes. Distinct patterns of self/other differences in development-related conceptions reflect different strategies of using social comparison to enhance feelings of self-efficacy in either past, current, or future personal development (J. Heckhausen & Krueger, 1991). Self-efficacy, in turn, is a fundamental requirement for the potential to act and exert control over one's environment and self (Bandura, 1982).

The human life course can be conceived as a context for action, action directed at development (J. Heckhausen, 1990a). Across the life course, an individual's potential to actively control her environment undergoes dramatic changes (Baltes & Baltes, 1986; Baltes, 1987). At birth and during early infancy the individual is almost completely unable to manipulate and change objects in the external world. Control during this time of life is, to the most part, exerted by getting more mature others such as caregivers, to act (J. Heckhausen, 1987; Kaye, 1982). During childhood and adolescence the individual rapidly gains motor abilities, skills, knowledge, and understanding, and thereby becomes increasingly aware of his own competence (Harter, 1975; J. Heckhausen, 1988) and autonomy from caregivers and other socialization agents (e.g., Steinberg & Silverberg, 1986). In early adulthood it is not only increasing motorphysical and cognitive abilities but also the age-graded allocation of multiple social roles in the work and family domain (Marini, 1984) which increase the individual's scope for exerting control over various life ecologies. During middle adulthood control potentials in many domains of life reach their maximum, but thereby also render over-ambitious life goals out of reach due to a lack of remaining life time (Brim, 1988; Neugarten, 1968). Finally, during old age physical powers decline, motor and mental activites become slowed (Salthouse, 1985), and social roles allocated by society diminish (Riley & Riley, 1986).

If self-efficacy beliefs would simply reflect absolute levels of personal control, such radical shifts in control potential as experienced throughout the human life course would render self-efficacy a very unstable feature of the human mind. Self-efficacy, however, has been shown to be a key resource for motivated action in humans (Bandura, 1977, 1982, 1986). Self-efficacy can only serve this important function if it is a stable and reliable resource, that is not jeopardized by obstacles and drawbacks, but instead helps to overcome difficult spells in life. The present paper attempts to line out and demonstrate some of the ways in which the human mind uses secondary, as opposed to more direct primary, control strategies (Rothbaum, Weisz, & Snyder, 1982) in order to maintain long-term self-efficacy in spite of constrained and declining control potential over the life course (J. Heckhausen & Schulz, 1991; Schulz, Heckhausen, & Locher, in press). Special emphasis is given to strategies of secondary control relying on selective social comparison. These issues are discussed with regard to the role of lay-persons' normative conceptions about development in adulthood.

The life course provides a unique time-graded structure of opportunities and risks for developmental gains and losses. Attempts to actively influence one's own development are constrained in specific age-related ways. Some of these restrictions are fairly rigid, such as the timing of school entry or retirement, some are more lenient. In any event, these age-related constraints provide guideposts for assessing an individual's current developmental status in the life course, and for advising future life planning. Three types of life course constraints can be discerned: (1) constraints in terms of the life time remaining till death (absolute), (2) constraints associated with chronological age (cross-sectional or vertical), and (3) constraints resulting from sequential patterns (longitudinal or horizontal) (J. Heckhausen, 1990a; J. Heckhausen & Schulz, 1991).   First, *life time remaining* till death restricts the potential future time extension of developmental goals and life plans. This is relevant, for instance, when in midlife the feasability of career changes is considered. Second, *age norms* set deadlines for various life events, and thereby slice the life span in vertical segments. Such norms can be set on a societal level, such as in the case of school entry or retirement (Hagestad & Neugarten, 1985; Neugarten, Moore, & Lowe, 1965), or be the product of universal biological processes such as in the case of puberty as the onset and menopause as the close of fertility. Third, *age-sequential* (horizontal) constraints can also be identified on the societal and the biological plane. Biologically they are shown in universal sequential patterns of maturation and aging. On the societal plane, age-sequential constraints result from the canalization of development and life course patterns into developmental or biographical tracks, involving more or less fixed sequences and timing of life events (Geulen, 1981; Mayer, 1986), for instance during the transition to adulthood (Marini, 1984; Modell, Furstenberg, & Hershberg, 1976).

These constraints in and of themselves—not even considering the substantial losses associated with aging—reveal that we are far from being in complete control over our lives. Instead, we have to adapt our hopes, goals, and plans to a fairly restricted repertoire of options over which we have at least some control. If our feelings of self-efficacy were perfect reflections of all these constraints we would be close to paralytic helplessness. In order to generate and maintain the potential for action directed at development and the life course, two requirements have to be fulfilled. On the one hand, the individual needs a fairly valid conception about options, possible life paths, suitable action means, and probability of success, in order to generate effective action. On the other hand, the motivational management of action requires feelings of self-efficacy and thus, hope for success; otherwise the individual would be overwhelmed by uncertainty and fear of failure. Given the constraints and radical life-span shifts in control potential, these two requirements are bound to get into conflict (J. Heckhausen & Schulz, 1991). When, for instance, physical strength drastically declines in old age, personal aspirations for athletic activities have to reflect this loss in order to keep in touch with reality. However, feelings of self-efficacy and self-worth also have to be protected in order to motivate the individual to keep up appropriate activity.

One most effective way in which both these partly contradictory requirements can be met is strategic social comparison. Festinger (1954) has proposed that social comparison may serve self-assessment and self-improvement functions. In order to assist self-assessment the individual compares with others who are similar on relevant performance dimensions, so that the evaluation of one's own performance is calibrated. Self-improvement is promoted if one compares with others who are a little superior on a relevant dimension. Incidently, such upward social comparison converges with the selection of a just-above-medium level of aspiration, which is identified as most promotive for performance and learning by achievement motivation research (see review in H. Heckhausen, 1991). Wood (1989) has recently proposed a three-fold model of social comparison adding self-enhancement as a major function of comparison to self-assessment and self-improvement, as proposed by Festinger (1954). Self-enhancement via social comparison is achieved by selecting a reference group which is inferior to oneself on relevant dimensions. Vis-à-vis such a reference group one can see oneself in a more favorable light, even if one has experienced a loss of self-esteem. In fact, recent empirical research has shown that such "downward comparisons" (Wills, 1981) are particularly sought out under conditions of threatened life or self-esteem, and impaired health. Severe disability (Schulz & Decker, 1985), life-threatening illnesses (Taylor & Lobel, 1989; Taylor, Wood, & Lichtman, 1984), or crime-related victimization (Burgess & Holmstrom, 1979) represent such eliciting conditions for "downward comparisons."

With regard to age-graded phenomena strategic social comparison is especially suitable. Throughout their life course individuals experience major intra-individual changes, for better and worse. Many of these changes are universal and, thus, shared with age peers. Therefore, the peer group provides a most suitable reference for self-assessment.

If one compares oneself with age peers the standards of aspiration become realistic. At the same time feelings of self-efficacy are protected, because one compares oneself with others who undergo similar age-related changes (Baltes, in press; Baltes & Baltes, 1990). The self-enhancement function of social comparison becomes especially salient in old age, when self-esteem is threatened by aging-related decline. Selecting a suitable comparison group for downward comparison in old age, however, is hardly a problem, since old age and aging is viewed in a negative stereotype manner. Survey research about the image of old age and aging has revealed that old people view old age as a bleak period of the life span for "most old people," yet see themselves as favorable exeptions (Harris & Associates, 1975, 1981). O'Gorman (1980) has extended this conclusion by showing that elderly estimated "most other old people's" problems in various life domains (e.g., health, finances, loneliness) higher, if they themselves reported experiencing the respective problem. Thus, self-enhancement via downward social comparison may be a common and effective way of coping with aging-related decline (J. Heckhausen & Krueger, 1991).

Generalized images of age groups are needed to generate mental representations about a social comparions group. In this context, normative conceptions about development play a crucial role, because they provide common reference frames for expectations and evaluations of developmental change. One of the unique features of the life course as a context for action is that, although the developmental tasks involved might not be currently relevant to any one of us, they will be or have been at some point in our life course. The life course and its various challenges are therefore personally relevant to everyone. Some of its periods, such as old age, might seem somewhat far away for a young person, for instance. However, they will eventually become the critical context for that person's own life management. Expectations for oneself as well as social comparison with regard to age-graded phenomena is based on normative conceptions about development in adulthood. The human life course provides a more or less common repertoire of sequential developmental tasks to the members of a given society (J. Heckhausen, 1990b). Therefore, it is essential both, for the individual and for the society at large to have conceptions about development and the life course which are commonly shared. Such normative conceptions about development and the life course represent "social constructions of reality" (Berger & Luckmann, 1966). They provide the reference frame for the developmental changes in oneself and for social comparisons both within and across age groups.

Normative conceptions about life-span development probably influence our thinking and actions with respect to all three planes in time, future, present, and past. With regard to the *future*, they set the stage for one's own developmental prospects. Certain developmental changes, such as learning a language, might appear more obtainable at some ages than at others. The individual will therefore try to time respective efforts accordingly, or if that is unfeasible, will know that special effort has to be invested to bring about the untimely change. Moreover, if certain changes, such as becoming forgetful, are expected to occur inevitably at a certain age, the individual will not expect to modify his or her developmental trajectory and thus will not invest effort. This way, normative beliefs about development form our expectations about what we can do, what we cannot do, and where to invest special effort in trying to take charge of our developmental future.

Moreover, normative beliefs about development could serve as a frame of reference for evaluating *current* developmental change in the self. Think, for instance, of undesired developmental changes, such as becoming forgetful in advanced age, or being worn out by mid-life crisis. Here, normative expectations might lead to a downgrading of one's peer reference group, and thereby may help us to maintain self-esteem and well-being in spite of unpleasant developmental experiences. If we believe that most of our peers are experiencing the same, we are less likely to blame ourselves; and if we suffer less decline than, we think, most of our age peers do, we actually could pride ourselves to have come up against the stream of aging.

Finally, normative beliefs about development might help us to reconstruct and interpret our biographical *past*. The sequence of biographical events we encountered in our lives appears as one path in a limited repertoire of life courses possible or likely in a given socio-cultural context (Kohli, 1981). This way, normative conceptions of the life course provide structure to individuals' biographies. They inform us, in what ways we are the same, and in which ways we are different from most other people. Both aspects are critical for our personal well-being. We want to be connected to the social world around us, but still we also want to be unique and somehow different from others (Campbell, 1986; Snyder & Fromkin, 1980). Thus, the optimal relation between what is perceived to be normative or typical and what is descriptive of the self probably is one which strikes the balance between consensus and uniqueness.

The examples just given about the role of normative conceptions about development for future life planning, current life management, and past life review, illustrate two types of phenomena. On the one hand, normative developmental conceptions are used to provide valid information about chances and risks, so that the individual could optimize his or her active developmental interventions. On the other hand, normative conceptions serve to console the person by favorable comparison with less fortunate others, or by fending off blame. These two modes of exerting control exemplify the distinction between primary and secondary control (Rothbaum et al., 1982) for the context of development-related conceptions and action. Primary control refers to direct action on the external world. Conversely, secondary control refers to cognitive adjustments in terms of mental representations. The target of primary control is the external world, whereas the target of secondary control is the own self, one's goals, well-being, interpretations, and most importantly one's self-efficacy. This distinction between primary and secondary control is related to Piaget's conceptual distinction between assimilative and accomodative processing (Piaget, 1985). Brandtstädter and Renner have used these Piagetian concepts to characterize primary and secondary modes of coping in middle-aged adults, and identified complementary age trends in a cross-sectional study covering middle adulthood (Brandtstädter & Renner, 1990; see also Brandtstädter, this volume).

Given the radical life-span changes in the potential to control one's environment and development, it would appear functional if there was a gradual shift from a preference for primary control strategies to a predominance of secondary control strategies at later periods of the life course (J. Heckhausen & Schulz, 1991; Schulz et al., in press). This hypothesis converges with Brandtstädter and Renner's finding of decreased importance of assimilative as compared to accomodative control strategies throughout middle adulthood (Brandtstädter & Renner, 1990). To be sure, at each period of the life span both strategies are necessary to cope with the challenges and constraints characteristic for that life-span segment. Moreover, primary and secondary strategies of control have to be balanced such that action is optimized, while self-efficacy is protected. Leaning too much into either direction bears major hazards to developmental potential. Being too realistic about the constraints in control exposes the individual to depression (Alloy & Abramson, 1979; Lewinsohn, Mischel, Chaplin, & Barton, 1980; Taylor, 1989), and thus reduces motivational resources for action. Conversely, if self-efficacy is boosted so much that the individual loses contact to reality, cognitive requirements for planning and execution of action are jeopardized.

Some recent empirical work at the Max Planck Institute will be reported to demonstrate, how in the context of adult development primary and secondary control strategies are balanced in a functional way, such as to optimize long-term action potential in terms of both, its cognitive and motivational requirements. In this research, primary and secondary control strategies are identified in social comparison as operationalized in differences between development-related expectations for the self as compared to "most other people."

We can expect to find both strategies of successful life management reflected in people's conceptions about development, and particularly in the way they view their own developmental status vis-à-vis the normative context of developmental expectations for "most other people." Specifically, one can expect primary control to be reflected in a focus on the veridicality of development-related conceptions. An effort to arrive at veridical conceptions about development would be shown in largely similar conceptions for the self and "most other people." Thus, developmental expectations for the self would not be unrealistically biased towards optimism. Expected developmental trajectories for self and others should be largely congruent. And perceived controllability for late life change should be lower than for early onset developmental change.[1]

However, conceptions about development should, to some degree, also reflect secondary control processes. First, an overall optimistic view of developmental prospects in adulthood can be expected. This would be shown in a predominance of expected desirable as compared to undesirable developmental changes. Second, with regard to the comparison of self and other, more developmental gains should be expected for the self than for "most other people." And third, especially with regard to old age, when expected developmental losses might prevail, self-related expectations should be more optimistic than expectations held for "most other people." Before dealing with these specific findings the first question in our research is of course: Are there at all common normative conceptions about development in adulthood that most members of a given society would agree on? And if yes, what do these conceptions entail?

Three studies were conducted. The first two dealt with adults' and adolescents' expectations about developmental gains and losses in adulthood (J. Heckhausen, 1990c; J. Heckhausen, Dixon, & Baltes, 1989; J. Heckhausen, Krueger, & Hosenfeld, 1989; Hosenfeld, 1988). The third one focused on the perceived controllability of such expected changes (J. Heckhausen & Baltes, in press).

The procedures and materials used in these studies were similar. The sample contained young adolescents between 11 and 17 years of age (Hosenfeld, 1988), young adults between 20 and 35 years of age, middle-aged adults between 40 and 55 years, and old adults above 65 years (J. Heckhausen, 1990c; J. Heckhausen &

---

[1] It should be noted at this point that we have no means of knowing to what degree conceptions about development are veridical (i.e., mirror reality), and whether optimistic or self-enhancing views of development are true or false. Life-span developmental psychology is far from being able to chart all relevent developmental trajectories; and most likely this will never be possible nor make sense. Moreover, all relevant assessments rely on subjective ratings and are thus subject to effects of selective references and biases (Krueger & Heckhausen, 1991).

Baltes, in press; J. Heckhausen, Dixon, & Baltes, 1989). Subjects were given a large list of adjectives denoting a variety of psychological attributes, for instance, intelligent, wise, forgetful, bitter, and mentally healthy.

The subjects were asked to rate each of these attributes with regard to the following questions: (1) How much does this attribute increase in strength across the adult life span, or does it not increase? (2) How desirable versus undesirable is a developmental increase in this attribute? (3) At which age does this developmental increase typically begin, and at which age does it end? And finally, (4) to what extent can one control, that is promote or hinder, the developmental increase in this attribute[2]?

We had expected to find a pattern of life-span expectations which would reflect a negative view of aging, that is, a target-age related shift from a predominance of gains to a predominance of losses. However, the image of old age should not be entirely bleak, so that the elderly would not be left to despair. Figure 1 shows the overall ratio of gains and losses across the life span. Note that the abscissa shows the target ages, not the subjects' ages.

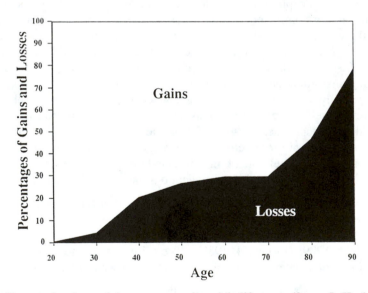

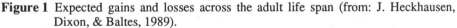

Figure 1 Expected gains and losses across the adult life span (from: J. Heckhausen, Dixon, & Baltes, 1989).

As shown in Figure 1, there is, as expected, a gradual shift from a predominance of gains expected for early adulthood to a predominance of losses in old age. Thus, people's conceptions about adults' developmental prospects reflect aging-related decline. However, Figure 1 also shows something else. Overall, the expected gains greatly outnumber the losses. Even in the 80s, about 20% of

---

[2] Perceived controllability was not assessed in the study on adolescents (Hosenfeld, 1988).

the total changes are expected to be gains. Thus, although the general pattern of normative beliefs about adult development reflects a negative view of aging, people of all age groups see some potential for growth even in advanced age. What about the perceived controllability of these expected changes? Controllability would appear to be the key variable to ameliorate the pretty unfavorable view of developmental prospects in old age.

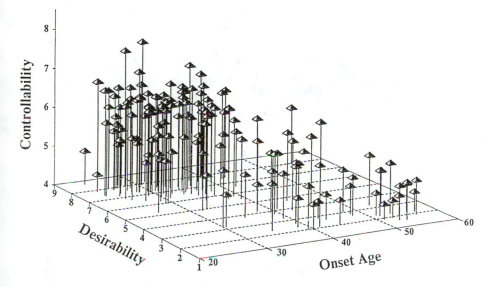

Figure 2 Three-dimensional representation of mean ratings of perceived controllability, desirability, and expected onset age for 163 change-sensitive attributes (from: J. Heckhausen & Baltes, in press).

Figure 2 provides a three-dimensional display of each attributes' mean ratings on three variables: Expected age of change onset, perceived controllability, and desirability. Each of the arrows refers to one attribute. The onset ages 20 through 60 years are shown on the horizontal scale in front; desirability from low *(very undesirable* = 1) to high *(very desirable* = 9) at the side; and controllability on the vertical scale, ranging from somewhat below medium *(medium controllability* = 5) to high *(very controllable* = 9). The controllability scale itself, which starts at a value of 4, shows that no attributes were perceived to be really low in controllability. Most mean ratings in fact were above the level of "medium controllability." This speaks to a fairly optimistic view about the scope of controllability, and thus plasticity of developmental change overall, even for advanced age.

Second, developmental changes expected to occur later in life were expected to be less desirable: As shown in Figure 2, arrows at the later target ages originate in front segments which correspond to low levels of desirability. This illustrates the shifting ratio of gains and losses, also depicted in Figure 1.

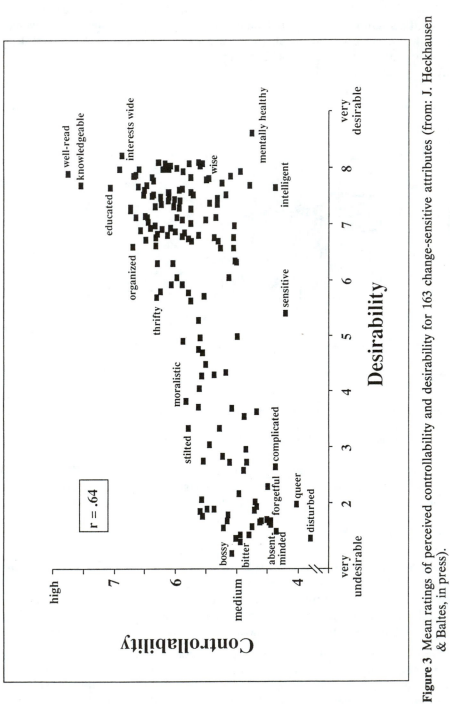

Figure 3 Mean ratings of perceived controllability and desirability for 163 change-sensitive attributes (from: J. Heckhausen & Baltes, in press).

With regard to perceived controllability there is also an age-related shift. At increasing target ages the arrows become shorter and shorter, indicating lower degrees of perceived controllability. Thus, later age periods in the adult life span are associated with less desirable and less controllable developmental changes. Note however, that even for changes expected very late in life a substantial degree of control was still expected, since even the short arrows indicate about medium controllability.

In order to illustrate more specifically the relationship between the perceived controllability and the desirability of developmental changes, Figure 3 provides a two-dimensional plot showing mean ratings of controllability and desirability for each attribute. In Figure 3 some of the attributes are identified. The undesirable and less controllable ones in the lower left corner, such as disturbed, absent minded, and forgetful, are prototypical features of decline in old age. Interestingly enough, the opposite cluster, that is those attributes which are very desirable and appear most controllable (see upper right corner), are virtues of life-long further education: well-read, knowledgeable, educated, wide interests; but not wisdom, which is highly desirable but appears by far not as controllable.

Figure 3 also illustrates the strong positive relation between desirability and perceived controllability of attributes. Desirable psychological features appeared clearly more controllable than undesirable features. This is reminiscent of the well known "attributional bias": People like to take credit for the positive events, but do not want to be blamed for negative ones (Bradley, 1978; H. Heckhausen, 1987; Kelley & Michela, 1980; Snyder, Stephan, & Rosenfield, 1978; Zuckerman, 1979). Such an attributional pattern is, of course, conducive to successful life management. It encourages the striving for improvement, but also consoles and avoids self-blame at times of losses. Thus, it is characteristic of the dual function of development-related conceptions: information and consolation, primary and secondary control. Interestingly, the relationship between desirability and perceived controllability was closer for the old and the middle-aged when compared to the young adults (J. Heckhausen & Baltes, in press). For old adults, who are surely confronted with more losses than younger adults, this attributional bias would be more essential than for younger people. The age difference in the degree of the attributional bias demonstrates the functionality of normative conceptions about development in terms of buffering potential negative effects of aging on self-efficacy.

In sum, on the one hand, normative conceptions about developmental change and its controllability do reflect a negative view of aging. With regard to old age processes of decline clearly predominate over processes of growth, and less controllability is expected for losses, losses that occur increasingly in old age. On the other hand, at all age periods some, however restricted, potential for growth is expected. And what is more, even the most severe losses seem not inevitable, but instead leave some hope for plasticity subject to active intervention.

In a second step in our research program, we extended our research paradigm to include self-related conceptions about development. In a recent study, our major goal was to explore how expectations about one's own development are related to normative conceptions about the development of "most other people" (J. Heckhausen & Krueger, 1991; Krueger & Heckhausen, 1991). As mentioned before, we view normative beliefs about development as social constructions of reality (Berger & Luckmann, 1966), which acquire the function of reference frames. They can guide action directed at the future, they help us in evaluating current developmental change, and they provide the scaffold to build interpretations of the past. We therefore predict that expected developmental trajectories for the self are similar to expected trajectories for "most other people." However, in certain respects self-related trajectories should differ from those attributed to "most other people." As argued already, normative beliefs about development might also serve to foster self-enhancement. For instance, if the developmental course of the typical age peer is expected to show decline, the self might be viewed as a praisable exception to this normative age trend. Thus, via social comparison with the expected typical age-related change, self-esteem is enhanced or at least maintained, even when facing actual age-related decline in functioning.

These theoretical expectations were investigated in a study comparing development-related conceptions regarding the self with those ascribed to "most other people" (J. Heckhausen & Krueger, 1991; Krueger & Heckhausen, 1991). The subject sample included 180 subjects with 60 subjects from each of three adult age groups: young (age range: 20 to 35 years), middle-aged (age range: 40 to 55 years), and old adults (age range: above 60 years). The age groups were equally divided by gender and by three levels of educational background: People who finished high school, people with some lower college education, and people who had earned college degrees. For reasons of parsimoniousness, between-subject differences due to age, sex, or educational background will not be discussed here but elsewhere (J. Heckhausen & Krueger, 1991; Krueger & Heckhausen, 1991). Instead, this article focuses on the within-subject factors in our design, that is, the difference between self and other, and the different changes expected for various decades of the adult life span.

Like in the first set of studies we used an attribute rating format. The variables, on which the attributes were rated, included "self description at present," "desirability," "perceived controllability" rated separately for the self and for "most other people," and the "expected change from 20 to 90 years of age" also rated separately for the self and "most other people." Ratings of expected change could be given as increases, ranging from +1 to +3, stability given as 0, or decreases, ranging from -1 to -3. Finally, we asked the subjects to indicate up to ten "developmental intentions," that is, to select attributes on which they intended to strive for a change (see also Hundertmark, 1990).

The pool of attributes was structured by five major psychological dimensions: Extraversion, Agreeableness, Conscientiousness, Emotional Stability, and Intellectual Functioning—commonly known as Norman's Big Five (Norman, 1963). Each of these factors consisted of two scales with ten attributes each, one scale for the desirable attributes, and one for the undesirable attributes. Analyses of the data showed that our previous finding of a shifting ratio of expected gains and losses across the adult life span was replicated. At increasing target ages, less and less gains, and more and more losses were expected, although as in our previous studies, some potential for growth was envisaged even for old age.

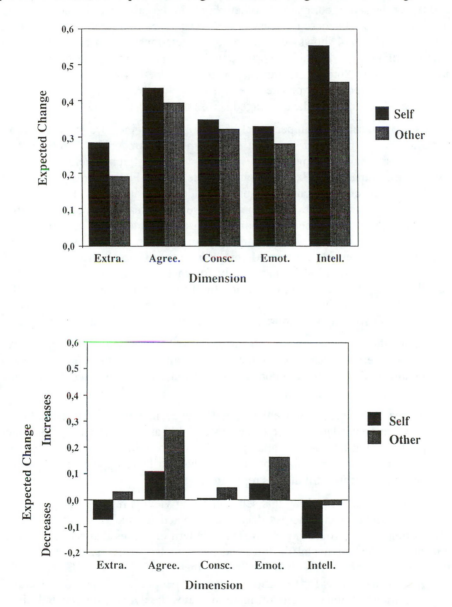

Figure 4 Expected change for self and "most other people" on five psychological dimensions, separately for desirable (upper panel) and undesirable (lower panel) attributes (from: J. Heckhausen, Krueger, & Hosenfeld, 1989).

With regard to the comparison between self and "most other people" in terms of expected developmental prospects, one should first consider the net change, that is, the expected change averaged across age decades in adulthood. In accordance with the self-enhancement hypotheses, people should expect more increases for the self as compared to other people in the case of desirable attributes, and less increases or more decreases for the self when undesirable attributes are concerned. Figure 4 shows developmental expectations for self and "most other people" relating to desirable (upper panel) and undesirable attributes (lower panel) of the five Norman dimensions. Ratings for the self are shown in the dark bars; those for "most other people" are given in lighter bars. On the vertical scale the expected net increase (i.e., averaged across decades) is plotted.

As one can see in the upper panel of Figure 4, more increase in the desirable attributes were expected for the self than for "most other people." However, separate analysis for each dimension revealed that this difference held statistically only for the dimensions Extraversion and Intellectual Functioning. The lower panel shows the complementary picture for undesirable attributes. Here, the vertical scale represents the expected net increase or decrease in undesirable attributes. For "most other people" more increases in undesirable attributes were expected than for the self. And accordingly for the decreases: Less decreases in undesirable features were expected for "most other people" than for the self. This pattern of finding holds statistically for each dimension, except for Conscientiousness. Hence, we find evidence for a self-enhancement effect, both for the desirable and for the undesirable attributes. The developmental prospects for the self are consistently seen more positively than those for "most other people."

Would this self-enhancement tendency also be reflected in perceptions of self-efficacy versus general controllability? Figure 5 gives the mean perceived controllability of desirable and undesirable attributes for the self and "most other people."

We see here again a self-enhancing tendency in perceptions of controllability. More controllability is ascribed to the self as compared to "most other people" both, for undesirable and desirable features. Moreover, our previous finding of an attributional bias, that is, desirable attributes appear more controllable than undesirable attributes, is replicated.

The next question is, how this self-enhancing view is reflected in the curves of developmental change across decades, expected for the self and for "most other people." We would expect to find a pattern of curves that reflects a postponement of developmental decline, and an extended maintenance of developmental growth for the self than for "most other people." Figure 6 depicts the expected change curves for self and "most other people" separately for desirable and undesirable attributes. The ordinate indicates the average degree and direction of change: Expected increases are shown above the dotted line, and expected decreases below. The trajectories expected for the self are plotted in solid lines. Those expected for "most other people" are shown in dotted lines.

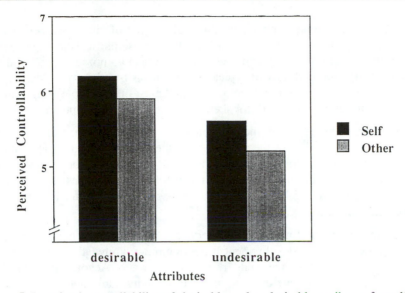

Figure 5 Perceived controllability of desirable and undesirable attributes for self and "most other people."

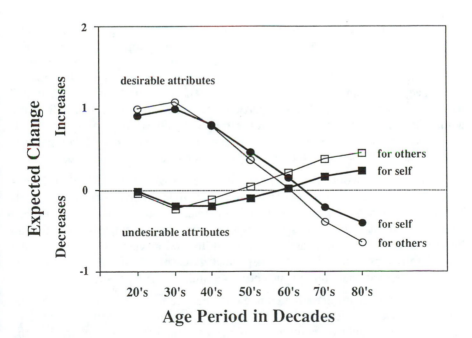

Figure 6 Expected change for self and "most other people" across the adult life span in desirable and undesirable attributes (from: J. Heckhausen, Krueger, & Hosenfeld, 1989).

At first glance, one is struck by the high degree of similarity between the expected trajectories for the self and "most other people".. This suggests that developmental expectations for the self closely reflect common and general conceptions about what normally or typically happens as people grow older. It thus seems, that conceptions about development in "most other people" might indeed serve as a normative framework for sketching one's own development.

However, there are also some differences. In fact, the pattern of curves confirms our prediction both for the desirable and the undesirable attributes. Starting from the age period of the 50s, the decline in the desirable attributes is viewed as less severe for the self than for "most other people." And also as early as for the 50s, increases in undesirable attributes are expected to be greater in "most other people" than in the self.

To summarize our findings: In a sequence of studies we have shown, that normative beliefs about development reflect common knowledge, widely shared among people varying in age, gender, and social strata. According to this common knowledge about development, aging throughout adulthood is a process of ever increasing risks for losses, and ever decreasing chances for gains. However, in spite of this negative view of the aging process, common conceptions about life-span development also involve optimism. Optimism with regard to potential for growth even in very advanced age, and optimism with regard to personal control to counteract decline.

Expectations about one's own developmental prospects largely follow similar trajectories as those expected to hold for "most other people." However, one's own development is viewed more optimistically. We believe to have more personal control over our own development than we ascribe to "most other people. We expect more gains and fewer losses for the self than for "most other people." This self-enhancement tendency is particularly salient for the second half of the adult life span, when increases in undesirable attributes are expected to occur earlier in "most other people" than in the self; likewise decline in positive features appears delayed for the self when compared to "most other people."

To conclude, I would like to briefly recapitulate what was said at the beginning of the chapter. The life course has a unique age-related structure of challenges. It confronts us with ever-changing demands, some of which we can face and meet with active attempts to intervene; but others seem to or actually do leave little scope for active, assertive control. Instead it seems they require some sort of re-interpretation, in order to protect a sense of self-efficacy, and thus safeguard motivational prerequisites of successful action.

To successfully master a life course one needs to have two sides. On the one hand, the efficient agent, who holds realistic expectations about his developmental prospects and strives for attainable goals. But also, on the other hand, the skillful self-manipulator, who always, even when confronted with losses, manages to maintain a balance of affect, and keeps up perceptions of self-efficacy. The task of balancing the two needs throughout the life course and in spite of radical changes in actual control potential, may sometimes appear like fitting a square peg in a round hole. However, the human mind finds ingenious ways to resolve the apparent paradox. One most suitable way is the strategic use of social reference groups, such that under conditions of stress one can make onself feel better by downward comparison.

In the service of control and agency we need to hold fairly realistic expectations about potential gains and losses. However, the constraints and losses encountered throughout the life span are so manifold that one cannot afford to be a realist. It looks like, the trick is to strike the balance. And that, I believe, the participants in our study have demonstrated beautifully.

REFERENCES

Alloy, L. B., & Abramson, L. Y. (1979). Judgement of contingency in depressed and non-depressed students: Sadder but wiser? *Journal of Experimental Psychology, 108*, 441-485.

Baltes, M. M., & Baltes, P. B. (Eds.). (1986). *The psychology of control and aging.* Hillsdale, NJ: Erlbaum.

Baltes, P. B. (1987). Theoretical propositions of life-span developmental psychology: On the dynamics between growth and decline. *Developmental Psychology, 23*, 611-626.

Baltes, P. B. (in press). The many faces of human aging: Toward a psychological culture of old age. *Psychological Medicine.*

Baltes, P. B., & Baltes, M. M. (1990). Psychological perspectives on successful aging: The model of selective optimization with compensation. In Baltes & Baltes (Eds.), *Successful aging: Perspectives from the behavioral sciences* (pp. 1-34). New York: Cambridge University Press.

Bandura, A. (1977). Self-efficacy: Toward a unifying theory of behavioral change. *Psychological Review, 84*, 191-215.

Bandura, A. (1982). Self efficacy in human agency. *American Psychologist, 37*, 122-147.

Bandura, A. (1986). *Social foundations of thought and action: A social cognitive theory.* Englewood Cliffs, NJ: Prentice-Hall.

Berger, P., & Luckmann, T. (1966). *The social construction of reality.* New York: Doubleday.

Bradley, G. W. (1978). Self-serving biases in the attribution process: A re-examination of the fact or fiction question. *Journal of Personality and Social Psychology, 36*, 56-71.

Brandtstädter, J., & Renner, G. (1990). Tenacious goal persuit and flexible goal adjustment: Explication and age-related analysis of assimilative and accomodative strategies of coping. *Psychology and Aging, 5*, 58-67.

Brim, O. G. (1988). Losing and winning. *Psychology Today, 9*, 48-52.

Burgess, A. W., & Holmstrom, L. (1979). *Rape: Crisis and recovery.* Bowie, MD: Brady.

Campbell, J. (1986) Similarity and uniqueness: The effects of attribute type, relevance, and individual differences in self-esteem and depression. *Journal of Personality and Social Psychology, 50*, 281-294.

Festinger, L. (1954). A theory of social comparison processes. *Human Relations*, 7, 117-140.

Geulen, D. (1981). Zur Konzeptionalisierung sozialisationstheoretischer Entwicklungsmodelle. In J. Matthes (Ed.), *Lebenswelt und soziale Probleme. Verhandlungen des 20. Deutschen Soziologentages* [Conceptualization of developmental models in socialization theory] (pp. 537-556). Frankfurt: Campus.

Hagestad, G. O., & Neugarten, B. L. (1985). Age and the life course. In R. H. Binstock & E. Shanas (Eds.), *Handbook of aging and the social sciences* (pp. 35-61). New York: Van Nostrand Reinhold.

Harris, L., & Associates (1975). *The myth and reality of aging in America.* Washington, DC: National Council on the Aging.

Harris, L., & Associates (1981). *Aging in the Eighties: America in transition.* Washington, DC: National Council on the Aging.

Harter, S. (1975). Developmental differences in the manifestation of mastery motivation on problem-solving tasks. *Child Development*, 46, 370-378.

Heckhausen, H. (1987). Causal attribution patterns for achievement outcomes: Individual differences, possible types, and their origin. In F. E. Weinert & R. H. Kluwe, (Eds.), *Metacognition, motivation, and understanding* (pp. 143-184). Hillsdale, N.J.: Erlbaum.

Heckhausen, H. (1991). *Motivation and action.* New York: Springer.

Heckhausen, J. (1987). Balancing for weaknesses and challenging developmental potential: A longitudinal study of mother-infant dyads in apprenticeship interactions. *Developmental Psychology*, 23, 762-770.

Heckhausen, J. (1988). Becoming aware of one's competence in the second year: Developmental progression within the mother-child dyad. *International Journal of Behavioral Development*, 11, 305-326.

Heckhausen, J. (1990a). *Life course patterns, developmental projects, and control beliefs in East- and West-Berliners born between 1920 and 1970: A study proposal.* Unpublished grant proposal, Max Planck Institute for Human Development and Education, Berlin.

Heckhausen, J. (1990b). Erwerb und Funktion normativer Vorstellungen über den Lebenslauf: Ein entwicklungspsychologischer Beitrag zur sozio-psychischen Konstruktion von Biographien [Acquisition and function of normative conceptions about the life course: A developmental psychology approach to the psychosocial construction of biographies]. *Kölner Zeitschrift für Soziologie und Sozialpsychologie*, Sonderheft 31: (K.-U. Mayer [Ed.], Lebensverläufe und sozialer Wandel)(pp. 351-373). Opladen: Westdeutscher Verlag.

Heckhausen, J. (1990c). Entwicklung im Erwachsenenalter aus der Sicht junger, mittelalter und alter Erwachsener [Development in adulthood as perceived by young, middle-aged, and old adults]. *Zeitschrift für Entwicklungspsychologie und Pädagogischer Psychologie*, 22, 1-21.

Heckhausen, J., & Baltes, P. B. (in press). Perceived controllability of expected psychological change across adulthood and old age. *Journal of Gerontology: Psychological Sciences.*

Heckhausen, J., Dixon, R. A., & Baltes, P. B. (1989). Gains and losses in development throughout adulthood as perceived by different adult age groups. *Developmental Psychology*, 25(1), 109-121.

Heckhausen, J., & Krueger, J. (1991). *Similarity and differences in developmental expectations for the self and "most other people" : Age-grading in three functions of social comparison*. Manuscript submitted for publication, Max Planck Institute for Human Development and Education, Berlin, FRG.

Heckhausen, J., Krueger, J., & Hosenfeld, B. (1989, July). *Normative beliefs about development: Their relation to developmental expectations for the self*. Paper presented at the Tenth Biennial Meeting of the Society for the Study of Behavioral Development (ISSBD) in Jyväskylä, Finland.

Heckhausen, J., & Schulz, R. (1991). *Primary and secondary control: Shifting trade-offs across the life span*. Unpublished Manuscript, Max Planck Institute for Human Development and Education, Berlin, FRG.

Hosenfeld, B. (1988). *Persönlichkeitsveränderungen im Erwachsenenalter aus der Sicht Jugendlicher* [Personality change in adulthood as perceived by adolescents]. Unpublished Masters thesis, Freie Universität Berlin.

Hundertmark, J. (1990). *Entwicklungsbezogene Intentionen im Lebenslauf: Selbstbild und normative Entwicklungsvorstellungen als Einflußfaktoren* [Development-related intentions throughout the life span: The impact of self-concept and normative conceptions about development]. Unpublished Master's thesis, Max Planck Institute for Human Development and Education, Berlin.

Kaye, K. (1982). *The mental and social life of babies: How parents create persons*. Chicago: The Harvester Press.

Kelley, H. H., & Michela, J. L. (1980). Attribution theory and research. *Annual Review of Psychology, 31*, 457-501.

Kohli, M. (1981). Zur Theorie der biographischen Selbst- und Fremdthematisierung [Theoretical perspectives on biographical conceptions about development]. In J. Matthes (Ed.), *Lebenswelt und soziale Probleme. Verhandlungen des 20. Deutschen Soziologentages* (pp. 502-520). Frankfurt: Campus.

Krueger, J., & Heckhausen, J. (1991). *Perception of growth and decline on five personality dimensions across the adult life span*. Manuscript submitted for publication, Max Planck Institute for Human Development and Education, Berlin, FRG.

Lewinsohn, P. M., Mischel, W., Chaplin, W., & Barton, R. (1980). Social competence and depression: The role of illusory self-perceptions. *Journal of Abnormal Psychology, 89*, 203-212.

Marini, M. M. (1984). Age and sequencing norms in the the transition to adulthood. *Social Forces, 63*, 229-244.

Mayer, K.-U. (1986). Structural constraints on the life course. *Human Development, 29*, 163-170.

Modell, J., Furstenberg, F. F., Jr., & Hershberg, T. (1976). Social change and transition to adulthood in historical perspectives. *Journal of Family History, 1*, 7-32.

Neugarten, B. L. (1968). The awareness of middle age. In B. L. Neugarten (Ed.), *Middle age and aging* (pp. 93-98). Chicago: University of Chicago Press.

Neugarten, B. L., Moore, J. W., & Lowe, J. C. (1965). Age norms, age constraints, and adult socialization. *American Journal of Sociology, 70*, 710-717.

Norman, W. T. (1963). Toward an adequate taxanomy of personality attitudes: Replicated factor structure in peer nomination personality ratings. *Journal of Abnormal and Social Psychology, 66*, 574-583.

O'Gorman, H. J. (1980). False consciousness of kind: Pluralistic ignorance among the aged. *Research on Aging, 2*, 105-128.

Piaget, J. (1985). *The equilibration of cognitive structures: The central problem of intellectual development*. Chicago: University of Chicago Press.

Riley, M. W., & Riley, J. W., Jr. (1986). Longevity and social structure: The added years. *Daedalus, 115,* 51-75.

Rothbaum, F., Weisz, J. R., & Snyder, S. S. (1982). Changing the world and changing the self: A two-process model of perceived control. *Journal of Personality and Social Psychology, 42,* 5-37.

Salthouse, T. A. (1985). *A theory of cognitive aging.* Amsterdam: North Holland.

Schulz, R., & Decker, S. (1985). Long-term adjustment to physical disability: The role of social support, perceived control, and self-blame. *Journal of Personality and Social Psychology, 48,* 1162-1172.

Schulz, R., Heckhausen, J., & Locher, J. (in press). Adult development, control, and adaptive functioning. *Journal of Social Issues.*

Snyder, C. R., & Fromkin, H. L. (1980). *The psychology of uniqueness.* New York: Plenum.

Snyder, M. L., Stephan, W. G., & Rosenfield, D. (1978). Attributional egotism. In J. H. Harvey, W. Ickes, & R. F. Kidd (Eds.), *New directions in attribution research* (Vol. 2, pp. 91-117). Hillsdale, NJ: Erlbaum.

Steinberg, L., & Silverberg, S. B. (1986). The vicissitudes of autonomy in early adolescence. *Child Development, 57,* 841-851.

Taylor, S. E. (1989). *Positive illusions: Creative self-deception and the healthy mind.* New York: Basic Books.

Taylor, S. E., & Lobel, M. (1989). Social comparison activity under threat: Downward evaluation and upward contacts. *Psychological Review, 96,* 569-575.

Taylor, S. E., Wood, J. V., & Lichtman, R. R. (1984). Attributions, beliefs about control, and adjustment to breast cancer. *Journal of Personality and Social Psychology, 46,* 489-502.

Wills, T. A. (1981). Downward comparison principles in social psychology. *Psychological Bulletin, 90,* 245-271.

Wood, J. V. (1989). Theory and research concerning social comparison of personal attributes. *Psychological Bulletin, 106*(2), pp. 231-248.

Zuckerman, M. (1979). Attribution of success and failure revisited, or: The motivational bias is alive and well in attribution theory. *Journal of Personality, 47,* 245-287.

PERSONAL CONTROL OVER DEVELOPMENT: SOME DEVELOPMENTAL IMPLICATIONS OF SELF-EFFICACY

Jochen Brandtstädter

The present contribution explores the various ways in which self-percepts of efficacy may contribute to optimal development and successful aging. Evidence from a larger cross-sequential investigation is presented supporting the view that self-referential beliefs of efficacy and control are of key importance in maintaining an optimistic perspective on personal development during middle and later adulthood. Notions of control and efficacy, however, cannot fully account for the mechanisms of coping with uncontrollable events and irreversible losses that typically cumulate in later phases of life. It is argued that besides self-percepts of efficacy, the capability or readiness to disengage from blocked developmental options and to flexibly readjust one's developmental goals is an important factor that reduces the risk of dissatisfaction and depression in later life. Empirical findings indicate that this second, accommodative mode of coping becomes increasingly dominant in later adulthood.

The present contribution attempts to highlight some implications that notions of personal control and self-efficacy have for issues of optimal development and successful aging. Such implications become readily apparent from an action perspective of development that focuses on the individuals' active contribution in shaping their personal development and circumstances of living (cf. Bandura, 1981; Brandtstädter, 1984). From this perspective, development over the life span has to be conceived as a process that to a large extent depends on the developing subject's self-referential cognitions, evaluations and actions. Life is a history of gains and losses in diverse areas of life and functioning (cf. Heckhausen, Dixon, & Baltes, 1989), but also a history of more or less successful attempts to keep this balance of gains and losses favorable. We are of course not the omnipotent producers of our development, as Bandura (1982a) has reminded us in his notion of "chance encounters." Schopenhauer, in his counsels and maxims concerning the wisdom of life, expressed this insight as follows: "...the course of a man's life is in no wise entirely of his own making; it is the product of two factors—the series of things that happened, and his own resolves in regard to them, and these two are constantly interacting upon and modifying each other" (Schopenhauer, 1851/1951, p. 84).

Extending notions of control and self-efficacy to the developmental domain spawns many interesting questions: e.g., how do self-beliefs of efficacy and control over development influence the person's construction of developmental gains and losses over the life span? How and to what extent do such self-referential beliefs determine the person's motivation of readiness to counteract anticipated developmental losses? What is their functional role in coping with critical life transitions, especially with those partly irreversible and uncontrollable losses that characterize the later phases of life? The following sections will address these questions.

PERCEIVED EFFICACY IN INSTRUMENTAL COPING EFFORTS: AN ACTION-THEORETICAL PERSPECTIVE

The action-theoretical model shown in Figure 1 may help to elucidate the functional role of self-efficacy beliefs in the context of personal control over development (see also Brandtstädter, 1989; Brandtstädter & Renner, 1991). The scheme roughly delineates cognitive, affective and behavioral factors involved in the process of coping with developmental losses and deficits. More specifically, it portrays a first phase or mode of coping where the individual actively tries to alter his or her behavior or developmental circumstances so that they match with, or are assimilated to, his or her developmental goals, life themes and desired "possible selves" (Markus & Nurius, 1986). We have denoted this stage in the coping process as the *assimilative* mode, in contrast to a second, *accommodative* mode that rather involves an accommodation of preferences and beliefs to given circumstances (cf. Brandtstädter, 1989; Brandtstädter & Renner, 1990). This second mode or phase of coping, and its relation to self-referential efficacy beliefs, will be considered more closely in a later section.

As shown in Figure 1, active-assimilative modes of coping are initially motivated by a perceived discrepancy or mismatch between factual and desired developmental prospects (the corresponding self-monitoring process is addressed in the Components 1 and 2 of the model). The ensuing affective and behavioral consequences now will critically depend on the individual's appraisal of his or her potentials for altering this unsatisfactory state. The different branching points in the scheme (4,7,9) denote different courses of events (for clarity, the branching points are conceived as alternatives: yes/no, +/-). If personal control potentials for altering the situation are seen as sufficient (5,+), the person will take measures to ameliorate his or her developmental circumstances and prospects (6). If, in contrast, personal potentials for action are seen as deficient (5,-), this will temporarily block development-related change efforts, but may not immediately bring about a state of helplessness or depression. Rather, it seems plausible to assume that at this stage of the coping episode, individuals will first try to augment their capacities and resources of action by searching for relevant

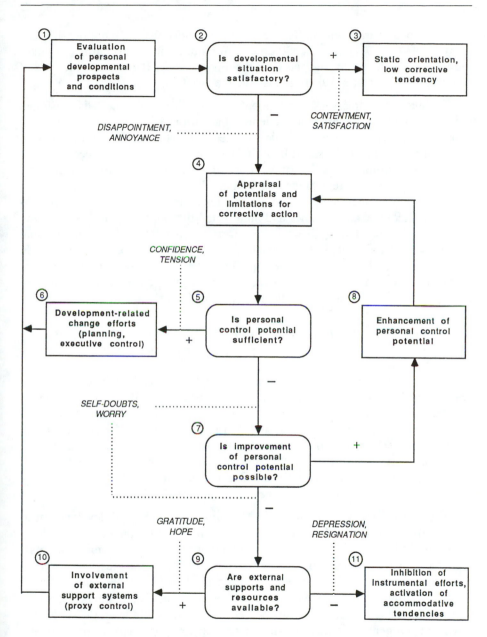

Figure 1 The assimilative mode of coping with developmental losses and deficits. Different active-assimilative strategies of coping are denoted by the paths < 1 → 2 (-) → 4 → 5 (+) → 6 >, < 1 → 2 (-) → 4 → 5 (-) → 7 (+) → 8 → 4 → 5 (+) → 6 >, < 1 → 2 (-) → 4 → 5 (-) → 7 (-) → 9 → 10 >. Efficacy beliefs intervene at the branching points of the scheme, which are linked with characteristic emotional states (according to this model, resignation and depression mark the shift from assimilative to accommodative processes of coping; see text for further explanations).

information, acquiring new skills, and so on—provided that such options are seen as available (5,-; 7,+). If such additional efforts turn out as unavailing, the individual may finally try to engage external support (7,-; 9, 10) or use some kind of proxy control (Bandura, 1982b) to manage the problem.

. Feelings of helplessness and hopelessness will arise when the different options for meliorative intervention depicted at various levels of the scheme seem exhausted (2,-; 5,-; 7,-; 9,-). Obviously, self-percepts of efficacy and control, which of course themselves will be influenced by experiences of success or failure in the assimilative phase of coping, function as differential moderating parameters at the different branching points of the modeled sequence. Persons harboring doubts about their potentials and resources to prevent personally undesired developmental outcomes and anticipated developmental losses will generally be less prone to engage in active efforts to ameliorate their developmental prospects or, if confronted with obstacles, to enhance their control potentials. In brief, the model shows how self-percepts of low efficacy pave the way into depression, or, conversely, how self-efficacy beliefs may enhance maintaining or regaining a positive, optimistic outlook on personal development.

PERCEIVED CONTROL OVER DEVELOPMENT AND QUALITY OF LIFE PERSPECTIVES

Against the backdrop of the action-theoretical model depicted above, it seems plausible to assume that differences in perceived self-efficacy or control over personal development should be closely related to indicators of optimal development and successful aging, and that strong percepts of efficacy will, at least in the long run, pay off in a more favorable balance of developmental gains and losses. In the following, I will present some selected findings that lend support to this general assumption. Before turning to results, let me briefly describe the research project where these findings come from.

The project[1] focuses on issues of personal self-regulation of development in adulthood. Our panel involves over 1,200 participants in the age range from 30 to 60 years. Within a cross-sequential research design which combines cross-sectional and longitudinal comparisons, structured questionnaires were used to assess various facets of the individual's appraisal of his or her own developmental situation. The ratings were done with respect to different goal dimensions (e.g., subjects were asked to rate the perceived importance of goal, the subjective distance from goal, the extent to which attainment of goals depends on personal efforts). We also asked our participants to describe their feelings with regard to their past and future development on selected adjective scales. From the basic ratings, various global indicators of development-related perceptions, beliefs and

[1] "Entwicklungserleben und Entwicklungskontrolle in Partnerschaften," funded by the German Research Foundation. The author is grateful to Bernhard Baltes-Götz, Werner Greve, Günter Krampen, Gerolf Renner and Dirk Wippermann, who assisted in various phases of this research.

action tendencies were derived. Further measures were included to assess inter-individual differences in personality traits, generalized control beliefs, marital adjustment, and life satisfaction. The longitudinal replications were separated by a two-year interval; to date, three waves have been completed which together span a longitudinal interval of four years (for more detailed descriptions of the research approach, see Brandtstädter & Baltes-Götz, 1991).

Development-Related Control Beliefs
and Perceived Developmental Deficits

A first series of analyses centered on the question of how self-percepts of control over development relate to perceived developmental deficits, or distances from developmental goals. Figure 2 summarizes the findings for the first wave, which were found to be stable across all longitudinal replications. The figure relates the distance ratings for 17 different goal dimensions of personal development ("How far are you presently from achieving this goal?") to an index variable of personal control over development (PCD; the two profiles shown in Figure 2 compare subgroups equal to or above and below the median of the PCD variable). The PCD index was aggregated from ratings concerning the perceived impact of controllable or autonomous and uncontrollable or heteronomous factors on personal development; validation studies have confirmed its usefulness as a measure of perceived control or development-related self-efficacy (see Brandt-städter, 1989). Across all goal dimensions, individuals scoring low in perceived control over development report significantly higher developmental deficits. There is also a control by goal dimensions interaction: Subjects having self-percepts of low control over development were found to report greater deficits above all on dimensions related to health, occupational efficiency, prosperity, and intellectual efficiency. A quite similar pattern of findings emerges when we take as a dependent variable the self-attributed potential for further developmental progress on the different dimensions (see Brandtstädter, Krampen, & Greve, 1987). These results indicate that subjects having self-percepts of high personal control over development give a more favorable account of their actual developmental situation. At the same time, they also see a greater latitude for improving their situation through determined efforts. Since no interactions involving age or gender were observed, it seems that we can generalize our findings across these factors.

Emotional Implications of Perceived Control Over Development

As may already be extrapolated from the previous findings, self-percepts of control over development should go with an optimistic and zestful outlook on personal development. Persons with self-confident action-outcome expectancies should be less threatened by aversive developmental prospects, and less vulnerable to feelings of despondency and depression. Parenthetically, we may note that such feelings may not only result from distinct "bad events" (Peterson &

Seligman, 1984) that are perceived as irreversible, but also from the experience of a gradual worsening in the balance of gains and losses with advancing age (cf. Heckhausen, Dixon, & Baltes, 1989). To some extent, the emotional implications of perceived control potentials or deficits are already revealed by analyzing the conceptual structure of emotion terms (e.g., Brandtstädter, 1985).

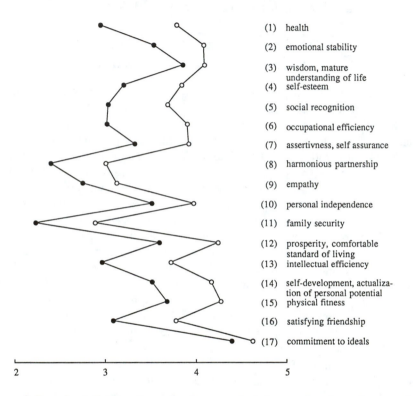

(1)	health
(2)	emotional stability
(3)	wisdom, mature understanding of life
(4)	self-esteem
(5)	social recognition
(6)	occupational efficiency
(7)	assertivness, self assurance
(8)	harmonious partnership
(9)	empathy
(10)	personal independence
(11)	family security
(12)	prosperity, comfortable standard of living
(13)	intellectual efficiency
(14)	self-development, actualization of personal potential
(15)	physical fitness
(16)	satisfying friendship
(17)	commitment to ideals

Figure 2 Perceived distance from developmental goals as a function of personal control over development (PCD). The profiles of means compare subgroups equal to or above (●) and below (○) the median of the PCD index (Brandtstädter, Krampen, & Greve, 1986).

In our research, the postulated cognitive-emotional relationhips were borne out in many convergent observations. As a paradigm case, we may consider the multiple regression of perceived control over development (as measured by the PCD index, see above) on ratings of emotional attitudes towards past and future development. The findings are based on data from the third wave (1987), but are highly consistent across all measurement points (Brandtstädter & Baltes-Götz, 1991).

Inspection of the regression structures shows that subjects scoring high in perceived control over development (PCD) tend to describe themselves *proud, happy, glad, satisfied, grateful* when looking back on their past development; looking toward their future, they feel more *hopeful, calm, confident, venturesome*.

To get a more detailed picture, we have decomposed here the aggregated index of personal control (PCD) into its separate components of Autonomous Control and Heteronomous Control over Development (in the aggregation procedure,

Table 1
Multiple Regression of Personal Control Over Development (PCD), Autonomous Control Over Development (CDA), and Heteronomous Control Over Development (CDH) on Ratings of Emotional Attitude Toward Past and Future Personal Development (Multiple Correlations and Regression Structure Coefficients)

Predictor variables	PCD	CDA	CDH
Retrospective Emotions			
Distressed	-.63	-.41	.43
Proud	.36	.44	.02
Happy	.45	.39	-.20
Exhausted	-.51	-.28	.46
Depressed	-.62	-.30	.60
Glad	.57	.50	-.25
Resigned	-.60	-.32	.55
Indifferent	-.21	-.30	.41
Satisfied	.50	.45	-.20
Powerless	-.61	-.31	.56
Angry	-.48	-.23	.47
Grateful	.43	.50	.06
Sad	-.62	-.36	.49
Prospective Emotions			
Hopeful	.71	.74	-.15
Calm	.55	.52	-.20
Uneasy	-.52	-.30	.44
Cheerful	.16	.08	-.15
Discouraged	-.71	-.41	.61
Worried	-.16	-.21	-.04
Anxious	-.63	-.31	.66
At a loss	-.71	-.36	.67
Fearful	-.70	-.31	.75
Confident	.61	.50	-.34
Troubled	-.57	-.30	.56
Venturesome	.71	.83	.00
Depressed	-.69	-.36	.62
R	.40**	.41**	.31**
N	757	813	794

Note. ** $p \leq .01$ (listwise deletion of missing data).

PCD was constructed as the difference between the indexes of Autonomous and Heteronomous Control). For Autonomous Control, we find largely the same pattern of relationships as for the global PCD index, whereas Heteronomous Control predicts a converse pattern of depression, worry and despondency (*distressed, exhausted, depressed, discouraged, fearful*, etc.). The finding of diametrically opposed correlational patterns for Autonomous and Heteronomous Control is not trivial, because these indicators do not form the opposite poles of a one-dimensional construct, but, on the contrary, were found to constitute statistically independent aspects of perceived control. This means, for example, that people who consider their personal development as strongly influenced by external and uncontrollable factors may nevertheless be convinced that they can play an active role in optimizing their balance of gains and losses. According to our observations, especially older people tend to adopt such a two-sided view, which obviously does not easily fit with traditional bipolar (e.g., internal versus external) conceptions of control.

A very similar pattern of relationships emerges when we correlate longitudinal change scores in the control and emotion variables. Over a longitudinal interval of four years, positive changes in self-percepts of Autonomous Control over Development are generally accompanied by shifts toward a positive evaluation of personal developmental achievements and prospects, as well as by other favorable changes in developmental circumstances and development-related beliefs (e.g., increases in general life satisfaction and perceived marital support, decreases in various indicators of depression; see Brandtstädter & Baltes-Götz, 1991). Conversely, increases in Heteronomous Control over Development go with a general worsening of developmental prospects. Inspection of cross-lagged panel correlations, however, did not suggest a specific causal ordering. As already mentioned above, self-percepts of low control over development should perhaps be considered as constitutive, rather than as causal, conditions of despondency and depression.

Self-Percepts of Control and Subjective Impact of Stressful Events

Critical or stressful life events—especially events or life changes which, from the subject's point of view, involve a worsening of personal developmental prospects—are generally seen as risk factors for depression and for a broad spectrum of pathophysiological changes, even if the mechanisms that mediate the documented statistical relationships are yet under dispute (e.g., Schroeder & Costa, 1984). Control-theoretical approaches have underscored the potential buffering effect of action-outcome expectancies on this relationship. As argued above, such expectancies should determine how much effort people will expend and how long they will persist in active-assimilative coping efforts; furthermore, self-percepts of efficacy and control should enhance threat-reducing interpretations of the impending situation (cf. Bandura, 1981; Lazarus & Folkman, 1984; Peterson & Seligman, 1984; Rodin, 1986; Scheier & Carver, 1985). Generally, the belief that one cannot improve one's developmental prospects or cannot attain personally valued goals is—almost by definition—an essential feature of help-lessness, depression and alienation.

Besides the assessments already described, we have asked the participants in our panel study to report critical or stressful events that they had experienced in the recent past and to rate the degree of strain experienced during the episode. In a first exploratory step, we correlated these ratings with age, depressive outlook on personal development and different measures of perceived control. Together with the indicators of Autonomous and Heteronomous Control over Develop-ment, a German adaptation of Levenson's scales (IPC-questionnaire; Krampen, 1981) was included in this analysis as a measure of generalized control beliefs. Depressive tendencies were measured by an index variable derived from self-ratings on selected adjective scales (cf. Brandtstädter & Baltes-Götz, 1991). Table 2 shows the relationships for different categories of events (the data come from the third wave, 1987; similar findings were obtained for the earlier waves).

First of all, the findings presented in Table 2 confirm the expected relation-ship of experienced strain in critical episodes with depressive tendencies; the event categories of unemployment, conflicts in familial or occupational contexts, change in financial state, change in residence and personal illness seem to stand out in this relationship. To further trace the effects of critical events reported for a given two-year longitudinal interval, we also looked at changes in depression rat-ings over that interval. Persons afflicted by personal illness, occupational con-flicts and by conflicts with family members or friends showed a significantly greater increase in depressive tendency (and a corresponding decrease in life satisfaction) than the complementary subsample of individuals not reporting the given event. For the other categories of events, longitudinal changes mostly pointed in a similar direction but—partly due to restrictions in sample size for the given event type—fell short of significance (noticeable exceptions are the cate-gories pregnancy/birth of child, change of residence and occupational change, which tended to go with a reduction in depressive tendencies over the corresponding longitudinal interval).

The focus of interest here, of course, is on the associations of experienced strain with indicators of control and self-efficacy. As a general tendency, control beliefs indicating low self-efficacy or an external locus of control (Heteronomous Control, IPC-Powerful others, IPC-Chance control) seem positively related to the strain experienced in a given critical episode. This relationship appears most clear-cut for personal illness, unemployment, and occupational conflicts. Inter-estingly, these data also hint that in specific cases, self-percepts of control over development may go with greater emotional strain in critical situations. A plaus-ible post factum explanation would be that persons attributing themselves a high degree of control over their development may to a greater extent feel personally responsible for failures and setbacks.

Within a hierarchical regression format, we further looked for moderating effects of control beliefs on the relationship between exposure to critical events and emotional strain, using simple and autoregressively residualized differences

Table 2
Subjective Impact of Stressful Events: Relations With Age, Depressive Outlook, and Measures of Control

Reference Variable	Type of Event [a]											
	1 (82)	2 (254)	3 (426)	4 (204)	5 (29)	6 (40)	7 (195)	8 (109)	9 (191)	10 (388)	11 (193)	12
Age	.01	.03	.18**	.00	-.24	-.22	-.03	-.02	-.01	-.01	-.01	-.04
Depressive outlook (DEP)	.31**	.27**	.15**	.17**	-.08	.44**	.36**	.10	.33**	.31**	.38**	.17**
Autonomous control over development (CDA)	-.07	.00	.12*	.11	.12	.22	.22**	.13	.02	.16**	.09	.02
Heteronomous control over development (CDH)	-.02	.24**	.22**	.07	-.04	.35*	.14	.28**	.27**	.09	.02	.08*
Personal control over development (PCD)	.00	-.16*	.03	.03	.11	-.09	.03	-.07	-.17*	.05	.03	-.05
Internality (IPC-I)	-.26*	-.07	-.02	-.12	-.30	.04	-.02	.09	-.14	-.04	-.01	-.06
Powerful others (IPC-P)	.10	.24**	.09	.08	-.06	.38*	.18*	.23*	.23**	.01	.16*	.12**
Chance control (IPC-C)	.10	.22**	.18**	.03	-.09	.22	.28**	.08	.24**	.08	.19**	.10**

Note. [a] 1: Change in residence, 2: Personal illness, 3: Illness of family member, 4: Death of family member, 5: Pregnancy/birth of child, 6: Unemployment, 7: Change in financial state, 8: Occupational change, 9: Occupational conflicts, 10: Conflicts with family members or friends, 11: Other stressful event (open category), 12: Sum of reported critical events. Numbers in parentheses refer to frequency of the given event within the sample ($N = 998$).
$**p < .01; *p < .05.$

between pre- and post-event depression ratings (obtained at the second and third occasion of measurement, respectively) as dependent variables. Space considerations allow for only a condensed overview here. Observed moderation effects were highly specific for the type of event considered. In part, the effects were consistent with the presumed buffering effect of perceived control; for example, it was found that higher scores on IPC-internality and on Autonomous Control over Development dampen the negative emotional impact of occupational conflict. Such effects came out more clearly when pertinent domain-specific ratings of perceived control over development were considered (considering, e.g., the emotional impact of personal illness, health-related control beliefs seem to have a stronger moderating effect than general indicators of perceived control). The global picture of our findings, however, does not support the unconditional conclusion that self-percepts of control and self-efficacy are under all circumstances contributive to emotional resilience and effective coping. For example, our results hint that the emotional impact of the event "death of family member" is not mitigated, but rather aggravated by perceived control or self-efficacy. This indicates that active-assimilative efforts at control may be dysfunctional in situations of loss which are factually irreversible.

It is possible, then, that the arguments considered so far, which largely centered on salutory effects of self-efficacy, give only an incomplete grasp of the factors that help individuals to cope with life crises and make them less vulnerable to depression in situations of loss. In the following, I will briefly sketch the outlines of a more comprehensive theoretical perspective.

BROADENING THE THEORETICAL SCOPE: TENACIOUS PURSUIT AND FLEXIBLE ADJUSTMENT OF DEVELOPMENTAL GOALS

To sum up, there are good empirical and theoretical reasons supporting the view that self-referential beliefs of efficacy and control are of key importance in maintaining a positive and optimistic outlook on personal development in middle and later adulthood. But—as intimated above—I think that this is only one element of a more complex story. We have a thorough theoretical understanding of the different ways in which self-percepts of efficacy may contribute to effective coping, and why persons entertaining doubts in their control potentials are more vulnerable to helplessness and depression when faced with obstacles or failures. From a control-theoretical or learned helplessness perspectives, however, it is by far less clear how people manage to recover from resignation and depression, especially in cases where they are confronted with permanent and definitely irreversible loss.

Accommodative Modes of Coping

To approach this question theoretically, we should recognize that a discrepancy between actual and desired developmental prospects may be handled in two basically different ways: on the one hand, the situation may be transformed—in the sense of assimilative efforts given above—to correspond more closely to personal goals and aspirations; on the other hand, the discrepancy may be neutralized by alterations in the system of personal goals, aspirations and evaluative cognitions that make the previously aversive situation more acceptable.

It follows that besides self-referential beliefs of control and efficacy, the capability or readiness to disengage from thwarted developmental options and to flexibly revise and readjust one's developmental goals and life design may be an important (and hitherto largely neglected) factor that serves to diminish the impact of aversive and stressful experiences and to reduce the individual's vulnerability to depression. Apparently, we are dealing here with a mode of coping that is basically different from active-assimilative efforts. This second mode of coping, which I have termed as *accommodative*, should become predominant to the extent that active, instrumental efforts to master the situation seem futile, or when generalized or specific beliefs of self-efficacy have been eroded through repeated unsuccessful attempts. In a certain sense, these considerations lead us beyond notions of control and learned helplessness. Note that accommodative readjustments of goals, aspirations and evaluative standards involve to a considerable extent reactive, automatic or effortless processes that do not involve intentional action. There are of course techniques of self-management and self-instruction that may be deliberately applied by the individual in an attempt to alter aversive cognitions and emotional states (e.g., Karoly & Kanfer, 1982; cf. also the notions of "emotion-focused coping" by Lazarus, 1977, or of "secondary control" by Rothbaum, Weisz, & Snyder, 1982). The fact, however, that we can to some extent modify our cognitive and emotional processes does not imply that these processes should be considered as intentionally controlled actions (just as the fact that we can deliberately bring about some bodily reflexes does not mean that these reflexes are intentional acts). We cannot give up our beliefs and commitments merely because it seems advantageous to us; if we could, problems of depression and despair would presumably not exist. To make a longer story short: The paradigm of intentional action does not apply to the cognitive and motivational processes that form the basis of intentional actions (see also Lanz, 1987). Rather, the process of generating palliative cognitions in aversive situations depends on their availability in a given situation; research on the mood congruence of cognitions has shed some light on the subpersonal mechanisms involved (for an overview, see Blaney, 1986). It becomes apparent at this juncture that feelings of hopelessness and helplessness are not simply the deplorable end state of unavailing efforts to master a problem, but may be important parameters in the shift from assimilative to accommodative phases of coping. When faced with factually uncontrollable events and irreversible losses, persons having a strong sense of personal control and self-efficacy may even have greater difficulties in adjusting their goals and life plans to the new circumstances (cf. Brandtstädter & Renner, 1990; Janoff-Bulman & Brickman, 1982).

The accommodative phase of coping involves a reorganization of goals, beliefs, aspirations and evaluational standards on different levels. We assume that, on a first level, reappraisals of the situation are activated; as the emotional evaluation of a given situation largely depends on the expectations and meanings (semantic and instrumental) associated with that situation, changes in subjective probabilities of specific consequences may have a palliative effect and enhance disengagment from blocked goals and action tendencies (cf. Klinger, 1975). Such palliative processes critically depend on the subjective availability of alternative interpretations, which may be enhanced by exploratory and ruminative processes (search for new information, consideration of new arguments, changing the analytic focus, etc.). Within the boundaries of rationality, there is usually some latitude for alternative interpretations of a given situation (cf. also Taylor & Brown, 1988); when alternative interpretations are available, individuals usually tend to endorse those that are consistent with, and have positive implications for, their self-conception and personal view of the world (cf. Greenwald, 1980). If palliative interpretations are not accessible, individuals may alter their evaluative standards and reference points. For example, developmental losses in old age may seem more acceptable to individuals who compare themselves with same-aged rather than with younger persons. Generally, a situation may appear less aversive when we contrast it with some worse alternative or, conversely, avoid contrasting it with a counterfactual better world (cf. Kahneman & Miller, 1986; Taylor, Wood, & Lichtman, 1983; Wills, 1981). Bandura (1982b, 1989) has discussed the mediating role of such processes in selective activation of self-corrective tendencies; here, the emphasis is on their functional role in the process of disengaging from barren goals and in revising developmental perspectives. On a final level, accommodative processes may eventually involve a radical shift in the person's conception of self and the world, comparable to a paradigm shift in science. Such more radical changes may be expected in cases when palliative reappraisals and readjustments of aspirations are not available for the individual (for further theoretical elaborations, see Brandtstädter & Renner, 1991).

Age-Related Changes in Coping Style: From Active-Assimilative to Accommodative Modes of Coping

The theoretical perspective outlined provides a conceptual scheme for dealing with some notorious puzzles of successful aging. How can we explain that older people do not report a general or dramatic loss in life satisfaction, even though they face morbidity, death, and an increasingly unfavorable balance of developmental gains and losses (Stock, Okun, Haring, & Wilter, 1983)? Why is there no increase in the prevalence rates of depression in old age (cf. Bolla-Wilson & Bleeker, 1989; Kasl & Berkman, 1981; Lewinsohn, Hoberman, Teri, & Hauzinger, 1985; Newmann, 1989)? As Blazer (1989, p. 198) summarizes the evidence, we should "seriously consider the possibility that older adults...may be...protected from the development of major or clinical depression." To illustrate this point, Figure 3 shows cross-sequential gradients for self-reported life satisfaction that were obtained from the first and third wave of our panel study ($N = 998$). The gradients span a cross-sectional range from 30 to 63 years and a longitudinal interval of four years (as a measure of life satisfaction, we used an item selection from scales developed by Neugarten, Havighurst, & Tobin, 1961). Apart from a slight decrease in subjective quality of life for the early phase of middle adulthood (30-41 years), the general picture from both cross-sectional and longitudinal comparisons is one of stability over the age range considered. Even for the cohorts approaching later adulthood, there is no indication of a decrease in life satisfaction.

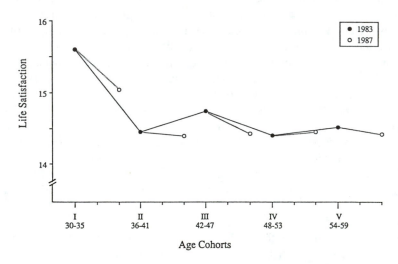

Figure 3 Subjective quality of life in adulthood: cross-sectional comparisons and four-year longitudinal changes in life satisfaction (occasions 1983 and 1987; age ranges for cohorts refer to first occasion).

From a control-theoretical or learned helplessness point of view, these facts become even more puzzling when we assume that older people see their life and personal development as increasingly dependent on factors beyond personal control, as several studies have documented (cf. Brandtstädter & Baltes-Götz, 1991; Lachman, 1986; Rodin, 1987). These apparent inconsistencies may be resolved when we assume a gradual age-related shift from assimilative to accommodative modes of coping. We have investigated this assumption by means of a questionnaire which specifically was designed to assess preferences of assimilative and accommodative modes of coping on a dispositional level. The instrument comprises two nearly orthogonal scales that we have denoted as "Tenacious Goal Pursuit" and "Flexible Goal Adjustment." Tenacious individuals cling to goals and commitments even in the face of obstacles or under high risk of failure (e.g., "When faced with obstacles, I usually double my efforts"; "Even when a situation seems hopeless, I still try to master it"). Flexible individuals disengage easily from barren commitments, and try to see the best in difficult situations (e.g., "I adapt quite easily to changes in plans or circumstances"; "If I don't get something I want, I take it with patience"). In spite of their statistical independence, both scales correlate consistently and positively with indicators of successful development such as optimism, life satisfaction, absence of depressive tendencies, and greater resilience in stressful life situations (see Brandtstädter & Renner, 1990).

Figure 4 shows cross-sectional age gradients for Flexibility and Tenacity for a large sample ($N = 1,433$). These results are obtained by pooling observations from our panel study (third wave, 1987; cf. also Brandtstädter & Renner, 1990) and several independent investigations in which the Flexibility and Tenacity scales were used. Over the age range considered, the age cohort by coping style (Flexibility, Tenacity) interaction is highly significant and clearly corresponds to the predicted shift from assimilative to accommodative modes of coping; the linear correlations of Flexibility and Tenacity with age are -.23 and +.23, respectively (the difference between these coefficients is highly significant). Inspection of the data for the oldest cohort indicates that these trends continue beyond the age of 65. The pattern of clearly opposite regressions of Flexibility and Tenacity on age is all the more noteworthy considering the independence of the scales (for the total sample, the correlation is .12). These findings seriously call into doubt widespread assumptions according to which "...older people...cope in much the same way as younger people" (McCrae, 1982, p. 459); at the same time, they underscore the importance of dispositional factors that have been hitherto largely neglected in coping research (see also Carver, Scheier, & Weintraub, 1989).

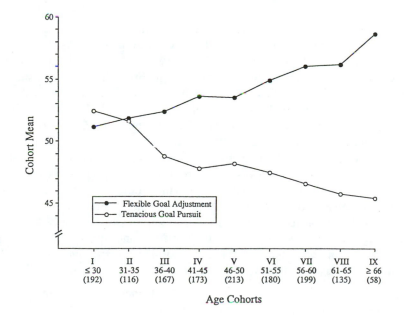

Figure 4 Age gradients for Tenacious Goal Pursuit and Flexible Goal Adjustment.

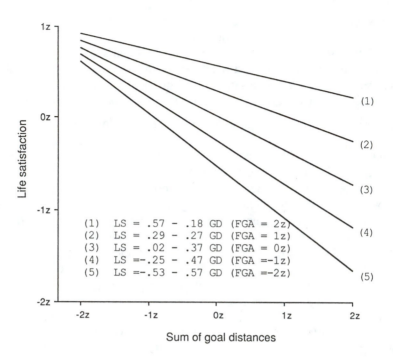

Figure 5 Conditional regressions of Life Satisfaction (LS) on subjective developmental deficits (sum index of perceived distances from 17 developmental goals, GD) for different levels.

Analyses of moderation effects further support this line of argument. Considering the presumed palliative functions of accommodative processes, we should expect that for highly flexible persons, perceived developmental losses or deficits should be less detrimental to subjective quality of life. Figure 5 shows the conditional regressions of life satisfaction on the sum of perceived goal distances over 17 developmental goals for different levels of Flexibility (N = 885; these data come from the third wave of our panel study where the Flexibility scale was first introduced; see also Brandtstädter & Renner, 1990). While being significantly negative (-.43) for the total sample, the correlation between life satisfaction and the sum of perceived distances from developmental goals is less pronounced for higher levels of Flexibility (this moderation effect is also obtained when age is statistically controlled). Apparently, the observed age-related shift from assimilative to accommodative modes of coping should not be interpreted as reflecting an insidious trend toward resignation and apathy, but rather as a process that is functional in maintaining an optimistic perspective, perhaps also a sense of power and self-efficacy, in old age.

At this juncture, the question may be raised whether the notions of power and self-efficacy should not be considered as diametrically opposed to the accommodative adjustment of preferences. But things are obviously not quite this simple.

On the one hand, it is certainly true that as long as there are no reasons to doubt one's efficacy in attaining personally valued goals, there is no point for accommodative adjustments. But if getting what one wants is central to the concept of power, it follows that a way to retain a sense of efficacy may be to adjust one's preferences to the range of the feasible.

REFERENCES

Bandura, A. (1981). Self-referent thought: A developmental analysis of self-efficacy. In J. H. Flavell & L. Ross (Eds.), *Social cognitive development. Frontiers and possible futures* (pp. 200-239). Cambridge: Cambridge University Press.

Bandura, A. (1982a). The psychology of chance encounters and life paths. *American Psychologist, 37,* 747-755.

Bandura, A. (1982b). The self and mechanisms of agency. In J. Suls (Ed.), *Psychological perspectives on the self* (Vol. 1, pp. 3-40). Hillsdale, NJ: Erlbaum.

Bandura, A. (1989). Self-regulation of motivation and action through internal standards and goal systems. In L. A. Pervin (Ed.), *Goal concepts in personality and social psychology* (pp. 19-85). Hillsdale, NJ: Erlbaum.

Blaney, P. H. (1986). Affect and memory: A review. *Psychological Bulletin, 99,* 229-246.

Blazer, D. (1989). Depression in late life: An update. *Annual Review of Gerontology & Geriatrics, 9,* 197-215.

Bolla-Wilson, K., & Bleecker, M. L. (1989). Absence of depression in elderly adults. *Journal of Gerontology: Psychological Sciences, 44,* P53-55.

Brandtstädter, J. (1984). Personal and social control over development: Some implications of an action perspective in life-span developmental psychology. In P. B. Baltes & O. G. Brim Jr. (Eds.), *Life-span development and behavior* (Vol. 6, pp. 1-32). New York: Academic Press.

Brandtstädter, J. (1985). Emotion, Kognition, Handlung: Konzeptuelle Beziehungen [Emotion, cognition, action: Conceptual relationships]. In L. H. Eckensberger & E.-D. Lantermann (Eds.), *Emotion und Reflexivität* [Emotion and reflexivity] (pp. 252-261). München: Urban & Schwarzenberg.

Brandtstädter, J. (1989). Personal self-regulation of development: Cross-sequential analyses of development-related control beliefs and emotions. *Developmental Psychology, 25,* 96-108.

Brandtstädter, J., & Baltes-Götz, B. (1991). Personal control over development and quality of life perspectives in adulthood. In P. B. Baltes & M. M. Baltes (Eds.), *Successful aging. Perspectives from the behavioral sciences* (pp. 197-224). New York: Cambridge University Press.

Brandtstädter, J., Krampen, G., & Greve, W. (1987). Personal control over development: Effects on the perception and emotional evaluation of personal development in adulthood. *International Journal of Behavioral Development, 10,* 99-120.

Brandtstädter, J., & Renner, G. (1990). Tenacious goal pursuit and flexible goal adjustment: Explication and age-related analysis of assimilative and accommodative strategies of coping. *Psychology and Aging, 5,* 58-67.

Brandtstädter, J., & Renner, G. (1991). Coping with discrepancies between aspirations and achievements in adult development: A dual-process model. In L. Montada,

S.-H. Filipp, & M. R. Lerner (Eds.), *Crises and experiences of loss in adulthood.* Hillsdale, NJ: Erlbaum, in press.

Carver, C. S., Scheier, M. F., & Weintraub, S. K. (1989). Assessing coping strategies: A theoretically based approach. *Journal of Personality and Social Psychology, 56,* 267-283.

Greenwald, A. G. (1980). The totalitarian ego: Fabrication and revision of personal history. *American Psychologist, 35,* 603-618.

Heckhausen, J., Dixon, R. A., & Baltes, P. B. (1989). Gains and losses in development throughout adulthood as perceived by different adult age groups. *Developmental Psychology, 25,* 109-121.

Janoff-Bulman, R., & Brickman, P. (1982). Expectations and what people learn from failure. In N. T. Feather (Ed.), *Expectations and actions: Expectancy-value models in psychology* (pp. 207-237). Hillsdale, NJ: Erlbaum.

Kahneman, D., & Miller, D. T. (1986). Norm theory: Comparing reality to its alternatives. *Psychological Review, 93,* 136-153.

Karoly, P., & Kanfer, F. H. (Eds.). (1982). *The psychology of self-management. From theory to practice.* New York: Plenum.

Kasl, S. V., & Berkman, L. F. (1981). Some psychosocial influences on the health status of the elderly: The perspective of social epidemiology. In J. L. McGaugh & S. B. Kiesler (Eds.), *Aging: Biology and behavior* (pp. 345-377). New York: Academic Press.

Klinger, E. (1975). Consequences of commitment to and disengagement from incentives. *Psychological Review, 82,* 1-25.

Krampen, G. (1981). *IPC-Fragebogen zu Kontrollüberzeugungen* [IPC-questionnaire of Perceived Control]. Göttingen: Hogrefe.

Lachman, M. E. (1986). Locus of control in aging research. *Journal of Psychology and Aging, 1,* 34-40.

Lanz, P. (1987). *Menschliches Handeln zwischen Kausalität und Rationalität* [Human action between causality and rationality]. Frankfurt a. M.: Athenäum.

Lazarus, R. S. (1977). Cognitive and coping processes in emotion. In A. Monat & R. S. Lazarus (Eds.), *Stress and coping* (pp. 145-158). New York: Columbia University Press.

Lazarus, R. S., & Folkman, S. (1984). *Stress, appraisal and coping.* New York: Springer.

Lewinsohn, P. M., Hoberman, H. M., Teri, L., & Hautzinger, M. (1985). An integrative theory of depression. In S. Reiss & R. R. Bootzin (Eds.), *Behavioral issues in behavior therapy* (pp. 331-362). New York: Academic Press.

Markus, H., & Nurius, P. (1986). Possible selves. *American Psychologist, 41,* 954-969.

McCrae, R. R. (1982). Age differences in the use of coping mechanisms. *Journal of Gerontology, 37,* 454-460.

Neugarten, B. L., Havighurst, R. J., & Tobin, S. S. (1961). The measurement of life satisfaction. *Journal of Gerontology, 16,* 134-143.

Newmann, J. P. (1989). Aging and depression. *Psychology and Aging, 4,* 150-165.

Peterson, C., & Seligman, M. E. P. (1984). Causal explanations as a risk factor for depression: Theory and evidence. *Psychological Review, 91,* 347-374.

Rodin, J. (1986). Health, control and aging. In M. M. Baltes & P. B. Baltes (Eds.), *The psychology of control and aging* (pp. 139-165). Hillsdale, NJ: Erlbaum.

Rodin, J. (1987). Personal control through the life course. In R. P. Abeles (Ed.), *Life-span perspective and social psychology* (pp. 103-119). Hillsdale, NJ: Erlbaum.

Rothbaum, F., Weisz, J. R., & Snyder, S. S. (1982). Changing the world and changing the self. A two-process model of perceived control. *Journal of Personality and Social Psychology, 42*, 5-37.

Scheier, M. F., & Carver, C. S. (1985). Optimism, coping, and health: Assessment and implications of generalized outcome expectancies. *Health Psychology, 4*, 219-247.

Schopenhauer, A. (1951). *Essays from the parerga and paralipomena.* London: Allen and Unwin (Original: 1851).

Schroeder, D. H., & Costa, P. T. Jr. (1984). The influence of life stress on physical illness: Substantive effects of methodological flows? *Journal of Personality and Social Psychology, 46*, 853-863.

Stock, W. A., Okun, M. A., Haring, M. J., & Wilter, R. A. (1983). Age and subjective well-being: A meta-analysis. In R. J. Light (Ed.), *Evaluation studies: Review annual* (Vol. 8, pp. 279-302). Beverly Hills, CA: Sage.

Taylor, S., & Brown, J. D. (1988). Illusion and well-being: A social psychological perspective of mental health. *Psychological Bulletin, 103*, 193-210.

Taylor, S. E., Wood, J. U., & Lichtman, R. R. (1983). It could be worse: Selective evaluation as a response to victimization. *Journal of Social Issues, 39*, 19-40.

Wills, T. A. (1981). Downward comparison principles in social psychology. *Psychological Bulletin, 91*, 245-271.

III

SELF-EFFICACY,
STRESS,
AND EMOTION

PERCEIVED SELF-EFFICACY AND PHOBIC DISABILITY

S. Lloyd Williams

This chapter reviews theory and evidence regarding self-efficacy judgments as causal determinants of phobia. Theories based on anxiety and/or stimulus exposure have serious conceptual and empirical weaknesses. In contrast, self-efficacy theory fares appreciably better. The author's and colleague's research with more than 200 severely phobic individuals found that the accuracy of self-efficacy judgments in predicting therapeutic changes in phobic behavior is not due to mere methodological artifacts or to correlation with alternative cognitive factors. Self-efficacy was a consistently accurate predictor of therapeutic outcome even with the influence of perceived danger and anticipated fear and panic held constant. When agoraphobic people were given treatment for some phobic areas while leaving other areas untreated, the variable generalized changes in the untreated phobias were most accurately predicted by changes in self-efficacy. And "guided mastery" treatment based on self-efficacy theory was more effective than standard exposure treatments for reducing phobic disability and distress. These findings indicate that self-efficacy theory can advance the understanding and treatment of phobia.

Phobia is a most striking and puzzling psychological phenomenon. It illustrates well the "neurotic paradox" of persistent self-defeating behavior, in which one is disabled despite perceiving every incentive to function normally, having the basic cognitive/motoric faculties needed to do so, and being well aware that one's disability is senseless. Many psychological theories have sought to explain this fascinating problem, and phobia was the first phenomenon to which self-efficacy theory was extensively applied (Bandura, 1977; Bandura & Adams, 1977; Bandura, Adams, & Beyer, 1977). Since that early experimentation, considerable research has examined the role of perceived self-efficacy in phobia. This paper will review some of the major findings from a series of experiments colleagues and I have conducted to evaluate self-efficacy theory. One purpose was to clarify the psychological mechanisms that cause phobic behavior. I use the word "cause" throughout this paper to refer to a current determining factor rather than an historical etiological factor. In particular, the research sought to evaluate whether self-efficacy perceptions are causal of phobic behavior. The second purpose was to apply knowledge about causal processes to developing improved treatment techniques. A natural starting place in this inquiry is the phobic phenomenon itself, which theories are trying to explain and treatments to remedy.

PHOBIA: NATURE AND CURRENT TREATMENTS

Phobia is a highly prevalent problem, and it impairs people's lives in many ways (Williams, 1985). People with phobias have difficulty carrying out routine social, vocational, and recreational activities, as they must avoid the possibility of having to cope with the phobic object. They feel marked subjective fear, and they experience physiological stress reactions such as pounding heart, nausea, and intense sweating when attempting phobia-related activities. Even successful avoidance doesn't shield them from distress, since they dwell on, and magnify, their own vulnerabilities, and ruminate about potential harms that might befall them. Some phobic people have attacks of terror and panic even when remote from phobic threats. Some phobias are specific to a particular object or activity, such as spiders or public speaking, whereas other phobic patterns are more generalized and encompass a wide variety of activities. An example of the latter is agoraphobia, which involves phobias of multiple activities away from home, such as shopping, driving, walking along the street, public transportation, bridges, restaurants, elevators, and others. Even specific phobias can be profoundly incapacitating and distressing (Bandura, 1977, 1978a), and agoraphobias are the more likely to be so.

Over the past 30 years substantial progress has been made in helping phobics recover. The first major therapeutic breakthrough was the introduction of systematic desensitization (Wolpe, 1958), in which phobic clients imagined themselves coping with feared activities. The next major advance was the use of performance-based treatments in which clients cope with phobic activities in actuality. Performance treatments proved to be substantially more effective than imaginal treatments for both generalized and specific phobias (Barlow, 1988; Leitenberg, 1976; Williams, 1987).

The performance treatment methods currently in widespread use consist of the therapist encouraging phobic individuals to expose themselves to what they fear. However, it is one thing to urge phobics to confront the worst for prolonged periods, yet another to actually enable them to do it, and to guide them to do it in ways that they truly master their phobias. As currently implemented, "exposure" treatments fail to benefit about 25% of those with generalized phobias, and leave the majority with at least moderate disability after treatment (Barlow, 1988; Gelder, 1977). Further therapeutic advances are therefore clearly necessary. Developing more effective phobia treatments requires understanding the psychological mechanisms of phobia.

THE FAILURE OF ANXIETY THEORY

Traditionally, theories of phobic behavior emphasized anxiety arousal as the main determinant of phobic behavior (e.g., Mowrer, 1960; Wolpe, 1958). [Note: the terms "fear" and "anxiety" are here considered synonyms]. This anxiety theory of phobia has always suffered from serious explanatory weaknesses

(Bandura, 1969; Rachman, 1976; Seligman & Johnston, 1973; Williams, 1987, 1988). In the first place, the term "anxiety" long has been a catch-all label for a bewildering assortment of disparate phenomena, so that simply measuring "it" can potentially be a complicated and highly uncertain task. Some analyses of anxiety, such as the "three systems" approach, went so far as to include phobic behavior into the very definition of anxiety. This renders into circular nonsense the proposition that anxiety causes phobic behavior, since a thing cannot cause itself. The proliferation of meanings was partly due to the longstanding failure of any particular index of anxiety to strongly predict avoidant behavior.

Perhaps the most usual ways of defining anxiety are (a) as a feeling of fear, rated on a subjective intensity scale, and (b) as autonomic arousal. But no matter how anxiety is defined and measured, its various indices prove to be only weakly correlated with one another, and only weakly correlated with phobic behavior (Bandura, 1969, 1978b, 1988; Lang, 1971; Rachman, 1976). People can be very anxious but not avoid, as with many people who suffer from panic attacks but nevertheless function normally. And people can be not very anxious but do avoid, as in the bridge phobic person who calmly drives far out of the way to stay clear of a large bridge.

Attempts to explain the therapeutic effects of various phobia treatments as due to anxiety inhibition, anxiety evocation, or anxiety extinction proved to lack merit. Whether anxiety was minimized, evoked, or ignored during treatment made little difference, and across numerous studies the anxiety people experienced during treatment correlated little with how much they benefited from treatment (Mathews, Gelder, & Johnston, 1981; Williams, 1987, 1990).

The negative evidence did not extinguish enthusiasm for anxiety theory in all quarters. A recent variation on anxiety theory has it that panic is the primary determinant of agoraphobic behavior. Since panic is defined using a list consisting mostly of conventional attributes of anxiety, especially different kinds of autonomic arousal as perceived by the client, and since autonomic arousal is rather labile and poorly related to phobic behavior (Williams, 1987, 1988), panic would seem from the outset an unlikely candidate to explain the persistent patterns of agoraphobia. Panic does appears to have some significant role in the historical etiology of agoraphobia, but panic bears little relation to it once agoraphobia develops. Many severe agoraphobics have not had a panic attack for months or years; moreover, many current panickers are not particularly agoraphobic. Therefore, it is hardly surprising that the correlation between panic attacks and severity of agoraphobia tends to be very low (Craske, Rapee, & Barlow, 1988). Later I will discuss the role of anticipated anxiety and panic in agoraphobia, which is a somewhat different matter, but here it suffices to say that panic and anxiety per se appear to have at best a modest relationship with phobic behavior.

Correlation is a necessary condition for causation. That is, if two variables are not correlated with one another, then the one cannot cause the other; if two variables are weakly correlated with one another, then at most the one can only weakly cause the other. Phobia theorists and researchers seem often to have lost sight of this basic principle, perhaps because of an overemphasis on the principle that correlation is not sufficient for causation. It may not be sufficient, but it is quite necessary. The weak correlations show that fearful feelings, panic attacks, and autonomic arousal cannot be major determinants of phobic behavior.

There is no doubt that fear arousal can accompany phobia, and that anxiety is a concomitant that that phobia theories must explain and phobia treatments remedy. But anxiety is better conceived as part of the problem to be solved, than as the mechanism of therapeutic change.

THE DYSFUNCTIONAL "EXPOSURE" CONCEPT

With the growing realization that anxiety mechanisms had little power to explain phobia, some proposed accounting for therapeutic changes in terms of "exposure" to fearsome stimuli. By this view, therapeutic improvement is due simply to the amount of time the person remains in the presence of scary stimuli, and one need not consider internal psychological processes. This view gained a wide following, and now disparate phobia treatments are known almost universally as "exposure" therapies.

The exposure notion and associated terminology are unfortunate because they emphasize external stimuli while neglecting inner psychological processes (Rosenthal & Bandura, 1978; Williams, 1987, 1988, 1990). The exposure principle encounters serious difficulties explaining why a given amount and kind of treatment will benefit one person very much but another person very little. Indeed, exposure has not been plainly operationally defined by its advocates so as to permit one to empirically test the relationship between exposure and therapeutic change. Some have even incorporated treatment benefit into the very definition of exposure, thereby rendering it circular and devoid of meaning (Williams, 1988).

The exposure principle also gives therapists little specific guidance, and indeed, diverts attention from the specifics of treatment procedures, because the term "exposure" is applied to various dissimilar treatments, including many that do not even involve performing phobia-related activities. If almost any behavioral treatment is "exposure therapy", then the exposure term and concept have little distinct meaning or value. Developing more effective phobia treatments requires specifying operationally the psychological processes of phobia, rather than a principle merely reminding us that learning requires domain-relevant material.

SELF-EFFICACY THEORY

Recent years have witnessed a growing convergence of theory and evidence on the influential role of cognitive factors in defensive behavior, and especially on the role of perceived control in determining avoidance and stress reactions. To the extent that people believe they can manage potential threats, they have little reason to fear and avoid them. People who judge themselves unable to cope dwell on their vulnerabilities and perceive situations as fraught with danger. As a result, they experience a high level of cognitively generated distress, autonomic arousal, and inability to function. The central proposition of the self-efficacy theory of phobias is that people's judgments about their coping capabilities largely determine the behavioral, cognitive, emotional, and physiological responses that characterize phobia. These various responses are conceived primarily as correlated coeffects of low perceived self-efficacy.

In the self-efficacy view, treatments alleviate phobic disability and distress by instilling a sense of confidence that one can effectively cope with what one formerly feared and avoided. This theory emphasizes not the amount of exposure to stimuli, but rather the quality and amount of information people gain from their transactions with the environment about their ability to manage challenging activities. A sense of control and self-efficacy is important not only with respect to overt behavior, but also with respect to exercising control over one's thinking processes and emotional arousal (Bandura, 1988). The firm belief that one can act effectively, turn off any scary trains of thought that might arise, and moderate one's emotions, should foster confident, calm, assured performance.

Research on Self-Efficacy: Initial Findings

A number of different methodologies have been used in examining the relationship between self-efficacy and phobia. The most basic first step in validating a theory of phobia is showing that the postulated cause does indeed correlate strongly with the effect to be explained, i.e., phobic disability. For any given pattern of behavior, one can generally find many different factors that will correlate moderately with it; but high correlations, and strong causes, are much harder to come by. Therefore, this preliminary test of showing high correlation between postulated cause and behavioral effect, though only a minimal criterion of validity, is one that many theories fail. Before and after treatment, coping self-efficacy is measured by having people rate their confidence for doing increasingly challenging phobia-related tasks. Phobic disability is measured by having them try to actually do the tasks. This kind of behavioral test is a highly reliable, valid, and meaningful measure of phobic behavior (Williams, 1985).

The results of diverse studies with diverse phobic conditions show that regardless of whether treatment is vicarious, imaginal, or performance-based, a close correspondence exists between the level to which self-efficacy is raised and the level of actual functional capabilities instated (Bandura & Adams, 1977; Bandura et al., 1977; Bandura, Adams, Hardy, & Howells, 1980; Bandura, Reese, & Adams, 1982; Biran & Wilson, 1981; Bourque & Ladouceur, 1980; Emmelkamp & Felten, 1985; Ladouceur, 1983; Southworth & Kirsch, 1988; Williams, Dooseman, & Kleifield, 1984; Williams, Kinney, & Falbo, 1989; Williams & Rappoport, 1983; Williams, Turner, & Peer, 1985; Williams & Watson, 1985). The obtained correlations between self-efficacy and subsequent coping behavior are usually in the range of .60 to .90, i.e., self-efficacy generally accounts for one-third to three-fourths or more of the variance in behavior. This was an auspicious beginning for a theory of phobic behavior, but the causal potency of self-efficacy perceptions did not go unchallenged.

Some Objections to Self-Efficacy Theory

Over the years, many objections have been raised against the proposition that people's beliefs about their own coping abilities influence their coping behavior. These objections include whether self-efficacy is a cause or an effect of behavioral change, whether the correspondence between self-efficacy and behavior is a mere methodological artifact, and whether self-efficacy and behavior are both caused by a "third variable". I will concentrate on several such issues that the current series of studies addressed directly. Readers interested in a more wide ranging discussion can consult a series of commentaries on self-efficacy theory by diverse authors, and the responses to those commentaries by Bandura (1978b, 1982, 1984, 1986, 1991).

One cannot manipulate self-efficacy directly. Some criticisms have amounted to rejecting internal psychological causation of behavior altogether, namely, that because one cannot directly manipulate self-efficacy perceptions, the theory is untestable. Of course, this line of argument can be applied readily to any internal psychological factor, including every one of the responses said to indicate anxiety; these also generally cannot be directly manipulated as can, say, the light intensity in a room. Internal psychological variables often can only be manipulated in a probabilistic way. This is done by first deterministically manipulating an external cause (e.g., a treatment procedure), then observing the [probabilistic] effect on the proposed internal cause (e.g., anxiety or self-efficacy), then examining the correspondence between the status of the internal cause and the status of the criterion behavioral effect. This general strategy is somewhat more complex than that required to test external causes, but it is appropriate for evaluating "mental" causation, and leads few to reject the proposition that thoughts and feelings can cause behavior.

Clinical relevance. Another criticism, now outdated, is worth addressing because it still persists in the minds of some. This is that self-efficacy studies used subjects with animal phobias, but animal phobias are infrequently encountered in clinics, therefore the findings are irrelevant to clinical practice. A variation of this criticism is that self-efficacy research has been mostly "analog" research, i.e., the subjects were somehow not authentic phobics or the treatments were somehow not authentic therapies. The negative implications of ignoring research with animal phobic people, and of carelessly labeling research as "analogue", have been discussed at length in a thoughtful essay by Bandura (1978a). Here it is worth pointing out that the high correspondence between self-efficacy perceptions and coping performance is found not only in animal phobias, but in agoraphobia (Arnow, Taylor, Agras, & Telch, 1985; Bandura et al., 1980; Southworth & Kirsch, 1988; Telch, Agras, Taylor, Roth, & Gallen, 1985; Williams et al., 1984,

1989; Williams & Rappoport, 1983), and in specific non-animal phobias as well (Biran & Wilson, 1981; Bourque & Ladouceur, 1980; Emmelkamp & Felten, 1985; Williams et al., 1984, 1985; Williams & Watson, 1985).

Contrary to the "analogue" mislabeling, the self-efficacy research cited in this paper, whether with animal or other phobias, was conducted with phobic people drawn from the community at large (i.e, the subjects were not undergraduates from the subject pool). A "small animal phobia" involves a small object, but a very large problem in people's lives. Unlike much if not most phobia research, all of these self-efficacy research subjects were selected using stringent objective behavioral criteria of phobic disability and distress. And in every study, whether of animal or non-animal phobia, this genuine psychological problem was alleviated with genuine psychological therapies (Bandura, 1978a). Whether animal phobic behavior is governed by basic principles different from those governing other kinds of phobic behavior is an open empirical question rather than a presumptive basis for dismissing research findings. In any case, the nine studies that I will be primarily concerned with in this paper (Arnow et al., 1985, Telch et al., 1985, Williams, 1991; Williams et al., 1984, 1985, 1989; Williams & Rappoport, 1983; Williams & Watson, 1985; Williams & Zane, 1989), employed as subjects 168 severe agoraphobics and 69 severe height phobics, whose relevance to the "real world" of human psychological distress is difficult to dispute.

Subjects match their behavior to their efficacy judgment. Some commentators expressed concern that the superior predictive accuracy of self-efficacy judgments over indices of anxiety and previous behavior indicated only that subjects felt social pressure to match their performances on behavioral tests to their earlier efficacy judgments. This interpretation is invalidated by direct empirical evidence, and in any case is highly implausible in light of the methodology for studying the efficacy-behavior relationship, and the phenomenology of phobic subjects undergoing behavioral assessment procedures. The methodologies for studying self-efficacy are designed to minimize subject concern about the efficacy ratings per se. Subjects are asked to judge what they believe they are capable of doing, using a confidence scale with many intermediate values reflecting uncertainty; they are not asked to "predict" what they "will" do. Subjects complete the forms in relative or complete privacy, and in my own research the self-efficacy forms are embedded among many other rating forms, thereby reducing their salience considerably. The psychological context of behavioral tests with phobic subjects also renders highly implausible that subjects would be much preoccupied during behavioral tests with their prior self-efficacy ratings. People are asked to do as much as they can, and this is in fact what they feel motivated to do. They have come for treatment of what they see as a serious personal problem, and they have a strong personal interest in knowing for themselves what they can do. During the test they are coping with real phobic threats that they find personally significant and often quite stressful as well. To claim that subjects trying to cope with scary stressful tasks would be preoccupied with matching their behavior to some marks they made many minutes, hours, or even days ago on a piece of paper embedded among other pieces of paper, strains the limits of credulousness. To the contrary, phobic subjects are every bit as interested as the experimenter, if not much more so, in just what their disabilities and capabilities are. When their behavioral test performance surpasses their earlier efficacy judgment, far from being embarassed or disappointed, they are generally pleased and delighted, understandably so since it shows them to be less disabled than they had thought. In short, phobic subjects give no appearance of playing efficacy-behavior matching games.

This conclusion is supported by formal evidence as well. If subjects were motivated to match their behavior to their efficacy judgments, the efficacy-behavior data should show an asymmetry in which subjects would rarely do more than they judged, because once their behavior reached the level of the previous judgment, they would simply quit so as to produce an exact match. In fact, however, the distribution of discrepancies between self-efficacy and subsequent behavior in my own program of research, based on analyses of more than a thousand behavioral tests with subjects having diverse phobias, shows a bias toward behavior somewhat more often surpassing the previous efficacy judgment than falling short of it. This hardly suggests a strong motivation to produce efficacy-behavior matches; rather to the contrary. In experimentation on the point, studies have shown that the mere act of rating one's self-efficacy has no bearing on subsequent coping behavior, unless the experimenter deliberately introduces distorting factors (Bandura, 1982; Gauthier & Ladouceur, 1981; Telch, Bandura, Vinciguerra, Agras, & Stout, 1982).

Reflection, not cause, of behavioral change. One line of argument was that self-efficacy was simply a "reflection" of behavioral change, not a cause of it. In other words, behavioral change occurs first, then self-efficacy change occurs. It is certain that self-efficacy perceptions can change in response to previous performance successes and failures. But the conclusion that self-efficacy perceptions simply reflect past behavior, without influencing future behavior, can be rejected on several grounds. First, the strong relationship between self-efficacy and subsequent behavior holds true even following treatments with vicarious or imaginal methods that involve no actual coping with phobic activities or objects, and that therefore provide no behavioral basis for judging one's self-efficacy (Bandura & Adams, 1977; Bandura et al., 1977, 1980, 1982). For example, in vicarious treatments, severely snake phobic subjects who all view an identical therapeutic film nevertheless experience widely varying degrees of improvement in their ability to cope with snakes, typically ranging from almost no improvement, through intermediate levels of benefit, to virtual complete elimination of the phobia. The individual degrees of behavioral improvement are well predicted by changes in self-efficacy measured prior to subjects having any opportunity to enact phobia-related tasks (Bandura et al., 1977). The changes in overt behavior come after the changes in self-efficacy.

Second, even when the treatments consist of overt performance of phobic activities, posttreatment coping behavior tends to be more accurately predicted by self-efficacy perceptions than by the level of behavioral accomplishment achiev-ed during treatment (e.g., Bandura et al., 1977, 1980; Williams et al., 1984, 1989). This is because previous behavior does not perfectly determine self-efficacy judgments. People who have achieved a certain level of performance during treatment, and then are tested a subsequent day, will in some cases think they can do less than before, and in other cases that they can do more than before. When there are such discrepancies between past performance and current self-efficacy, it is self-efficacy that tends to be the more accurate predictor of subse-quent performance.

Third, when agoraphobics are given performance-based treatment for one of their phobias (e.g., driving), while another phobia (e.g., grocery shopping) is left untreated, generalized improvement occurring in the untreated phobia is accu-rately predicted by degree of improvement in self-efficacy for that phobia, despite subjects having no behavioral experience during treatment with tasks related to the untreated phobia. [Below I will review this generalization study in more detail.] These findings make clear that self-efficacy changes are much more than mere "reflections" of behavioral change.

Self-Efficacy Judgments and Anticipated Outcomes

Most cognitively oriented theories of learning and motivation have empha-sized anticipated outcomes of behavior, that is, the consequences the person expects would follow from a given course of action. Self-efficacy theory, in contrast, concerns one's perceived ability to execute and sustain a given course of action in the first place. This includes self-judgments about performing both overt actions and mental actions, such as maintaining or terminating a certain train of thought. The contrast between self-efficacy judgments and outcome expectations is thus clear and straightforward. With respect to bridge phobia, for example, my judgment that I can walk only half way across a certain bridge is a perception of self-efficacy; my belief that I would faint (or die, or experience panic) if I were to walk half way across that bridge is an anticipated outcome.

Some have proposed that perceptions of self-efficacy might reduce to or derive from anticipated outcomes. In this view, people refrain from coping and experience coping attempts as aversive because they anticipate harmful or painful outcomes, and it is the expectation of negative outcomes that underlies their per-ceptions that they cannot cope with the activity. Self-efficacy theory acknowl-edges that outcome expectations can affect behavior independently of self-efficacy perceptions (Bandura, 1977). Obviously, when other factors are equal, people are much more likely to do things they expect to be enjoyable and reward-ing than things they expect to be aversive and harmful. But judgments of self-efficacy are partly independent of anticipated outcomes and thus constitute a partly independent source of motivation. I can judge myself quite capable of doing something that I think would produce undesirable outcomes (e.g., park illegally in Manhattan); and I can judge myself quite unable to do something that

I think would produce desirable outcomes (e.g., compose lovely music). But efficacy judgments and outcome expectations are not entirely independent. Sometimes anticipated outcomes are inferred largely from how well one believes one can execute effective coping actions. When proficient actions produce desirable outcomes but inept actions produce undesirable outcomes, as is commonly the case, then people's beliefs about their ability to execute actions proficiently should affect the outcomes they expect to result from the attempts. Poor musical compositions will result in caustic reviews and scornful audiences, whereas good compositions will result in favorable reviews and appreciative audiences. Similarly, in the domain of social functioning, inept social approach likely will result in rejection and embarassment, whereas adept approach likely will result in welcoming acceptance. In these cases, the outcome one expects should be strongly influenced by how well one judges one can perform the action. Although the sense of self-efficacy is by no means all-determining of expected outcomes (and indeed, there are circumstances in which outcomes bear no relation to antecedent performances), under the many circumstances in which actions precede and influence outcomes, self-efficacy perceptions logically must precede and influence outcome expectations.

Perceived Danger

One kind of outcome expectation often held to underly phobia is the belief that phobia-related activities will produce physical or psychosocial harm (Beck, 1976; Beck, Emery, & Greenberg, 1985), an outcome expectation that might be called perceived danger. In Beck's (1976) analysis, phobia is always linked to a particular theme of danger; for example, height phobics fear falling, social phobics fear humiliation and rejection, agoraphobics fear loss of control and death, and so on. Beck (1976) argues further that although phobic people are, by definition, aware of the irrationality of their fears, "the phobic individual is usually better able to appraise realistically the actual danger of his feared situations from a distance" (Beck et al., 1985, p. 117). At a distance, a phobic man may rate the probability of harm as being at near zero, but "as he approaches the situation, the odds change. He goes to 10%, to 50%, and finally in the situation, he may believe 100% that harm will occur" (Beck, 1976, p. 176).

This proposition encounters some difficulty in explaining why much phobic avoidance takes place when the individual is far removed in time and space from feared settings. Social phobics decline invitations to parties from the safety of their living rooms, and bridge phobics plan and follow circuitous routes precisely to be certain that they never have to face a big bridge. Nevertheless, it remains an empirical question whether perceived danger contributes independently to phobic behavior. Although phobic people often do mention beliefs in danger, it is possibile that such danger perceptions, like feelings of anxiety, are diffuse and variable accompaniments of phobia with little direct bearing on the severity of phobic disability.

Anticipated Anxiety and Anticipated Panic

Another kind of anticipated consequence that has been emphasized in explaining phobic behavior, and especially agoraphobic behavior, is the expectation that engaging in phobia related activities will produce aversive feelings of distress or panic. Anticipated anxiety is the expectation that phobic activities will produce aversive feelings of fear and distress. A second kind of anticipated outcome, which is closely related to the first, is anticipated panic, the judged likelihood that a panic attack would occur were one to engage in phobia-related tasks. Note that this differs substantially from anticipated anxiety, because it is a prediction of the likelihood of panic, rather than level of anxiety.

Earlier I pointed out actual anxiety and panic do not have a strong influence on phobic behavior, but the argument here is that irrespective of actual anxiety or panic, the belief that coping behavior will produce intense fear is sufficient to inhibit coping attempts. Of course, even before considering the evidence, there is the question of the source of the anticipated fear, that is, why someone should expect to be fearful in the first place. This source is usually assumed to be a thought of danger.

Self-Efficacy Judgments and Expected Outcomes Compared

The ultimate test of competing causal hypotheses is to establish empirically which cause most accurately predicts the criterion behavioral effect. The studies I am concerned with here each measured phobic subjects' perceived self-efficacy for tasks within one or more areas of phobic dysfunction, and also measured at least one kind of anticipated negative consequences for the same tasks. Then subjects completed behavioral tests of their ability to do the tasks. These assessment procedures were repeated after treatment and again at follow-up. The object was to see which type of thought would emerge as the most accurate predictor of phobic behavior.

Self-efficacy perceptions were measured in all studies using the method described above (p. 153). Perceived danger was measured in four studies using Beck's (1976) procedure of having subjects indicate the likelihood of a harmful consequence occurring were they to perform each task. In two studies with height phobics, subjects were asked to rate the likelihood that they would fall were they to ascend to a balcony at each level of a tall building and look down. In two studies in which agoraphobic subjects were behaviorally tested for a variety of phobic areas, subjects were first asked to specify a harmful event that they thought could occur if they were to do the target test activity. They then rated its likelihood for each task of the behavioral test. If they thought no harmful event could occur, perceived danger was scored as zero. Anticipated anxiety was measured in seven studies, having subjects indicate how anxious they thought they would become if they were to perform each task of the behavioral test. Anticipated panic was measured in two studies, as the likelihood of having a panic attack during the tasks.

The result across all studies showed that self-efficacy was consistently a highly accurate predictor of posttest approach behavior (*r* averaging about .80), anticipated anxiety and anticipated panic were also consistently quite accurate behavioral predictors (*r* for both averaging about -.70), whereas perceived danger was an inconsistent and on the average relatively poor predictor of behavior (*r* averaging about -.25). To determine the capacity of each of the anticipated outcome measures to predict coping behavior independently of self-efficacy, and of self-efficacy to predict coping behavior independently of each kind of anticipated outcome, partial correlation analyses were performed. First I will present the results for all the studies except for the Williams et al. (1989) study of generalization because that study is present separately in detail later in this paper.

Perceived Danger Compared with Self-Efficacy

The results for perceived danger are presented in Table 1. Self-efficacy consistently remained a very strong predictor of behavior when perceived danger was held constant, whereas perceived danger consistently lost its capacity to predict behavior when self-efficacy was held constant. The modest relationship between thoughts of danger and phobic behavior appears to derive from phobic people's awareness of the irrationality of their phobias. They often really believe that the activity is not dangerous. It is not at all unusual for clients, whether severe agoraphobics or height phobics, even when in the phobic situation and experiencing a high level of fear, to resolutely deny harboring any belief in danger. Often they will admit it seems foolish to be terrified about nothing that they can identify, but they will insist that they know they will not die, go crazy, and so on. Moreover, recent analyses of think-aloud protocols of driving phobic agoraphobics, gathered as they were actually driving alone on scary routes, revealed essentially no occurrence of danger-related ideation (Williams, 1990). It appears that thoughts of danger, like feelings of anxiety, are only diffuse and variable accompaniments of phobia, with little influence on phobic behavior.

Anticipated Anxiety/Panic Compared With Self-Efficacy

The analyses of anticipated anxiety with partial correlations are presented in Table 2. The first column shows that across the studies and assessment phases, self-efficacy tended to remain strongly correlated with approach behavior when anticipated anxiety was held constant, whereas anticipated anxiety tended to lose its capacity to predict behavior when self-efficacy was held constant.

Finally, anticipated panic was measured in the study by Williams (1991), as well as in the generalization study described later. The pattern of results closely resembles that for anticipated anxiety. In the Williams (1991) data, 37 phobic areas were measured in a series of 26 subjects who recently completed research procedures in the Lehigh Phobia Program. The results showed that when the perceived likelihood of panicking was held constant, self-efficacy still strongly predicted approach behavior at pretreatment, *r* = .64, posttreatment *r* = .81, and follow-up $r = .86$; all $ps < .001$. In contrast, with self-efficacy held constant, anticipated panic did not significantly predict behavior at any of the three phases, $rs = .07, -.05$, and $.07$, respectively, all nonsignificant.

Table 1

Partial Correlations Between Self-Efficacy and Behavior (Perceived Danger Held Constant) and Between Perceived Danger and Behavior (Self-Efficacy Held Constant), by Study and Assessment Phase

Study/ Test Phase	n^a	Self-Efficacy Predict Behavior (perceived danger held constant)	Perceived Danger Predict Behavior (self-efficacy held constant)
Williams & Watson, 1985			
Pretreatment	15	.62**	.19
Posttreatment	15	.75***	-.38
Williams et al., 1985			
Pretreatment	38	.45**	-.05
Posttreatment	38	.91***	.34^b
Follow-up	38	.90***	-.10
Williams, 1991			
Pretreatment	37	.35*	-.20
Posttreatment	37	.82***	-.08
Follow-up	26	.84***	-.02

Note. ^{a} The *ns* in this study refer to the number of phobias rather than the number of subjects (26), because multiple phobias were evaluated within some subjects, and the analyses' logic requires correlating at the level of phobias.
^{b} Significant in the direction contrary to expectation, $p < .05$.
$* p < .05.$ $** p < .01.$ $*** p < .001.$

These data certainly support the view that perceptions of self-efficacy are primary, and that self-efficacy theory cannot be dismissed by simply assuming the primacy of some other kind of cognitive process. The results from the generalization research, described next, further support the conclusion that perceptions of self-efficacy play a central role in phobic disability.

Generalization of Therapeutic Change

Because agoraphobia refers to multiple phobias of a variety of activities away from home, such as shopping, driving, walking, elevators, heights, restaurants, bridges, and many others (Williams, 1985), a vitally important question is whether performance treatments produce changes that generalize beyond the situations and activities specifically treated. It is clear that changes generalize fairly well within a given area of functioning, e.g., from a particular supermarket to other supermarkets (Bandura et al., 1980; Williams & Rappoport, 1983), but little previous research had examined generalization across different domains of functioning, for example, from shopping to driving. Paper-and-pencil ratings sometimes showed substantial generalized benefit to untreated phobias, but these data must be regarded with scepticism because brief global self-rating measures possess only modest validity, and they can sometimes markedly overestimate the degree of actual behavioral improvement (Kinney & Williams, 1988; Williams, 1985; Williams & Rappoport, 1983).

Table 2

Partial Correlations Between Self-Efficacy and Behavior (Anticipated Anxiety Held Constant) and Between Anticipated Anxiety and Behavior (Self-Efficacy Held Constant), by Study and Testing Phase

Study/ Test Phase	n^a	Self-Efficacy Predict Behavior (anticipated anxiety held constant)	Anticipated Anxiety Predict Behavior (self-efficacy held constant)
Williams & Rappoport, 1983			
Pretreatment 1	20	.40*	-.12
Pretreatment 2	20	.59**	-.28
Posttreatment	20	.45*	.13
Follow-up	18	.45*	.06
Williams et al., 1984			
Pretreatment	32	.22	-.36*
Posttreatment	32	.59**	-.21
Williams et al., 1985			
Pretreatment	38	.25	-.36*
Posttreatment	38	.72***	.05
Follow-up	38	.66***	-.12
Arnow et al., 1985			
Pretreatment	24	.77***	.17
Posttreatment	24	.43*	-.08
Follow-up	22	.88***	-.06
Telch et al., 1985			
Pretreatment	29	-.28	-.56***
Posttreatment	29	.48**	.15
Follow-up	25	.42*	-.05
Williams, 1991			
Pretreatment	37	.35*	-.20
Posttreatment	37	.82***	-.08
Follow-up	26	.84***	-.02

Note. [a] The *n*s in this study refer to the number of phobias rather than the number of subjects (26), because multiple phobias were evaluated within some subjects, and the analyses' logic requires correlating at the level of phobias.
* $p < .05$. ** $p < .01$. *** $p < .001$.

The limited evidence based on measures of actual behavior had been less encouraging. One early report by Crowe and colleagues (Crowe, Marks, Agras, & Leitenberg, 1972; see also Meyer & Gelder, 1963) found essentially no generalized benefit from treated to untreated phobias, but in that study a relatively weak treatment was used so there was not much change from which to generalize. In a preliminary study, Erin Kleifield and I found only a slight degree of generalized change to untreated phobias in four agoraphobic subjects (Williams & Kleifield, 1985). These findings indicate that generalization is by no means automatic, yet at the same time they are discrepant with clients' reports, and self-ratings, that they experience generalized benefit.

We therefore mounted a study to get a fuller picture of the extent and pattern of generalization, by studying many more subjects and a wider range of typical agoraphobic activities. Our strategy was to select subjects who showed marked behavioral disability in several phobic areas, then give them performance-based treatment for only some of the phobias, then measure their disability for all the phobias again. A control group provided data on change in the phobias without any intervening treatment. To study generalization within phobias, we conducted the behavioral tests in settings different from those used for treatment, then compared the performance subjects achieved during treatment to their performance on the posttest. To study generalization across phobias, we compared the changes in (a) the treated phobias, (b) the untreated "transfer" phobias, and (c) a control group of phobias in subjects given no treatment for any of their phobias.

The study also addressed the psychological mechanisms of generalization. In most traditional learning theories, generalization is analyzed largely in terms of stimulus similarity, with transfer thought to occur in direct proportion to the number of stimulus features shared by the learning situation and the transfer situation. This approach is problematic for several reasons, a major one of which is the difficulty in quantifying the amount of stimulus overlap between distinct complex situations. A grocery store and a busy downtown street contain a virtual infinitude of potentially relevant (and irrelevant) stimulus features, and the features that define relevance appear to be idiosyncratic for each agoraphobic person (Williams, 1985). Even if it were possible to quantify the degree of stimulus overlap, there would remain the equally vexing problem of quantifying the amount the person was "exposed" to the shared stimuli; as mentioned earlier, definitions of exposure that have been offered are either circular, or yield empirical data that stimulus exposure has little bearing on therapeutic benefit. Given these seemingly insurmountable problems, it is not surprising that stimulus-oriented approaches have not led to a theory of generalized change in phobia. A successful theory of generalization effects will have to consider not just factors external to the person, but psychological factors within the person.

A much more promising approach to generalization is offered by cognitive theories of phobia, which hold that transfer of behavior change is determined by change in people's cognitive appraisal of the transfer situations and activities. Thus, for example, Beck's (1976) theory would predict transfer according to changes in people's perceptions of danger, whereas self-efficacy theory would predict generalization by the extent to which people acquire confidence for coping with the transfer activities.

To put these various theories to the test, the research measured not only agoraphobic behavior in several areas of disability for each person, but also subjects' self-efficacy, perceived danger, anticipated anxiety, and anticipated panic for each phobia. Our goal was to evaluate which of the various mediators has the strongest bearing on behavioral outcome in the treated phobias and the transfer phobias. The design of the study provided a novel opportunity for testing whether the various proposed internal mediators are independent causes of behavior, not just direct reflections of previous behavior. In the research described earlier, subjects were giving their cognitive appraisals of posttreatment activities similar to activities they had directly performed during treatment. A still more stringent test of cognitive mediators is their capacity to predict generalized changes in phobic areas given no treatment whatsoever, as this would eliminate direct experience with the activities as a basis for having altered one's thoughts and actions.

The subjects were 27 agoraphobics who showed severe behavioral disablity in at least 2 of 9 areas of functioning tested in the study. The nine areas included driving, walking along a busy street, heights, grocery shopping, walking through a shopping mall, bridges, restaurants, elevators, and enclosed places. Only the areas in which they showed severe disability were selected as target phobias, and the number of target phobias per subject ranged from 2 to 7. After pretesting, subjects were given performance treatment for one or two of their phobias selected at random, while their other phobias were left untreated. Then subjects completed a midtreatment assessment procedure for all their target phobic areas. The midtest is the final stage of the experiment with which I am concerned at this point. (The remaining procedure for each subject included a second treatment phase then a posttreatment assessment phase, and later a follow-up evaluation. I will present the posttest and follow-up data in correlational analyses, below). A few subjects were randomly assigned to a control condition in which they initially completed the measures on two occasions without any intervening treatment. We only had a few control subjects because severe agoraphobic disability typically changes little or not at all over a several-week period without treatment, so more control data were not needed. In all, there were 37 treated phobias, 63 transfer phobias, and 12 control phobias.

The mean changes in behavioral performance among the three groups of phobias from pretreatment to midtreatment are presented in Figure 1. This Figure reveals clearly that the treated phobias improved more than the transfer phobias, and that the transfer phobias improved more than the control phobias. The differences between the three groups of phobias were all statistically significant, not only for behavior, but also for the various measures of cognition (self-efficacy and anticipated outcomes), which changed in parallel with behavior. It is important to note here that all subjects were strictly prohibited from practicing coping with phobic activities on their own in between the pretest and the posttest, and we had subjects keep detailed diary records that confirmed that they did not try to tackle the transfer phobias on their own. So the improvement in the transfer phobias was not the result of any extraexperimental self-treatment. Thus this is a clear demonstration that performance-based treatment produces generalized behavioral change across distinct areas of agoraphobic disability that have not been treated directly.

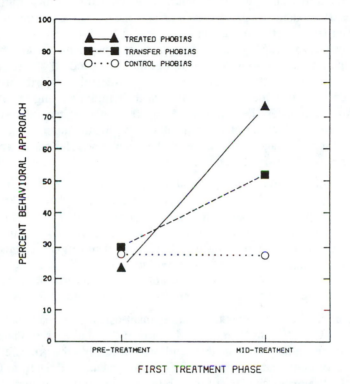

Figure 1 Mean changes in approach behavior during the first treatment phase among the treated, transfer, and control phobias (from Williams, Kinney, & Falbo, 1989).

At the same time, however, the findings also clearly show that untreated phobias do not change nearly as much as treated phobias. Not only in behavior, but in all four cognitive variables the treated phobias improved significantly more than the transfer phobias. The partial independence and situational specificity of agoraphobic phobias are even more evident when the data for individual subjects are considered separately. So far I have discussed average changes in treated and transfer phobias. Although such average effects are clearly important, they conceal a rather striking degree of variability in generalization effects between subjects and, perhaps even more interesting, within subjects. That is, in a single individual, large change in a treated phobia can be simultaneously accompanied by both large and small changes in transfer phobias. Of the 18 subjects with two or more transfer phobias, 9 showed a discrepancy in improvement between pairs of transfer phobias of more then 40 percentage points on the 100-point behavioral performance scale. Also striking was that seemingly similar pairs of phobias, e.g., bridges and heights, or enclosed places and elevators, often showed quite different degrees of change in a given subject.

In addition to transfer across phobias, we examined transfer within the treated phobias, from subjects' performance level achieved in the treatment setting to their performance in the similar posttest setting. Prior to treatment, subjects started only able to do 25% of the approach tasks. They achieved a mean level of 87% task performance during treatment, but then achieved 70% performance on the matched posttest. Subjects transfered to the posttest the majority of what they had gained during treatment (compared with their initial starting level of 25%), but the loss of transfer (i.e., from 87% to 70%), was statistically significant. Given the careful matching of assessment sites to treatment sites, the degree of transfer loss serves as another reminder that agoraphobic fears can be sensitive to even apparently subtle situational differences.

These findings suggest strongly that despite the unitary label, "agoraphobia" is not entirely a unitary condition, and that the various phobias that together constitute agoraphobia are partly independent of one another. The findings also show that treatment and transfer effects are governed partly by situation-specific factors in people and not only by broad response dispositions; in other words, that it is not a simply a matter of an individual being a "good generalizer" or a "poor treatment responder." The variable and idiosyncratic changes also seriously challenge the predictive power of theories of therapeutic mechanisms.

As mentioned earlier, after the midtreatment assessment, each subject completed a second treatment phase in which some of the phobic areas that remained disabling at the midtest were treated, and the others served as transfer phobias. Then subjects completed a posttreatment assessment, and later a follow-up assessment. The major challenge for each proposed cognitive mediator is to provide the best prediction of behavioral outcome in the transfer phobias at the midtest and posttest. It is also of interest to look at the results for the treated phobias, and for all the phobias at the pretest and follow-up. Self-efficacy was compared not only to other cognitive factors, but also to previous behavior in predicting subsequent behavior. In the case of the treated phobias, the behavioral level subjects achieved during treatment served as the index of previous behavior. For the transfer phobias (and for all phobias at follow-up), previous behavior was subjects' performance on the most recent behavioral test.

The correlational analyses examined the capacity of self-efficacy to predict behavior with the alternate factors (outcome expectations and previous behavior) held constant, and the capacity of the alternate factors to predict behavior with self-efficacy held constant. These analyses are presented in Table 3.

Table 3

Partial Correlations Between Self-Efficacy and Behavior (Alternate Factors Held Constant) and Between Alternate Factors and Behavior (Self-Efficacy Held Constant), in Generalization Study by Williams et al., 1989

Self-Efficacy Predict Behavior (alternate factor held constant)

Alternate Factor	Treated Phobias			Transfer Phobias		
	Pre	Mid	Post	Mid	Post	Follow-Up
Perceived danger	.71***	.79***	.56***	.75***	.75***	.87***
Anticipated anxiety	.45***	.65***	.47**	.53***	.36	.71***
Anticipated panic	.71***	.63***	.41*	.51***	.41*	.75***
Previous behavior	—	.67***	.40*	.59***	.58**	.74***
df	99	35	25	61	16	78

Alternate Factor Predict Behavior (self-efficacy factor held constant)

Alternate Factor	Treated Phobias			Transfer Phobias		
	Pre	Mid	Post	Mid	Post	Follow-Up
Perceived danger	.02	-.21	-.20	.09	.11	-.02
Anticipated anxiety	-.13	-.15	.02	-.15	-.16	-.03
Anticipated panic	-.10	-.17	-.04	-.20*	-.40*	.05
Previous behavior	—	.49***	.33*	.19	.39	.54***
df	99	35	25	61	16	78

Note. All tests are one-tailed. Pre = Pretreatment assessment; Mid = Midtreatment assessment; Post = Posttreatment assessment. The *df* are based on the number of phobias rather than the number of subjects (26), because multiple phobias were evaluated within some subjects, and the analyses' logic requires correlating at the level of phobias. There are many fewer phobias at posttreatment than midtreatment because the analysis at posttreatment considers only those phobias that remained severe at the midtreatment assessment phase.
* *p* < .05. ** *p* < .01. *** *p* < .001.

These results are entirely consistent with the findings reported earlier. Self-efficacy remained significantly predictive of behavioral outcome at all phases, and for both the treated and the transfer phobias, with outcome expectations and prior behavior held constant. In contrast, the alternate factors lose most or all of their predictive capacity with self-efficacy held constant. The findings show that performance-based treatments for agoraphobia lead to generalized behavioral changes both within phobias (from one setting to another) and between distinct phobias. The beneficial generalized changes are not limited to overt behavior but also include various patterns of thought and feeling.

Generalization proved to be highly variable within and between individual subjects, and on the average, untreated phobias changed less than treated phobias. The transfer of therapeutic gain appears to be limited by discriminatory processes that lead people to discount the relevance of their prior successes to future performances. The loss of transfer from treatment to matched assessment settings implies that such discriminations can occur even toward circumstances only slightly different from those present during treatment.

The findings lend support to the proposition that perceptions of self-efficacy are the primary mediators of generalized behavioral changes. Self-efficacy was the dominant predictor of therapeutic changes whether the changes were produced directly or indirectly by treatment for other phobias. This finding adds to the sizable body of findings from studies of diverse phobias and treatment methods, that perceptions of self-efficacy are independent causes of coping behavior rather than mere by-products of other processes. It seems clear that when people successfully cope with a phobic activity, the breadth of their enhanced functioning is directly a function of the breadth of their gains in self-efficacy.

TREATMENT BASED ON SELF-EFFICACY THEORY: GUIDED MASTERY

Guided Mastery Conception

Theories of psychological problems must be judged in part by their capacity to generate effective means of helping people overcome them. As mentioned in the introductory comments, most accounts of phobia treatment heavily emphasize the concept of "exposure" to phobic stimuli. The exposure principle not only has serious conceptual failings, but fails to give therapists much guidance as to the best specific procedures to follow, because a wide variety of methods embody some kind of commerce with phobic stimuli. This leaves considerable room for uncertainty, and failure, as therapists must arbitrarily select, or improvise their own, techniques for therapeutically "exposing" clients.

Self-efficacy theory does not leave such wide latitude for procedural uncertainty (Williams, 1990). In self-efficacy theory, treatments alleviate phobia by conveying information that increases people's perceptions that they can cope effectively. The emphasis is not upon the amount of exposure to stimuli or the extinction of anxiety, but rather on the quality and amount of information people gain about what they can manage and the sense of mastery they thereby develop. Because firsthand experiences of performance success provide the most reliable evidence that one can function effectively, self-efficacy theory prescribes performance-based mastery experiences as the most potent means of raising and strengthening perceptions of self-efficacy. In this conception, during treatment people are not passively absorbing stimuli but actively trying to master a difficult challenge. This cognitively and behaviorally active role also applies, or should apply, to therapists.

In most treatment based on the exposure principle, the therapist's role is largely limited to encouraging people to expose themselves to phobic situations for prolonged periods until fear extinguishes itself. For example, when a height phobic is frozen in terror three steps from a balcony railing, the exposure view would say that he is at "maximum exposure," and should remain there until fear declines. One prominent exposure theorist recommended that a shopping phobic woman who experiences panic in a grocery store should simply sit down and do knitting until the anxiety declines, whereupon she should resume her shopping. Evidently the exposure perspective regards the quality of the person's performance as irrelevant as long as intimidating stimuli are nearby.

Self-efficacy theory would take an entirely different view of these circumstances. The goal is not maximum exposure, but maximum enhancement of self-efficacy. The most potent source of information for increasing self-efficacy is performance accomplishments. Therefore, clients should be assisted to continue striving for coping effectiveness, which means the therapist must foster rapid achievements that build a sense of mastery. Of course, it is one thing to urge people to succeed, but a very different thing to actually enable them to do so. In efficacy-based therapy, also called "guided mastery" treatment (Williams, 1990), when people are having difficulty making progress, the therapist assumes a highly active role in giving direct performance-related assistance designed to enhance their confidence and ability to manage new tasks. The guided mastery therapist also gives people specific guidance in how to perform activities proficiently so as to gain a robust sense of confidence. Once the person's progress and proficient performance are restored, the therapist withdraws the assistance, and arranges for people to have varied and independent success experiences so that their sense of mastery will be robust.

In the self-efficacy view, the shopping phobic woman should be guided to continue to engage in shopping tasks, if necessary with the direct assistance of the therapist, so as to gain a sense of efficacy for functioning effectively, whether anxious or not. The height phobic man frozen in terror on a balcony should be given immediate assistance so that he can continue to advance. For example, he might well gain renewed confidence if the therapist offers an arm for support, or suggests a more manageable route of approaching the railing. In the exposure view, however, such assistance could very easily be construed as reducing exposure because it might reduce anxiety and the threat value of the stimuli.

Therefore, it is not surprising that in writings on the theory and practice of exposure treatment, direct therapist assistance is almost entirely neglected. For example, in most studies of exposure treatment with agoraphobics the therapists do not even accompany the people to community treatment settings beyond the first one or two sessions, if at all. Usually they prefer instead to dispatch clients from the office to go out and cope with phobic situations on their own, in other words, to go treat themselves. Such "treatment by remote control" is consistent with the exposure principle, but it is not compatible with self-efficacy theory and, as we will see, it is not especially good treatment. Whereas the exposure principle emphasizes confronting scary stimuli for prolonged durations of time, self-efficacy theory emphasizes rapidly gaining a sense of mastery. In this conception, time is incidental, and feelings of fear, although sometimes present during treatment, are not fundamentally necessary for therapeutic change to occur. What is necessary, is that the client gain a sense of self-efficacy and mastery.

Self-efficacy theory also specifies what kinds of assistance are not likely to be very beneficial. Because physiological and verbal/persuasive modes of therapy have only a limited effect on self-efficacy perceptions, the guided mastery therapist does not rely heavily on relaxation, biofeedback, or verbal reasoning and persuasion to bring about change. Although non-performance therapies might be developed that would help facilitate change, self-efficacy theory emphasizes performance mastery as the foundation of phobia treatments.

Guided Mastery and Exposure Effectiveness Compared

The question is whether performance treatment based on self-efficacy theory is more effective than performance treatment based on the exposure principle. To investigate this question, my colleagues and I conducted three experiments that compared "guided mastery" treatment to standard exposure treatments.

The first study (Williams et al., 1984) compared guided mastery to a "flooding" exposure treatment. Subjects were 32 driving and height phobics (about half of whom were agoraphobic) selected using stringent criteria of phobic disability and unresponsiveness to treatment. They were randomly assigned to three hours of individual guided mastery treatment, three hours of individual flooding exposure treatment, or no treatment. In flooding exposure, the therapist accompanied subjects to the treatment setting and strongly urged them to ascend to progressively higher balconies or to tackle progressively more difficult driving routes, and to quickly confront the worst despite anxiety. In guided mastery treatment, the therapist also accompanied subjects and encouraged rapid progress, but in addition the therapist took a highly active role in giving direct efficacy-based assistance and guidance when subjects were having trouble progressing. The therapeutic changes in approach behavior and self-efficacy are shown in Figure 2.

Guided mastery treatment was significantly and substantially more effective than exposure in terms of increased behavioral capabilities, enhanced self-efficacy (both shown in Figure 2), and decreased fear arousal. Both treatments were significantly more effective than the control condition. I should add that this was yet another study in which performance on the posttest was more accurately predicted by posttest self-efficacy than by performance during treatment.

The second study (Williams et al., 1985) compared guided mastery treatment to performance desensitization, an exposure variant that seeks to help clients

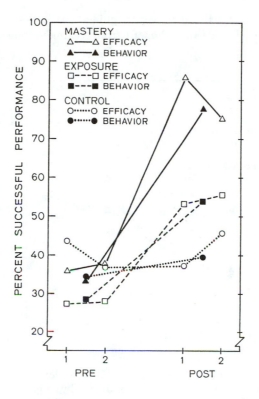

Figure 2 Mean percent of tasks performed and mean level of self-efficacy reported before and after treatment, by subjects in the guided mastery, stimulus exposure, and control conditions. Note that self-efficacy was measured both before and after the behavioral test at each assessment phase (from Williams, Dooseman, & Kleifield, 1984).

remain at low levels of anxiety during exposure, and it is generally regarded as being about as effective as flooding. Subjects were 38 severe height phobics. The desensitization therapist accompanied subjects to provide support, and he encouraged them to progress as rapidly as possible while remaining calm and relatively free of anxiety. All subjects rated their anxiety periodically during treatment, and desensitization subjects were encouraged to advance only when their anxiety was at a level of 2 or below on a 10-point scale. Treatment in both conditions was given for a maximum of three hours or until the subject performed all therapeutic tasks. Measures were gathered at pretreatment, posttreatment, and at a one-month follow-up. The results are shown in Figure 3.

Again, guided mastery was significantly and substantially more effective than desensitization exposure, and the therapeutic differences remained clearly in evidence at the follow-up. It is also worth noting that in this study, guided mastery subjects received significantly shorter durations of exposure than desensitization subjects because guided mastery subjects made more rapid progress to maximal performance. In other words, guided mastery subjects received less exposure time, but derived more benefit from treatment than did desensitization subjects.

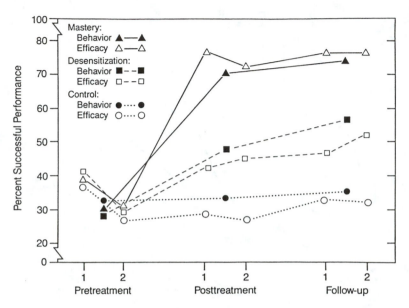

Figure 3 Mean percent of tasks performed and mean level of self-efficacy reported before and after treatment and at follow-up, by subjects in the guided mastery, performance desensitization, and control conditions. Note that self-efficacy was measured both before and after the behavioral test at each assessment phase (from Williams, Turner, & Peer, 1985).

The most recent study compared guided mastery and flooding exposure therapy for 26 agoraphobics who became highly anxious during pretreatment behavioral tests but were able to perform most or all tasks of the test (Williams & Zane, 1989). Such subjects challenge the capacity of therapeutic techniques to reduce feelings of fear. In the self-efficacy analysis, a major factor sustaining fearful performance is that clients engage in a variety of defensive rituals and self-protective maneuvers while doing scary tasks. Defensive maneuvers and self-restrictions on how one performs the task take a multitude of forms. One example is the freeway phobic who drives the freeway staying in the slow lane only, holding the steering wheel by leaning forward with "white knuckles" and wide eyes, and who has the radio blaring loudly at all times. These defensive maneuvers undermine self-efficacy in two ways: First, they vividly remind the person of her own driving ineptitude, and second, they lead her to attribute any success in freeway driving to the defensive maneuvers rather than to her own driving capabilities. Therefore, in people who are performing at a high level, but with anxiety, the mastery therapist helps them identify defensive maneuvers and gives guidance in eliminating the devices.

Subjects were randomly assigned to guided mastery treatment, exposure treatment, or to a no-treatment control condition. Both methods embodied one hour of treatment for each area of phobia treated in each subject. Guided mastery treatment emphasized the quality of performance and how subjects could perform tasks with fewer defensive maneuvers and self-protective activities, as well as performing the tasks in a varied manner. Exposure treatment emphasized remaining in the presence of the phobic stimuli.

The results for the focal dependent variable, level of anxiety reached during the behavioral tests are shown in Figure 4. Guided mastery treatment clearly produced a much more striking reduction in anxiety than did exposure treatment, and the difference between treatments was statistically significant. The advantage of guided mastery over exposure significantly increased over the follow-up period. Mastery subjects continued to show significant gains, whereas exposure subjects remained unchanged over the follow-up period.

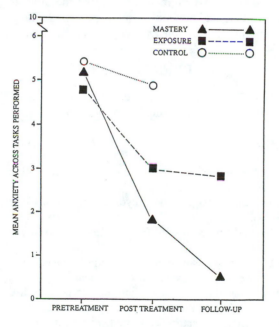

Figure 4 Mean anxiety (averaged across the tasks of the behavioral test) reported before and after treatment and at follow-up, by subjects in the guided mastery, stimulus exposure, and control conditions.

Taken together, these studies suggest that when the focus shifts from stimulus exposure and anxiety extinction to promoting rapid proficient performance accomplishments that build a strong sense of self-efficacy, the therapist can go beyond merely urging commerce with threats, to aiding people in effectively mastering them.

CONCLUSIONS

Self-efficacy theory has demonstrated power to account for behavioral change brought about by diverse treatments for diverse phobias. Perceptions of self-efficacy appear to be causal determinants of behavior in their own right. Their accuracy in predicting behavior is not a mere methodological artefact, and efficacy perceptions cannot easily be explained in terms of other factors. Especially important is that the theory appears capable of helping promote more effective means of reducing phobic disability and distress.

Most previous efforts to generate more effective treatments have reflected a predominantly piecemeal process of trial-and-error learning in which failures typically far outnumbered successes. Self-efficacy theory provides a welcome change from this kind of haphazard and low-yield approach. Of course, much work remains to be done. It is necessary to explore in greater depth the sources of self-efficacy and self-doubt, which means exploring the outer influences, as well as inner mechanisms, that lead to people's self-appraisals. The evidence reviewed here suggests that it will be profitable to accept this challenge.

REFERENCES

Arnow, B. A., Taylor, C. B., Agras, W. S., & Telch, M. J. (1985). Enhancing agoraphobia treatment outcome by changing couple communication patterns. *Behavior Therapy, 16*, 452-467.

Bandura, A. (1969). *Principles of behavior modification.* New York: Holt, Rinehart, & Winston.

Bandura, A. (1977). Self-efficacy: Toward a unifying theory of behavioral change. *Psychological Review, 84*, 191-215.

Bandura, A. (1978a). On paradigms and recycled ideologies. *Cognitive Therapy and Research, 2*, 79-103.

Bandura, A. (1978b). Reflections on self-efficacy. *Advances in Behaviour Research and Therapy, 1*, 237-269.

Bandura, A. (1982). The assessment and predictive generality of self-percepts of efficacy. *Journal of Behavior Therapy and Experimental Psychiatry, 13*, 195-199.

Bandura, A. (1984). Recycling misconceptions of perceived self-efficacy. *Cognitive Therapy and Research, 8*, 231-255.

Bandura, A. (1986). The explanatory and predictive scope of self-efficacy theory. *Journal of Clinical and Social Psychology, 4*, 359-373.

Bandura, A. (1988). Self-efficacy conception of anxiety. *Anxiety Research, 1*, 77-98.

Bandura, A. (1991). Human agency: The rhetoric and the reality. *American Psychologist, 46*, 157-162.

Bandura, A., & Adams, N. E. (1977). Analysis of self-efficacy theory of behavioral change. *Cognitive Therapy and Research, 1*, 287-308.

Bandura, A., Adams, N. E., & Beyer, J. (1977). Cognitive processes mediating behavior change. *Journal of Personality and Social Psychology, 35*, 125-139.

Bandura, A., Adams, N. E., Hardy, A., & Howells, G. (1980). Tests of the generality of self-efficacy theory. *Cognitive Therapy and Research, 4*, 39-66.

Bandura, A., Reese, L., & Adams, N. E. (1982). Microanalysis of action and fear arousal as a function of differential levels of perceived self-efficacy. *Journal of Personality and Social Psychology, 43*, 5-21.

Barlow D. H. (1988). *Anxiety and its disorders*. New York: Guilford.

Beck, A. T. (1976). *Cognitive therapy and the emotional disorders*. NY: International Universities Press.

Beck, A. T., Emery, G., & Greenberg, R. L. (1985). *Anxiety disorders and phobias: A cognitive perspective*. NY: Basic Books.

Biran, M., & Wilson, G. T. (1981). Treatment of phobic disorders using cognitive and exposure methods: A self-efficacy analysis. *Journal of Consulting and Clinical Psychology, 49*, 886-899.

Bourque P., & Ladouceur R. (1980). An investigation of various performance-based treatments with agoraphobics. *Behaviour Research and Therapy, 18*, 161-170.

Craske, M. G., Rapee, R. M., & Barlow, D. H. (1988). The significance of panic-expectancy for individual patterns of avoidance. *Behavior Therapy, 19*, 577-592.

Crowe, M., Marks, I., Agras, W., & Leitenberg, H. (1972). Time-limited desensitization, implosion, and shaping for phobic patients: A crossover study. *Behavior Research and Therapy, 10*, 319-328.

Emmelkamp, P. M. G., & Felten, M. (1985). The process of exposure in vivo: Cognitive and physiological changes during treatment of acrophobia. *Behaviour Research and Therapy, 23*, 219-223.

Gauthier, J., & Ladouceur, R. (1981). The influence of self-efficacy reports on performance. *Behavior Therapy, 12*, 436-439.

Gelder, M. (1977). Behavioral treatment of agoraphobia. Some factors which restrict change after treatment. In J. C. Boulougouris & A. D. Rabavilas (Eds.), *The treatment of phobia and obsessive compulsive disorders* (pp. 7-12). NY: Pergamon.

Kinney, P. J., & Williams, S. L. (1988). Accuracy of fear inventories and self-efficacy scales in estimating agoraphobic behavior. *Behaviour Research and Therapy, 26*, 513-518.

Ladouceur, R. (1983). Participant modeling with or without cognitive treatment of phobias. *Journal of Consulting and Clinical Psychology, 51*, 942-944.

Lang, P. J. (1971). The application of psychophysiological methods to the study of psychotherapy and behavior modification. In A. E. Bergin & S. L. Garfield (Eds.), *Handbook of psychotherapy and behavior change* (pp. 75-125). New York: Wiley.

Leitenberg, H. (1976). Behavioral approaches to the treatment of neuroses. In H. Leitenberg (Ed.), *Handbook of behavior modification and behavior therapy* (pp. 124-167). Englewood Cliffs, NJ: Prentice-Hall.

Mathews, A. M., Gelder, M. G., & Johnston, D. W. (1981). *Agoraphobia: Nature and treatment*. New York: Guilford.

Meyer, V., & Gelder, M. G. (1963). Behaviour therapy and phobic disorders. *British Journal of Psychiatry, 109*, 19-28.

Mowrer, O. H. (1960). *Learning theory and behavior*. New York: Wiley.

Rachman, S. (1976). The passing of the two-stage theory of fear and avoidance: Fresh possibilities. *Behaviour Research and Therapy, 14*, 125-131.

Rosenthal, T. L., & Bandura, A. (1978). Psychological modeling: Theory and practice. In S. L. Garfield & A. E. Bergin (Eds.), *Handbook of psychotherapy and behavior change* (pp. 621-658). New York: Wiley.

Seligman, M. E. P., & Johnston, J. C. (1973). A cognitive theory of avoidance learning. In F. J. McGuigan & D. B. Lumsden (Eds.), *Contemporary approaches to conditioning and learning* (pp. 69-110). Washington, DC: Winston & Sons.

Southworth, S., & Kirsch, I. (1988). The role of expectancy in exposure-generated fear reduction in agoraphobia. *Behaviour Research and Therapy, 26*, 113-120.

Telch, M. J., Agras, W. S., Taylor, C. B., Roth, W. T., & Gallen, C. C. (1985). Combined pharmacological and behavioral treatment for agoraphobia. *Behaviour Research and Therapy, 23*, 325-335.

Telch, M. J., Bandura, A., Vinciguerra, P., Agras, A., & Stout. A. L. (1982). Social demand for consistency and congruence between self-efficacy and performance. *Behavior Therapy, 13*, 694-701.

Williams, S. L. (1985). On the nature and measurement of agoraphobia. *Progress in Behavior Modification, 19*, 109-144.

Williams, S. L. (1987). On anxiety and phobia. *Journal of Anxiety Disorders, 1*, 161-180.

Williams, S. L. (1988). Addressing misconceptions about phobia, anxiety, and self-efficacy: A reply to Marks. *Journal of Anxiety Disorders, 2*, 277-289.

Williams, S. L. (1990). Guided mastery treatment of agoraphobia: Beyond stimulus exposure. *Progress in Behavior Modification, 26*, 89-121.

Williams, S. L. (1991). Unpublished data.

Williams, S. L., Dooseman, G., & Kleifield, E. (1984). Comparative effectiveness of guided mastery and exposure treatments for intractable phobias. *Journal of Consulting and Clinical Psychology, 52*, 505-518.

Williams, S. L., Kinney, P. J., & Falbo, J. (1989). Generalization of therapeutic changes in agoraphobia: The role of perceived self-efficacy. *Journal of Consulting and Clinical Psychology, 57*, 436-442.

Williams, S. L., & Kleifield, E. (1985). Transfer of behavioral change across phobias in multiply phobic clients. *Behavior Modification, 9*, 22-31.

Williams, S. L., & Rappoport, A. (1983). Cognitive treatment in the natural environment for agoraphobics. *Behavior Therapy, 14*, 299-313.

Williams, S. L., Turner, S. M., & Peer, D. F. (1985). Guided mastery and performance desensitization treatments for severe acrophobia. *Journal of Consulting and Clinical Psychology, 53*, 237-247.

Williams, S. L., & Watson, N. (1985). Perceived danger and perceived self-efficacy as cognitive determinants of acrophobic behavior. *Behavior Therapy, 16*, 237-247.

Williams, S. L., & Zane, G. (1989). Guided mastery and stimulus exposure treatments for severe performance anxiety in agoraphobics. *Behaviour Research and Therapy, 27*, 237-247.

Wolpe, J. (1958). *Psychotherapy by reciprocal inhibition.* Stanford, CA: Stanford University Press.

Author Notes

The preparation of this paper and much of the research reported in it was supported by United States Public Health Service grants R03-MH41595 and R29-MH42385.

SELF-EFFICACY AND DEPRESSION

David J. Kavanagh

There is now substantial support for a correlation between depression and reduced judgments of self-efficacy. However, there are several possible paths to this result: For example, lower self-efficacy may be making people depressed, the depression may be undermining their self-efficacy, or depression may be indirectly affecting self-efficacy through an impact on performance attainments. The current evidence suggests that all three effects are probably occurring. A model is presented, where self-efficacy judgments, performances and moods have reciprocal influences on each other, and limiting conditions for the effects are discussed.

"I am totally hopeless," a depressed woman said to me recently. "I'm no good at anything. I can't get any good ideas for my projects, I keep saying dumb things when I'm around other people. I look at my friend—she has a great job, she's popular, she always seems to know what to say. I'm never going to be like her. There's no point in trying."

An important aspect of this person's cognition is her low self-efficacy. This may be a major factor in her depression being maintained, since it is likely to influence the activities that she chooses to engage in and the effort and persistence she invests in them (Bandura, 1982; Kavanagh, 1983). When she gives up trying, it reduces the opportunities for her to experience positive outcomes, and increases the frequency of aversive events for her (Lewinsohn & Libet, 1972).

Her low self-efficacy does not just seem to affect her performance: It also seems to be affecting her emotional state directly. When she talks about her perceived incapability in areas that she values highly, she becomes visibly upset. This does not seem to be solely because she anticipates negative external outcomes, but because she is violating her own standards. The impact appears to be compounded by an unflattering comparison with other people and a sense that this is a permanent problem.

The phenomenon is modelled in Figure 1. Depressive feelings that are triggered by cognitions, aversive events or physiological states is thought to have a reciprocal relationship with both self-efficacy and performance. As with the client just described, a low sense of self-efficacy often deepens the person's sadness, especially when it makes the opportunity for positive outcomes seem remote or when the performance domain is crucial to the person's self-esteem. When aversive outcomes occur, these also feed into the depressive mood (the arrow on the bottom right). Emotional states are expected to affect self-efficacy both directly and through an impact on performance. Aspects of this model are supported by the current state of the research, although some of the influences appear to be less strong than others, and some only occur in restricted circumstances.

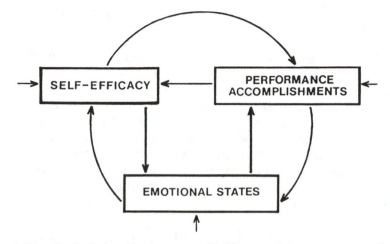

Figure 1 Theorized relationships between self-efficacy, performance accomplishments and depression. From Yusaf and Kavanagh (1990).

Is Depression Associated With Low Self-Efficacy?

Depressed people often display reductions in self-efficacy (Cane & Gotlib, 1985; Davis & Yates, 1982; Kanfer & Zeiss, 1983; Miller, 1984). However this could arise from a number of processes: The depressive mood might be reducing self-efficacy, self-efficacy may be producing sadness, or the effects may be mediated by differences in performances. It may even be the case that something outside the model is producing the effects.

To determine whether emotional states are influencing self-efficacy we need to manipulate the emotion. In Kavanagh and Bower (1985), students were asked to visualize three situations under hypnosis. One of these was neutral in tone (sitting at home reading a textbook). The other two were more emotive situations, involving an interaction with a romantic partner. In one they had communicated well and had a successful interaction, in the other they had failed completely and had been rejected. They were asked to re-create the feelings of sadness or happiness that they had experienced in the situation. Then, they were asked to rate their self-efficacy on a wide range of activities. Students who had visualized a positive romantic event had higher average levels of self-efficacy than those who recalled a disastrous experience (Figure 2). This effect did not only occur on activities that were associated with romantic relationships, but also on more general social skills, and on miscellaneous activities from athletic tasks to weight reduction or handling snakes. Since the change in self-efficacy ratings did not significantly differ across these domains, we argued that the results were unlikely to be due to a generalization of self-efficacy (which would be expected to produce a generalization gradient).

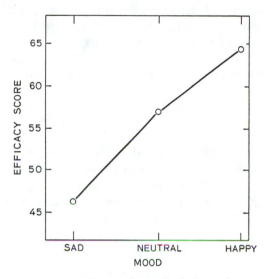

Figure 2 Efficacy scores averaged across items for judges who were happy, neutral, or sad. From Kavanagh and Bower (1985).

Later experiments have attempted to confirm that the effects could be obtained if the emotion induction had no mention of success or failure (Kavanagh, 1983; Kavanagh & Hausfeld, 1986). The outcome has been that the effect is obtained on some tasks, but—at least for emotions that are induced in the laboratory—the impact of the emotions is relatively small. For example, in Kavanagh and Hausfeld (1986) happiness produced higher self-efficacy than sadness on one of the tasks (push-ups), but not on the other (handgrip). When subjects were happy they thought they could do 2.6 more push-ups than when they were sad. Since differences of this size are liable to be overshadowed by within-group variation, the phenomenon is more easily observed in repeated measures on the same subjects than in between-subject designs (Kavanagh, 1987).

What then is producing the self-efficacy changes, and why aren't they stronger? There is some evidence that the changes in self-efficacy are mediated by differences in recalled performances under happy and sad moods. In Wright and Mischel (1982), sadness or happiness was induced, and then subjects were given bogus feedback about performance on a perceptual task. At the end of the task, self-efficacy was assessed and subjects were asked to recall their success over the session. When the affective tone of the feedback was consistent with their mood, the subjects' predictions about future performances were close to the actual feedback information they had received. However, a mismatch between the emotion and the feedback information skewed the subjects' predictions. Happy subjects who had "failed" predicted higher future performance than their feedback suggested, and sad subjects who had "succeeded" thought they would do worse.

Since the recalled feedback was similarly skewed, the self-efficacy effect appeared to be based on differences in memory for the performance information.

The Wright and Mischel study (1982) did not clarify whether the impact of the emotions was primarily occurring at encoding or at retrieval. We know from other research that substantial effects can be observed on encoding. People who are sad or depressed attend to negative aspects of their experience more than happy people do (Bower, 1983; Lishman, 1972; Lloyd & Lishman, 1975). They also evaluate their own performance more negatively (Forgas, Bower, & Krantz, 1984; Lobitz & Post, 1979; Smolen, 1978) and reward themselves less readily (Gotlib, 1981), although they are not necessarily less "accurate" in their self-evaluations (Lewinsohn, Mischel, Chaplin, & Barton, 1980; cf. Dykman, Horowitz, Abramson, & Usher, 1991). But influences on self-efficacy that arise from the encoding of performance information rely on the person having undertaken the activity while sad. Sometimes this has not occurred—for example, the person may have never felt sad when playing billiards. Or their performance on this particular task may not have been poorer than usual at times when they were sad.

Selective retrieval of mood-consistent information can also occur (e.g., Clark & Teasdale, 1982; cf. Bower & Mayer, 1985), and current thinking suggests that it is mediated by a differential evaluative response to the judgment target under happiness or sadness (Bower, 1991; Schwartz & Bless, 1991). There is still substantial controversy about the nature of this phenomenon. In the view of Schwartz and Clore (1988), people often misread their current affective state as a response to the target. This predicts that the effects of current emotions on both evaluations and retrieval of consistent memories will be greater when the reason for the person's affective state is not salient, and there is some evidence to support that idea (e.g., Schwartz & Clore, 1983). Bower's network theory predicts an impact of the emotion whether the reason for the emotion is salient or not (Bower, 1981, 1991).

Bower (1991) has drawn attention to the parallels between cognitive dissonance and effects of emotions on judgments. But the situation where people make successive judgments under different moods is somewhat different from the traditional dissonance paradigm. If subjects become aware of the discrepancy between their judgments over different days, this might itself create cognitive dissonance. This new dissonance might only be resolved by discounting the mood effects. Such an effect could explain the results of Schwartz and Clore (1983). Verbal reports from subjects suggest that this is precisely what has occurred in some of my mood induction experiments: A very common statement was along the lines, "I felt that I couldn't do the task, but then I realised that it was just because I was feeling unhappy just now, so I put down what I usually can do." That is, some subjects seem to be aware of the effect that the emotion has had on their judgments or recollections, and actively adjust for it.

The example also suggests that these subjects have access to performance information that conflicts with their prevailing emotion. This illustrates the point that both encoding and retrieval effects from emotions may be overridden by other salient performance information (Bandura, 1982). I vividly recall another subject's response to a self-efficacy question about lifting weights. "This question's easy," he said. "I've just come from the gym and I know what I can lift today." It would be very difficult for a change in his mood to affect that self-efficacy judgment!

Sometimes the impact of emotions on self-efficacy may be produced by mechanisms that have little to do with recall. In this case, the different recollections of performance may follow the judgment, rather than producing it. There are at least two candidates for the alternative mechanisms. One is that cognitions about low generalised capabilities have been rehearsed so frequently in the negative mood that they have become very highly available in that mood. For example, the statement "I am totally hopeless" by the client at the beginning of the chapter was made several times during the first interview. When she made a judgment about a specific capability, this general proposition may have immediately sprung to mind. This would tend to act as a low anchor for the self-efficacy judgment. We know from data on numerical anchors (Cervone & Peake, 1986) that people do not correct sufficiently for changes in their starting point when they judge their self-efficacy. As a result, her self-efficacy when she felt "totally hopeless" would be lower than when she felt happy and "reasonably competent."

A final possible source of the reductions in self-efficacy is that people may feel unable or unwilling to muster the effort that will be required to perform the task. This will be more likely when the task is expected to require substantial effort for success (see below).

Major depressive episodes and dysthymia may be especially prone to lowered self-efficacy because the conditions for all of these processes may often be present. The aggregated duration of the disorder makes it very likely that a wide range of activities will have been experienced under a dysphoric mood. If the depression has strong endogenous features, its origin will often be unclear to the person—the situation where Schwartz and Bless (1991) predict that judgmental effects will be most prominent. Depressed people are prone to rehearse generalised negative cognitions about themselves (Beck, 1991), and their judgments may well be subject to anchoring effects. Unlike the mood induction subjects, they also know that their emotional state will probably continue for some time, and as a result it may not seem adaptive for them to adjust their expectations upwards. No wonder that they feel unable to do well!

Effects of Depression on Performance

Low expectations of depressed people are rendered even more plausible when they notice reductions in their performance. Poorer performance is often observed in depression (e.g., Cohen, Weingartner, Smallberg, Pickar, & Murphy, 1982; Miller, 1975). Some tasks involve a non-depressed presentation for optimal performance: For example smiling often enters an assessment of social performance, and a reduction of smiling by depressed people may partially explain their poorer social performance scores (e.g., Lewinsohn et al., 1980). In addition, depressed people are more self-absorbed (Ingram & Smith, 1984), and this decreases their ability to pay attention to others' contributions and offer empathic responses. Perhaps because of the preoccupation with negative thoughts, depressed people also do poorly on complex laboratory tasks that make high attentional demands (Cohen et al., 1982). People who are suffering from a severe Major Depressive Episode may also feel lethargic (e.g., because of sleep disturbance and a reduced food intake) and physiological effects on psychomotor speed can occur: These features have a direct impact on timed responses.

However, most depressive deficits occur in situations (a) where subjects can withdraw from the activity, or (b) where effort makes an impact on the performance (Ciminero & Steingarten, 1978; Loeb, Beck, & Diggory, 1971; Miller, 1984). Frequently an apparent deficit can be eliminated by just encouraging people to persist in their attempts (e.g., Friedman, 1964). These reductions in persistence and effort resemble deficits that are produced by self-efficacy (Bandura, 1982). In terms of the model in Figure 1, the route of influence for these particular performance deficits may be primarily through the changes in self-efficacy discussed in the previous section.

Kavanagh (1987) examined this possibility in a mood induction experiment. Happy and sad moods were induced by using a combination of appropriate music and recollections of romantic experiences in which connotations of success or failure were minimized. A between-subjects design was used, and a neutral mood condition was also included. Strong behavioral differences resulted from the mood inductions: Subjects who were happy persisted 50% longer at solving anagrams than did those who were sad (Figure 3), and spent a smaller proportion of their time on the easiest anagrams. Happy subjects also solved more anagrams, but this was mainly due to the women. Sad women not only worked on the task for a shorter time, they also took four times longer on average to solve each anagram. On the other hand, men responded to both happiness and sadness by increasing their efficiency.

Despite the occurrence of at least some of the expected performance effects, there were no parallel effects on self-efficacy before the anagrams task. In fact, rather than demonstrating the mediation of self-efficacy on the performance changes, the performance attainments produced alterations in self-efficacy. After the task, happy subjects did have higher self-efficacy than those who were sad. While later performances may be affected by flow-on effects from these self-efficacy changes, the initial impact of the emotions on the anagram performance seemed to be produced by other mechanisms.

What could these other mechanisms be? One possibility is the *maintenance of positive mood*. In Kavanagh (1987), verbal reports suggested that some subjects terminated the anagrams task because it was giving an insufficient rate of positive outcomes, and they aniticipated more positive experiences (and hence a better chance of improving their mood) from other activities. In the case of women, there was also an impact on *cognitive efficiency*—perhaps because of cognitive intrusions that were triggered by the sad recollection. Why this did not occur for men is unclear. Other data suggests that they are more likely to actively correct for mood effects on self-efficacy and performance (Kavanagh, 1983), and may become more task-oriented as a way of distracting themselves from negative recollections. If so, this may be an important reason for the lower risk of depression that is observed in men (Nolen-Hoeksema, 1987). Where the predominant incentives for performance are positive, there may also be an effect on performance through a *reduction in expected pleasure during sadness*. When subjects are in a negative mood, they expect less enjoyment from activities (Carson & Adams, 1980). Positive incentives therefore have less weight.

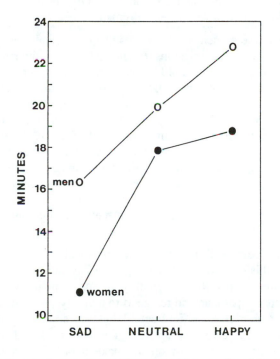

Figure 3 Persistence on an anagrams task under sad, neutral and happy moods. From Kavanagh (1987).

Self-Efficacy and Skills as Determinants of Depression

In the example at the beginning of the chapter, the client reported feeling worse when she thought about her lack of capabilities. This suggests that associations between depression and self-efficacy may partly be due to an influence of self-efficacy on emotion. If so, this has important implications for the treatment and prevention of depressive episodes.

Despite considerable debate over the role of cognitions in depression (e.g., Coyne & Gotlib, 1983), cognitive-behavioral approaches to depression have a strong influence on current psychological theory and practice (e.g., Beck, 1991; Beck, Rush, Shaw, & Emery, 1979; Rehm, 1977). One of the influential theories has been learned helplessness theory (Abramson, Seligman, & Teasdale, 1978; Seligman, 1975). In the original theory, an independence of responses and outcomes was seen as a cause of depression. When people experienced negative outcomes that were not contingent on their responses, they displayed cognitive, behavioral and emotional responses that were similar to those of depressed people. However, Bandura (1978) argued that the experience of non-contingent negative outcomes only produces despondency when the person ascribes the negative outcome to their personal inefficacy. This was highly consistent with the results that were emerging from the laboratory research on learned helplessness (e.g., Klein, Fencil-Morse, & Seligman, 1976).

In response to the evident inadequacies of the original theory, Abramson et al. (1978) advanced a revision distinguishing "universal helplessness" —approximately the same as the old helplessness concept—from "personal helplessness." In personal helplessness, people expect that the outcome is contingent on the responses of relevant others, but is not contingent on any response in their own repertoire. Except in cases of personal victimization, this is approximately equivalent to the concept of low comparative self-efficacy: Like the client at the beginning of the chapter, these people usually see themselves as being unable to achieve the outcome solely because of their own inability. In Abramson et al. (1978), either type of helplessness was expected to produce despondency if the outcome was sufficiently aversive, but greater negative affect was predicted in personal helplessness, and an association between internal attributions and depression was expected.

Bandura has continued to assert that personal inefficacy is the key to despondency. In his own words: "When people have a low sense of personal efficacy and no amount of effort by themselves or comparative others produces results, they become apathetic and resigned to a dreary life. The pattern in which people perceive themselves as ineffectual but see similar others enjoying the benefits of successful effort is apt to give rise to self-disparagement and depression. Evident successes of others make it hard to avoid self-criticism" (Bandura, 1982, p. 141).

So, the distress of the client at the beginning of the chapter appears to be exacerbated by the comparison with her friend's capabilities and achievements ("I look at my friend—she has a great job, she's popular, she always seems to know what to say. I'm never going to be like her.").

Bandura's emphasis on personal inefficacy is supported by the observation that depressed and nondepressed people do not differ in their predictions of how others will do—only on how well they themselves will perform a task (e.g., Garber & Hollon, 1980). In particular, depressed people lose the self-enhancing bias in efficacy judgments that is seen when nondepressed people make social comparisons (Ahrens, Zeiss, & Kanfer, 1988). Pessimism about future outcomes is also linked to the degree of illusory personal control: If someone else throws some dice, depressed people expect a higher degree of success than when they throw the dice themselves (Golin, Terrell, Weitz, & Drost, 1979). In contrast, nondepressed people are more optimistic when their personal control seems higher. An emphasis on personal inefficacy is also supported by a relationship between proneness to depressive mood and a tendency to ascribe poor perform-ances to oneself (Seligman, Abramson, Semmel, & von Baeyer, 1979). Further-more, improvements in depressive mood during treatment appears to be corre-lated with increases in perceived mastery or self-efficacy (e.g., Teasdale, 1985; Zeiss , Lewinsohn, & Muñoz, 1979).

While these studies support the focus on personal self-efficacy in depression, a critical test of self-efficacy as a determinant of depressive mood would require an examination of the effects from manipulating self-efficacy. Studies that have reduced self-efficacy do demonstrate that a depressive mood can be triggered, and the effect is more likely when others appear able to emit the response (e.g., Davis & Yates, 1982).

The focus on self-efficacy rather than just on attributions draws attention to the fact that depressed people are not only concerned about the cause or blame for past events—as important as this can be. They are also concerned about the implications of the events for the future (cf. Beck et al., 1979). This is a similar point that Abramson et al. (1978) made when they emphasised attributions to "stable" factors. If the person expects that potentially aversive situations may recur, and that they will once again be unable to prevent a negative outcome, this is likely to compound their reactions to a current event. As a result, depression levels are expected to be related both to the *aversiveness of past events* and to *self-efficacy about control of situations* they will be facing in the future. The point is illustrated in a study by Cutrona and Troutman (1986). As any new par-ent will attest, the sound of their crying infant induces significant emotional distress in the parents (Frodi, Lamb, Leavitt, & Donovan, 1978). When the baby has a more stormy temperament, the mother is expected to be at a greater risk of postpartum depression, and this was indeed the case in the Cutrona and Troutman study. But at least some of the relationship between infant difficulty and depression was mediated by changes in parenting self-efficacy. When the infant's crying was seen by the mother as showing her lack of capability as a parent, the risk of depression was amplified.

Low self-efficacy about future situations can of course produce a range of negative emotional responses apart from sadness. For example, anxiety or fear seems to occur when people anticipate that they may be unable to control a potentially aversive situation (Bandura, 1988). On the other hand, the focus in sadness appears to be the anticipated loss of positive or pleasurable experiences (Bandura, 1982). The reductions in self-efficacy achieve special significance when these expected losses are greater—for example, when the self-efficacy defi-cit covers a wide range of task domains and the person sees no chance of future improvement. Unfortunately global deficits are very likely in sadness (Kavanagh

& Bower, 1985), and like the woman at the beginning of the chapter, many depressed people say they are "no good at anything" and they will "never" improve.

Not only are the losses predicted from external sources: Sadness is often triggered by the person's self-reactions. In this case, the expected loss involves a withdrawal of self-valuation. While the self-standards of depressed people may not exceed those of other people, they frequently are below the level they think they can achieve (Kanfer & Zeiss, 1983). When the performance domain is central to the person's self-esteem, awareness of the discrepancy between the standard and the self-efficacy level may have a powerful immediate impact on the emotional state.

When we take a view of depression that emphasises both the aversiveness of experiences and the self-efficacy and skills that people have in dealing with the situation, this opens up exciting possibilities for predicting the course of depression and for developing better methods to prevent its recurrence.

In considering these issues, I have recently become interested in the process of recovery from a bereavement (Kavanagh, 1990). Here is a situation that generates extremely strong emotional reactions and often produces major changes to goals and incentives. Yet even after the death of a spouse, only about a third of people develop a major depressive episode (Bornstein, Clayton, Halikas, Maurice, & Robins, 1973) and most people report some relief from dysphoria within 1-3 months after the bereavement (Parkes, 1970). This is an extreme example of the low correspondence that is typically found between life events and depression, where events per se account for only about 10% of the variance in depression (Brown & Harris, 1986).

Some of the reasons for recovery probably include features of the bereavement situation such as the difficulty in avoiding extended stimulus exposure and resultant habituation. It is also difficult to avoid some re-engagement in activities. But a substantial contributor to the high recovery rate seems to be the skills that survivors already have in dealing with aversive events—coping skills that they have developed from their previous encounters with a variety of situations, from broken love affairs to failed examinations or job retrenchment. At least some of the existing coping skills can be applied to the bereavement and moderate its aversive emotional impact. Consistent with this idea, Bornstein et al. (1973) found a lower risk of depression among widows who had experienced a previous bereavement than for those who had not (4%, compared with 25%).

The tasks that are posed by a bereavement seem to fall into four groups. One group involves *attacking cognitive sources of negative mood* (Beck, 1991; Beck et al., 1979). This consists of paying attention to negative cognitions and examining their evidence base. A second group involves *solving practical problems and coping with day-to-day demands* such as managing finances, finding new employment, or arranging child care (D'Zurilla & Goldfried, 1971). Both of these task areas involve thinking about the bereavement and its effects. However in the short term these thoughts will invoke sadness, especially since many of the negative cognitions are not easily discounted and the central problem is not readily resolved ("the person is gone and will never come back"). Therefore a third set of tasks involves restoring a more positive mood through *attention diversion and enjoyable activity* (Lewinsohn & Libet, 1972). Here, people use both activities and cognitive strategies such as fantasy or humour to divert their attention from depressive thoughts and to invoke positive emotion. Finally, the person may need to be mobilising assistance from other people, to supplement deficiencies in their performance of the other tasks (Cohen & Wills, 1985).

When the circumstances of the death make it very difficult to successfully undertake these tasks, we would expect people to be more at risk of depression. This does seem to be so. When the death involves some blame being attached to the survivor—such as when a child dies accidentally (Nixon & Pearn, 1977), or a spouse suicides (Parkes & Weiss, 1983)—there is a severe challenge to cognitive restructuring skills, and the survivor is at special risk of depression. If the death was violent the grief reaction can last for many years (Lehman, Wortman, & Williams, 1987): In this case, the person is often plagued by vivid and extremely distressing images of the death that are very difficult to suppress. Ongoing legal action offers further complications by reinvoking the negative emotions and continuing to disrupt activities.

While the specific challenges in bereavement are often different from other instances of sadness or depression, the same task areas apply. There is often a set of problems to be resolved, negative thoughts are triggered, the person needs to find ways to restore a positive mood, and assistance from others may be required. Consistent with this view, cognitive-behavioral treatments of depression that build skills and performance in these task domains have achieved impressive results in controlled trials (Wilson, 1989). We can also predict future occurrences of depression from reports of past achievements in handling daily hassles and life events, even when the effects of current depression levels are taken into account (Holahan & Holahan, 1987). Other research demonstrates that depressed people who use active coping strategies (increasing activity levels, engaging in interpersonal activity, or rehearsing positive cognitions) have shorter and less severe depressive episodes than those who ruminate about their depression (Morrow & Nolen-Hoeksema, 1990). From studies of unselected subjects we also know that most people have intrusive negative thoughts from time to time and that they regularly use cognitive restructuring, problem solving and attention diversion strategies to deal with them (Edwards & Dickerson, 1987).

Given these data, self-efficacy judgments about depression-related task domains have special significance for understanding the process of recovery from depression and predicting its later course (Kavanagh & Wilson, 1989; Yusaf & Kavanagh, 1990). In Kavanagh and Wilson (1989), depressed subjects were treated with cognitive therapy, and their outcomes over a 12-month follow-up period were observed. Self-efficacy questions asked about the subjects' expected self-control of emotion and cognition over the next 12 months, and attempted to capture both their capabilities in attacking cognitive sources of depression and in positive mood induction. The questions were: (a) "How much time can you make at least moderately enjoyable?", (b) "How much time can you have without any sad, discouraging or unpleasant thoughts," and (c) "What percentage of the negative thoughts that pop into your mind can you effectively challenge?" In each case, there were ten levels of performance, from 30 minutes each day to 12 hours or more (or from 0 to 100% in the case of the last question). Confidence ratings on the three skill areas were averaged to form a single score of self-efficacy strength for each subject. Changes in these self-efficacy scores over the course of treatment accounted for 50% of the variance in the depression improvement. Furthermore, the self-efficacy scores at post-treatment strongly predicted the number of three-month periods that the subjects were in remission ($r = .59$), and the prediction remained significant even after the post-treatment depression level was taken into account. The results parallel work that suggests self-efficacy about control of anxious thoughts is an important determinant of anxiety reactions (Kent, 1987; Kent & Gibbons, 1987; Ozer & Bandura, 1990). They also join a range of studies in other problem domains that have attested the importance of self-efficacy for predicting sustained behavioral improvement after treatment (e.g., Kavanagh, Pierce, Lo, & Shelley, 1991; Sitharthan & Kavanagh, 1990).

The precise tasks that will be important for the depression will of course alter according to the circumstances that the person is facing. So, for example, self-efficacy for assertion turned out to be a very powerful predictor of follow-up status in the sample used by Yusaf and Kavanagh (1990). In Cutrona and Troutman's (1986) sample of postpartum women, parenting self-efficacy appeared especially important.

Up to now, I have not been examining the role of self-efficacy about mobilising assistance, but this would appear to be a useful area to begin looking at. We know that social support can moderate the aversive impact of life events (e.g., Cohen & Wills, 1985) and that it has a function in reducing the risk of relapse after recovery from a depressive episode (Belsher & Costello, 1988). We also know that people often find it aversive to talk with people who are depressed (Coyne, 1976), and that depressed college students offer negative self-disclosures in situations that others find inappropriate (Jacobsen & Anderson, 1982; Kuiper & McCabe, 1985). While most of the literature has focused on initial acquaintances among college students, it suggests that skills in effectively eliciting support and in preserving the sources of support for future crises may turn out to be an important focus for assessment and intervention.

Summary

There is now substantial support for the model described in Figure 1, and we now know in more detail what the limiting conditions are for the effects that are described. Reductions in self-efficacy and performance appear to be both consequences of depression and determinants of it. The direct influence of sadness on self-efficacy is broad in scope but—at least in studies on induced moods—it is often small in degree. The impact of depression on performance occurs primarily through an impact on task selection, persistence and effort, although some direct effects from depressive symptoms may also be observed. Poorer performances are most likely to affect later depression (a) when they mean that a valued external outcome is not obtained (or an aversive situation is not terminated), (b) when they induce negative self-reactions, or (c) when the task involves the control of negative mood. These are also the conditions in which low self-efficacy has an emotional impact. Self-efficacy judgments appear to affect emotional state both directly (when people imagine the future consequences of their inefficacy), and through their effect on later performance. However, these indirect effects of the self-efficacy judgments are better substantiated by studies on the prediction of depressive episodes than by laboratory experiments on induced mood.

The work on sadness and self-efficacy has contributed to the theory and research on self-efficacy in two ways. First, it has extended the role that emotion has on the formation of self-efficacy judgments. We now know that emotions not only act as one of the pieces of information that people use (as in Bandura, 1977), but that within constraints, they have the potential to color the other information that is gained from the other sources (Bandura, 1986). The second contribution is the extension of self-efficacy theory on the prediction and causation of depressive episodes. The current data provide further evidence of the significance of self-efficacy for the production and maintenance of behavioral change, and offer exciting prospects for further research.

REFERENCES

Abramson, L. Y., Seligman, M. E. P., & Teasdale, J. D. (1978). Learned helplessness in humans: Critiques and reformulation. *Journal of Abnormal Psychology, 87,* 49-74.

Ahrens, A. H., Zeiss, A. M., & Kanfer, R. (1988). Dysphoric deficits in interpersonal standards, self-efficacy, and social comparison. *Cognitive Therapy and Research, 12,* 53-67.

Bandura, A. (1977). Self-efficacy: Toward a unifying theory of behavioral change. *Psychological Review, 84,* 191-215.

Bandura, A. (1978). Reflections on self-efficacy. *Advances in Behavior Research and Therapy, 1,* 237-269.

Bandura, A. (1982). Self-efficacy mechanism in human agency. *American Psychologist, 37,* 122-147.

Bandura, A. (1986). *Social foundations of thought and action: A social cognitive theory.* Englewood Cliffs, NJ: Prentice-Hall.

Bandura, A. (1988). Self-efficacy conception of anxiety. *Anxiety Research, 1,* 77-98.

Beck, A. T. (1991). Cognitive therapy: A 30-year retrospective. *American Psychologist, 46,* 368-375.

Beck, A. T., Rush, A. J., Shaw, B. F., & Emery, G. (1979). *Cognitive therapy of depression.* New York: Guilford.

Belsher, G., & Costello, C. G. (1988). Relapse after recovery from unipolar depression: A critical review. *Psychological Bulletin, 104,* 84-96.

Bornstein, P. E., Clayton, P. J., Halikas, J. A., Maurice, W. L., & Robins, E. (1973). The depression of widowhood after thirteen months. *British Journal of Psychiatry, 122*, 561-566.

Bower, G. H. (1981). Mood and memory. *American Psychologist, 36*, 129-148.

Bower, G. H. (1983). Affect and cognition. *Philosophical Transactions of the Royal Society of London, Series B, 302*, 387-402.

Bower, G. H. (1991). Mood congruity of social judgments. In J. P. Forgas (Ed.). *Emotion and social judgments* (pp. 31-53). Oxford: Pergamon.

Bower, G. H., & Mayer, J. D. (1985). Failure to replicate mood-dependent retrieval. *Bulletin of the Psychonomic Society, 23*, 39-42.

Brown, G. W., & Harris, T. (1986). Establishing causal links: The Bedford College studies of depression. In H. Katschnig (Ed.). *Life events and psychiatric disorders: Controversial issues* (pp. 107-187). Cambridge: Cambridge University Press.

Cane, D. B., & Gotlib, I. H. (1985). Depression and the effects of positive and negative feedback on expectations, evaluations, and performance. *Cognitive Therapy and Research, 9*, 145-160.

Carson, T. P., & Adams, H. E. (1980). Activity valence as a function of mood change. *Journal of Abnormal Psychology, 89*, 368-377.

Cervone, D., & Peake, P. K. (1986). Anchoring, efficacy and action: The influence of judgmental heuristics on self-efficacy judgments and behavior. *Journal of Personality and Social Psychology, 50*, 492-501.

Ciminero, A. G., & Steingarten, K. A. (1978). The effects of performance standards on self-evaluation and self-reinforcement in depressed and nondepressed individuals. *Cognitive Therapy and Research, 2*, 179-182.

Clark, D. M., & Teasdale, J. D. (1982). Diurnal variation in clinical depression and accessibility of positive and negative experiences. *Journal of Abnormal Psychology, 91*, 87-95.

Cohen, R. M., Weingartner, H., Smallberg, S. A., Pickar, D., & Murphy, D. L. (1982). Effort and cognition in depression. *Archives of General Psychiatry, 39*, 593-597.

Cohen, S., & Wills, T. A. (1985). Stress, social support and the buffering hypothesis. *Psychological Bulletin, 98*, 310-357.

Coyne, J. D. (1976). Depression and the response of others. *Journal of Abnormal Psychology, 85*, 186-193.

Coyne, J. C., & Gotlib, I. H. (1983). The role of cognition in depression: A critical appraisal. *Psychological Bulletin, 94*, 472-505.

Cutrona, C. E., & Troutman, B. R. (1986). Social support, infant temperament, and parenting self-efficacy: A mediational model of postpartum depression. *Child Development, 57*, 1507-1518.

Davis, F. W., & Yates, B. T. (1982). Self-efficacy expectancies versus outcome expectancies as determinants of performance deficitis and depressive affect. *Cognitive Therapy and Research, 6*, 23-35.

Dykman, B. M., Horowitz, L. M., Abramson, L. Y., & Usher, M. (1991). Schematic and situational determinants of depressed and nondepressed students' interpretation of feedback. *Journal of Abnormal Psychology, 100*, 45-55.

Edwards, S., & Dickerson, M. (1987). On the similarity of positive and negative intrusions. *Behaviour Research and Therapy, 25*, 207-211.

Forgas, J. P., Bower, G. H., & Krantz, S. (1984). The influence of mood on perceptions of social interactions. *Journal of Experimental Social Psychology, 20*, 497-513.

Friedman, A. S. (1964). Minimal effect of severe depression on cognitive functioning. *Journal of Abnormal and Social Psychology, 69,* 237-243.

Frodi, A. M., Lamb, M. E., Leavitt, L. A., & Donovan, W. L. (1978). Fathers' and mothers' responses to infant smiles and cries. *Infant Behavior and Development, 1,* 187-198.

Garber, J., & Hollon, S. D. (1980). Universal versus personal helplessness: Belief in uncontrollability or incompetence? *Journal of Abnormal Psychology, 89,* 56-66.

D'Zurilla, J. J., & Goldfried, M. R. (1971). Problem solving and behavior modification. *Journal of Abnormal Psychology, 78,* 107-126.

Golin, S., Terrell, F., Weitz, J., & Drost, P. L. (1979). The illusion of control among depressed patients. *Journal of Abnormal Psychology, 88,* 454-457.

Gotlib, I. H. (1981). Self-reinforcement and recall: Differential deficits in depressed and nondepressed psychiatric patients. *Journal of Abnormal Psychology, 90,* 521-530.

Holahan, C. K., & Holahan, C. J. (1987). Life stress, hassles, and self-efficacy in aging: A replication and extension. *Journal of Applied Social Psychology, 17,* 574-592.

Ingram, R. E., & Smith, T. W. (1984). Depression and internal versus external focus of attention. *Cognitive Therapy and Research, 8,* 139-152.

Jacobsen, N. S., & Anderson, E. A. (1982). Interpersonal skill and depression in college students: An analysis of the timing of self-disclosures. *Behavior Therapy, 13,* 271-282.

Kanfer, R., & Zeiss, A. M. (1983). Depression, interpersonal standard-setting, and judgments of self-efficacy. *Journal of Abnormal Psychology, 92,* 319-329.

Kavanagh, D. J. (1983). Mood and self-efficacy: *Influence of joy and sadness on efficacy and task selection.* (Doctoral d issertation, Stanford University, 1983). Dissertation Abstracts International, 44, 2922B.

Kavanagh, D. J. (1987). Mood, persistence and success. *Australian Journal of Psychology, 39,* 307-318.

Kavanagh, D. J. (1990). Toward a cognitive-behavioural intervention for adult grief reactions. *British Journal of Psychiatry, 157,* 373-383.

Kavanagh, D. J., & Bower, G. H. (1985). Mood and self-efficacy: Impact of joy and sadness on perceived capabilities. *Cognitive Therapy and Research, 9,* 507-525.

Kavanagh, D. J., & Hausfeld, S. (1986). Physical performance and self-efficacy under happy and sad moods. *Journal of Sport Psychology, 8,* 112-123.

Kavanagh, D. J., Pierce, J. P., Lo, S. K., & Shelley, J. (1991). Self-efficacy and social support as predictors of smoking after a quit attempt. University of Sydney (manuscript submitted for publication).

Kavanagh, D. J., & Wilson, P. H. (1989). Prediction of response to cognitive therapy for depression. *Behaviour Research and Therapy, 27,* 333-343.

Kent, G. (1987). Self-efficacious control over reported physiological, cognitive and behavioural symptoms of dental anxiety. *Behaviour Research and Therapy, 25,* 341-347.

Kent, G., & Gibbons, R. (1987). Self-efficacy and the control of anxious cognitions. *Journal of Behaviour Therapy and Experimental Psychiatry, 18,* 33-40.

Klein, D. C., Fencil-Morse, E., & Seligman, M. E. P. (1976). Learned helplessness, depression, and the attribution of failure. *Journal of Personality and Social Psychology, 33,* 508-516.

Kuiper, N. A., & McCabe, S. B. (1985). The appropriateness of social topics: Effects of depression and cognitive vulnerability on self and other judgments. *Cognitive Therapy and Research, 9*, 371-379.

Lehman, D. R., Wortman, C. R., & Williams, A. F. (1987). Long-term effects of losing a spouse or child in a motor vehicle crash. *Journal of Personality and Social Psychology, 52*, 218-231.

Lewinsohn, P. M., & Libet, J. (1972). Pleasant events, activity schedules, and depression. *Journal of Abnormal Psychology, 79*, 291-295.

Lewinsohn, P. M., Mischel, W., Chaplin, W., & Barton, R. (1980). Social competence and depression: The role of illusory self-perceptions. *Journal of Abnormal Psychology, 89*, 203-212.

Lishman, W. P. (1972;). Selective factors in memory, Part 2: Affective disorders. *Psychological Medicine, 2*, 248-253.

Lloyd, G. G., & Lishman, W. R. (1975). Effect of depression on the speed of recall of pleasant and unpleasant experiences. *Psychological Medicine, 5*, 173-180.

Lobitz, W. C., & Post, R. D. (1979). Parameters of self-reinforcement and depression. *Journal of Abnormal Psychology, 88*, 33-41.

Loeb, A., Beck, A. T., & Diggory, J. (1971). Differential effects of success and failure on depressed and nondepressed patients. *Journal of Nervous and Mental Disease, 152*, 106-114.

Miller, G. (1984). *An assessment of self-efficacy, performance and cognitive distortion following success and failure, in moderately depressed and nondepressed female college students.* Unpublished Honours Project, University of Sydney.

Miller, W. R. (1975). Psychological deficit in depression. *Psychological Bulletin, 82*, 238-260.

Morrow, J., & Nolen-Hoeksema, S. (1990). Effects of responses to depression on the remediation of depressive affect. *Journal of Personality and Social Psychology, 58*, 519-527.

Nixon, J., & Pearn, J. (1977). Emotional sequelae of parents and siblings following the drowning or near-drowning of a child. *Australian and New Zealand Journal of Psychiatry, 11*, 265-268.

Nolen-Hoeksema, S. (1987). Sex differences in depression: Evidence and theory. *Psychological Bulletin, 101*, 259-282.

Ozer, E. M., & Bandura, A. (1990). Mechansims governing empowerment effects: A self-efficacy analysis. *Journal of Personality and Social Psychology, 58*, 472-486.

Parkes, C. M. (1970). The first year of bereavement: A longitudinal study of the reaction of London widows to the death of their husbands. *Psychiatry, 33*, 444-467.

Parkes, C. M., & Weiss, R. S. (1983). *Recovery from bereavement.* New York: Basic Books.

Rehm, L. P. (1977). A self-control model of depression. *Behavior Therapy, 8*, 787-804.

Schwartz, N., & Bless, H. (1991). Happy and mindless, but sad and smart? The impact of affective states on analytic reasoning. In J. P. Forgas (Ed.). *Emotion and social judgments* (pp. 55-71). Oxford: Pergamon.

Schwartz, N., & Clore, G. L. (1983). Mood, misattribution and judgments of well-being: Informative and directive functions of affective states. *Journal of Personality and Social Psychology, 45*, 513-523.

Schwartz, N., & Clore, G. L. (1988). How do I feel about it? The informative functions of affective states. In K. Fiedler & J. Forgas (Eds.). *Affect, cognition, and social behavior* (pp. 44-62). Toronto: Hogrefe.

Seligman, M. E. P. (1975). *Helplessness: On depression, development and death.* San Francisco: W. H. Freeman.

Seligman, M. E. P., Abramson, L. Y., Semmel, A., & von Baeyer, C. (1979). Depressive attributional style. *Journal of Abnormal Psychology, 88*, 242-247.

Sitharthan, T., & Kavanagh, D. J. (1990). Role of self-efficacy in predicting outcomes from a programme for controlled drinking. *Drug and Alcohol Dependence, 27*, 87-94.

Smolen, R. C. (1978). Expectancies, mood and performance of depressed and non-depressed psychiatric inpatients on chance and skill tasks. *Journal of Abnormal Psychology, 87*, 91-101.

Teasdale, J. D. (1985). Psychological treatments for depression How do they work? *Behaviour Research and Therapy, 23*, 157-165.

Wilson, P. H. (1989). Cognitive-behaviour therapy for depression: Empirical findings and methodological issues in the evaluation of outcome. *Behaviour Change, 6*, 85-95.

Wright, J., & Mischel, W. (1982). The influence of affect on cognitive social learning person varaibles. *Journal of Personality and Social Psychology, 43*, 901-914.

Yusaf, S., & Kavanagh, D. J. (1990). The role of self-efficacy in the treatment of depression. *Journal of Cognitive Psychotherapy, 4*, 51-70.

Zeiss, A. M., Lewinsohn, P. M., & Muñoz, R. F. (1979). Nonspecific improvement effects in depression using interpersonal skills training, pleasant activity schedules, or cognitive training. *Journal of Consulting and Clincial Psychology, 47*, 427-439.

SELF-EFFICACY AS A RESOURCE FACTOR IN STRESS APPRAISAL PROCESSES

Matthias Jerusalem and Ralf Schwarzer

According to the cognitive-relational theory of stress, emotions, and coping, cognitive appraisals are seen as mediating processes that refer to the stakes a person has in a stressful encounter and to the coping options. They result in either challenge, threat, or harm/loss. It is undetermined, however, how these appraisals are interrelated over time and whether they can occur simultaneously. An idealized motivation model has been established to stimulate research on this issue. The present experiment has been set up to assess the dynamic pattern of cognitive appraisals at nine points in time under stress, defined as continuous failure at demanding academic tasks. General self-efficacy is considered to represent a personal resource among other antecedents of appraisals. Therefore, self-efficacy was used as a between-groups factor. Very different patterns of appraisals emerged for low and high self-efficacious subjects, indicating that high self-efficacy buffers the experience of stress, whereas low self-efficacy puts individuals at risk for a dramatic increase in threat and loss appraisals.

The present study deals with the prediction of cognitive appraisal processes by dispositional antecedents and by stressful conditions. It is based on the cognitive-relational theory which defines stress as "a particular relationship between the person and the environment that is appraised by the person as taxing or exceeding his or her resources and endangering his or her well-being" (Lazarus & Folkman, 1984b, p. 19). Appraisals are determined simultaneously by perceiving environmental demands and personal resources. They can change over time due to coping effectiveness, altered requirements, or improvements in personal abilities.

The cognitive-relational theory of stress emphasizes the continuous, reciprocal nature of the interaction between the person and the environment. Since its first publication (Lazarus, 1966), it has not only been further developed and refined, but it has also been expanded recently to a meta-theoretical concept of emotion and coping processes (Lazarus, 1991a; Lazarus & Folkman, 1987). The present paper deals with an experimental study based partly on this meta-theory of emotions and coping. Therefore, it is necessary to describe briefly some aspects of this theory that are relevant for the understanding of the study.

Meta-Theoretical Considerations

Within a meta-theoretical system approach Lazarus and Folkman (1987) conceive the complex processes of emotion as composed of causal antecedents, mediating processes, and effects. *Antecedents* are person variables like commitments or beliefs on the one hand and environmental variables, such as demands or situational constraints, on the other. *Mediating processes* refer to cognitive appraisals of situational demands and personal coping options as well as to coping efforts aimed at more or less problem-focused and emotion-focused behavior (Jerusalem & Schwarzer, 1989; Krohne, 1988; Laux & Weber, 1987; Lazarus & Folkman, 1987; McCrae & Costa, 1986). Stress experiences and coping results bring along immediate effects, such as affects or physiological changes, and long-term results concerning psychological well-being, somatic health and social functioning (Lazarus & Folkman, 1984a, 1984b).

There are *three meta-theoretical assumptions: transaction, process,* and *context.* It is assumed, first, that emotions occur as a specific encounter of the person with the environment and that both exert a reciprocal influence on each other; second, that emotions and cognitions are subject to continuous change; and third, that the meaning of a transaction is derived from the underlying context, i.e., various attributes of a natural setting determine the actual experience of emotions and the resulting action tendencies (Lazarus, 1991a, 1991b).

For obvious reasons, prior research has mostly neglected these meta-theoretical assumptions in favor of unidirectional, cross-sectional, and rather context-free designs. Within methodologically sound empirical research it is hardly possible to study complex phenomena such as emotions and coping without constraints. Also, on account of its complexity and transactional character leading to interdependencies between the involved variables, the meta-theoretical system approach cannot be investigated and empirically tested as a whole model. Rather, it represents a heuristic frame that may serve to formulate and test hypotheses in selected subareas of the theoretical system only. Thus, in practical research one has to compromise with the ideal research paradigm. Investigators have often focused on structure instead of on process, measuring single states or aggregates of states. In the present study, however, *stress* is analyzed and investigated as an *active, unfolding process.* More precisely, stress appraisal processes are predicted by environmental and personal variables as antecedents, whereas coping strategies and long-term effects are not considered. From the meta-theoretical system perspective, the study concentrates on stress antecedents and actual stress as a process, but has its limits with respect to transaction and context.

In view of the research intention and the variables involved in the present empirical study, the concept of stress appraisals will be discussed first. Second, some environmental and personal antecedents of stress evaluations are considered. Finally, we will refer to the phenomena of mixed appraisal patterns and their development over time.

Stress Appraisals

The cognitive relational theory (Lazarus & Folkman, 1984a, 1987) defines stress as an encounter in which the demands tax or exceed the available resources. Cognitive appraisals include two component processes, primary and secondary appraisals. *Primary appraisal* refers to the stakes a person has in a certain encounter. In primary appraisals, a situation is perceived as being either irrelevant, benign-positive or stressful. Those events classified as stressful can be further subdivided into the categories of challenge, threat and harm/loss.

A stress-relevant situation is appraised as challenging when it mobilizes physical and psychological activity and involvement. In the appraisal of *challenge*, a person may see an opportunity to prove herself or himself, anticipating gain, mastery or personal growth from the venture. The situation is experienced as pleasurable, exciting, and interesting, and the person is hopeful, eager, and confident to meet the demands.

Threat occurs when the individual perceives being in danger, and it is experienced when the person anticipates future harm or loss. Harm or loss can refer to physical injuries and pain or to attacks on one's self-esteem. Although in threat appraisal future prospects are seen in a negative light, the individual still seeks ways to master the situation faced. The individual is partly restricted in his or her coping capabilities, striving for a positive outcome of the situation in order to gain or to restore his or her well-being. "Rather, threat is a relational property concerning the match between perceived coping capabilities and potentially hurtful aspects of the environment" (Bandura, 1991, p. 90).

In the experience of *harm/loss*, some damage to the person has already occurred. Damages can include the injury or loss of valued persons, important objects, self-worth or social standing. Instead of attempting to master the situation, the person surrenders, overwhelmed by feelings of helplessness. Beck's cognitive theory of anxiety and depression (Beck & Clark, 1988) is in line with these assumptions, mentioning threat as the main cognitive content in anxiety compared to loss as its counterpart in depression.

Primary appraisals are mirrored by *secondary appraisals* which refer to one's available coping options for dealing with stress, i.e., one's perceived resources to cope with the demands at hand. The individual evaluates his competence, social support, and material or other resources in order to readapt to the circumstances and to reestablish an equilibrium between person and environment. In academic situations mostly the task-specific competence or the prerequisite knowledge to cope with the task is of primary importance. There is no fixed time order for primary and secondary appraisals. The latter may come first. Moreover, they depend on each other and often appear at the same time. Instead of primary and secondary, the terms "demand appraisal" and "resource appraisal" might be more appropriate. Hobfoll (1988, 1989) has expanded the stress and coping theory with respect to the conservation of resources as the main human motive in the struggle with stressful encounters.

Antecedents of Stress Appraisals

Stress appraisals result from perceived situational demands in relation to perceived personal coping resources. Despite this relational conception one can imagine environmental conditions that are more likely to induce stress than others, provided the same person is confronted with them. One can also imagine individual differences in perceived personal resources that make people more or less vulnerable to the same environmental requirements.

With respect to the relevance of *situational stressors*, Lazarus and Folkman (1984b) mention formal properties, such as novelty, event uncertainty, ambiguity and temporal aspects of the stressing conditions. For example, demands that are difficult, ambiguous, unannounced, not preparable, to be worked on both for a long time and under time pressure, are more likely to induce threat perceptions than easy tasks which can be prepared for thoroughly and can be solved under convenient pace and time conditions. Regarding *content*, environmental aspects can be distinguished with respect to the stakes involved by the kind of a given situation. For example, threatening social situations imply interpersonal threat, the danger of physical injury is perceived as physical threat, and anticipated failures endangering self-worth indicate ego-threat (McGrath, 1982; Spielberger, 1985). Lazarus (1966) additionally distinguishes between task-specific stress, including cognitive demands and other formal task properties, from failure-induced stress, including evaluation aspects such as social feedback, valence of goal, possibilities to fail, or actual failures. By and large, unfavorable task conditions combined with failure-inducing situational cues are likely to provoke feelings of distress.

With respect to the relevance of perceived *personal resources*, Lazarus and Folkman (1984b) mention commitments and beliefs. Commitments represent motivational structures such as personal goals and intentions that in part determine perceptions of situational stress relevance and the stakes at hand (Novacek & Lazarus, 1990). Provided the stakes are really relevant, beliefs as personal antecedents of stress appraisals come into play. Beliefs are convictions and expectations of being able to meet situational requirements. With "generalized beliefs"—as opposed to situation-specific appraisals of control—dispositional resource or vulnerability factors are meant, such as locus of control, general self-efficacy, trait anxiety, or self-esteem (Folkman, 1984; Hobfoll, 1989; Jerusalem, 1990a, 1990b; Lazarus & Folkman, 1987). Given a stressful situation, low dispositional control expectancies make people vulnerable to distress, whereas perceptions of high dispositional competence represent a positive resource factor.

Since the present study is concerned with achievement tasks to be solved under ego-threatening conditions, general self-efficacy can be conceived of as a personal resource or vulnerability factor (Bandura, 1986, 1989, 1991, 1992; Jerusalem, 1990a). People who generally trust in their own capabilities to master all kinds of environmental demands also tend to interpret difficult achievement tasks as more challenging than threatening. Their generalized belief of a positive self-efficacy in this sense serves as a resource factor that should buffer against distress experiences furthering "eustress" perceptions instead. Individuals, however, who are characterized by generally low self-efficacy expectations are prone to self-doubts, state anxiety, threat appraisals and perceptions of coping deficiencies when confronted with critical achievement demands. Moreover, previous research on anxiety and self-related cognitions has demonstrated that generalized beliefs of weak self-efficacy make persons vulnerable toward distress experiences because they tend to be permanently worried, have weak task-specific competence expectancies, interpret physiological arousal as an indicator of anxiety, regard achievement feedback as social evaluations of their personal value, and feel more responsible for failure than for success (Bandura, 1992; Carver & Scheier, 1988; Dweck & Wortman, 1982; Epstein, 1986; Jerusalem, 1990a, 1990b; Ozer & Bandura, 1990; Sarason, 1988; Schwarzer, 1986; Schwarzer & Wicklund, 1991; Spielberger, 1972, 1985; Wine, 1980, 1982; Wood & Bandura, 1989). Like other trait-like person characteristics, weak general competence expectancies have numerous causes. A history of success and failure combined with a lack of supportive feedback and an unfavorable attributional style by parents, teachers and peers may lead to the development of a tendency to scan the environment for potential dangers ("sensitizing"), to appraise demands as threatening, and to cope with problems in a maladaptive way. In the present context it can be summarized that general self-efficacy is seen as a personal resource factor with respect to distress experiences such as threat and loss perceptions, which are assumed to come up faster and to a higher degree for low compared to high self-efficacious subjects. The latter are expected to feel more challenged instead. These assumptions do not apply to the absolute level of each distinct stress appraisal, but rather to the prediction of appraisal patterns and their changes over time. For a better understanding of this phenomenon, the issue of appraisal patterns and processes is to be discussed in more detail.

Appraisal Patterns and Processes

The experience of challenge, threat or loss does not happen exclusively, but can overlap or even occur simultaneously. Challenge, threat and loss are not to be considered as clearly distinct modes of experience, but rather as interrelated cognitive-emotional states that exist simultaneously. For example, a person might be challenged by the demanding characteristics of a situation, while expecting injury to his or her well-being at the same time. Since life often confronts us with situations that are unforeseen, difficult, novel or ambiguous, the corresponding appraisals can be complex states with more or less favorable and unfavorable evaluations of these environmental demands. Moreover, the structure of this mixture is likely to change over time unless the problem is solved immediately. Once a transactional stress process has commenced, the pattern of positive and negative evaluations changes from one encounter to the next. Challenge appraisals might be stronger than threat at one time, both could be perceived as equal size the next time, and another time threat might exceed challenge. The actual pattern at each point in time reflects the momentary subjective uncertainty of being able to cope with the demands at hand. In a study by Folkman and Lazarus (1985), for example, 94% of a student sample facing an examination experienced feelings of both threat and challenge two days before the exam. Afterwards these appraisals diminished; in case of poor grades they were replaced by loss perceptions. Similar patterns were found for emotions connected to cognitive appraisals (Folkman & Lazarus, 1985; Gall & Evans, 1987; Smith & Ellsworth, 1985, 1987).

According to these research findings, stressful encounters are dynamic, unfolding processes that imply complex appraisal patterns, rather than static, unitary events. More scientific knowledge is required about the nature of the interrelationships among challenge, threat, and loss over time under certain precisely defined environmental conditions in general, and about the role of individual differences in particular. The following theoretical considerations lead to an idealized model of the potential development and change of appraisal processes under certain environmental circumstances and for specific individual differences.

A Process Model

We have developed a process model of cognitive appraisals (Schwarzer, Jerusalem, & Stiksrud, 1984; Jerusalem, 1990a) which extends Lazarus' original stress theory by integrating ideas from Seligman's helplessness theory (Abramson, Seligman, & Teasdale, 1978; Brown & Siegel, 1988; Seligman, 1975). A state of helplessness is predicted as a long-term consequence of cumulative experience of personal uncontrollability. Accordingly, the theoretical model of appraisal processes was built for the special case of continuous failures. Its purpose was to describe the potential development of loss of control and personal helplessness by means of cognitive appraisal processes in academic failure situations. We argue that at almost any point in time, all three cognitive appraisals may occur simultaneously, but to differing degrees, therefore leading to different emotions: Challenge causes curiosity, exploration and productive arousal threat causes anxiety and loss of control causes helplessness or even depression.

Looking at the process model in Figure 1, the x-axis represents the number of failures. The curves characterize the idealized potential development and change of challenge, threat and loss perceptions. With continued experience of failures, challenge diminishes, while loss enhances from one point in time to the next. Threat perceptions first increase and then decrease. Unexpected failures might be interpreted as challenges to one's competence, whereas threat or even loss are less relevant. If this happens repeatedly, the person will begin to feel more threatened than challenged, but will still persist with the task. The highest degree of threat is located at the point where complete subjective uncertainty about the next outcome prevails. Later, when subsequent failure is expected with higher certainty, the individual will experience loss of control while feeling less threatened because the loss becomes certain. According to this model, four *idealized motivational stages* can be distinguished:

1. The *Challenge Stage* is a kind of "*reactance stage.*" Although the person is challenged by one or more failures, she retains confidence in her ability to cope with the demands. High self-efficacy may be combined with productive arousal, i.e., the tendency to explore the nature of the task.

2. The *First Threat Stage* occurs when failures mount and threat surpasses challenge appraisal anxiety is the dominant emotion. The combination of anxiety with productive arousal here can be called "facilitating anxiety" because the person is still self-confident and persists with the task.

3. The *Second Threat Stage* occurs at the culminating point, when there is complete uncertainty about the next outcome. The threat appraisal is combined with less challenge and some loss of control. This mode can be called "debilitating anxiety state" because intrusive self-related cognitions distract from the task. The person worries about his or her performance, capability, and the potential for further failures.

4. Finally, there is a *Loss-of-Control Stage*. Loss of control is dominant, replacing the appraisal of threat. The student becomes helpless and disengages; the next failure is almost certain. Cognitive appraisals cannot be predicted by the situation at hand exclusively, for example by *task-specific failure experiences.*

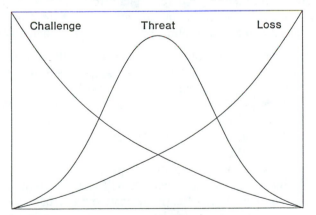

Development of Primary Appraisals

Challenge   Threat   Loss

Failure Experiences

Figure 1 Idealized process model of the development of cognitive appraisals under continuous failure.

The model is restricted to the special case of continuous failures, a condition which is rather exceptional than commonplace under real-life circumstances. Besides, human beings confronted with achievement demands differ with respect to their acquired competencies and their generalized beliefs. Thus, there are also *subject-matter-specific factors* producing differences with respect to the proportional amounts of challenge, threat and loss. Life-long learning experiences establish subjective perceptions of individual resources in the sense of more or less stable personality traits. For example, anxious individuals or those with unfavorable generalized expectancies of self-efficacy often have a learning history which includes a number of individual failures or perceived threats in a variety of more or less taxing situations. High trait anxiety or low general self-efficacy make one vulnerable to demands which endanger self-worth.

When confronting stressful academic demands, individuals with high general self-efficacy expectancies or low trait anxiety will most likely start at the left side of the model curve. Positive self-evaluation retains the confidence in the ability to cope with the demands. This is the *reactance stage*. Less self-efficacious people, however, are more likely to display state anxiety and develop only little, if any, positive competence expectancies. When failures mount and the task is perceived as becoming more difficult, incremental threat instead of challenge would be experienced but the person can still be self-reliant and persistent with the task. This person may arrive at the *first threat stage*. Supposing she suffers from her generalized belief of low self-efficacy to such a degree that her expectancy for failure is stronger than that for success, she would start the sequence at a point where more loss than challenge is experienced. She then worries about performance, has self-doubts and is not at all confident about her competence. This refers to the *second threat stage*. For depressed individuals or those with high helplessness scores, a dominance of loss perceptions can be expected. Only few failures suffice for them to give up further efforts because the next failure is almost certain. This is equivalent to the *loss-of-control stage*. Similar stages have been proposed by Wortman and Brehm (1975) and by Heckhausen (1991).

Empirical evidence was obtained in a study with high-school students (Schwarzer et al., 1984). Within a two-year period, different student subpopulations became more or less anxious and more or less helpless over time. As predicted, the anxiety level of some subjects declined, but only at the expense of helplessness. Particularly long-term low achievers developed a tendency to perceive less threat and more loss of control in face of academic demands. Regarding the model of appraisal processes, this was a preliminary pilot field study. The present research questions are how far similar processes can be observed within a laboratory experiment and whether general self-efficacy as a resource factor serves to predict the hypothesized appraisal patterns and processes. Only some few longitudinal field studies have addressed cognitive appraisal processes (e.g., Covington, Omelich, & Schwarzer, 1986; Folkman & Lazarus, 1985; Jerusalem, 1990a; Schwarzer et al., 1984). The strength of these studies was that they tried to capture the dynamic character of the theory by measuring cognitions in naturalistic settings at different points in time, but the joint consideration of individual differences and experimental factors is still lacking.

Research Question

In the present study, the research question is directed at appraisal processes depending on experimental treatment and personality traits. Stress appraisals are linked to one personal resource factor (general self-efficacy) and to one environmental demands factor (difficult academic tasks). When the tasks become more complex and failures mount, all subjects should lower their initial level of challenge appraisal and experience more threat and more loss of control until a person's maximal level is attained. It is also expected that low general self-efficacy represents a major vulnerability condition which predisposes the corresponding individuals to appraise the situation as little challenging, but more threatening, and—later—as uncontrollable. Thus, *two independent factors*, *general self-efficacy* and *demanding experimental tasks* are seen as influential for the development of three cognitive appraisals over nine points in time. Further research questions are the following: Can overlapping appraisal patterns be observed, i.e., do different cognitive appraisals turn up at the same time? Do cognitive appraisals change during a stressful encounter? How do appraisals of challenge, threat, and loss develop over time in face of continuous failure? Is there a differential development with respect to dispositional self-efficacy levels? How is continuous failure experienced by low self-efficacious subjects?

METHOD

Sample and Procedure

Subjects were 210 adults (108 females and 102 males between 21 and 52 years, with a mean age of 29.8 years) who responded to advertisements in city magazines and newspapers. The design of the study is depicted in Figure 2. Subjects filled in a series of various personality scales, among them a general self-efficacy scale. They were then confronted with nine series, each consisting of difficult performance tasks, performance feedback, and self-report items.

The experimental setting contained task-specific stressors (ambiguity, time pressure, difficulty, etc.) and ego-threatening failure conditions. Each of the first six task sequences was composed of 15 *anagrams* presented on a computer-screen. Within each set of anagrams the degree of difficulty increased from the first to the fifteenth, and all but the last ones were solvable. Three further task sequences, consisting of *intelligence test items*, were given by the experimenter in a paper-and-pencil version. All tasks were described as cognitive problem-solving, to be performed under time pressure, designed to measure the more academic and the more practical aspects of intellectual ability, respectively. Each anagram was presented individually on the computer monitor with a number appearing under each letter. Subjects were to type a new sequence of numbers

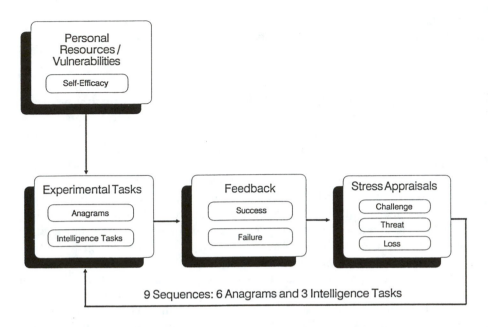

Figure 2 Design of the experiment.

according to the correct order of the letters forming the word that was looked for. A maximum of 40 seconds was allowed for each anagram. Subjects were instructed to call the next item by pressing a certain key if they found the solution before the time was up. Otherwise, a tone was sounded and the next anagram appeared automatically. The introductory information on how to work with the computer was provided by the computer program. Paper-and-pencil intelligence items were given under comparable difficulty and time conditions.

After each task episode, one group consistently received fictitious success feedback and the other group fictitious failure feedback. The feedback was partly related to actual performance by a programming device so the outcome seemed more credible. The feedback referred both to individual performance (number of points achieved) and to the performance within their age group (social comparison information). In the success group, subjects were told that the number of points achieved was above average; in the failure group individual performance was reported as being below average. Achievement feedback was followed by 21 items addressing various aspects of self-related cognitions, among them perceptions of challenge, threat and loss.

This cycle (experimental tasks, feedback, stress appraisals) was repeated nine times, six with anagrams and three with intelligence items. Afterwards, subjects were paid and debriefed about the manipulated feedback. The whole procedure lasted about three hours. The present analysis deals with the *failure condition* and with *general self-efficacy* as a resource/vulnerability factor for individual appraisal processes. The failure group consisted of half the sample (105 subjects).

Instruments

General self-efficacy was measured by a scale we developed with respect to the self-efficacy theory of Bandura (1977, 1986; Jerusalem & Schwarzer, 1986). In this study a six-item version was used (e.g., "When facing difficulties, I can always trust my abilities."). Its internal consistency was alpha = .82. In order to assess *cognitive appraisals as dependent variables*, we developed psychometric scales which had to be short because they were presented nine times; appraisals should not take more time and should not be emphasized more than the problem-solving itself. The *Challenge* scale consisted of four items, such as "I am already curious about how I will manage the next tasks" (alpha = .78); the *Threat* scale contained three items, such as "I am afraid of not being equal to the next tasks" (alpha = .81); and the *Loss* scale was represented by four items, such as "I feel discouraged and depressed now" (alpha = .83). The internal consistencies within each appraisal category were averaged over time. The response format was a four-point-scale ranging from *not at all* to *a great deal*.

RESULTS

The failure group was subdivided by use of median split of the self-efficacy scores. Scores below average are conceived of as weak resources indicating high vulnerability ($n = 46$), those above average as strong resources indicating low vulnerability accordingly ($n = 59$). By use of 2 x 9 analyses of variance with re-peated measurements, the self-efficacy factor then served as one predictor of the intensity and change of primary appraisals over time.

At any point in time, the three cognitive appraisals occurred simultaneously. Throughout the nine sequences, all appraisals remained present, but to different degrees. In short, as predicted, there were *patterns of appraisals* to be observed instead of mutually exclusive states of challenge, threat or loss perceptions.

First, the overall results are given separately for the experimental and the personality factors. Analyses of repeated measurements revealed that all apprais-als were changing over time. The corresponding F values were computed accord-ing to the correction procedure proposed by Geisser and Greenhouse (1958). Due to *continuous failures*, challenge appraisals declined ($F[8, 824] = 20.32$, $p < .001$), whereas threat and loss perceptions increased over time ($F[8, 824] = 1.98$, $p < .05$ for threat and $F[8, 824] = 5.45$, $p < .001$ for loss). The nature of all changes can be characterized by linear trend components (Challenge: $F[1, 103] = 78$, $p < .001$; Threat: $F[1, 103] = 6.7$, $p < .05$; Loss: $F[1, 103] = 18.8$, $p < .001$).

As expected, *general self-efficacy* turned out to be an important predictor of subjective perceptions following failure experiences. With respect to all appraisal qualities, low self-efficacious subjects reported less favorable stress cognitions than high self-efficacious subjects. Low self-efficacy was accompanied by con-siderably lower challenge and higher threat and loss evaluations (challenge: $F[1, 103] = 17.5$, $p < .001$); threat: $F[1, 103] = 18.5$, $p < .001$; loss: $F[1, 103] = 14.9$,

$p < .001$). There were even additional Self-Efficacy x Time interactions predicting both threat and loss appraisals and indicating a stronger increase of these unfavorable distress experiences for low self-efficacy compared to high self-efficacy subjects (threat: $F[8, 824] = 4, p < .001$; loss: $F[8, 824] = 3.1, p < .01$). The observed interaction effects are mainly due to linear trend differences (threat: $F[1, 103] = 6.7, p < .05$; loss: $F[1, 103] = 9.8, p < .05$). In sum, both environmental failure conditions and individual self-efficacy differences were powerful antecedents of the unfolding process of stress appraisals.

The *dominance structure* of primary appraisals was affected by the two stress factors, too. At the *beginning*, different structures were observed for *both self-efficacy groups*. High self-efficacy individuals felt more challenged than threatened, and they perceived more threat than loss, as predicted by the theoretical model. This was similar for low self-efficacy subjects, but the difference between challenge on the one hand and threat or loss on the other hand was to a lesser extent. Compared with the high self-efficacy group, low self-efficacy subjects reported less challenge and more threat and loss—at the very beginning as well as overall (when summed up over all points in time).

The results for high self-efficacious persons are presented in Figure 3, those for low self-efficacious persons in Figure 4. The corresponding means and standard deviations are reflected in Tables 1 and 2, respectively. Scores in challenge, threat and loss were each divided by the respective number of scale items in order to attain the same unit of measurement.

Table 1
Means and Standard Deviations of Challenge, Threat and Loss for High Self-Efficacy and Failure Experiences (n = 59)

Points in Time	Challenge		Threat		Loss	
	M	*SD*	*M*	*SD*	*M*	*SD*
1	2.96	.56	1.85	.65	1.66	.57
2	2.74	.66	2.00	.71	1.70	.62
3	2.62	.69	2.01	.78	1.80	.70
4	2.61	.72	2.02	.79	1.72	.69
5	2.49	.73	2.00	.78	1.77	.72
6	2.50	.78	2.00	.84	1.77	.75
7	2.67	.69	1.84	.68	1.73	.74
8	2.58	.66	1.83	.74	1.71	.67
9	2.57	.69	1.84	.73	1.82	.74

Table 2

Means and Standard Deviations of Challenge, Threat and Loss for Low Self-Efficacy and Failure Experiences (n = 46)

Points in Time	Challenge		Threat		Loss	
	M	*SD*	*M*	*SD*	*M*	*SD*
1	2.54	.47	2.25	.65	1.98	.50
2	2.32	.60	2.36	.67	2.05	.62
3	2.19	.63	2.38	.70	2.05	.74
4	2.14	.69	2.40	.73	2.17	.82
5	2.05	.67	2.40	.72	2.26	.84
6	1.95	.76	2.55	.77	2.32	.78
7	2.15	.74	2.50	.63	2.33	.82
8	2.04	.64	2.55	.70	2.35	.78
9	2.02	.68	2.60	.71	2.39	.81

With respect to *changes over time* (linear trend components), both groups can clearly be differentiated. For *high self-efficacy* subjects, challenge perceptions decreased with continued failure experiences ($F[1,58] = 15.2$, $p < .001$). However, threat and loss did not change significantly but remained on a low and constant level, although failures were repeatedly reported. Throughout the entire sequence, challenge cognitions exceeded threat and loss appraisals.

In contrast, *low self-efficacy* subjects were *much more affected by failure*. Challenge perceptions declined ($F[1,45] = 34.5$, $p < .001$), whereas threat and loss perceptions increased over time (threat: $F[1,45] = 9.8$, $p < .01$; loss: $F[1,45] = 18$, $p < .001$). The strength of these temporal trends is slightly weakened by motions that take place after measurement point six: Contrary to the trend an increase in challenge perceptions and a similar, but comparably smaller, decrease in threat evaluations was observed. These effects were probably due to the fact that at this point the task material changed from anagrams to intelligence items. In face of the altered demands, both reappraisals of coping options and corresponding primary reappraisals occurred. Accordingly, subjective evaluations were not generalized from anagrams to intelligence tasks, at least not for challenge. However, these "recovery effects" were limited to a short time period. Due to the fact that failure feedbacks did not dissipate—although the task quality was different—appraisals again became less favorable.

Looking at the results in terms of temporal patterns, it is obvious that the appraisal pattern remained stable for high self-efficacy subjects in the sense that challenge exceeded threat and loss perceptions at all nine points in time. In comparison, the results for *low self-efficacy* subjects were completely different. The temporal dominance structure of stress appraisals in this group was reversed: At

Temporal Pattern of Primary Appraisals

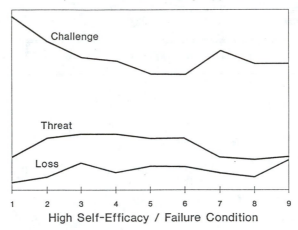

High Self-Efficacy / Failure Condition

Figure 3 Temporal pattern of cognitive appraisals for high self-efficacy subjects.

Temporal Pattern of Primary Appraisals

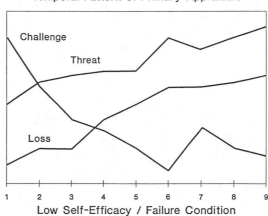

Low Self-Efficacy / Failure Condition

Figure 4 Temporal pattern of cognitive appraisals for low self-efficacy subjects.

first challenge clearly dominated threat and loss, but at the end threat and loss had become the prevailing appraisals. Accordingly, two intersection points were observed: Challenge was surpassed by threat at Point 2 and by loss at Point 4. Referring to the theoretical model, these intersection points indicate shifts from the reactance stage (Stage 1) to the first threat stage (Stage 2), and from the first to the second threat stage (Stage 3), respectively. However, loss never exceeded threat perceptions, which would have been required to indicate a state of helplessness (Stage 4).

DISCUSSION

The reported findings demonstrate mainly that situation variables and person variables are prominent predictors of perceived challenge, threat and loss in stressful situations. In an experimental setting these appraisals differed in dependence on evaluative feedback and general self-efficacy. In face of continuous failures stress appraisals changed from favorable to unfavorable evaluations in the long run. At the same time, low self-efficacious individuals felt more distressed than high self-efficacious individuals. As predicted, stress appraisals did not come up as single states that are switched either "on" or "off." Instead, dynamic patterns of appraisals do exist that are related to each other and that are also changeable according to the transactional processes involved. By this, the entire pattern is continuously changing, but at no time will any of the appraisals disappear unless the situation is no longer perceived as stressful.

With respect to these complex and dynamic appraisal processes the role of general self-efficacy as a resource/vulnerability factor could be clearly demonstrated. Moreover, the results could be mostly explained with the help of a theoretical model. In general, *high self-efficacious individuals* seem to be scarcely vulnerable to the stressing situational conditions since they hardly show any reactions to experimental manipulations. Obviously, high general self-efficacy is equivalent to or leads to positive personal beliefs providing people with good capacities to resist stress. Even though failures are consistently given at nine points in time, appraisals remain predominantly positive, and their relative strengths do not change. During the whole time sequence, subjects remain within the challenge or reactance stage, and they do not enter threat or loss stages at all. The stressing situational conditions do not take much effect because they are confronted with a personality who can resist on account of his or her powerful resources and low vulnerability, respectively. By and large, the experimental situation faced by low vulnerability persons seems not to be stressful enough to induce strong negative emotional experiences.

Contrary to this obvious stress resistence, *low self-efficacious subjects* seem to be especially vulnerable for difficult demand characteristics and failure experiences. They come up with less favorable evaluations, consistently developing to a more negative way of appraising situational demands. By and by, they shift from reactance to the first threat stage, and later on to the second threat stage as well. In this case, the experimental demands and failure feedbacks do take much effect because they are perceived by a personality who is handicapped by his or her weak resources and high vulnerability, respectively. However, the experimental situation has its constraints in so far as it is not powerful enough to make subjects turn to stage four in the process model, that is, to elicit predominant loss-of-control evaluations and overwhelming feelings of helplessness. However, for ethical reasons one should not complain about this specific result.

Concerning the theoretical model, the predicted slope of threat appraisals that could not be fitted exactly in this investigation might be particularly sensitive to the stakes given. Regarding the above-mentioned field study (Schwarzer et al., 1984), long-term low grades endanger the academic career of the respective students. Since this concerns an important real-life stake almost everyone strives for, the low graders have enough reason to feel helpless and depressed in the long run. Within an experimental situation one has to undertake and then is able to leave again, it is more likely that real-life stakes are not so deeply involved, i.e., central values and commitments might be less emphasized. In order to feel severely helpless, individuals most likely have to suffer from failures in more stress-relevant real-life situations than only from negative achievement feedback in a laboratory setting where ethical limits are given in this respect.

Appraisal processes also turned out to be sensitive to variations in task material or problem structure at hand. Movements of challenge and threat contrary to the trend appeared when a shift from anagrams to intelligence problems occured. One explanation would be that by this shift several demand characteristics are changing, too, for example situational ambiguity, familiarity with the tasks at hand, or their perceived validity for assessing intellectual ability. The distinctiveness of task material may cause new hope to be better able to meet the requirements of the upcoming problems. However, this renewed confidence disappears again as soon as further failures are faced.

It is interesting to note that predominantly low self-efficacious individuals show strong reactions to task shifts in this way, whereas high self-efficacious subjects seem to be less sensitive to differing task materials. For the latter, their generalized beliefs obviously provide a shelter from all kinds of failure feedback, at least from those experienced in the experimental session. Maybe they are so confident in their abilities so as not to attach any importance to the artificial problems given by the experimenter because they do not believe in the tasks' validity for intelligence measurement and/or the ecological validity of the experimental condition. In contrast, low self-efficacious individuals do not possess such a strong shelter from external feedback because they are much less secure with respect to their actual abilities. Due to their lack of self-confidence they are guided to a large extent by situational cues which have a strong impact on stress appraisals, be it failure, task material change, or other conditions.

General self-efficacy as a resource/vulnerability factor towards feeling distressed when confronted with achievement demands serves as a moderator for the impact of these demands on actual stress experience as represented by cognitive appraisals. High self-efficacy subjects rather select positive cues, such as stable and favorable self-evaluations, than negative signals, such as situational failures, in appraising the stressing person-environment relationship. Low self-efficacy subjects see themselves confronted with negative achievement cues and negative self-evaluations. Thus, both information sources are combined and attached to high importance, leading to distressful experiences which turn from bad to worse in the long run.

REFERENCES

Abramson, L. Y., Seligman, M. E. P., & Teasdale, J. (1978). Learned helplessness in humans: Critique and reformulation. *Journal of Abnormal Psychology, 87*, 49-74.

Bandura, A. (1977). Self-efficacy: Toward a unifying theory of behavioral change. *Psychological Review, 84*, 191-215.

Bandura, A. (1986). *Social foundations of thought and action: A social cognitive theory.* Englewood Cliffs, N.J.: Prentice-Hall.

Bandura, A. (1989). Human agency in social cognitive theory. *American Psychologist, 44*, 1175-1184.

Bandura, A. (1991). Self-efficacy conception of anxiety. In R. Schwarzer & R. A. Wicklund (Eds.), *Anxiety and self-focused attention* (pp. 89-110). London: Harwood Academic Publishers.

Bandura, A. (1992). Exercise of personal agency through the self-efficacy mechanism. In R. Schwarzer (Ed.), *Self-efficacy: Thought control of action.* New York: Hemisphere (this volume).

Beck, A. T., & Clark, D. A. (1988). Anxiety and depression: An information processing perspective. *Anxiety Research, 1*, 23-36.

Brown, J. D., & Siegel, J. M. (1988). Attributions for negative life events and depression: The role of perceived control. *Journal of Personality and Social Psychology, 55*, 316-322.

Carver, C. S., & Scheier, M. F. (1988). A control-process perspective on anxiety. *Anxiety Research, 1*, 17-22.

Covington, M., Omelich, C., & Schwarzer, R. (1986). Anxiety, aspirations and self-concept in the achievement process. A longitudinal model with latent variables. *Motivation and Emotion, 10*, 71-88.

Dweck, C. S., & Wortman, C. B. (1982). Learned helplessness, anxiety and achievement motivation. In H. W. Krohne & L. Laux (Eds.), *Achievement, stress, and anxiety* (pp. 93-125). Washington, DC: Hemisphere.

Epstein, S. (1986). Anxiety, arousal, and the self-concept. In C. D. Spielberger & I. G. Sarason (Eds.), *Stress and anxiety. A sourcebook of theory and research* (pp. 265-305). Washington, DC: Hemisphere.

Folkman, S. (1984). Personal control and stress and coping process: A theoretical analysis. *Journal of Personality and Social Psychology, 46*, 839-852.

Folkman, S., & Lazarus, R. S. (1985). If it changes it must be a process: Study of emotion and coping during three stages of a college examination. *Journal of Personality and Social Psychology, 48*, 150-170.

Gall, T. L., & Evans, D. R. (1987). The dimensionality of cognitive appraisal and its relationship to physical and psychological well-being. *The Journal of Psychology, 121*, 539-546.

Geisser, S., & Greenhouse, S.W. (1958). An extension of Box's results on the use of the F-distribution in multivariate analysis. *Annals of Mathematical Statistics, 29*, 885-891.

Heckhausen, H. (1991). *Motivation and action.* Heidelberg: Springer.

Hobfoll, S. E. (1988). *The ecology of stress.* Washington, DC: Hemisphere.

Hobfoll, S. E. (1989). Conservation of resources: A new attempt at conceptualizing stress. *American Psychologist, 44* (3), 513-524.

Jerusalem, M. (1990a). *Persönliche Ressourcen, Vulnerabilität und Streßerleben* [Personal resources, vulnerability, and stress experience]. Göttingen: Hogrefe.

Jerusalem, M. (1990b). Temporal patterns of stress appraisals for high- and low-anxious individuals. *Anxiety Research, 3*, 113-129.

Jerusalem, M., & Schwarzer, R. (1986). Selbstwirksamkeit [Self-efficacy]. In R. Schwarzer (Ed.), *Skalen zur Befindlichkeit und Persönlichkeit* (pp. 15-28). Berlin: Freie Universität, Institut für Psychologie.

Jerusalem, M., & Schwarzer, R. (1989). Anxiety and self-concept as antecedents of stress and coping: A longitudinal study with German and Turkish adolescents. *Personality and Individual Differences, 10* (7), 785-792.

Krohne, H. W. (1988). Coping research: Current theoretical and methodological developments. *The German Journal of Psychology, 12*, 1-30.

Laux, L., & Weber, H. (1987). Person-centred coping research. *European Journal of Personality, 1*, 193-214.

Lazarus, R. S. (1966). *Psychological stress and the coping process*. New York: McGraw-Hill.

Lazarus, R. S. (1991a). *Emotion and adaptation*. New York: Oxford University Press.

Lazarus, R. S. (1991b). Cognition and motivation in emotion. *American Psychologist, 46*, 352-367.

Lazarus, R. S., & Folkman, S. (1984a). Coping and adaptation. In D. Gentry (Ed.), *The handbook of behavioral medicine* (pp. 282-325). New York: Guilford.

Lazarus, R. S., & Folkman, S. (1984b). *Stress, appraisal, and coping* . New York: Springer.

Lazarus, R. S., & Folkman, S. (1987). Transactional theory and research on emotions and coping. *European Journal of Personality, 1*, 141-170.

McCrae, R. R., & Costa, R. T. (1986). Personality, coping, and coping effectiveness in an adult sample. *Journal of Personality, 54*, 385-405.

McGrath, J. E. (1982). Methodological problems in research on stress. In H. W. Krohne & L. Laux (Eds.), *Achievement, stress, and anxiety* (pp. 19-50). Washington, DC: Hemisphere.

Novacek, J., & Lazarus, R. S. (1990). The structure of personality commitments. *Journal of Personality, 58*, 693-715.

Ozer, E., & Bandura, A. (1990). Mechanisms governing empowerment effects: A self-efficacy analysis. *Journal of Personality and Social Psychology, 58*, 472-486.

Sarason, I. G. (1988). Anxiety, self-preoccupation and attention. *Anxiety Research, 1*, 3-8.

Schwarzer, R. (Ed.) (1986). *Self-related cognitions in anxiety and motivation*. Hillsdale, NJ: Erlbaum.

Schwarzer, R., Jerusalem, M., & Stiksrud, A. (1984). The developmental relationship between test anxiety and helplessness. In H. M. van der Ploeg, R. Schwarzer, & C. D. Spielberger (Eds.), *Advances in test anxiety research* (Vol. 3, pp. 73-79). Lisse, The Netherlands/Hillsdale, NJ: Swets & Zeitlinger/Erlbaum.

Schwarzer, R., & Wicklund, R. A. (Eds.) (1991). Anxiety and self-focused attention. London: Harwood Academic Publishers.

Seligman, M. E. P. (1975). *Helplessness. On depression, development and death*. San Francisco: Freeman.

Smith, C. A., & Ellsworth, P. C. (1985). Patterns of cognitive appraisal in emotion. *Journal of Personality and Social Psychology, 48*, 813-838.

Smith, C. A., & Ellsworth, P. C. (1987). Patterns of appraisal and emotion related to taking an exam. *Journal of Personality and Social Psychology, 52*, 475-488.

Spielberger, C. D. (1972). Conceptual and methodological issues in anxiety research. In C. D. Spielberger (Ed.), *Anxiety: Current trends in theory and research* (Vol. 2, pp. 481-493). New York: Academic Press.

Spielberger, C. D. (1985). Anxiety, cognition and affect: A state-trait perspective. In H. Tuma & J. Maser (Eds.), *Anxiety and anxiety disorders* (pp. 171-182). Hillsdale, NJ: Erlbaum.

Wine, J. D. (1980). Cognitive-attentional theory of test anxiety. In I. G. Sarason (Ed.), *Test anxiety: Theory, research, and applications* (pp. 349-385). Hillsdale, NJ: Erlbaum.

Wine, J. D. (1982). Evaluation anxiety: A cognitive-attentional construct. In H. W. Krohne & L. Laux (Eds.), *Achievement, stress, and anxiety* (pp. 207-219). Washington, DC: Hemisphere.

Wood, R. E., & Bandura, A. (1989). Impact of conceptions of ability on self-regulatory mechanisms and complex decision making. *Journal of Personality and Social Psychology, 56*, 407-415.

Wortman, C. B., & Brehm, J. W. (1975). Responses to uncontrollable outcomes: An integration of reactance theory and the learned helplessness model. In L. Berkowitz (Ed.), *Advances in experimental social psychology* (Vol. 8, pp. 277-336). New York: Academic Press.

IV

SELF-EFFICACY AND
HEALTH BEHAVIORS

SELF-EFFICACY IN THE ADOPTION AND MAINTENANCE OF HEALTH BEHAVIORS: THEORETICAL APPROACHES AND A NEW MODEL

Ralf Schwarzer

Health behavior theories endeavor to explain and to predict human behaviors that contribute either to the risk or to the prevention of disease onset. There are considerable individual differences with regard to the adoption and maintenance of health behaviors. These differences have been attributed to a variety of factors, such as vulnerability to illness, perceived threat, or attitude towards a particular behavior. So far, there has been little agreement on which of these factors is the most important one, and if and how they interact. Current theoretical approaches offer different explanations as to which causal mechanism shapes the intention to change risk behaviors or helps to maintain health behaviors. This paper provides a critical analysis of four theories: Self-Efficacy Theory, Health Belief Model, Theory of Planned Behavior, and Protection Motivation Theory. Based on this comparison, an attempt is made to reconceptualize the process by which people adopt precaution strategies, change detrimental health habits, maintain desired health behaviors, and abstain from risky habits. From a social-cognitive perspective, a causal model is proposed, the so-called Health Action Process Approach, which focuses on the role of expectancies and covers self-regulatory processes in the maintenance phase. It is assumed that a complex set of expectancies, one of them being self-efficacy expectancy, results in a behavioral intention. In order to carry out the behavior and to prevent relapse, action-related cognitions are required, including action plans and action control. Additionally, situational factors are considered that reflect the risk potential involved in a particular environment as well as social support coming forward in a particular context.

Health behavior theories aim at behavioral change, in particular at the causal mechanisms that either shape an intention to change one's behavior or help to maintain a specific health behavior (such as abstinence). These two lines of theorizing and research follow separate traditions. Models have been designed to explain and to predict a behavioral intention, whereas different models have been established to better understand why people fail to maintain the health behaviors to which they had committed themselves. A comprehensive approach that accounts for all aspects of health behavior, however, is missing. This paper provides a critical analysis of theories of health behavior and attempts to reconceptualize the process by which people adopt precaution strategies, change detrimental health habits, and maintain desired health behaviors as well as abstain from risky habits.

Expectancies and Health Behavior: Benefits From Social Cognitive Theory

According to the Social Cognitive Theory (Bandura, 1977, 1986), behavior is governed by expectancies and incentives. An incentive pertains to the subjective importance of a particular outcome or object; behavior is regulated by its consequences (reinforcements) as perceived by the person. Expectancies can be subdivided into three types: (a) situation-outcome expectancies, i.e., which consequences will occur without interfering personal action; (b) outcome expectancies, i.e., the assumed normal consequences of action, and (c) self-efficacy expectancies, i.e., perceiving one's competence to perform a specific action required to attain a desired outcome.

The likelihood that people adopt a valued health behavior (such as physical exercise) or change a detrimental habit (such as quitting smoking) therefore may depend on three cognitions: (a) the expectancy that a life situation is dangerous (smoking and lack of exercise may trigger diseases), (b) the expectancy that behavioral change will reduce the threat, and (c) the expectancy that one is sufficiently competent to adopt the positive behavior or to quit the negative behavior.

Outcome Expectancies and Self-Efficacy Expectancies

The self-sustaining power of risk behaviors is best illustrated in the case of addictions, quitting attempts and relapse (for a review see Marlatt, Baer, Donovan, & Kivlahan, 1988). Why are risky habits maintained over an extended period of time, why is it so hard to initiate change, and why do people seldom persist when trying to quit the habit? These difficulties cannot be attributed to the pharmacological properties of the substance only, but also have to be explained by cognitive factors. Two kinds of cognitions proved to be of critical importance, namely outcome expectancies and self-efficacy expectancies.

Considerable research attention has been devoted to outcome expectancies. One kind of outcome expectancy is represented by the belief that certain risk behaviors will produce a desired outcome, for example, pleasant emotions, or at least the avoidance or minimization of negative emotions. Alcohol expectancies, for example, have been shown to include physical pleasure, improved social facilitation, increased self-esteem and assertiveness, enhanced sexual performance, and relief from tension (Critchlow, 1986; Critchlow Leigh, 1989). Substance-related outcome expectancies are already developed before the first use of a drug, and they are reinforced and stabilized by subsequent risk behavior followed by seemingly rewarding consequences. For example, the belief that alcohol reduces tension is often confirmed when alcohol is consumed in a stress situation. Another kind of outcome expectancy refers to behavior change, such as the belief that quitting drinking would improve health. It is this kind of conviction that is necessary to overcome addictions, and therefore its establishment has been a major treatment goal (Marlatt, 1985).

Self-efficacy expectancies, on the other hand, represent the belief that addictive behavior can be changed by employing one's skills to resist temptation or to control the amount of drug intake (e.g., controlled drinking). Behavior change is seen as dependent on one's perceived capability to cope with stress and boredom and to mobilize one's resources and courses of action required to meet the situational demands. Self-efficacy affects the intention to change risk behavior, the effort expanded to attain this goal, and the persistence to continue striving in spite of barriers and setbacks that may undermine motivation (Bandura, 1991). Self-efficacy has become a widely applied theoretical construct in models of addiction and relapse (e.g., Annis & Davis, 1988; Baer & Lichtenstein, 1988; Donovan & Marlatt, 1988; Marlatt & Gordon, 1985). These theories assume that the way people cope with high-risk situations depends partly on believing that they operate as active agents of their own actions and that they possess the necessary skills to reinstate control should a slip occur. Empirical research on this phenomenon has only recently begun.

Both outcome expectancies and self-efficacy expectancies play a role in the adoption of health behaviors, in the change of detrimental habits, and in the maintenance of change (Bandura, 1991). When adopting a desired behavior, individuals first form an intention and then attempt to execute the action. Outcome expectancies are seen as particularly important in intention formation but less so in action control. Self-efficacy, on the other hand, seems to be crucial in both stages. A positive outcome expectancy, for example, could be of the following kind: "If I were to eat more fiber and less fat, I would lose weight." A corresponding positive self-efficacy could be: "I am capable of resisting fatty foods even if healthier alternatives are not available." The former cognition helps one to make a decision about behavior change; after this has happened, however, the outcome expectancy may often be dispensable because a different problem is at stake, namely the actual performance of the behavior and its maintenance. At this stage, self-efficacy expectancies continue to serve a purpose. There is a large array of recent research on these latter expectancies, findings of which will be mentioned in the following sections.

Some theories focus on disease severity and personal vulnerability as well as on benefits and costs of preventive actions (Becker, 1974; Rosenstock, 1966; Weinstein, 1988). However, the motivation to engage in health behaviors is influenced not only by perceived threat, perceived barriers, and outcome expectancies, but also by self-efficacy expectancies. In fact, there is ample evidence today that self-efficacy is a powerful determinant of behavioral intentions as well as of actual health behavior. Bandura (1977, 1986, 1988, 1989, 1991) has shown that behavior change is mediated through changes in the belief that one possesses the capability to perform a certain action in order to attain a desired outcome. Self-efficacy can be acquired through (a) direct or mastery experience, (b) indirect or vicarous experience, and (c) verbal persuasion or symbolic experience. The *magnitude* or level of efficacy refers to one's estimate of one's best possible performance, the *strength* or certainty of efficacy refers to one's confidence in this estimate, and the *generality* of efficacy refers to more or less specific or global situations where the behavior could be performed successfully.

Measurement of self-efficacy often focuses on its strength because this has turned out to be the most important aspect. For example, Bandura, in his own work on physical exercise (personal communication), uses the following question: "Please rate your confidence that you can continue your exercise program on a regular basis (five or more times each week)." Then 19 situations are described, and the subject assigns them numbers from 0 (*cannot at all*) to 100 (*certain to do*). Example items are, "When I am feeling generally tired," "During bad weather," and "When I have other time commitments."

A comparison between the Theory of Reasoned Action (see below) and Social Cognitive Theory has been performed by Dzewaltowski (1989) in the field of exercise motivation. The exercise behavior of 328 students was recorded for seven weeks and then related to prior measures of cognitive constructs. The behavioral intention was measured by asking the individuals whether it is likely or unlikely that they will perform exercise behavior. The author also assessed the attitude toward the action as well as its corresponding behavioral beliefs, and the subjective norm as well as its corresponding normative beliefs. The Theory of Reasoned Action fit the data, as indicated by a path analysis. Exercise behavior correlated with intention (.22), attitude (.18), and behavioral beliefs (.13). In addition, three social cognitive constructs were assessed: (a) self-efficacy was measured as the strength of efficacy expectancy toward participation in an exercise program when faced with impediments; (b) outcome expectancies were assessed as 13 outcomes multiplied by the evaluation of those outcomes; finally, (c) self-evaluated dissatisfaction with the multiple outcomes of exercise were also considered. It turned out that exercice behavior was correlated with self-efficacy (.34), outcome expectancies (.15), and dissatisfaction (.23), as well as with their interactions.

Those who exercised more days per week had scored initially higher in these three social cognitive constructs. Persons who were confident that they could adhere to a strenuous exercise program and, in addition, were dissatisfied with their present standing on the outcomes and who expected positive outcomes, appeared to exercise more. The Theory of Reasoned Action variables did not account for any unique variance in exercise behavior over these constructs, as indicated by a commonality analysis. The data support the assumption that the Social Cognitive Theory provides the most powerful explanatory constructs.

Further Evidence on Self-Efficacy Expectancies and Health Behaviors

Self-efficacy has been found to predict intentions and actions in different domains of human functioning. In the health domain, self-efficacy has proven to be a powerful resource in coping with stress (Lazarus & Folkman, 1987). There is also evidence that perceived self-efficacy in coping with stressors affects the immune function (Wiedenfeld et al., 1990). Subjects with high self-efficacy tolerate more pain than those with low self-efficacy (Litt, 1988; Manning & Wright, 1983). Self-efficacy has been shown to affect blood pressure, heart rate and serum catecholamine levels in challenging or threatening situations (Bandura, Cioffi, Taylor, & Brouillard, 1988; Bandura, Reese, & Adams, 1982; Bandura, Taylor, Williams, Mefford, & Barchas, 1985). Recovery of cardiovascular function in postcoronary patients is enhanced by self-percepts of coping resources (Taylor, Bandura, Ewart, Miller, & DeBusk, 1985). Patients with rheumatoid arthritis were treated with a cognitive-behavioral program that resulted in the enhancement of perceived self-efficacy, reduced pain and joint inflammation, and improved psychosocial functioning (O'Leary, Shoor, Lorig, & Holman, 1988).

The intention to engage in a certain health behavior and the actual behavior itself are positively associated with confident beliefs in one's personal efficacy (for a review see Bandura, 1991; O'Leary, 1985; Yalow & Collins, 1987). A number of studies on adopting health practices beyond the very limited impact made by fear appeals have measured self-efficacy in order to identify its potential benefits. As people proceed from considering precautions in a general way toward shaping a behavioral intention, contemplating detailed action plans, and actually performing a health behavior on a regular basis, they become aware of their more or less sufficient capabilities to initiate change. In an early study on this problem, Beck and Lund (1981) have exposed dental patients to a persuasive communication designed to manipulate their beliefs about periodontal disease. Perceived disease severity and outcome expectancy turned out to be no longer predictive when self-efficacy was entered into the equation. Self-efficacy emerged as the best predictor of the intention to floss ($r = .69$) and of the actual behavior, frequency of flossing ($r = .44$). Seydel, Taal, and Wiegman (1990) have found that outcome expectancies as well as self-efficacy expectancies are good predictors of the intention to engage in behaviors to prevent the consequences of breast cancer (such as breast self-examination) (see also Meyerowitz & Chaiken, 1987; Rippetoe & Rogers, 1987).

Self-efficacy has been studied with respect to preventive aspects of sexual behavior, e.g., the resistance of sexual advances and the use of contraceptives to avoid unwanted pregnancies. For example, teenage women with a high rate of unprotected intercourse have been found to use contraceptives more effectively if they believed they could exercise control over their sexual activities (Levinson, 1982). Gilchrist and Schinke (1983) taught teenagers through modeling and role-playing how to deal with contraceptives and other sexual matters, and by this treatment approach significantly raised their self-efficacy and protective skills. Sexual risk-taking behavior such as not using condoms has also been studied among homosexual men with multiple partners. Longitudinally, self-beliefs in one's capability of turning to low-risk practices emerged as the most important predictor of such behaviors (McKusick, Coates, Morin, Pollack, & Hoff, 1990).

Influencing health behaviors that contribute to the prevention of AIDS has become an urgent issue, and self-efficacy appears to play a role in such behaviors. Kok, De Vries, Mudde, and Strecher (1990) report a study from their Dutch laboratory that analyzed condom use and clean needle use by drug addicts. Intentions and behaviors were predicted by attitudes, social norms, and especially by self-efficacy. Self-efficacy correlated with the intention to use clean needles (.35), with reported clean needle use (.46), with the intention to use condoms (.74), and with reported condom use (.67) (Paulussen, Kok, Knibbe, & Kramer, 1989). Bandura (1990) has described the role of perceived self-efficacy in the exercise of control over HIV infection in more detail.

Within a smoking prevention program with Dutch adolescents, Kok et al. (1990) conducted several studies on the influence of self-efficacy on non-smoking intentions and behaviors. Cross-sectionally, they could explain 64% of the variance of intentions as well as of behavior, which was due to the over-whelming predictive power of self-efficacy ($r = .66$ for intention, $r = .71$ for reported behavior) (De Vries, Dijkstra, & Kuhlman, 1988). Longitudinally, these relationships were replicated, although with somewhat less impressive coefficients (De Vries, Dijkstra, & Kok, 1989).

In the field of weight control and eating behavior, various studies have used self-efficacy measures (Bernier & Avard, 1986; Chambliss & Murray, 1979; Glynn & Ruderman, 1986; Slater, 1989; Weinberg, Hughes, Critelli, England, & Jackson, 1984).

Compliance with medical regimens has been improved after patients suffering from chronic obstructive pulmonary diseases received a self-efficacy training; self-efficacy predicted moderate exercise ($r = .47$) (Kaplan, Atkins, & Reinsch, 1984). Ewart, Gillian, Kalemen, Manley, and Kalemen (1986) found self-efficacy useful in predicting overexertion during programmed exercise in coronary artery disease patients. The role of self-efficacy in initiating and maintaining a regular program of physical exercise has been studied by Desharnais, Bouillon, and Godin (1986), Sallis et al. (1986), and Wurtele and Maddux (1987). In an unpublished study, Reinhard Fuchs and myself found that self-efficacy was highly correlated with intentions to adopt an exercise regimen ($r = .55$). Endurance in physical performance was found to be dependent on self-efficacy in a series of experiments by Weinberg, Gould, and Jackson (1979), Weinberg, Yukelson, and Jackson (1980), and Weinberg, Gould, Yukelson, and Jackson (1981). In terms of competitive performance, the role of self-efficacy in tennis playing has been investigated with the result that perceived competence was related to 12 rated performance criteria (Barling & Abel, 1983).

Most research on the change of detrimental behaviors has been conducted with respect to smoking cessation (see Baer & Lichtenstein, 1988). The number of cigarettes smoked ($r = -.62$), the amount of tobacco per smoke ($r = -.43$), and the nicotine content ($r = -.30$) were inversely related to self-efficacy in a treatment sample (Godding & Glasgow, 1985). Several studies point to the phenomenon that pretreatment self-efficacy does not predict relapse, but posttreatment self-efficacy does. Mudde, Kok, and Strecher (1989) found that self-efficacy increases after treatment and that successful quitters were those who had acquired the highest self-efficacy levels during a one-year period (see also Kok et al., 1990). Various authors have identified relationships between relapse occurrence, time of relapse, and self-efficacy with correlations ranging from -.34 to -.69 (Colletti, Supnick, & Payne, 1985; Condiotte & Lichtenstein, 1981; DiClemente, Prochaska, & Gibertini, 1985; Garcia, Schmitz, & Doerfler, 1990; Wilson, Wallston, & King, 1990).

Self-efficacy has proven to be a very powerful behavioral determinant in many studies, and its inclusion in theories on health behavior, therefore, is warranted. By summing up direct and indirect effects, it can be stated that the total effect of self-efficacy on health behaviors exceeds the effects of any single variable. Self-efficacy determines the appraisal of one's personal resources in stressful encounters and contributes to the forming of behavioral intentions. The stronger their self-efficacy beliefs, the higher are the goals people set for themselves, and the firmer their commitment to engage in the intended behavior, even if failures mount.

The Health Belief Model and its Reinterpretation

A second major theoretical orientation that should be considered is identified with the term "health belief model." The discussion about health behavior theory has been stimulated and nurtured for many years by the early work on health beliefs and the formulation of the health belief model in the 1950s and 1960s (Becker, 1974; Rosenstock, 1966). This model assumes that individuals base health behavior on rational thinking. Individual perceptions and modifying factors then determine the likelihood of action (Figure 1).

According to the model, perceived *susceptibility* to illness and perceived *severity* of a disease result in the experience of *threat*. This is modified by individual differences in demographic variables, social pressure, and personality. Threat is also influenced by *cues to action* such as mass media campaigns, advice from others, reminders for dentist appointments, etc. Finally, the likelihood of action is determined by the threat as well as by a subjective *cost-benefit analysis* that compares the perceived benefits of a recommended preventive action with the perceived barriers to this action, including financial costs and efforts needed.

A number of studies testing the explanatory and predictive power of this Health Belief Model (Janz & Becker, 1984; Mullen, Hersey, & Iverson, 1987) have yielded consistent but weak relationships among the model's components.

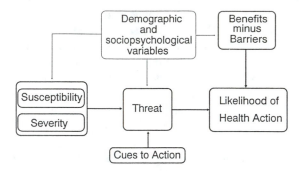

Figure 1 Simplified version of the Health Belief Model.

Although this model has stimulated discussions of health behavior, it also has some shortcomings:

1. The model lacks the specification of at least two indispensable cognitive mediators, one being a behavioral intention (as was done in the Theory of Reasoned Action; Fishbein & Ajzen, 1975), the other being self-efficacy expectancy.

2. The model overestimates the direct effect of threat on action. It does so because is makes obsolete assumptions about the effect of fear appeals on preventive behavior. It now seems likely that threat should be specified as a more distal antecedent variable that triggers other cognitions such as expectancies or behavioral intentions.

3. The path from cues to threat seems to be misspecified. Instead, cues should lead more directly to intentions and behavior. Further, it would be wise to distinguish between perceived and actual situational cues.

4. The cost-benefit analysis as one single model component confounds outcome expectancies associated with a health action (response effectiveness) with situational obstacles and thus reduces these complex cognitions to a single value.

5. There is no distinction between a motivation phase that is dominated by cognitions and a volition phase where the action is planned and performed in detail. The model is static and does not refer to processes.

In recent years, the Health Belief Model has been reinterpreted by its authors (Becker & Rosenstock, 1987) in comparing it to the Social Learning Theory. They summarize their model in the following words: "...health-related action depends on the simultaneous occurrence of three classes of factors, (a) the existence of sufficient *motivation*, or health concern, to make health issues salient or relevant; (b) the belief that one is *susceptible* or vulnerable to a *serious* problem, or to sequelae of that health problem; this is often termed "perceived *threat*"; and (c) the belief that following a particular health recommendation would be *beneficial* in reducing the perceived threat at subjectively acceptable *cost*, where "cost" refers to perceived *barriers* to following the health recommendation..." (p. 246). Becker and Rosenstock (1987) claim similarity with the Social Learning Theory in comparing the concepts of both models. An incentive is equated with the health motive (value of reduction of perceived threats to health). The situation-outcome expectancy (what leads to what) parallels the perceived threat including susceptibility to and severity of illness. Perceived benefits of following a recommendation have been interpreted as outcome expectancies; the Health Belief Model confounds this with the perceived costs, whereas the Social Learning Theory does not. Finally, self-efficacy expectancies are not explicitly included in the Health Belief Model, but is, according to the authors, implied in "perceived barriers," which appears to be somewhat far-fetched. In concluding, the authors admit that self-efficacy expectancy is the only necessary ingredient that is missing or underrepresented in the Health Belief Model and therefore should deserve more attention (see also Rosenstock, Strecher, & Becker, 1988; Strecher, DeVellis, Becker, & Rosenstock, 1986). This reinterpretation of the Health Belief Model, however, does not invalidate the criticism made above. Instead, it would be wiser to include the major ingredients of the Health Belief Model in a modern comprehensive theory of health behavior (see below).

An innovative approach has been taken by Weinstein (1988), who focused on the factors vulnerability, severity, and precaution effectiveness (outcome expectancies), subdividing each factor into three stages with different qualitities. The first stage refers to general knowledge about the existence of a health threat ("AIDS is a terminal disease") or precaution strategy; the second stage is attained when people believe that someone in their social environment could be the victim of a disease ("I know someone who has AIDS"); the third stage describes personal vulnerability ("It may be possible that I could contract the HIV virus"), personal belief about severity ("I could die from AIDS"), or effectiveness of one's own precaution strategy ("There is nothing I can do about it"). This new perspective adds a self-reference component to the Health Belief Model as well as a more developmental view that claims the existence of cognitive thresholds which have to be overcome before a behavioral intention is likely to be formed. Thus, Weinstein introduces cognitive mediators and underscores the process character of adopting health behaviors. Although he did not explicitly attempt to improve the Health Belief Model, his approach might nevertheless serve this purpose, and including an explicit self-efficacy factor would make a further improvement.

In sum, the Health Belief Model is misspecified in various ways, for example by confounding outcome expectancies with perceived barriers instead of separating specific causal pathways that involve both factors distinctly. It underestimates the role of cognitive processes involved in the adoption of health practices and in the change of detrimental habits. There is no distinction between a motivational phase that is dominated by cognitions and a volitional phase where the action is planned and performed in detail. The model is static and does not refer to processes.

Behavioral Intention Models

The Theory of Reasoned Action

Many health behaviors can be thought of as being under volitional control. If, for example, a person who is ill goes to the doctor, this behavior is a direct result of a deliberate attempt made by this individual. By a motivational process, the person develops an intention to engage in a health behavior or disengage from a risk behavior. It is assumed that a strongly intended behavior will occur with great likelihood. Thus, an intention is regarded as a behavioral disposition with high predictive power. Barring unforeseen events, human beings are expected to behave in accordance with their intentions. The Theory of Reasoned Action (Fishbein & Ajzen, 1975) has originally been designed for this case of willful behavior. It has been applied to various domains, including smoking cessation (Fishbein, 1982; Sutton, 1989).

One of the two determinants of an intention is the individual's *attitude toward a behavior*, i.e., the positive or negative evaluation of performing this specific behavior. Antecedents of the attitude are behavioral beliefs which can be seen as outcome expectancies, such as "going to the doctor leads to the prescription of relieving medication" (outcome expectancies are multiplied with belief strength in accordance with expectancy-value-models in order to provide an indirect measure of attitude).

The other determinant of an intention reflects social influence and is called the *subjective norm*. It is the individual's perception of social pressure to perform or not perform the specific action. Antecedents of the subjective norm are *normative beliefs*, i.e., beliefs that one's reference persons approve or disapprove of performing the behavior (normative beliefs are multiplied with one's motivation to comply in order to provide an indirect measure of the subjective norm).

The Theory of Planned Behavior

This theory has been extended to the Theory of Planned Behavior by one of its founders (Ajzen, 1988) for the case of incomplete volitional control. For example, if an overweight person goes on a diet, there is a considerable chance that this person will fail in spite of strong intentions. Goal attainment not only depends on the strength of an intention but also on nonmotivational factors such as resources or obstacles. There are internal control factors (information, personal deficiencies, skills, abilities, emotions or compulsions) and external control factors (opportunities, dependence on others, obstacles or other obstructing factors). Further, it has to be considered whether these factors are actually present or whether the individual merely perceives them as being present.

The main feature of the Theory of Planned Behavior lies in the specification of a third predictor variable called *perceived behavioral control* that exerts an

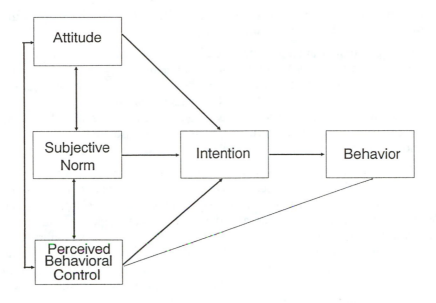

Figure 2 The Theory of Planned Behavior.

additional influence on intention formation (Figure 2). Individuals who believe that they do not possess the resources to perform a specific behavior are unlikely to develop a strong intention to engage in it, even if they hold favorable attitudes towards it and expect that significant others would approve of their performing the behavior. Antecedents of perceived behavioral control are *control beliefs* that are based on past experience or on second-hand information.

A second feature of the Theory of Planned Behavior lies in the possibility of a direct path from perceived behavioral control to the behavior. Perceived behavioral control can predict an action independent of the intention, especially in cases where there is no actual control over the behavior. Perceived behavioral control may reflect actual control and may be considered a partial substitute for a measure of actual control. For example, a person may have a strong intention to start exercising, but due to a bodily handicap he or she is unable to perform the behavior. Schifter and Ajzen (1985) have studied weight loss intention and actual weight reduction among female college students. Goal attainment was linked directly to perceived behavioral control with a zero-order correlation of $r = .41$, whereas, after including the intention in the regression equation, the multiple correlation increased to $R = .44$ only. The increment was negligible, and perceived behavioral control could be considered the major direct determinant of weight reduction. The author (Ajzen, 1988) explains this phenomenon with the problems of volitional control inherent in weight loss attempts. In such cases with a low degree of volitional control, behavior may be predicted by perceived behavioral control, but in cases where control was very high, the determinant perceived behavioral control may be dispensable, and the model reduces to the former Theory of Reasoned Action.

The operationalization of perceived behavioral control has simply been equated with perceived difficulty of goal attainment or subjective success probability by asking questions such as "How much control do you have over [this specific risk behavior]?" or "To perform [this behavior] is easy :_:_:_:_:_:_difficult" (see Ajzen & Madden, 1986; Schifter & Ajzen, 1985). If one would add a self-reference such as "Dieting is difficult *for me*," the measurement would become identical with attempts to assess self-efficacy (see Kok et al., 1990).

The Theory of Planned Behavior requires a reconceptualization of the attitude factor, which has been described as an emotional component by the authors. Attitudes and their preceding behavioral beliefs appear to be interchangeable; there is no temporal or even causal order among them, as several studies have demonstrated (Ajzen & Madden, 1986; De Vries et al., 1988). Behavioral beliefs yield the same predictive power as attitude does. Therefore, it is suggested to substitute the attitude factor by the behavioral beliefs. In addition, replacing the label "behavioral beliefs" by the term "outcome expectancies" would be possible without changing the content. Further, the factor "perceived behavioral control" could be relabeled "self-efficacy." In sum, there is some evidence that the Theory of Planned Behavior could be reduced to two antecedents of intentions, namely the "behavioral beliefs" and the "perceived behavioral control" without losing its predictive power. Relabeling these two into "outcome expectancies" and "self-efficacy expectancies" would integrate this theory with the Social-Cognitive Theory (normative beliefs could also be translated into social outcome expectancies).

It remains an open question to which extent perceived behavioral control is similar to self-efficacy expectancy. The latter is a well-established psychological construct that is embedded in social learning theory and has proven valid and useful in many studies. Ajzen and Madden (1986, p. 457) refer to the similarity between both constructs, but refrain from adopting self-efficacy at the expense of their own construct.

However, exactly this has been done by a group of Dutch researchers (De Vries et al., 1989; De Vries & Kok, 1986; Kok et al., 1990), who replaced perceived behavioral control by self-efficacy as one determinant of intention formation and behavior. A research example may illustrate their approach (De Vries et al., 1988). In a smoking prevention project, 85 students aged 14 to 17 years were studied in terms of the above-mentioned variables. Cross-sectional assessment of all variables involved in the model resulted in standardized regression coefficients of .66 (from attitude to intentions), .47 (from subjective norm to intention), and .66 (from self-efficacy to intention). Self-efficacy turned out to be an excellent predictor of reported non-smoking behavior (.71), and the intention not to smoke was an equally strong determinant (.74). Together they yielded a multiple correlation of $R = .80$. In a longitudinal replication, the intention was correlated $r = .80$, and self-efficacy was correlated $r = .50$, with non-smoking as the target behavior. In both cases, a direct link between self-efficacy and behavior was established, endorsing the assumption that this behavior can be considered as being only partially under volitional control.

The Kok et al. (1990) model, although superior, suffers from the same short-coming as the Theory of Planned Behavior as far as the attitude factor is concern-ed. They also share the weakness of not making explicit assumptions about cognitive processes at the initiation and maintenance stages of preventive actions.

Protection Motivation Theory

Protection Motivation Theory by Rogers (1975, 1983, 1985) combines some of the features of the Health Belief Model, the Theory of Reasoned Action and the Self-Efficacy Theory (see also Maddux, Norton, & Stoltenberg, 1986; Maddux & Rogers, 1983; Rippetoe & Rogers, 1987). This approach is based on four components: (a) perceived severity of a disease, (b) perceived vulnerability to illness, (c) response effectiveness of a certain health action, and (d) self-efficacy expectancy towards a health action. The third component could be relabeled "outcome expectancy." Thus, Protection Motivation Theory combines the three major approaches in modeling the motivation towards health behavior. These four components are considered to jointly allow a good prediction of a behavioral intention and—indirectly—of the actual health behavior.

However, Protection Motivation Theory is less a coherent theory than a cumulative number of varying assumptions that differ from publication to publi-cation of the authors. Originally, it was designed to investigate the effects of per-suasive messages and fear appeals on the adoption of recommended health behaviors. In the "revised theory," Maddux and Rogers (1983) incorporate self-efficacy as a fourth component in addition to (a) outcome expectancy—current behavior, (b) outcome expectancy—alternative behavior, and (c) the relative value of the different sets of outcomes. Rippetoe and Rogers (1987) introduce a complex scheme of Protection Motivation Theory where sources of information and resulting coping modes are mediated by a cognitive process. In this cogni-tive process, which is the focus of the model, severity and vulnerability are fac-tors that decrease a maladaptive response, whereas self-efficacy and response efficacy are factors that increase an adaptive response. "Threat appraisal" results from subtracting severity/vulnerability from internal/external rewards, and "coping appraisal" results by subtracting response costs from response efficacy/self-efficacy. These two appraisals, finally, yield protection motivation, which is considered a synonym of a behavioral intention. Stated thus, the model is hardly testable, and empirical studies on this model restrict themselves to a simpler way of looking at the data. This simplified approach, which is clearly testable, could be illustrated as in Figure 3.

The first three predictors are adopted from the Health Belief Model; self-efficacy is added; the general design resembles the Theory of Reasoned Action

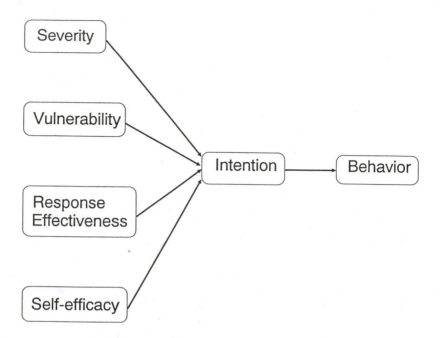

Figure 3 Simplified version of the Protection Motivation Theory.

and the Theory of Planned Behavior. The Protection Motivation Theory seems to be superior to the Theory of Planned Behavior because it explicitly includes self-efficacy as the most powerful single determinant of intentions and behavior change that is known today (see above). Rippetoe and Rogers (1987, p. 602) also transform their variables into a path analysis design where "fear," however, has been included as a fifth mediator. Independent (experimental) variables such as threatening information influence the five mediators, which, in turn, determine two kinds of coping modes, maladaptive ones (such as avoidance) and adaptive ones (such as behavioral intentions). In the latter study, women were given different information about breast cancer, and those model components that influence their intentions to practice breast self-examinations were estimated. Response efficacy (.43), severity (.32), and self-efficacy (.19) emerged as the three predictors of breast self-examination intention.

Beck and Lund (1981) exposed dental patients to a persuasive communication designed to manipulate their beliefs about periodontal disease. Experimental levels of severity aroused greater levels of fear. Severity items were correlated with intention to floss ($r = .32$) and frequency of flossing ($r = .35$), but in a regression equation self-efficacy emerged as the most powerful predictor, closely related to intention ($r = .69$) and behavior ($r = .44$). Outcome expectancy did not contribute to the explanation of variance. The intention-behavior correlation was .49.

The Protection Motivation Theory was successfully applied to the prediction of regular exercise (Wurtele & Maddux, 1987) and smoking cessation (Maddux

& Rogers, 1983). In the study by Wurtele and Maddux (1987), 160 undergraduate women were given persuasive appeals for increasing physical exercise which varied on the four components vulnerability, severity, outcome efficacy, and self-efficacy. Vulnerability and self-efficacy enhanced exercise intentions, but none of the four variables succeeded in predicting self-reported exercise behavior. The intention-behavior correlation was only $r = .30$, which could have been due to the lack of specificity of the measures involved. A triple interaction between vulnerability, self-efficacy and outcome expectancy on intentions revealed that the subjects intended to adopt the target behavior even though they held only weak convictions about its health benefits. Although this was a good study overall, there were a few problems with the assessment of the essential theory components because they had been measured by only two heterogeneous items each (vulnerability by three items). For example, outcome efficacy (response efficacy) was tapped by the following two items: "Exercising regularly is more effective than changing one's diet or quitting smoking in preventing heart attacks and strokes," and "Exercise stimulates the growth of new blood vessels." The internal consistency was only .19! Self-efficacy was measured by the items "I am capable of starting and continuing a regular program of exercise," and "Sticking with a regular program of exercise would be very difficult for me to do (reversed)." This yielded an internal consistency of .25. In spite of this weakness, self-efficacy emerged from the multiple regression analyses as the most powerful predictor of exercise intentions, replicating an earlier finding by Maddux and Rogers (1983). It is likely that the Protection Motivation Theory as a whole could be empirically validated more convincingly if measurement would be improved.

The weakest component of the model was the illness severity aspect. No main effect of threat severity was found in both studies, neither in that by Maddux and Rogers (1983) nor in that by Wurtele and Maddux (1987). In the study by Beck and Lund (1981), experimental manipulation of severity aroused greater levels of threat, but did not predict either intentions or behaviors when self-efficacy was included in the same equation. According to the Health Belief Model, threat can be considered as a result of severity and vulnerability, but this three-variable interplay has not been researched carefully (see also Rippetoe & Rogers, 1987). Instead of simply dropping the severity component from the model, as implicitly suggested by Wurtele and Maddux (1987, p. 463), it would be wiser to identify its causal status in more detail, for example by specifying it as a more distal antecedent.

Seydel et al. (1990) conducted two studies on cancer-related preventive behaviors with the aim in mind to compare the Health Belief Model and the Protection Motivation Theory. What they actually did was an assessment of the predictive power of a restricted model (denoted "Health Belief Model") consisting of severity, vulnerability, and outcome expectancy, compared to the power of a full model (denoted "Protection Motivation Theory") where self-efficacy was added as a fourth determinant of intentions, reported behavior, and actual behavior. Vulnerability appeared to be a negligible factor; severity emerged in only one third of the analyses as a useful predictor, but always less significantly than the two kinds of expectancies. Outcome and self-efficacy expectancies, in contrast, explained most of the criterion variance. The full model explained between 19% and 48% of the intention as well as between 11% and 14% of the behavior variance. This study again showed that these expectancies are crucial variables in behavioral change and that the other variables can hardly compete within the same regression equation. This need not mean, however, that the latter are dispensable. It could be, for example, that they play a role at an earlier stage of the decision process (see Weinstein, 1988), and that they would emerge as being more influential if the causal model would be specified appropriately. Protection Motivation Theory does not make explicit assumptions about cognitive processes at the initiation and maintenance stages of preventive actions.

The Health Action Process Approach

The preceding sections have reviewed recent advances in health behavior theories without exhaustively incorporating all suggestions made in the literature. The two major approaches in the 1970s, the Health Belief Model and the Theory of Reasoned Action, have been revised or reinterpreted by their authors, and other authors have continued to improve them further (e.g., the Protection Motivation Theory and the Kok et al. model). The emergence of the self-efficacy theory, which is not restricted to health matters, has strongly influenced the scientific debate and analysis of preventive behaviors. Cognitive processes, in particular expectancies, have been identified as the crucial determinants of changes in health practices.

Today, a model is required which is refined beyond the previous approaches, acknowledging the superior role of self-efficacy for predicting preventive actions, changing risky habits, and maintaining health-beneficial behaviors. In this section, I attempt to account for the cumulated research findings by specifying a causal model I termed the social-cognitive "health action process approach." Its main feature lies in the explicit distinction between a decision-making or motivation stage and an action or maintenance stage. Thus, a time perspective is added to the previous models, with a more detailed analysis of cognitions that guide on-going behavior. In the past, the maintenance phase has been subject to only few theories, such as relapse prevention theory (Marlatt, 1985) and volition theory (Heckhausen, 1991; Heckhausen & Kuhl, 1985; Kuhl, 1983, 1985, 1986; Kuhl & Krasna, 1990), but has not been an integral part of a comprehensive health behavior theory (for a five-stage approach see DiClemente et al., 1985; Velicer, DiClemente, Rossi, & Prochaska, 1990). Figure 4 displays the complete model, the left part representing the motivation phase, the right part the action phase.

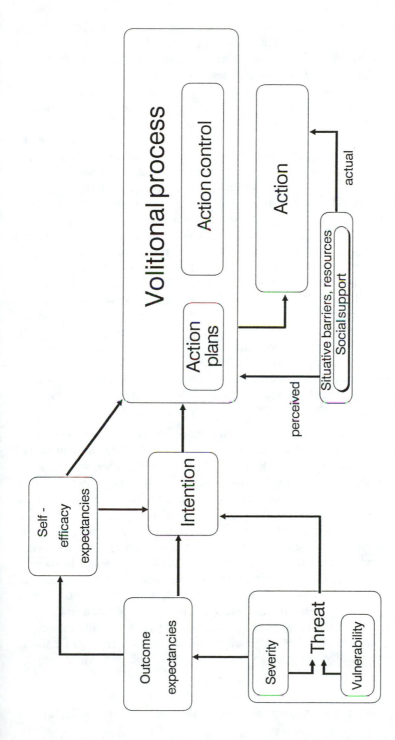

Figure 4 The Health Action Process Approach.

The Motivation Phase

In the motivation phase, the individual forms an intention to either adopt a precaution measure or change risk behaviors in favor of other behaviors. This has also been conceived as a "decision-making stage" by some authors (Eiser, 1983; Eiser & Sutton, 1977; Fishbein & Ajzen, 1975). It is now known that self-efficacy and outcome expectancies are the major predictors of an intention. Most previous models, however, treat these two as being unrelated, whereas Bandura (1989) has repeatedly underscored that their interrelationship should be taken into consideration: "...the effects of outcome expectancies on performance motivation are partly governed by self-beliefs of efficacy. There are many activities that, if performed well, guarantee valued outcomes, but they are not pursued if people doubt they can do what it takes to succeed...Self-perceived inefficacy can thus nullify the motivating potential of alluring outcome expectations...When variations in perceived self-efficacy are partialed out, the outcomes expected for given performances do not have much of an independent effect on behavior" (p. 1180). *Outcome expectancies* can be seen as precursors of self-efficacy because people usually make assumptions about the possible consequences of behaviors before inquiring whether they can take the action themselves (Schwarzer, 1981, 1992). If *self-efficacy* is specified as a mediator between outcome expectancies and intention, the direct influence of outcome expectancy on intention may dissipate. But the research findings on this issue are very inconsistent, rendering both cognitions primary candidates for motivating change. Under conditions where individuals have no experience with the behavior they are contemplating, we assume that outcome expectancies may have a stronger direct influence. Only after a sufficient level of experience is attained does self-efficacy receive the lion's share of the intention variance.

A specific subset of outcome expectancies, namely *social outcome expectancies*, should also be considered explicitly as determinants within the motivation phase, as proposed in the Theory of Reasoned Action and the Theory of Planned Behavior, where this has been called the "normative beliefs." People often develop intentions because they perceive social pressures to do so. Individuals comply with the perceived expectations of significant others in order to avoid conflict or disregard, or because of naive trust in the opinion of others. We cannot always contemplate expectancies and undertake cost-benefit analyses in order to arrive at a sound decision to act. Instead, we often have to adapt to the circumstances quickly. For example, we sometimes purchase vitamin supplements or health foods not because we are convinced that they will be beneficial, but simply because others, including the media, have recommended them and because the ample availability of such products suggests that health-conscious people make regular use of this offer. Social expectations may represent a shortcut to intentions; socially conforming behavior saves time and energy in the motivation process.

Previous findings on the predictive value of the "subjective norm" (or normative beliefs) have not been overwhelming, which is possibly due to limited theoretical elaboration and to measurement. The perceived social expectation factor should be looked at from two additional vantage points, i.e., (a) from a *social comparison* perspective which suggests that our intentions and actions are governed by our desire to maintain or enhance self-esteem or self-consistency within normative reference groups (see Wills, 1990; Wood, 1989), and (b) from a *social support* perspective which suggests that people draw on their social networks and resources when making decisions, e.g., the intention to quit smoking being facilitated by a network of non-smokers (Cohen et al., 1988). The link between social outcome expectancies and intentions has to be reconsidered with these research perspectives in mind.

The previous discussion pertained to specific outcome expectancies, not to generalized ones. However, there is increasing research evidence that generalized outcome expectancies, labeled "optimism," can contribute significantly to the adoption and maintenance of health behaviors (Scheier & Carver, 1985, 1987; Scheier, Weintraub, & Carver, 1986).

The interplay between perceived *severity* of an illness, perceived *vulnerability*, and the resulting *threat*, as hypothesized in the Health Belief Model, is still undetermined (there is some evidence that experimental manipulations of severity raise threat levels [Beck & Lund, 1981]). An analogy to transactional stress theory could be established (Lazarus & Folkman, 1984, 1987). Severity resembles primary appraisal, where one defines what is at stake and what are the situation characteristics that pose demands on the individual; on the other hand, vulnerability pertains to secondary appraisal, where one's options are under investigation. Vulnerability is defined as a lack of coping resources. Both appraisals result in the experience of more or less threat. Threat is, among others, considered a starting point for coping processes, whether they are adaptive or maladaptive. This analogy may underscore the usefulness of these concepts (see also Weinstein, 1988, 1989). On the other hand, threat has been overestimated in past research and interventions. Fear appeals are of limited value; the message has to be framed in a way that allows individuals to draw on their coping resources and to exercise skills to control health threats. In persuasive communications, a focus should be made on self-percepts of personal coping capabilities to manage effective precaution strategies (Bandura, 1991, 1990). This suggests a causal order where threat is specified as a distal antecedent that helps to stimulate outcome expectancies which further stimulate self-efficacy. A minimum level of threat or concern must exist before people start contemplating the benefits of possible actions and ruminate their competence to actually perform them. The direct path from threat to intention may become negligible if expectancies are already well-established.

In establishing a rank order among the three direct paths that lead to intention, it is assumed that self-efficacy dominates, followed by outcome expectancies, whereas threat may fail to contribute any additional direct influence. As indirect factors, however, threat and outcome expectancies may be of considerable significance within the motivation phase. As mentioned above, the context and one's personal experience play a role and may change the pattern of weights.

The Action Phase

It is common knowledge that good intentions do not necessarily guarantee corresponding actions. Correlations between intentions and behaviors vary tremendously. The previously mentioned theories refer more generally to "barriers" or "costs" as the reasons for this gap, and they list a number of impediments, such as situational constraints or lack of willpower. The Theory of Planned Behavior, which was designed for the case of incomplete control over the behavior, makes an attempt to quantify this problem by specifying a direct link between perceived behavioral control and behavior, thus circumventing the intention. More theoretical elaborations are required, however, to better understand the processes involved. Relapse prevention theory (Marlatt, 1985), volition theory (Heckhausen, 1991; Heckhausen & Kuhl, 1985; Kuhl, 1983), and self-efficacy theory (Bandura, 1977, 1986) have sparked the following ideas.

While in the motivation phase it is described what people choose to do, in the subsequent action or volition phase it is described how hard they try and how long they persist. The right-hand part of Figure 4 consists of three levels: cognitive, behavioral, and situational. The focus is on cognitions that instigate and control the action, i.e., a volitional or self-regulative process which is subdivided into action plans and action control.

When a preference for a particular health behavior has been shaped, the intention has to be transformed into detailed instructions of how to perform the desired action. If, for example, someone intends to lose weight, it has to be planned how to do it, i.e., what foods to buy, when and how often to eat which amounts, when and where to exercise, and maybe even whether to cease smoking as well. Thus, a global intention can be specified by a set of subordinate intentions and action plans which contain proximal goals and algorithms of action sequences. The volition process seems not to be influenced by outcome expectancies, but more strongly by self-efficacy, as the number and quality of action plans have to be dependent on one's perceived competence and experience. Self-efficacy beliefs influence the cognitive construction of specific action plans, for example by visualizing scenarios that may guide goal attainment. These pre-actional cognitions are necessary because otherwise the person would impulsively act in a trial-and-error fashion and would not know where to allocate the available resources.

Once an action has been initiated, it has to be controlled by cognitions in order to be maintained. The action has to be protected from being interrupted and from being given up prematurely due to incompatible competing intentions which may become dominant while a behavior is being performed. Meta-cognitive activity is needed to complete the primary action and to suppress distracting secondary action tendencies. Daily physical exercise, for example, requires self-regulatory processes in order to secure effort and persistence and to keep other motivational tendencies at a distance (such as the desire to eat, social-ize, or sleep) until these tendencies obtain their chance to prevail for a limited time period.

When the action is being performed, self-efficacy determines the amount of effort invested and the perseverance. People with self-doubts are more inclined to anticipate failure scenarios, worry about their possible performance deficien-cies, and abort their attempts prematurely. People with an optimistic sense of self-efficacy, however, visualize success scenarios that guide the action and let them persevere in face of obstacles. When running into unforeseen difficulties they quickly recover.

Performing an intended health behavior is an action, just as is not performing a risk behavior. The suppression of health-detrimental actions also requires effort and persistence, and therefore is also guided by a volitional process that includes *action plans* and *action control*. If one intends to quit smoking or drink-ing, one has to plan how to do it. For example, it is important to avoid high-risk situations where the pressures to relapse are overwhelming (Marlatt, 1985). Attaining proximal subgoals contributes to increase the difficulty level of situa-tions until one can resist under all possible circumstances. If someone is craving for a cigarette or a drink, action control helps to "survive" the critical situation. For example, individuals can make favorable social comparisons, refer to their self-concept, or simply pull themselves together. The more these meta-cognitive skills and internal coping dialogues are developed and the better they are matched to specific risk situations, the easier the urges can be controlled. Self-efficacy helps to reestablish the perseverant efforts needed for the accomplish-ment of self-imposed goals.

One of the major action control paradigms is the "delay of gratification pat-tern." Children already possess the meta-cognitive skills to suppress the craving for a small piece of candy if they are promised to obtain a bigger one at a later point in time; they apply cognitive distraction and other techniques for this pur-pose (Mischel, 1966, 1973; Mischel & Mischel, 1983). A similar paradigm can be found in disease prevention. If children comply to brush and floss their teeth regularly, they are "promised" not to suffer from tooth decay or periodontal dis-ease several decades later. Evidently, it requires an immense volitional strength (after the necessary intention is given) to obtain this kind of "gratification," which can hardly be expected from the majority of human beings. After a cir-cumscribed action has been completed, the individual evaluates it as successful or failing and attributes the perceived outcome to possible causes (Weiner, 1980). Dependent on this cognitive event, emotions and expectancies are varied, and the volitional strength may be increased or decreased for subsequent similar actions. Self-reinforcement is seen as a favorable meta-cognitive strategy.

Finally, situational barriers as well as opportunities have to be considered. If situational cues are overwhelming, meta-cognitive skills fail to protect the individual and the temptation cannot be resisted. Actions are not only a function of intentions and cognitive control, but are also influenced by the perceived and the actual environment. A social network, for example, that ignores the coping process of a quitter by smoking in his presence, creates a difficult stress situation which taxes the quitter's volitional strength. If, on the other hand, the spouse decides to quit too, then a social support situation is created that enables the quitter to remain abstinent in spite of lower levels of volitional strength.

In sum, the action phase can be described along three levels: cognitive, behavioral, and situational. The cognitive level refers to self-regulatory processes that mediate between the intentions and the actions. This "volitional process" contains action plans and action control and is strongly influenced by self-efficacy expectancies, but also by perceived situational barriers and support.

Conclusions

Expectancies have proven to be highly predictive for the adoption of precautions, the change of detrimental habits, and the maintenance of health behaviors. The Health Belief Model has been reinterpreted in terms of expectancies, but still underestimates them and lacks specificity as well as mediating cognitions. The Theory of Reasoned Action has been revised to the Theory of Planned Behavior, but still lacks explicit outcome and self-efficacy expectancies. The Protection Motivation Theory has been revised to account for expectancies, but needs further improvement with respect to causal and temporal order.

The theories mentioned so far do not explain either the transition from intentions to actions or the maintenance and relapse process. Therefore, a causal model has been proposed, the Health Action Process Approach, that is based on the influential role of expectancies and also covers self-regulatory processes during the action phase.

REFERENCES

Ajzen, I. (1988). *Attitudes, personality, and behavior.* Milton Keynes: Open University Press.

Ajzen, I., & Madden, J. T. (1986). Prediction of goal-directed behavior: Attitudes, intentions, and perceived behavioral control. *Journal of Experimental Social Psychology, 22,* 453-474.

Annis, H. M., & Davis, C. S. (1988). Assessment of expectancies. In D. M. Donovan & G. A. Marlatt (Eds.), *Assessment of addictive behaviors* (pp. 84-111). New York: Guilford Press.

Baer, J. S., & Lichtenstein, E. (1988). Cognitive assessment. In D. M. Donovan, & Marlatt, G. A. (Eds.), *Assessment of addictive behaviors* (pp. 104-110). New York: Guilford Press.

Bandura, A. (1977). Self-efficacy: Toward a unifying theory of behavioral change. *Psychological Review, 84,* 191-215.

Bandura, A. (1986). *Social foundations of thought and action.* Englewood Cliffs, NJ: Prentice-Hall.

Bandura, A. (1988). Self-efficacy conception of anxiety. *Anxiety Research, 1,* 77-98.

Bandura, A. (1989). Human agency in social cognitive theory. *American Psychologist*, *44*(9), 1175-1184.

Bandura, A. (1990). Perceived self-efficacy in the exercise of control over AIDS infection. *Medienpsychologie*, *2*, 23-43.

Bandura, A. (1991). Self-efficacy mechanism in physiological activation and health-promoting behavior. In J. Madden (Ed.), *Neurobiology of learning, emotion and affect* (pp. 229-270). New York: Raven Press.

Bandura, A., Cioffi, D., Taylor, C. B., & Brouillard, M. E. (1988). Perceived self-efficacy in coping with cognitive stressors and opioid activation. *Journal of Personality and Social Psychology*, *55*, 479-488.

Bandura, A., Reese, L., & Adams, N. E. (1982). Micro-analysis of action and fear arousal as a function of differential levels of perceived self-efficacy. *Journal of Personality and Social Psychology*, *43*, 5-21.

Bandura, A., Taylor, C. B., Williams, S. L., Mefford, I. N., & Barchas, J. D. (1985). Catecholamine secretion as a function of perceived coping self-efficacy. *Journal of Consulting and Clinical Psychology*, *53*, 406-414.

Barling, J., & Abel, M. (1983). Self-efficacy and tennis performance. *Cognitive Therapy and Research*, *7*, 265-272.

Beck, K. H., & Lund, A. K. (1981). The effects of health threat seriousness and personal efficacy upon intentions and behavior. *Journal of Applied Social Psychology*, *11*, 401-415.

Becker, H. M. (1974). *The health belief model and personal health behavior*. Thorofare, NJ: Slack.

Becker, M. H., & Rosenstock, I. M. (1987). Comparing social learning theory and the health belief model. In W. B. Ward (Ed.), *Advances in health education and promotion* (Vol. 2, pp. 245-249). Greenwich, CT: JAI Press.

Bernier, M., & Avard, J. (1986). Self-efficacy, outcome and attrition in a weight reduction program. *Cognitive Therapy and Research*, *10*, 319-338.

Chambliss, C. A., & Murray, E. J. (1979). Efficacy attribution, locus of control, and weight loss. *Cognitive Therapy and Research*, *3*, 349-353.

Cohen, S., Lichtenstein, E., Mermelstein, R., Kingsolver, K., Baer, J. S., & Kamarck, T. W. (1988). Social support interventions for smoking cessation. In B. H. Gottlieb (Ed.), *Marshaling social support. Formats, processes, and effects* (pp. 211-240). Beverly Hills, CA: Sage.

Colletti, G., Supnick, J. A., & Payne, T. J. (1985). The smoking self-efficacy questionnaire (SSEQ): Preliminary scale development and validation. *Behavioral Assessment*, *7*, 249-260.

Condiotte, M. M., & Lichtenstein, E. (1981). Self-efficacy and relapse in smoking cessation programs. *Journal of Consulting and Clinical Psychology*, *49*, 648-658.

Critchlow, B. (1986). The powers of John Barleycorn: Beliefs about the effects of alcohol on social behavior. *American Psychologist*, *41*, 751-764.

Critchlow Leigh, B. (1989). In search of the seven dwarves: Issues of measurement and meaning in alcohol expectancy. *Psychological Bulletin*, *105*, 361-373.

De Vries, H., Dijkstra, M., & Kok, G. (1989, July). *Self-efficacy as a determinant of the onset of smoking and interventions to prevent smoking in adolescents*. Paper presented at the First European Congress of Psychology. Amsterdam, The Netherlands.

De Vries, H., Dijkstra, M., & Kuhlman, P. (1988). Self-efficacy: The third factor besides attitude and subjective norm as a predictor of behavioural intentions. *Health Education Research*, *3*, 273-282.

De Vries, H., & Kok, G. J. (1986). From determinants of smoking behavior to the implications for a prevention programme. *Health Education Research*, *1*, 85-94.

Desharnais, R., Bouillon, J., & Godin, G. (1986). Self-efficacy and outcome expectations as determinants of exercise adherence. *Psychological Reports*, *59*, 1155-1159.

DiClemente, C. C., Prochaska, J. O., & Gibertini, M. (1985). Self-efficacy and the stages of self-change of smoking. *Cognitive Therapy and Research*, *9*, 181-200.

Donovan, D. M., & Marlatt, G. A. (Eds.). (1988). *Assessment of addictive behaviors*. New York: Guilford Press.

Dzewaltowski, D. A. (1989). Toward a model of exercise motivation. *Journal of Sport & Exercise Psychology*, *11*, 251-269.

Eiser, J. R. (1983). Smoking, addiction and decision-making. *International Review of Applied Psychology*, *32* , 11-28.

Eiser, J. R., & Sutton, S. R. (1977). Smoking as a subjectively rational choice. *Addictive Behaviors*, *2*, 129-134.

Ewart, C. K., Gillian, R. E., Kalemen, M. H., Manley, S. A., & Kalemen, M. D. (1986). Usefulness of self-efficacy in predicting overexertion during programmed exercise in coronary artery disease. *American Journal of Cardiology*, *57*, 557-561.

Fishbein, M. (1982). Social psychological analysis of smoking behavior. In J. R. Eiser (Ed.), *Social psychology and behavioral medicine* (pp. 179-197). Chichester: Wiley & Sons.

Fishbein, M., & Ajzen, I. (1975). *Belief, attitude, intention, and behavior: An introduction to theory and research*. Reading, MA: Addison-Wesley.

Garcia, M. E., Schmitz, J. M., & Doerfler, L. A. (1990). A fine-grained analysis of the role of self-efficacy in self-initiated attempts to quit smoking. *Journal of Consulting and Clinical Psychology*, *58*, 317-322.

Gilchrist, L. D., & Schinke, S. P. (1983). Coping with contraception: Cognitive and behavioral methods with adolescents. *Cognitive Therapy and Research*, *7*, 379-388.

Glynn, S. M., & Ruderman, A. J. (1986). The development and validation of an eating self-efficacy scale. *Cognitive Therapy and Research*, *10*, 403-420.

Godding, P. R., & Glasgow, R. E. (1985). Self-efficacy and outcome expectations as predictors of controlled smoking status. *Cognitive Therapy and Research*, *9*, 583-590.

Heckhausen, H. (1991). *Motivation and action*. Berlin: Springer.

Heckhausen, H., & Kuhl, J. (1985). Form wishes to actions: The dead ends and short cuts on the long way to action. In M. Frese & J. Sabini (Eds.), *Goal-directed behavior: The concept of action in psychology* (pp. 134-159). Hillsdale, NJ: Erlbaum.

Janz, N. K., & Becker, M. H. (1984). The health belief model: A decade later. *Health Education Quarterly*, *11*, 1-47.

Kaplan, R. M., Atkins, C. J., & Reinsch, S. (1984). Specific efficacy expectations mediate exercise compliance in patients with COPD. *Health Psychology*, *3*, 223-242.

Kok, G., De Vries, H., Mudde, A. N, & Strecher, V. J. (1990). Planned health education and the role of self-efficacy: Dutch research. *Health Education Research*, *5*.

Kuhl, J. (1983). *Motivation, Konflikt und Handlungskontrolle* [Motivation, conflict, and action control]. Berlin: Springer.

Kuhl, J. (1985). Volitional mediators of cognition-behavior consistency: Self-regulatory processes and action versus state orientation. In J. Kuhl & J. Beckmann (Eds.), *Action control: From cognition to behavior* (pp. 101-128). New York: Springer.

Kuhl, J. (1986). Motivation and information processing. A new look at decision making, dynamic change, and action control. In R. M. Sorrentino & E. T. Higgins (Eds.), *Handbook of motivation and cognition* (pp. 404-434). New York: Wiley.

Kuhl, J., & Krasna, K. (1990). Self-regulation and metamotivation: Computational mechanisms, development, and assessment. In R. Kanfer, P. L. Ackerman, & R. Cudeck (Eds.), *Learning and individual differences* (pp. 343-374). Hillsdale, NJ: Erlbaum.

Lazarus, R. S. (1991). *Emotion and adaptation*. London: Oxford University Press.

Lazarus, R. S., & Folkman, S. (1984). *Stress, appraisal, and coping*. New York: Springer.

Lazarus, R. S., & Folkman, S. (1987). Transactional theory and research on emotions and coping. *European Journal of Personality, 1*, 141-170.

Levinson, R. A. (1982). *Teenage women and contraceptive behavior: Focus on self-efficacy in sexual and contraceptive situations*. Unpublished Doctoral Dissertation. Stanford University, Stanford, CA.

Litt, M. D. (1988). Self-efficacy and perceived control: Cognitive mediators of pain tolerance. *Journal of Personality and Social Psychology, 54*, 149-160.

Maddux, J. E., Norton, L. W., & Stoltenberg, C. D. (1986). Self-efficacy expectancy, outcome expectancy, and outcome value: Relative effects on behavioral intentions. *Journal of Personality and Social Psychology, 51*, 783-789.

Maddux, J. E., & Rogers, R. W. (1983). Protection motivation and self-efficacy: A revised theory of fear appeals and attitude change. *Journal of Experimental Social Psychology, 19*, 469-479.

Manning, M. M., & Wright, T. L. (1983). Self-efficacy expextancies, outcome expectancies, and the persistence of pain control in childbirth. *Journal of Personality and Social Psychology, 45*, 421-431.

Marlatt, G. A. (1985). Cognitive factors in the relapse process. In G. A. Marlatt & J. R. Gordon (Eds.), *Relapse prevention: Maintenance strategies in the treatment of addictive disorders* (pp. 128-200). New York: The Guilford Press.

Marlatt, G. A., Baer, J. S., Donovan, D. M., & Kivlahan, D. R. (1988). Addictive behaviors: Etiology and treatment. *Annual Review of Psychology, 39*, 223-252.

Marlatt, G. A., & Gordon, J. R. (Eds.). (1985). *Relapse prevention: Maintenance strategies in the treatment of addictive behaviors*. New York: Guilford.

McKusick, L., Coates, T. J., Morin, S. F., Pollack, L., & Hoff, C. (1990). Longitudinal predictors of reductions in unprotected anal intercourse among gay men in San Francisco: The AIDS behavioral research project. *American Journal of Public Health, 80*, 978-983.

Meyerowitz, B. E., & Chaiken, S. (1987). The effect of message framing on breast self-examination attitudes, intentions, and behavior. *Journal of Personality and Social Psychology, 52*, 500-510.

Mischel, H. N., & Mischel, W. (1983). The development of children's knowledge of self-control strategies. *Child Development, 54*, 603-619.

Mischel, W. (1966). Theory and research on the antecedents of self-imposed delay of reward. In B. A. Maher (Ed.), *Progress in experimental personality research* (Vol. 3, pp. 85-132). New York: Academic Press.

Mischel, W. (1973). Toward a cognitive social learning reconceptualization of personality. *Psychological Review*, 80, 252-283.

Mudde, A., Kok, G., & Strecher, V. (1989, July). *Self-efficacy and success expectancy as predictors of the cessation of smoking*. Paper presented at the First European Congress of Psychology. Amsterdam, The Netherlands.

Mullen, P. D., Hersey, J. C., & Iverson, D. C. (1987). Health behavior models compared. *Social Science and Medicine, 24*, 973-983.

O'Leary, A. (1985). Self-efficacy and health. *Behavioral Research Therapy, 23*, 437-451.

O'Leary, A., Shoor, S., Lorig, K., & Holman, H. R. (1988). A cognitive-behavioral treatment for rheumatoid arthritis. *Health Psychology, 7*, 527-542.

Paulussen, T., Kok, G. J., Knibbe, R., & Kramer, T. (1989). AIDS en intraveneus drug-gebruik [AIDS and IV-drug use]. *Tijdschrift voor Sociale Gezondheitszorg* [Dutch Journal of Social Health Care], 68, 129-136.

Rippetoe, P.A., & Rogers, R.W. (1987). Effects on components of protection motiva-tion theory on adaptive and maladaptive coping with a health threat. *Journal of Personality & Social Psychology, 52*, 596-604.

Rogers, R.W. (1975). A protection motivation theory of fear appeals and attitude change. *Journal of Psychology, 91*, 93-114.

Rogers, R. W. (1983). Cognitive and physiological processes in fear appeals and atti-tude change: A revised theory of protection motivation. In J. R. Cacioppo & R. E. Petty (Eds.), *Social psychology: A sourcebook* (pp. 153-176). New York: Guilford.

Rogers, R. W. (1985). Attitude change and information integration in fear appeals. *Psychological Reports, 56*, 179-182.

Rosenstock, I. M. (1966). Why people use health services. *Milbank Memorial Fund Quarterly, 44*, 94.

Rosenstock, I. M., Strecher, V. J., & Becker, M. H. (1988). Social learning theory and the Health Belief Model. *Health Education Quarterly, 15*, 175-183.

Sallis, J. F., Haskell, W. L., Fortmann, S. P., Vranizan, K. M., Taylor, C. B., & Solomon, D. S. (1986). Predictors of adoption and maintenance of physical activity in a community sample. *Preventive Medicine, 15*, 331-341.

Scheier, M. F., & Carver, C. S. (1985). Optimism, coping, and health: Assessment and implications of generalized outcome expectancies. *Health Psychology, 4*, 219-247.

Scheier, M. F., & Carver, C. S. (1987). Dispositional optimism and physical well-being: The influence of generalized outcome expectancies on health. *Journal of Personality, 55*, 169-210.

Scheier, M. F., Weintraub, J. K., & Carver, C. S. (1986). Coping with stress: Divergent strategies of optimists and pessimists. *Journal of Personality and Social Psychology, 51*, 1257-1264.

Schifter, D. B., & Ajzen, I. (1985). Intention, perceived control, and weight loss: An application of the theory of planned behavior. *Journal of Personality and Social Psychology, 49*, 843-851.

Schwarzer, R. (1981). *Streß, Angst und Hilflosigkeit* [Stress, anxiety, and helplessness]. Stuttgart: Kohlhammer.

Schwarzer, R. (1992). *Psychologie des Gesundheitsverhaltens* [Psychology of health behavior]. Göttingen: Hogrefe.

Seydel, E., Taal, E., & Wiegman, O. (1990). Risk-appraisal, outcome and self-efficacy expectancies: Cognitive factors in preventive behavior related to cancer. *Psychology and Health, 4*, 99-109.

Slater, M. D. (1989). Social influences and cognitive control as predictors of self-efficacy and eating behavior. *Cognitive Therapy and Research, 13*, 231-245.

Strecher, V. J., DeVellis, B. M., Becker, M. H., & Rosenstock, I. M. (1986). The role of self-efficacy in achieving health behavior change. *Health Education Quarterly, 13*, 73-91.

Sutton, S. (1989). Smoking attitudes and behavior: Applications of Fishbein and Ajzen's Theory of Reasoned Action to predicting and understanding smoking decisions. In T. Ney & A. Gale (Eds.), *Smoking and human behavior* (pp. 289-312). Chichester: Wiley.

Taylor, C. B., Bandura, A., Ewart, C. K., Miller, N. H., & DeBusk, R. F. (1985). Exercise testing to enhance wives' confidence in their husbands' cardiac capability soon after clinically uncomplicated acute myocardial infarction. *American Journal of Cardiology, 55,* 635-638.

Velicer, W. F., DiClemente, C. C., Rossi, J. S., & Prochaska, J. O. (1990). Relapse situations and self-efficacy: An integrative model. *Addictive Behaviors, 15,* 271-283.

Weinberg, R. S., Gould, D., & Jackson, A. (1979). Expectations and performance: An empirical test of Bandura's self-efficacy theory. *Journal of Sport Psychology, 1,* 320-331.

Weinberg, R. S., Gould, D., Yukelson, D., & Jackson, A. (1981). The effect of preexisting and manipulated self-efficacy on competitive muscular endurance task. *Journal of Sport Psychology, 4,* 345-354.

Weinberg, R. S., Hughes, H. H., Critelli, J. W., England, R., & Jackson, A. (1984). Effects of preexisting and manipulated self-efficacy on weight loss in a self-control program. *Journal of Research in Personality, 18,* 352-358.

Weinberg, R. S., Yukelson, D., & Jackson, A. (1980). Effects of public and private efficacy expectations on competitive performance. *Journal of Sport Psychology, 2,* 340-349.

Weiner, B. (1980). The role of affect in rational (attributional) approaches to human motivation. *Educational Researcher, 9,* 4-11.

Weinstein, N. D. (1988). The precaution adoption process. *Health Psychology, 7,* 355-386.

Weinstein, N. D. (1989). Effects of personal experience on self-protective behavior. *Psychological Bulletin, 105,* 31-50.

Wiedenfeld, S. A., O'Leary, A., Bandura, A., Brown, S., Levine, S., & Raska, K. (1990). Impact of perceived self-efficacy in coping with stressors on immune function. *Journal of Personality and Social Psychology, 59,* 1082-1094.

Wills, T. A. (1990). Multiple networks and substance use. *Journal of Social and Clinical Psychology, 9,* 78-90.

Wilson, D. K., Wallston, K. A., & King, J. E. (1990). Effects of contract framing, motivation to quit, and self-efficacy on smoking reduction. *Journal of Applied Social Psychology, 20,* 531-547.

Wood, J. (1989). Theory and research concerning social comparisons of personal attributes. *Psychological Bulletin, 106,* 231-248.

Wurtele, S. K., & Maddux, J. E. (1987). Relative contributions of protection motivation theory components in predicting exercise intentions and behavior. *Health Psychology, 6,* 453-466.

Yalow, E. S., & Collins J. L. (1987). Self-efficacy in health behaviour change: Issues in measurement and research design. In W. B. Ward (Ed.), *Advances in health education and promotion* (Vol. 2, pp. 181-199). Greenwich, CT: JAI Press.

Author Notes

The author is grateful to Albert Bandura, Charles Carver, and two anonymous referees for their valuable comments on an earlier draft of this chapter.

SELF-EFFICACY AND ATTRIBUTION THEORY IN HEALTH EDUCATION

Gerjo Kok, Dirk-Jan Den Boer,
Hein De Vries, Frans Gerards,
Harm J. Hospers, and Aart N. Mudde

Self-efficacy is defined as the estimation of the person about his/her ability to perform a specific behavior. The important role of self-efficacy in health education is argued, illustrated with Dutch research, which shows that self-efficacy is an important determinant of health behavior, of future health behavior, and of health behavior change. It will be discussed how attribution theory is related to self-efficacy theory and how insights from attribution theory can be applied in health behavior interventions. Programs to improve self-efficacy by attributional retraining have been developed successfully, mostly based on relapse prevention theory.

Health education is a form of planned behavior change (see Green & Lewis,1986; Kok, 1988). Research shows that the effectiveness of health education activities is determined by the quality of this planning process (Jonkers, De Haes, Kok, Liedekerken, & Saan, 1988): analysing the problem, analysing the related behaviors, analysing the determinants of that behavior, developing interventions to change that behavior, organising implementation, and finally evaluating of the effects on the problem or, at least, the behavior. An important step in this planning process is the analysis of the determinants of the target behavior. We will focus on self-efficacy as a determinant of behavior and as a predictor of future behavior and behavioral change, using illustrations from our own research. We will then suggest strategies to improve self-efficacy, based on attribution theory and relapse prevention theory.

DETERMINANTS OF BEHAVIOR

Social psychological theory and research, fundamental as well as applied, has traditionally provided an important contribution to the understanding of the determinants of behavior. Fishbein and Ajzen (1975) integrated a series of models from attitude theory and social influence theory in their model of reasoned behavior. They stimulated a whole field of fundamental and especially applied research (Ajzen & Fishbein,1980; De Vries & Kok, 1986). Gradually it became clear that the Fishbein and Ajzen model was very useful, but limited. The model could not sufficiently account for the important role of behavioral costs and barriers in performing the behavior. In theory, costs and barriers should appear as beliefs about performing the behavior, but in practice researchers found better prediction of behavior when costs and barriers were measured independently of the attitude. In addition to the model of reasoned behavior, researchers focussed on Bandura's concept of self-efficacy (Bandura, 1986; Strecher, DeVellis, Becker, & Rosenstock, 1986) as a determinant of behavior. Self-efficacy is the estimation of the person about his/her ability to perform a specific behavior in a specific situation. Self-efficacy expectations are based on own experience with the behavior (and especially the attributions that people make about success and failure), observations of others, persuasion by others, and physiological information (e.g., nervousness). Self-efficacy has to be distinguished from outcome expectancy, the latter being an estimation of the effectiveness of the behavior to reach a desired goal. For a smoker, outcome expectancy is the estimation of the improvement in health and life by stopping smoking, while self-efficacy is the estimation of own ability to really give up smoking. Several researchers reported an improvement in the prediction of behavior by combining attitudes, social norms, and self-efficacy (Ajzen, 1987; De Vries, Dijkstra & Kuhlman, 1988). This "Determinants of Behavior Model" is represented in Figure 1.

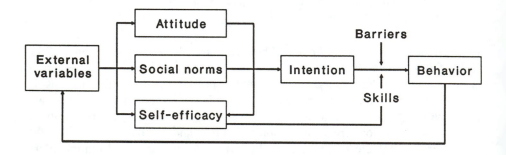

Figure 1 Determinants of behavior model.

Attitudes, social norms and self-efficacy predict the intention, which in turn predicts the behavior. External variables (outside the model), like demographic ones, are supposed to influence behavior via the three determinants and the intention. Between intention and behavior there can be barriers or lack of skills. Attitudes, social norms and self-efficacy can be measured in advance, while barriers and skills play a role when the behavior is actually performed. The intention predicts the behavior, but the model also indicates that self-efficacy is an estimation of the skills that are needed in the actual situation and the possibilities to overcome barriers. For that reason an influence from self-efficacy via skills on behavior is proposed. The actual performance of the behavior leads to a feedback process that influences in turn the three determinants. Attitudes, social norms and self-efficacy are not completely independent from each other. Mostly the correlations between the three are substantial. All three determinants can be characterised as beliefs. But empirical data indicate that a separate measurement of each determinant improves the prediction of behavior significantly.

There is as yet no tradition in the measurement of self-efficacy. Bandura (1986) has argued that self-efficacy expectations vary along dimensions of magnitude, generality, and strength. This implies that self-efficacy estimates must be viewed as situation dependent. The perception of subjects' ability to perform a certain behavior is determined, and varies, by the perceived task difficulty and the situation. Measurement of perceived difficulty does not necessarily imply an estimation of ability. A person can see a behavior in a certain situation as very difficult, but also as something that can be done. Measuring ability in relation to situational aspects, however, is likely to include perceived difficulty levels of both situation and behavior. A person asked to rate his confidence of being able to perform a certain behavior in a certain situation, will probably weigh ability against task difficulty and situation difficulty. This leads to the conclusion that instruments to measure perceived ability ("Do you think you are able to...") assess both the dimensions strength and magnitude. Including a sample of relevant situations provides an assessment of the dimension generality.

In the following we will present some of our studies about the role of self-efficacy as a determinant of behavior and behavioral change (for a review of the international literature, see Strecher et al.,1986). Most of these studies are cross-sectional, measuring the determinants and the behavior at the same time. In addition we will present two of our studies that are longitudinal, predicting future behavior from former measures of determinants. This makes it possible to infer causal relationships.

Dutch Research on Self-Efficacy as a Determinant of Behavior

De Vries (1989) analyzed the determinants of the onset of smoking in youth. Eighty-five third grade Dutch pupils of various secondary schools participated in his study, 40% male and 60% female, with age varying between 14 and 17 years. Sixteen questions assessed the attitude by focussing on both short- and long-term consequences, and personal, social and health consequences. Social norms were assessed by nine questions about the norms of parents, siblings, peers and adults. The nine questions on self-efficacy comprised: finding it difficult/easy not to smoke when friends smoke, explaining to other people that "I do not want to smoke," being able to refuse a cigarette when offered, when offered by parents, when offered by friends, in spite of being called a coward, being able to stop smoking when wanting to, knowing a reason to refuse a cigarette, succeeding in becoming/staying a non-smoker. One item measured the intention and one item measured the behavior. The nine self-efficacy questions formed a reliable scale, with Cronbach's alpha .80. Figure 2 shows the correlations and multiple correlations of the determinants with intention and behavior.

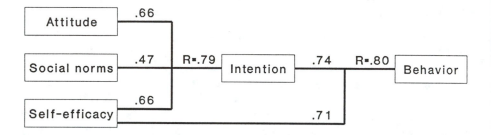

Figure 2 Correlations and multiple correlations of the three determinants with intention and smoking behavior ($N = 85$, all correlations are significant $p < .01$).

A hierarchical regression analysis showed that self-efficacy had a unique contribution in the prediction of the intention, when added after attitude and social norm. Self-efficacy explained another 15% of the variance in the intention. Moreover, self-efficacy had a unique contribution in the prediction of the behavior, when added after the intention, explaining another 9%. So in line with our expectations, De Vries found an influence from self-efficacy on the intention independent of attitude and social norm, and an influence on behavior independent of the intention. The latter is probably the result of the relation between self-efficacy estimations and the actual skills in performing the behavior and overcoming barriers. On seven of the nine self-efficacy items there was a significant difference between the smokers and the non-smokers (see De Vries, 1989).

We have presented a study that shows a relation between attitudes, social norms and self-efficacy on the one hand, and intention and behavior on the other. A number of other studies have found the same result. These were cross-sectional studies that cannot show any causal relationship. We know that attitudes cause behavior, but behavior in turn causes attitudes. The same applies to social norms. With respect to self-efficacy, the first assumption is that self-efficacy is the result of behavior. In our model, however, we have assumed that self-efficacy can also cause behavior. In the following we will present two studies that are longitudinal and that show that self-efficacy is a determinant of future behavior.

The reported study by De Vries (1989) was part of a research program about the prevention of smoking in youth, with a series of measures over time. The attitude, social norm and self-efficacy scores of the control group at the first measurement (Time 1), have been used to predict intention and behavior at a following measurement, one year later (Time 2). The correlations of the determinants at Time 1 with intention and behavior at Time 2 are depicted in Figure 3.

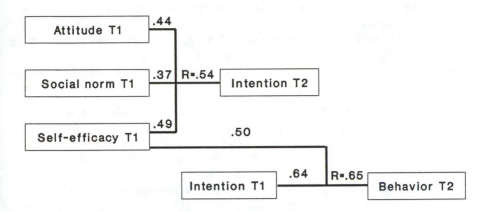

Figure 3 Correlations and multiple correlations of the three determinants at Time 1 with (1) the intention at Time 2, and (2) with smoking behavior at Time 2 ($N = 600$; all correlations are significant $p \leq .01$).

The results of a regression analysis showed that self-efficacy at Time 1 was the best predictor of smoking intention at Time 2 one year later, explaining 24% of the variance. Self-efficacy at Time 1 also had a unique contribution in the prediction of behavior at Time 2, when added after the intention Time 1. This study showed that self-efficacy, measured at a certain time, can predict future intentions and behavior.

The study of Mudde, Kok, and Strecher (1989) focussed on self-efficacy as a predictor of success in the cessation of smoking. Subjects were 123 participants in a three-week "Stop Smoking" program. The most important principles of the program were: (a) quitting at the first meeting, (b) concentrating on one's own potential to fight addiction through willpower, and (c) preparation for the physiological consequences of quitting.

Enhancing self-efficacy was not the focus of this program. Although certain components of the program are likely to enhance self-efficacy, no specific attention was paid to skills training or obtaining adequate coping responses. The possibility of relapse and how to handle it when it occurs received minimal attention. The program consisted of seven meetings, spread over three weeks. Both before and after treatment and after follow-up periods of six weeks and one year, self-efficacy and smoking behavior were measured by questionnaire. Two measures related to self-efficacy were used in this study:

1. A one-item perceived ability measure. Subjects were asked to rate their perceived ability in resisting the urge to smoke in every possible situation.

2. The "Smoking Self-Efficacy Questionnaire" (SSEQ), developed by Coletti, Supnick and Payne (1985). Subjects were asked to rate their perceived ability in resisting the urge to smoke in seventeen different situations.

At the pre-treatment self-efficacy measure, respondents were told to imagine that they were quitting without professional assistance, to minimize the effect of program-efficacy expectations. Assessment of smoking behavior was realised by self-report. The cutting point between smokers and quitters was set at one cigarette or more during the last seven days before measurement. Once a participant was missing at a follow-up, that person was treated as a smoker in the following analyses.

Success rates of the program were 54% after treatment, 44% after six-weeks follow-up, and 27% after one-year follow-up. Schwartz (1987) reports median success rates for group interventions of 24% to 36% after one-year follow-up, so the result of this treatment is comparable. There are no differences between the groups of quitters and smokers after one year, with respect to any measure on the pretest. We will focus on the role of self-efficacy after treatment in predicting smoking behavior after one year. Mudde et al. (1989) divided the participants that were successful after the treatment in three success/failure groups:

A: post-treatment success, post-six-weeks success, post-one-year success:

B: post-treatment success, post-six-weeks success, post-one-year failure;

C: post-treatment success, post-six-weeks failure, post-one-year failure.

Mudde et al. predicted the membership of Groups A, B and C after one year, from the self-efficacy scores at the post-treatment measure, and the increase in self-efficacy during treatment (see Table 1) (post-treatment failures were left out because their post-treatment self-efficacy scores will artificially be lower than those of the other groups). The post-treatment level of self-efficacy and the increase of self-efficacy during treatment, as measured by the one-item perceived ability measure, were predictors for success and failure after one year. In the SSEQ measures there is a slight trend. Again we find that self-efficacy at a certain time can predict behavior change in the future, in this case the long-term effects of a smoking cessation program.

Table 1

Self-Efficacy Scores at Post-Treatment Measures and Success and Failure Groups After One Year (N = 66)

	Post-Treatment Score		Increase During Treatment	
	One-Item	SSEQ	One-Item	SSEQ
Group A	3.8	4.5	2.2	2.2
Group B	3.4	4.1	1.6	1.9
Group C	3.2	4.4	1.2	1.7
$p <$	.05	.14	.01	.17

Improving Self-Efficacy by Health Education

We have presented research that shows the contribution of self-efficacy in the determination of behavior. We have also presented research showing that self-efficacy is predictive for future success and failure in behavioral change. However, the program in the study by Mudde et al. (1989) was not specifically meant to improve self-efficacy. An important question for health education is: Can we improve self-efficacy and thus stimulate the desired behavior change? This question cannot fully be answered positively at this moment, but we do have promising evidence. During the last decade there has been an increase in techniques based on attribution theory that can be used to induce people to change their behavior and based on attributional retraining and self-efficacy improvement (Weary, Stanley, & Harvey, 1989). We will now discuss attribution theory and show how this theory is related to self-efficacy theory. we will also show how attributional insights can be applied in health behavior change programs.

ATTRIBUTION THEORY

Figure 4 is a schematic depicting Weiner's attributional model (1985, 1986). The model indicates that when outcomes are negative, unexpected, or important a causal search is started, resulting in causal ascriptions that try to explain the outcomes. For example, a person who attempts to quit smoking but fails might attribute this outcome to a variety of reasons, e.g., low effort, the difficulty of the task, or nicotine dependency. According to attribution theory, perceived causal reasons have an underlying dimensional structure (Heider, 1958; Kelley, 1967).

Theoretically, three attributional dimensions have been distinguished. The first dimension, locus of causality, reflects the extent to which previous outcomes are attributed to causes either internal or external to the person. The second dimension, stability, reflects the extent to which previous outcomes are attributed to stable or unstable causes. Stable causes refer to perceptions that a failure or success was due to immutable, unalterable causes. Unstable causes refer to perceptions that a failure or a success was due to causes that were mutable. The third dimension, controllability, reflects the extent to which previous outcomes are attributed to controllable or uncontrollable causes. Empirical support is strongest for the dimensions locus of causality and stability, the support for the dimension controllability is weakest (Hewstone & Antaki, 1988; Weiner, 1986). Attribution theory contends that causal ascriptions influence cognitions and emotions related to success and failure. We will first describe the cognitive component and then turn to the affective component of attribution theory.

Cognitive Component of Attribution Theory

Weiner's model suggests that expectancy of success is determined by the perceived stability of the causes for success or failure. A person attributing a success to a stable cause (e.g., ability) will have a higher expectancy of success when having to perform the same task again, compared to somebody who attributes a success on the same task to an unstable cause (e.g., luck). After failure this effect is reversed. The rationale behind this assumption is that when there is no reason to expect the cause of failure to change, the second time the task will be performed the cause responsible for failure will still be present. If the cause for failure was unstable, there is no reason to expect the cause to be present the next time one performs the task.

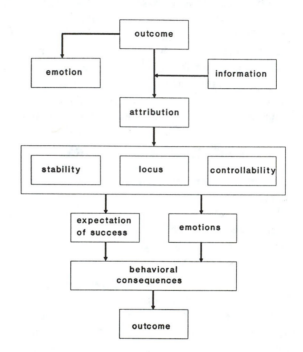

Figure 4 Schematic overview of Weiner's attribution theory.

Furthermore, it is assumed that a lowered expectancy of success leads to less adaptive task behavior. Because of the lowered expectation of success, persons will invest less energy in the task at hand, because they perceive a lower likelihood of succeeding. It is this lack of energy invested in the task which causes the low performance. This line of reasoning very closely parallels Bandura's ideas about self-efficacy. He assumes that a low self-efficacy leads to avoidance of the task at hand. Self-efficacy estimates resemble expectancies of success in the respect that both concepts are related to the estimate people make about the likelihood that a certain outcome or goal will be attained. Furthermore, both estimates are based on a cognitive appraisal of past experiences (Bandura, 1986, p. 349; Weiner, 1986, p. 181). Several studies on attributional processes have used self-efficacy ratings as a measure of expectancy of success, and some authors claim that self-efficacy and expectancy of success are identical concepts (e.g., Kirsch, 1985, 1986).

Support for the cognitive component of this theory can be found, among others, in a study by Eiser and Van der Pligt (1986) on smoking behavior, and a study by Hospers, Kok, and Strecher (1990) on weight reduction. Hospers et al. tested the cognitive component of the attributional model on 158 subjects who participated in a weight reduction program. They measured the number of previous attempts to lose weight, stability of attributions for previous failure, expectancy of success and goal attainment. Results of this study are shown in Figure 5.

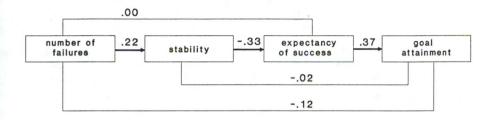

Figure 5 Path analysis with goal attainment as outcome variable; bold arrows indicate significant β-weights $(p < .01)$.

As hypothesized, goal attainment is positively associated with success expectancy which, in turn, is negatively associated with stability. Furthermore, stability was positively related to the number of former trials. Also as hypothesized, there was no significant association between the number of previous attempts and goal attainment, or stability and goal attainment. These results suggest that it is not the number of failures people experience that is important, but the way people interpret these failures. The more stable the causes attributed to failure, the lower the expectancy of success for the next attempt, and hence lower goal attainment.

As the results of the above-mentioned studies are all correlational, one should be careful in interpreting these results. These studies do not show that because subjects attribute their previous failures at losing weight (or quitting smoking [Eiser & Van der Pligt, 1986]) to stable causes they do not achieve their goals. Correlational studies can only show that a relationship between variables exists, they can never show that a change in one variable is the cause of the change in another variable. Only some studies have shown a causal relationship between attributional change and behavioral change (Den Boer, Meertens, Kok, & Van Knippenberg, 1990).

Affective Component of Attribution Theory

The relation between stability of attributions, expectation of success and behavior can be referred to as the cognitive component of Weiner's theory. The theory also consists of an affective component: the relation between perceptions of locus and controllability on the one hand and emotions and behavior on the other. It is assumed that different attributions lead to different emotions. An attribution of effort for failure (internal/controllable) will lead to guilt, while an attribution of ability (internal/uncontrollable) for failure will lead to shame. It is assumed that there are two kinds of emotions: motivating and debilitating. Motivating emotions (guilt for instance) will lead to a better task performance while debilitating emotions (shame) will lead to a worse task performance.

Attribution theory states that after failure guilt (as a result of an attribution to, for instance, effort) will lead to better task performance than shame (as a result of an attribution to, for instance, ability). This statement makes the results found by Clifford (1986) interesting. She presented subjects with a scenario in which students failed an exam because of lack of ability, choice of a wrong strategy or lack of effort. She found that subjects predicted the highest rate of success for those students who failed because of the choice of a wrong strategy, no differences where found between ability or effort attribution condition. She explains these results by stating that an extremely high or an extremely low level of guilt (associated with effort or ability respectively) will lead to a worse performance than a moderate level of guilt (associated with an attribution to strategy).

It seems that the relationship between emotions and task behavior is less clear than it is assumed to be in attribution theory. At this point it is safe to assume that a relationship between attributions and outcome expectancies exists that is related to task behavior. Different kinds of research paradigms have shown this to be true (Den Boer et al., 1990; Hospers et al., 1990). However, there remains doubt about the affective component of this theory. Especially the question of which emotions could be termed debilitating and which motivating, remains to be answered.

Applying Attributional Theories

Earlier we stated that attributional techniques can be, and are already, applied to many different situations and problem areas. Examples of attributional explanations can be found in problem areas as diverse as loneliness (Anderson, Horowitz, & French, 1983), alcoholism (McHugh, Beckman, & Frieze, 1979), smoking (Eiser & Van der Pligt, 1986), losing weight (Hospers et al., 1990), coping with critical life events like accidents, rape and illness (Janoff-Bulman, 1979). While the above-mentioned studies are all descriptive, there have also been attempts at changing people's behavior by changing their attributions (see Försterling, 1988, for a review). There have been attempts to improve reading skills of children (Fowler & Peterson, 1981), improve arithmetic skills of children (Schunk, 1984), improve the score of subjects on anagram tasks (Andrews & Debus, 1978), lower drop-out rates at high-school, and improve academic success (Wilson & Linville, 1982). All these studies are based on the following assumption: If different attributions lead to different behavioral consequences, it should be possible to change the behavior of people by changing the attributions they make. As most research within this paradigm is focused on attributions after failure, it is assumed that after failure an attribution to effort leads to "better" task behavior than an attribution to, for instance, ability. One could also say that an internal, stable and uncontrollable attribution for failure should be substituted by an internal, unstable and controllable attribution (Figures 6 and 7). Because of the change from stable to instable there is no need for the subjects to expect a renewed failure. Because of the controllability of the cause they can actively try to change it: They can invest more energy in the task, hoping that it will improve their performance. This implies that, because of the change in attribution, they will have a higher expectation of success, which in turn will increase their task performance. Helping people lose weight is a good example of how this theory can be applied. Research shows that the cause people perceive for their failure is predominantly internal, stable and uncontrollable (Hospers et al., 1990). People often think that they are incapable of losing weight because they perceive no relation between the amount of food they eat and their weight. They think that they will get fat anyway, even if they eat small amounts of low-calorie food. This is a typical case of dysfunctional attribution. Changing this stable, internal and uncontrollable attribution to unstable, internal and controllable will result in a higher possibility of a successful attempt at losing weight the next time. Another possibility is that they do perceive the relation between amount of food eaten and their weight, but do not think that they can control their behavior because they feel they do not have the willpower to change this behavior. Again an example of a dysfunctional attribution.

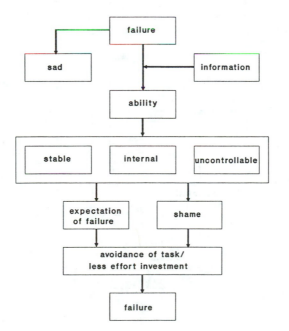

Figure 6 Undesirable attributional sequence.

Applications of attributional insights are plentiful (Den Boer, Meertens, Kok, & Van Knippenberg, 1989; Försterling, 1988; Schunk, 1984; Wilson & Linville, 1982). There remains, however, a significant amount of doubt about the causes of the positive effects found in these reattribution techniques. The fact that there has been hardly any research in which different attributions are compared with each other makes it difficult to state which attributions are "the best" to attribute failure or success to. The fact that providing subjects with a simple attributional questionnaire leads to increases in performances, sheds some doubt on the necessity of complex reattribution techniques as well. Despite these problems we will discuss an approach to maintenance of behavioral change that incorporates many of the above-mentioned insights: relapse prevention theory.

RELAPSE PREVENTION

A theory that uses both the concepts of attribution and self-efficacy is relapse prevention theory. Relapse prevention theory explains why people who try to quit a certain addictive behavior (e.g., smoking or drinking) often fail. Marlatt and Gordon (1985) have elaborated a relapse prevention theory that can be explained in attributional and self-efficacy concepts. An overview of the theory is presented in Figure 8.

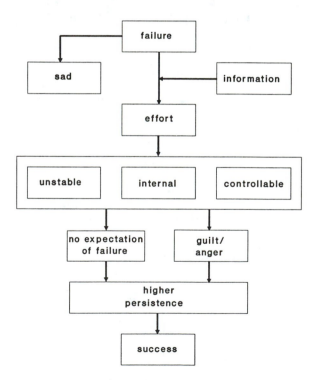

Figure 7 Desired attributional sequence.

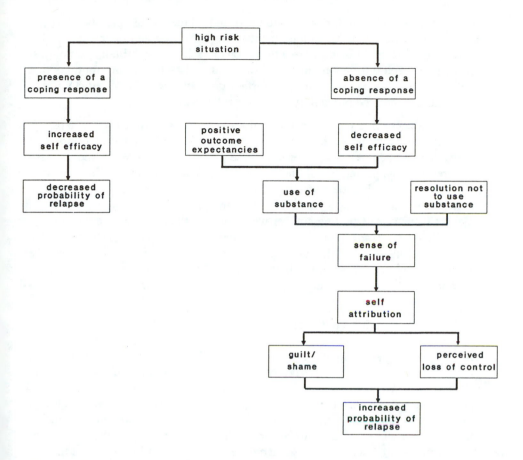

Figure 8 The relapse-prevention model (adapted from Marlatt & Gordon, 1985, p. 106).

An important concept in this theory is the so-called "high-risk situation." A high-risk situation is a situation in which a person is tempted to return to his or her old habit. For a smoker who tries to quit smoking, a meeting with friends who smoke or a day of hard work might be a high-risk situation. In order to cope with such a situation the person needs a coping response. This means that the person needs to anticipate the situation and know what to do when that situation arises. According to the theory the absence of a coping response will lead to decreased self-efficacy and initial use of the substance, resulting in a relapse. If there is a relapse, it is important to consider what caused this lapse, and what can be done to avoid such lapses in the future. The use of the word "caused" in the previous sentence already suggests the importance of attribution theory. There are causes that a person should not attribute to (for instance stable causes like ability or willpower) in this situation because that would result in an even lower self-efficacy. Attributing to stable, internal causes will also lead to shame and perceived loss of control. The smoker who has decided to quit and finds himself unable to cope with a high-risk situation resulting in the use of cigarettes, experiences a conflict between his commitment to stop smoking and his actions. This conflict could result in dissonance, attributions to self, and debilitating emotions. As we have seen attributions to stable, internal causes results in emotions like guilt which have a negative impact on further task behavior. In this situation that will mean an increased probability of further relapses.

The absence of a coping response does not necessarily lead to a lapse, it "only" increases the probability of a lapse. The basis for this assumption lies in the relationship between the presence or absence of the response and the increase or decrease of the perception of one's own self-efficacy in coping with the situation. This implies that the better ingrained and more automated the response is, the higher one's self-efficacy and the lower the probability of a relapse will be. Take for instance the quitting smoker who needs to think every time when he or she is offered a cigarette whether or not he/she will accept the cigarette compared with the quitting smoker who automatically says: "No thank you, I don't smoke anymore." The pressures on the latter person will be much smaller than on the one who has to make up his/her mind anytime he or she is offered the temptation of a cigarette.

One can conclude from the above-mentioned theories that it is not enough to motivate people to adopt healthier behaviors; one has to equip them with the necessary coping-skills to avoid the undesired behavior. This will decrease the probability of a relapse because it increases their self-efficacy. If a lapse occurs it is important to make sure that it is attributed to the "right" cause. This means that it should not be attributed to internal, stable causes like willpower or ability, as these attributions result in a lowered self-efficacy and a lower expectation of success which will result in a higher probability of a relapse. In the last part of this contribution we will discuss some examples of interventions to avoid the pitfalls mentioned.

One important source of self-efficacy information is one's own experience (Bandura, 1986). This implies that self-efficacy can be raised by letting people experience success. Marlatt and Gordon (1985) devised a procedure, consisting of four different stages, to influence the self-efficacy of their clients. These stages are: (a) influencing the frame of reference of the client, (b) searching for high-risk situations and the learning of coping-skills, (c) actual practice of these coping-skills, and (d) learning how to handle relapses.

The first stage consists of teaching the client that to achieve the desired behavior one has to learn certain skills. To quit smoking for instance is not a question of abilities or willpower but a question of skills. This replaces ideas like "I am a weakling who cannot quit smoking by himself" by the idea that one is going to learn the skills to quit smoking. As self-efficacy is related to experiences of success, it is important to state realistic subgoals. One such subgoal could be to stop smoking during the day. The second stage consists of looking at all the possible high-risk situations, by means of keeping a diary, self-monitoring or exploring the reasons why previous quitting attempts failed. For each high-risk situation a coping response should be devised. Thirdly, it is important to practice these responses. A possibility to practice lies in actively seeking the risk situations and discussing the experiences afterwards. If a lapse occurs, it is important to learn from this lapse by examining what caused it and how this can be avoided in the future. Reattribution studies showed that not all the causes are as good: Attributing to ability has different results from attributing to the situation. Relapse prevention theory states that attributing to the self is not a good attribution because it will lead to negative emotions and a lowered self-efficacy. One has to attribute to *external*, unstable and controllable aspects of the situation. This recommendation is at odds with that of reattribution research in which it is recommended to attribute to *internal*, unstable and controllable causes (specifically effort) after failure. One could say that the attribution recommended in relapse prevention consist of finding a (better) coping response for the situation in which one failed. The cause of the lapse is external, but one is responsible for finding a way to handle that specific cause and that is something one has to do by oneself. Relapse prevention and attribution theory do agree, however, on the subject of which attributions are not helpful after a lapse; stable or uncontrollable causes whether they are internal or external will result in a lowered self-efficacy or expectation of success and thus in a higher probability of a total relapse.

Hall, Rugg, Turnstall, and Jones (1984) have shown that such a coping-skills treatment can be successful. They recruited 135 smokers who followed an aversive-smoking program. For half of them this was followed by training in coping skills. The other half participated in a discussion group. Skills training was more effective in avoiding relapse than the discussion group. Analyses showed that this training was especially effective with subjects who smoked less than 20 cigarettes a day. Killen, McCoby, and Taylor (1984) also showed the effectiveness of skills-training. Fifty-four subjects were divided across three conditions; nicotine chewing gum, skills-training, and a combination of both. Follow-up measures after 10 months showed abstinence of smoking of respectively 23%, 30% and 50%. A combination of interventions was clearly the most effective, but skills-training alone was more effective than nicotine chewing gum.

CONCLUSIONS

Self-efficacy has been shown to be an important determinant of behavior and of behavior change. Self-efficacy expectations predict future success or failure in behavior change programs, like quitting smoking. Health education should focus on the improvement of self-efficacy in addition to motivating people to behave in a healthier way. Convincing people about the utility of the expected behavior is necessary but not sufficient. Especially people who have experienced multiple failures and interpret these failures as caused by stable, internal and uncontrollable causes should undergo some kind of reorientation period in which they are taught that they are indeed able to change their behavior. Furthermore we may say that the relapse prevention model can be described in attributional and self-efficacy concepts. This model states that it is not only important to convince people to adopt healthier habits and change their attributions but they have to be taught how to cope with difficult situations, that will surely arise, as well. Some of these difficulties will be caused by barriers which can be overcome by the person concerned. These difficulties can be dealt with within the theoretical—self-efficacy and attributional—framework, and the resulting relapse prevention interventions. Other difficulties will be caused by real barriers (Bandura, 1986). The difference between these two kinds of barriers is not unequivocally determined: Perhaps it is best to state that this difference lies in the perceived controllability of the barriers. Real barriers are beyond the person's control; others might be controllable.

Next to skills training, health educators should focus on health promotion strategies in which barriers beyond the individual's control, but controlled by government or community, are removed as well (De Leeuw, 1989; see also Bandura, 1986, p. 449, about collective efficacy and social action). Most of the studies that were presented focussed on smoking, but the basic ideas can be generalized to other areas in health education, for instance AIDS preventive behavior (Bandura, 1991), participation in fitness programs, and compliance.

REFERENCES

Ajzen, I. (1987). Attitudes, traits and actions: Dispositional prediction of behavior in personality and social psychology. In L. Berkowitz (Ed.), *Advances in experimental social psychology*, (Vol. 20, pp. 1-63). New York: Academic Press.

Ajzen, I., & Fishbein, M. (1980). *Understanding attitudes and predicting social behavior*. Englewood Cliffs, NJ: Prentice-Hall.

Anderson, C. A., Horowitz, L., & French, R. (1983). Attributional style of lonely and depressed people. *Journal of Personality and Social Psychology, 55*, 979-990.

Andrews, G. R., & Debus, R. L. (1978). Persistence and the causal perception of failure: Modifying cognitive attributions. *Journal of Educational Psychology, 70*, 154-166.

Bandura, A. (1986). *Social foundations of thought and action*. Englewood Cliffs, NJ: Prentice Hall.

Bandura, A. (1991). Self-efficacy mechanism in physiological activation and health-promoting behavior. In J. Madden (Ed.), *Neurobiology of learning, emotion and affect* (pp. 229-270). New York: Raven Press.

Clifford, M. M. (1986). The effects of ability, strategy and effort attributions for educational, business and athletic failure. *British Journal of Educational Psychology, 56*, 169-179.

Colletti, G., Supnick, J. A., & Payne, T. J. (1985). The smoking self-efficacy questionnaire (SSEQ): Preliminary scale development and validation. *Behavioral Assessment, 7*, 249-260.

De Leeuw, E. (1989). *The sane revolution. Health promotion: Backgrounds, scope, prospects*. Maastricht, The Netherlands: Van Gorcum.

Den Boer, D. J., Meertens, R. M., Kok, G. J., & Van Knippenberg, A. (1989). Measurement effects in reattribution research. *European Journal of Social Psychology, 19*, 553-559.

Den Boer, D. J., Meertens, R. M., Kok, G. J., & Van Knippenberg, A. (1990). *Weiner's attribution theory: A test of causal relations*. Internal report, University of Limburg, Maastricht, The Netherlands.

De Vries, H. (1989). *Smoking prevention in Dutch adolescents*. Dissertation, University of Limburg, Maastricht, The Netherlands.

De Vries, H., Dijkstra, M., & Kuhlman, P. (1988). Self-efficacy: The third factor besides attitude and subjective norm as a predictor of behavioural intentions. *Health Education Research, 3*, 273-282.

De Vries, H., & Kok, G. J. (1986). From determinants of smoking behavior to the implications for a prevention programme. *Health Education Research, 1*, 85-94.

Eiser, J. R., & Van der Pligt, J. (1986). Smoking cessation and smokers' perceptions of their addiction. *Journal of Social and Clinical Psychology, 37*, 261-272.

Fishbein, M., & Ajzen, I. (1975). *Belief, attitude, intention and behavior: An introduction to theory and research*. Reading, MA: Addison Wesley.

Försterling, F. (1988). *Attribution theory in clinical psychology*. New York: John Wiley and Sons.

Fowler, J. W., & Peterson, P. L. (1981). Increasing reading persistence and altering attributional style of learned helpless children. *Journal of Educational Psychology, 73*, 251-260.

Green, L. W., & Lewis, F. M., (1986). *Measurement and evaluation in health education and health promotion*. Palo Alto, CA: Mayfield.

Hall, S. H., Rugg, D., Turnstall, C., & Jones, R. T. (1984). Preventing relapse in cigarette smoking by behavioral skill training. *Journal of Consulting and Clinical Psychology, 3*, 372-382.

Heider, F. (1958). *The psychology of interpersonal relations*. New York: John Wiley and Sons.

Hewstone, M., & Antaki, C. (1988). Attribution theory and social explanations. In Hewstone, M., Stroebe, W., Codol, J. P., & Stephenson, G. M. (Eds.). *Introduction to social psychology. A European perspective* (pp 111-141). Oxford: Blackwell.

Hospers, H. J., Kok, G. J., & Strecher, V. J. (1990). Attributions for previous failures and subsequent outcomes in a weight reduction program. *Health Education Quarterly, 17*, 409-415.

Janoff-Bulman, R. (1979). Characterological versus behavioral self-blame: Inquiries into depression and rape. *Journal of Personality and Social Psychology, 37*, 1798-1809.

Jonkers, R., De Haes, W. F. M., Kok, G. J., Liedekerken, P., & Saan, J. A. M. (1988). *Effektiviteit van GVO* (Effectiveness of health education). The Hague, The Netherlands: Care.

Kelley, H. H. (1967). Attribution theory in social psychology. In Levine, D. (Ed.) *Nebraska symposium on motivation* (Vol. 15, pp 192-240). Lincoln: University of Nebraska Press.

Killen, D., McCoby, N., & Taylor, C. B. (1984). Nicotine gum and self-regulation training in smoking relapse-prevention. *Behavioral Therapy, 15*, 234-248.

Kirsch, I. (1985). Self-efficacy and expectancy: Old wine with new labels. *Journal of Personality and Social Psychology, 49*, 824-830.

Kirsch, I. (1986). Early research on self-efficacy: What we already know without knowing we knew. *Journal of Social and Clinical Psychology, 4*(3), 339-358.

Kok, G. J. (1988). Health motivation: Health education from a social psychological point of view. In S. Maes, C. D. Spielberger, P. B. Defares, & I. G. Sarasen (Eds.), *Topics in health psychology* (pp. 295-300). New York: Wiley.

Marlatt, G. A., & Gordon, J. R. (1985). *Relapse prevention. Maintenance strategies in the treatment of addictive behaviors*. New York: The Guilford Press.

McHugh, M., Beckman, L,. & Frieze, I. H. (1979). Analyzing alcoholism. In I. H. Frieze, D. Bar-Tall, & J. Carrol (Eds.). *New approaches to social problems* (pp 168-208). San Francisco: Jossey Bass.

Mudde, A. M., Kok, G. J., & Strecher, V. J. (1989, July). *Self-efficacy and success-expectancy as predictors of the cessation of smoking*. Paper presented at the First European Congress of Psychology, Amsterdam, The Netherlands.

Schunk, D. H. (1984). Sequential attributional feedback and children's achievement behaviors. *Journal of Educational Psychology, 76*, 1159-1169.

Schwartz, J. L. (1987). *Review and evaluation of smoking cessation methods: The United States and Canada. 1978-1985*. U.S. Department of Health and Human Services, Public Health Service. Bethesda, MD: National Institutes of Health.

Strecher, V. J., DeVellis, B. M., Beker, M. H., & Rosenstock, I. M. (1986). The role of self-efficacy in achieving health behavior change. *Health Education Quarterly, 13*, 73-91.

Weary, G., Stanley, M. A., & Harvey, J. H. (1989). *Attribution*. New York: Springer.

Weiner, B. (1985). An attributional theory of achievement motivation and emotion. *Psychological Review, 92*, 548-573.

Weiner, B. (1986). *An attributional theory of motivation and emotion*. New York: Springer.

Wilson, T. D., & Linville, P. W. (1982). Improving the academic performance of college freshman: Attribution therapy revisited. *Journal of Personality and Social Psychology, 42*, 367-376.

THE INFLUENCE OF EXPECTANCIES AND PROBLEM-SOLVING STRATEGIES ON SMOKING INTENTIONS

Martin V. Covington
and Carol L. Omelich

Educational researchers have proposed that children's health risk-taking behavior depends in part on how youngsters resolve social/interpersonal problems and on the personal expectations that arise in the course of their daily lives. The present research attempted to establish the usefulness of such a problem-solving/social-cognitive approach to anti-smoking interventions by (a) investigating the nature and causes of problem-solving deficiencies among students at high risk for cigarette smoking, and (b) by determining if various self-efficacy problem-solving elements influence smoking decisions so as to alter the level of temptation experienced in social situations. Some 4,000 sixth, eighth, and tenth graders (11- and 15-year-olds) reacted to hypothetical smoking scenarios by rating temptation level, intentions to smoke, and the likelihood of applying ten problem-solving strategies thought to mediate smoking intentions. Between-group analysis indicated consistent differences in problem-solving approaches among individuals with various smoking histories (e.g., non-smokers, regular smokers), regardless of grade, sex, ethnicity or ability level. Moreover, path analysis showed that self-efficacy strategies and outcome expectations acted as mediators of the temptation → intention relationship regardless of smoking history. Implications of these results for a social problem-solving approach to adolescent health education are considered.

Effective problem solving has long been a valued teaching goal in schools. In more recent years, social problem resolution has also come to occupy a central role in thinking about how to achieve the larger objectives of health education including long-term risk reduction and health maintenance, especially in the area of cigarette use (Botvin & Eng, 1980, 1982; Botvin, Eng, & Williams, 1982; Cohen et al., 1988; Gilchrist, Schinke, & Blythe, 1979; Kim, 1982; Schinke, Gilchrist, Snow, & Schilling, 1985; Williams & Arnold, 1980). Usually the working definition of a *problem* and its *solution* involves the resolution of an interpersonal conflict between family members or among peers in which health issues are not necessarily the paramount concern of the participants, but rather get resolved in the course of solving certain other issues involving children's needs for autonomy, recognition and affiliation.

According to this view, anti-smoking education should provide a range of problem-solving skills for coping with larger issues of personal/social significance, yet in a manner that also reduces the likelihood of problem resolution in favor of smoking. It is in this sense that smoking behavior should not be the sole, or even the primary, concern of anti-smoking interventions. If basic needs such as those for autonomy and affiliation underlie adolescent smoking decisions, educational interventions must work within the context of these naturally occurring motivations and not against them for short-term prevention of smoking. This growing concern with the problem-solving dynamics involved in health-risk reduction is further reflected in the concept of *informed* decision making. The operative notion here is that students should be taught the judgmental skills necessary to reach their own conclusions regarding personal, moral and social issues, thereby shifting the burden of defining the content of personally relevant education from the school and teacher to the student (Botvin, 1983; Botvin et al., 1980; Jones, Piper, & Matthews, 1970; Piper, Jones, & Matthews, 1974).

However, despite the widespread recognition of the potential health relevance of various problem-solving models, few health intervention programs are based primarily on social decision making (for a review, see D'Onofrio, 1983b). One of the reasons for this dearth, at least in the area of cigarette smoking, is the general absence of information on the problem-solving characteristics of smokers and nonsmokers. Missing is systematic evidence on the question of whether or not smokers differ from nonsmokers in how they approach a smoking decision; and how such differences, if they exist, enter into smoking decisions. Yet the inherent value of a problem-solving model to the goals of health education depends fundamentally on the presumption of such skill differences, and on their causal role as mediators of a smoking decision. For example, it may be that smokers arrive at different smoking decisions than do nonsmokers, not because they see the issues differently or choose different strategies to resolve interpersonal dilemmas, but simply because their peer culture encourages smoking or because their parents condone it. If this is true, a problem-solving approach offers little leverage for an increased understanding of smoking behavior for its interdiction. In this instance, educators would be better advised to direct their attention to other aspects of the process of smoking uptake and resistance, perhaps by focusing on parent education or by supporting more restrictive legislation on the use and availability of cigarettes among adolescents.

Obviously, then, an important initial step in establishing the usefulness of a problem-solving focus in health education is to investigate the nature and causes of problem-solving deficiencies among adolescents at risk for smoking. Such an investigation was the main purpose of the present study.

Several potential sources of problem-solving differences can be anticipated, each of which may lead to a decision to smoke or not, and each implying somewhat different intervention strategies. First, it may be that individual differences in the perception of smoking issues and in the availability of prosocial strategies are conditioned in part by variations in basic ability. Although many smokers are bright, well-informed individuals, there are enough scattered reports indicating that children who smoke tend to score lower on standard achievement tests and to have poorer scholastic records to make this hypothesis of basic cognitive differences between smokers and nonsmokers more than idle speculation (for a review, see Evans, Henderson, Hill, & Raines, 1979). Intervention strategies would likely differ markedly depending on the acceptance or rejection of this possibility.

A second and likely more important source of differences involves the individual's personal smoking history. Smokers and nonsmokers face fundamentally different decisions when confronted with the possibility of smoking. Nonsmokers feel considerable pressure to yield arising from personal curiosity and from peer pressure (Covington & Omelich, 1986), yet by definition are highly resistant to such temptation. Such resistance likely depends in part on a well-developed repertoire of problem-solving strategies which acts to diffuse situations in favor of not smoking. By comparison, the experienced smoker tends to yield more easily to temptation, irrespective of peer pressure and immediate circumstances, and sees little violation of his or her self-image by smoking. As a result, young smokers are likely to be less concerned with the issues surrounding smoking and with the probable consequences of their behavior, and to possess less well-formulated strategies to avoid smoking. Such concerns may simply be less salient to smokers, not only because the physical addictive process may have advanced to a point so as to render the decision to smoke automatic (Leventhal & Cleary, 1980), but also because young smokers possess well-entrenched rationalizations that minimize and distort the risks of having "just one more cigarette." Thus, unlike the calculated response of the nonsmoker to peer pressure, what is likely to dominate the decision for smokers is their perception of the value of cigarettes to achieve certain desired goals, the force of habit, and the whim and moods of the moment.

This line of reasoning suggests that we should be quite surprised if investigators failed to find differences in the characteristic ways smokers and nonsmokers typically approach a smoking decision. However, if it is so obvious as to why such differences should arise, then perhaps their existence is merely trivial from the perspective of intervention. In effect, we must also address a further question: Do such problem-solving differences actually exert a causal impact on important target behaviors such as one's intentions to begin smoking or to continue to smoke in the future? As we have argued, problem-solving differences may simply be an artifact of the individual's smoking experiences—more the *result* of smoking or of coping in a smoking milieu than a *cause* of smoking.

These causal questions are considered from a social-cognitive perspective which emphasizes the role of expectations as leading causes of behavioral intentions (Bandura, 1977, 1989). According to social-cognitive theory at least two kinds of expectations can be discerned: First, outcome expectancies which refer to the perceived consequences of one's actions and their importance to the individual; and second, self-efficacy expectations, namely, perceiving that one is capable of performing a specific action. Self-efficacy has proven an especially robust predictor of intentions to smoke or to abstain, even after other factors such as attitudes toward smoking have been taken into account (Ajzen & Madden, 1986; De Vries, Dijkstra & Kuhlman, 1988). Moreover, individuals report greater feelings of efficacy after episodes in which they resisted smoking than when they succumbed to the temptation to smoke (Garcia, Schmitz, & Doerfler, 1990). For purposes of this research we have focused on two aspects of outcome expectancies. First, there are the outcomes themselves, that is, the anticipated *consequences* of, say, one's parents finding out that a child has been smoking. Then, second, there is the *importance* the individual attaches to various outcomes, or what we refer to as *issues*: To extend our example, how important the anticipated parental reactions are to the child. *Issues and consequences* often interact in their influence on intentions. For example, the expectation of a swift reprisal from parents may have little to do with the child's decision to smoke or not if he or she does not care what the parents think or do. Additionally, we have represented the self-efficacy portion of Bandura's model as the perceived availability of *strategies* for effective action such as diffusing conflict and negotiating a positive, nonsmoker resolution which might include communicating one's values to others and redirecting attention from smoking to other more constructive activities.

These three components—perceived issues, consequences, and strategies—comprised the focus of this investigation. In order to evaluate the saliency of these three components to a smoking decision, we focused on the pervasive smoking temptation/intention linkage. It has been well established that the temptation value of a cigarette exerts a dominant, if not preemptive, influence on intentions to smoke among young adolescents (Best & Hakstian, 1978; Covington & Omelich, 1988), in effect, as temptation (desire) increases, so do intentions (desired action). For the child without a well-developed set of internalized controls, desire typically translates directly into action). Research on the development of moral and social reasoning suggests that such impetuousness only slowly comes under the control of evolving cognitive processes and self-interested reflection. Unfortunately, such self-regulating cognitions are not sufficiently established until most youngsters are well past junior high school (13-15 years old), which appears to be the most vulnerable periods to smoking temptation (Covington & Omelich, 1986). If we accept temptation level as a pivotal causal factor in smoking uptake, then a reasonable measure of the value of a problem-solving approach to moderating health risks would be reflected to the extent to which cognitive factors act to offset the dependency of intentions on temptation so that intentions to smoke will remain low, irrespective of the temptation of a given circumstance. This reasoning implies a causal model of the kind portrayed in Figure 1. The unidirectional arrows indicate the paths of influence that were examined in the present study. Put in causal terms, we asked whether or not present problem-solving skills will reduce the dependency of intentions on temptation: (a) by serving as an inhibitor of temptation (i.e., high temptation → problem-solving strategies → low intentions); and/or (b) by providing a direct, countervailing presence in their own right (problem-solving strategies → low intentions)?

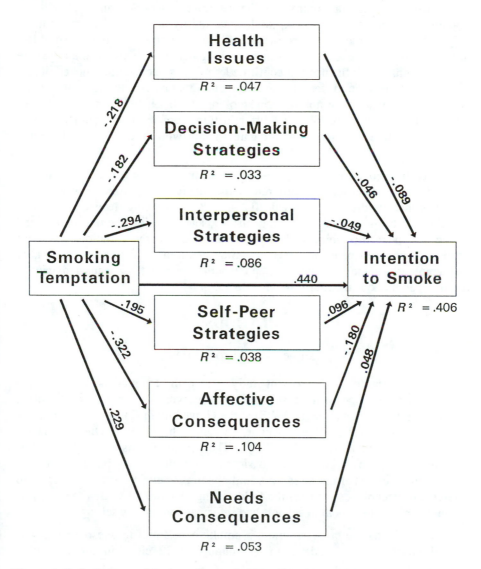

Figure 1 Path diagram of the hypothesized effect of problem solving in moderating the temptation/intention relationship in smoking decisions.

The history of research on problem solving is as rich and variegated as it is voluminous (for a review, see Covington, 1986; Herrnstein, Nickerson, Sanchez, & Swets, 1986; Nickerson, Perkins, & Smith, 1985). Surely, some approaches will prove more useful to the goals of health education than will others, but which ones? While issue, consequence and strategy components may all contribute to a decision to smoke or to resist, their impact is unlikely to be of equal weight across all individuals. Thus in order to provide a firm empirical basis for problem-oriented interventions, we must also know which of these components are most influential in controlling the smoking intentions and behavior of youngsters of differing ages, sex, intellectual ability and ethnic group membership. Most important, key problem-resolution components may also differ depending on the youngster's personal smoking history. In effect, the cognitive considerations that influence the confirmed smoker's decision to smoke another cigarette may be quite different from the factors that enter into the nonsmoker's decision about whether or not to begin smoking at all. Likewise, the dynamics of both of these groups are likely to differ in turn from those of youngsters who have experimented previously with cigarettes, but who have yet to continue the practice.

Given the above considerations, the specific purpose of the present study was twofold: (a) to determine if different expectancies and problem-solving approaches that children characteristically bring to a smoking decision vary as a function of the individual's smoking history, age, sex, intellectual ability, and ethnic group membership; and (b) to determine if any variations in these problem-solving elements influence smoking intentions in such a way as to alter the temptation value of cigarettes, and whether or not these causal dynamics differ depending on smoking-group membership.

METHODS

Subjects and Procedures

The data reported in the present study were gathered in connection with the research and development of a school-based intervention program by the Risk and Youth: Smoking Project (RAY:S) at the University of California at Berkeley (Covington, D'Onofrio, Thier, Schnur, & Omelich, 1983; D'Onofrio, Thier, Schnur, Buchanan, & Omelich, 1982). The project consisted of three interlocking phases: (a) a program of basic research and theory building; (b) the practical implication of these research findings in the development of educational intervention techniques; and (c) the field testing and formal evaluation of these instructional products both in schools and informal community settings.

As part of the research program, a smoking risk profile questionnaire was administered to 6,494 students in 51 schools in 12 cities in the great San Francisco Bay Area. Of these students, 49.2% (3,198) were sixth-graders (11-12 years old); 31.2% (2,025) were eighth-graders (13-14 years); and 19.6% (1,271) were in the tenth grade (15-16 years). The total sample comprised 8.7% Asians, 32.0% Blacks, 8.6% Hispanics, 48.6% Whites, and 2.1% who classified themselves as "Other." This ethnic distribution roughly approximated the population of the San Francisco Bay Area.

The 179-item questionnaire was designed to identify the prevalence of smoking and the causes of cigarette uptake, resistance and cessation. The predictor variables included distal antecedents (e.g., family characteristics), proximal antecedents (e.g., peer-group characteristics), beliefs regarding the instrumental value of cigarette use, and the quality of prosocial decision-making skills.

One section of the questionnaire presented several brief, life-like scenarios in which youngsters might be tempted to smoke. Each situation depicted temptation in a group setting varied along several dimensions including composition of the group (e.g., best friends versus casual acquaintances) and whether or not others in the group were already smoking. Because the reactions of subjects differing in degree of previous experience with cigarettes have been shown to be little influenced by these variations in circumstances (Covington & Omelich, 1988), all situational variables of interest were combined across scenarios for the present analysis.

Criterion Measures

All subjects responded to a series of Likert-type rating questions as follows:

Temptation. "In this situation, how much would you actually want to smoke?" (1 = *not at all*; 5 = *very much*)

Intentions. "Do you think you would actually smoke in this situation?" (1 = *definitely no*; 5 = *definitely yes*).

Problem-solving. Ten theoretically derived scales incorporating 28 items represented the basic problem-solving components thought to mediate smoking intentions (Covington, 1981; Fishbein, 1977; Sutton, 1989). As a group, these ten scales measured: (1) the extent to which youngsters were likely to consider various *issues* as important in making a smoking choice (3 scales); (2) the degree to which they were likely to entertain various prosocial *strategies* facilitative of a nonsmoking decision (4 scales); and (3) the extent to which children anticipated various *consequences* following a decision to smoke (3 scales). Preliminary principal components analyses of the total sample provided empirical validation of the conceptual structure of the 28 items selected to measure these ten problem-solving scales. The factor solutions accounted for 55.9% of the variance in the item set concerned with issues, 47.5% for strategies, and 43.0% for consequences. The actual items making up the various scales are available upon request from the authors.

Issues. Three Likert-type scales measured the perceived importance of affective issues, needs issues and health issues, respectively (item responses: 1 = *not important*; 4 = *very important*). The *affective issues* scale (range: 3-12) measured the importance of anticipated affective reactions of one's parents and peers, and self-reactions to a decision to smoke (M = 9.15, SD = 2.03, α = .48). The *needs issues* scale (range: 4-16) assessed the extent to which the subject considered needs for affiliation, for appearing mature, and for a sense of independence as important issues in making a decision about smoking) (M = 9.36, SD = 2.50, α = .51). The *health issues* scale (range: 2-8) measured whether or not concerns for potential health risk and addiction were important issues in a smoking decision (M = 6.93, SD = 1.51, α = .69).

Strategies. Four Likert-type sales appraised whether or not subjects would utilize a variety of prosocial, problem-solving skills (item responses: 1 = *definitely no*; 5 = *definitely yes*). A *decision-making strategy* scale (range: 2-10) measured whether or not subjects were inclined to reflect on a smoking decision rather than to act impulsively without deliberating (M = 7.08, SD = 2.61, α = .76). An *interpersonal strategy* scale (range: 5-25) appraised the subject's potential repertoire of interpersonal skills for defusing pressures to smoke (M = 16.99, SD = 4.86, α = .76). A *parent strategy* scale (range: 2-10) assessed the degree to which subjects would be likely to seek out and consider parental opinion (M = 6.73, SD = 2.29, α = .61). A *self/peer strategy* scale (range: 2-10) reflected a preoccupation with satisfying one's own wishes or those of one's peers in reaching a decision (M = 4.77, SD = 1.92, α = .21).

Consequences. Three Likert-type scales appraised the extent to which subjects anticipated various consequences should they decide to smoke (item responses: 1 = *not at all*; 5 = *very much*). The *affective consequences* scale (range: 3-15) measured the expected degree of parental, peer, and self displeasure should the subject smoke (M = 10.82, SD = 3.06, α = .61). The *needs consequences* (scale range: 3-15) indicated whether or not smoking would promote a sense of autonomy, maturity, and belonging for the subject (M = 7.18, SD = 2.78, α = .37). The *health consequences* scale (range: 2-10) assessed the degree to which subjects anticipated health problems as a result of smoking (M = 7.37, SD = 2.29, α = .38).

Individual Difference Measures

Smoking status. Current smoking status was measured by a single, self-report item as follows: "Check the *one* sentence below that best tells about you": "I have never smoked a cigarette (not even a few puffs)"; "I tried one or two cigarettes and never smoked again"; "I smoked for a while, but do not smoke anymore"; "I smoke cigarettes regularly." The incidence of cigarette use in the final sample of 3,994 students having a complete data file closely paralleled that found in national self-report surveys of adolescents in the United States (National Institute of Education, 1979). Some 1,804 subjects had *never smoked* (NS) (N = 1,127, N = 460, and N = 217 at grades 6, 8, and 10, respectively). Among the remaining subjects, three additional groups were differentiated. That group which had smoked only one or two cigarettes (*Experimental Smokers*; ES); that which had smoked for a while and then quit (*Ex-Smokers*; XS); and that which smoked regularly at the time of assessment (*Regular Smokers*; RS). There were 1,256 ES subjects ($N = 518$, $N = 424$, $N = 314$, at grades 6, 8 and 10, respectively); 433 XS subjects ($N = 125$, $N = 180$, and $N = 128$, respectively); and 510 RS subjects ($N = 89$, $N = 235$, and $N = 177$, respectively).

While the validity of adolescent self-reports of smoking has been questioned repeatedly, a study by Williams, Eng, Botvin, Hill, and Wynder (1979) demonstrated that when assured of anonymity (as was the case in the present research), adolescents do give accurate self-reports of smoking behavior. Additionally, by applying a bogus-pipeline procedure (Evans, Hansen, & Mittlemark, 1977) to a subsample ($N = 193$) of our sixth-grade and eighth-grade subjects, we also confirmed the validity of self-report measures. A comparison of this subsample with the main sample without bogus pipeline revealed no significant differences in reported smoking status, $p < .05$. The reported smoking levels for the main sample and the bogus pipeline subsample were comparable: NS (50.7% versus 54.0%), ES (29.5% versus 27.0%), XS (9.5% versus 9.0%), RS (10.3% versus 10.0%).

Sex and grade. Sampling was disproportionately heavier at the lower grades (11-14 years old) to allow for adequate numbers of youngsters with smoking experience ($N_6 = 1,859$, $N_8 = 1,299$, $N_{10} = 836$). Boys ($N = 1,949$) and girls ($N = 2,045$) were represented in roughly equal proportions across the three grade levels.

Ability. Academic ability was measured by an abbreviated 10-item form of the Comprehensive Test of Basic Skills (CTBS/McGraw Hill, 1973). Three forms, one appropriate to each grade level, were used so that items of increasing difficulty insured maximum discrimination across age.

Ethnicity. Subjects were also classified as to ethnic background based on their response to a single, six-category questionnaire item: Asian, Black, Hispanic, Latino, White, and Other. Since the Latino category was used by less than 1% of the sample, it was combined with the Hispanic category. Also, due to the undifferentiated nature of the "Other" category, these subjects (2.1%) were dropped from those analyses involving ethnicity as a factor.

Statistical Analysis

Between-group differences in smoking temptation level, smoking intentions, and all problem-solving variables were assessed by separate 3 (Grade) x 2 (Sex) x 2 (Ability) x 4 (Ethnicity) analyses of variance. Preliminary analysis indicated that the inclusion of Smoking Status in a five-way factorial design produced too many depleted cells and resulted in no significant interactions with the other individual difference factors. Accordingly, analysis of smoking-status group differences were investigated through separate one-way analyses of variance. Determination of the specific source of any significant group differences involved the use of Dunn's multiple-comparison procedures (Kirk, 1968) which permit testing a specific number of a priori contrasts at a predetermined level of significance ($\alpha = .05$). The postulated causal role of the various problem-solving elements and temptation in determining smoking intentionality were evaluated by a path-analytic interpretation of multiple regression. Path analysis (Pedhazur, 1982) allows for all determining factors as specified by a causal model to be incorporated into an overall predictive analysis, thereby permitting an estimation of the relative contribution (both direct and indirect) of each determinant to variations in dependent variables of interest. Hypotheses regarding the similarity of these causal relationships for subjects with varying smoking histories were assessed by comparing the differences in magnitude of regression slopes for the relevant groups.

RESULTS AND DISCUSSION

Between-Group Differences

Table 1 displays the mean values and standard deviations for smoking intentions and for the ten issue, strategy, and consequence variables by smoking status and grade. A 2 (Sex) x 3 (Grade) x 2 (Ability) x 4 (Ethnicity) analysis of variance was performed on each of the variables shown in Table 1. With the exception of grade level, the impact of these individual difference variables—although significant due to the large sample involved—was marginal in terms of magnitude of explained variance (ω^2). For this reason, these mean values are not tabled, nor are those for temptation level since these latter results are essentially identical to those found for intentions ($r = .57, p < .05$).

Ability. Brighter youngsters found each of the smoking issues, strategies, and consequences, with the exception of the self/peer strategy variables (NS), to be more salient to their thinking about a smoking decision than did less bright youngsters, all Fs $(1,3946) > 3.84$, $p < .05$. However, the amount of explained variance (ω^2) accounted for by ability in each dependent factor was negligible, accounting on average for less than 1% of the variance. The sole exception was the health consequences variable, for which ability level explained some 4% of the variance, $F(1,3946) = 122.79$, $\omega^2 = .044$. It appears that brighter youngsters weigh the health consequences of their actions more heavily ($N = 7.87$) than do less bright individuals ($M = 6.93$). Otherwise, however, we conclude that problem-solving dispositions are not particularly dependent on differences in basic cognitive ability. Nor did variations in ability influence smoking temptation level ($\omega^2 = .000$) or intentions to smoke ($\omega^2 = .004$), although the ability factor proved significant for temptation and intentions, Fs $(1,3946) = 5.55, 24.24$, respectively, $p < .05$, owing to the large sample size. One caution should be noted, however. The recognition mode of assessment used in this study may underrepresent the role of ability in real-life dilemma resolutions. For example, had our subjects been assessed under a free-response format, then ideational fluency factors, verbal skills, and analytic reasoning would have likely become more salient, thereby increasing the dependency of responses on ability level.

Table 1

*Mean Values and Standard Deviations on Intentions to Smoke and Problem-Solving
Skills by Current Smoking Status and Grade*

Dependent Variable		Smoking Status				Grade		
		NS	ES	XS	RS	6	8	10
(*N*)		(1804)	(1256)	(433)	(501)	(1859)	(1299)	(836)
Intentions	*M*	1.32	1.72	2.10	3.26	1.63	1.98	1.80
	SD	0.69	1.01	1.18	1.31	1.02	1.23	1.18
Issues								
Affective	*M*	9.55	9.06	8.67	7.97	9.35	8.99	8.66
	SD	2.01	1.95	2.02	1.92	1.99	2.05	2.10
Needs	*M*	9.34[a]	9.34[a]	9.37[a]	9.39[a]	9.51	9.28	9.06
	SD	2.70	2.44	2.23	2.15	2.79	2.23	2.15
Health	*M*	7.14	6.97	6.66	6.03	7.12	6.72[a]	6.63[a]
	SD	1.41	1.42	1.54	1.80	1.41	1.59	1.62
Strategies								
Decision-making	*M*	7.40	7.08	6.60	5.88	7.21	6.91[a]	6.75[a]
	SD	2.71	2.55	2.41	2.32	2.67	2.54	2.64
Inter-personal	*M*	18.24	17.04	15.38	13.54	18.02	16.19	15.64
	SD	4.62	4.56	4.61	4.45	4.71	4.68	4.88
Parent	*M*	7.27	6.71	6.05	5.64	7.26	6.36[a]	6.19[a]
	SD	2.23	2.18	2.28	2.25	2.25	2.25	2.24
Self/peer	*M*	4.39	4.89[b]	5.13[b]	5.44[a]	4.47	5.00[a]	5.05[a]
	SD	1.93	1.91	1.79	1.78	1.95	1.87	1.86
Consequences								
Affective	*M*	11.82	10.65	9.91	8.17	11.42	10.41	9.90
	SD	2.74	2.81	2.88	2.97	2.86	2.98	3.28
Needs	*M*	6.92	7.23[a]	7.33[a]	7.93	7.23	7.34[a]	6.89
	SD	2.83	2.72	2.67	2.67	2.88	2.64	2.72
Health	*M*	7.58	7.25[a]	7.10[a]	6.70	7.34[ab]	7.21[b]	7.41[a]
	SD	2.29	2.25	2.24	2.32	2.29	2.27	2.36

Note. Similarly superscripted values (e.g., [a, b]) are not significantly different (*p* < .05).
NS = Nonsmokers; ES = Experimental Smokers; XS = Ex-Smokers; RS =
Regular Smokers.

Sex and ethnicity. Like ability, both the sex and ethnic effects were significant, all *F*s < 3.84, .05 *p* < .05, but accounted for only negligible portions of the
problem-solving issues, strategies, and consequence factors. Typical ω^2 values
were less than .005, especially for the sex effect. One exception was the self/peer
strategy category for which ethnic-group membership accounted for approximately 3% of the variance. Several other exceptions occurred for ethnicity,
which explained some 2-3% of the variance in problem-solving behavior. For
example, it appears that Asians and, to a lesser degree, Whites, were more likely
than Blacks to reflect upon the issues involved in a smoking decision (decision-

making strategy). Moreover, the issues of greater importance to Asians and Whites were the negative reactions of others (affective issues) and the potential health hazards of smoking (health consequences). On the other hand, Hispanics and Blacks were less likely than Asians and Whites to be guided by peer group suggestions for resolving dilemmas (self/peer strategy). Finally, planned pairwise contrasts performed after the ethnicity effect proved significant for temptation level and intentions, $F(3,3946) = 14.65$, 18.93, respectively, indicated that Asians were less tempted to smoke and consequently had lower intentions to do so when compared to the other three ethnic categories, $p < .05$. By contrast, Whites, Blacks, and Hispanics did not differ among themselves with regard to degree of temptation and intentions to smoke, $p < .05$.

In summary, with only the occasional exceptions noted above, variations in ethnic group membership, ability, and sex proved to be only marginal contributors to characteristic approaches to smoking dilemmas. Nor were there any significant interactions among these group differences that accounted for more than negligible proportions of variance, all $\omega^2 < .005$. Thus, regarding the relative degree of problem-solving responsiveness, we conclude that it makes little difference if a youngster is male or female, Hispanic or Asian, or bright or less bright.

Grade level. Grade level proved to be a consistent, although modest, contributor to variations in the problem-solving components, as well as variations in temptation level and intentions, all $Fs(2,3946) < 3.00$, $p < .05$. The significance of all pairwise contrasts is indicated by superscripts in Table 1. Similarly, superscripted values were not significantly different from one another ($p < .05$). The results of pairwise contrasts generally revealed that the younger the child, the more salient were issues concerning affective reactions ($\omega^2 = .020$) and health ($\omega^2 = .026$), and the more likely he or she was to recognize the value of interpersonal strategies for problem resolution ($\omega^2 = .044$) and to seek parental advice (parent strategy: $\omega^2 = .044$) while rejecting peer suggestions and the paths of personal rebelliousness (self/peer strategy: $\omega^2 = .020$). Without such constraints, older students were more likely to be tempted by cigarettes ($\omega^2 = .017$) and to harbor stronger smoking intentions ($\omega^2 = .023$). These age trends were especially pronounced among eighth-grade students who experienced greater temptation and intentionality than either sixth- or tenth-graders.

Smoking status. The single overwhelming source of individual differences in the saliency of problem-solving components was the current smoking status of the individual (Table 1). Smoking status accounted for some 30% of the variation in intentions to smoke ($F[3,3946] = 704.73$, $p < .05$; $\omega^2 = .299$. A series of pairwise contrasts was performed between all smoking-status groups for each problem-solving factor separately and for both smoking intentions and temptation as well. Not unexpectedly, the four smoking-status groups were all significantly differentiated as to intentions (as seen by the absence of superscripts), with current smokers reporting greatest degree of intentionality and nonsmokers reporting the lowest (RS > ES > NS, $p < .05$). Feelings of temptation also depended largely on one's smoking history, $F(3,3946) = 426.96$, $p < .05$; $\omega^2 = .219$, with the same significant rank ordering by smoking-status category for temptation as was found for intentions.

Also, as expected, with the exception of the needs issues category (NS, as indicated by the "A" superscript in Table 1), the smoking status main effect for all problem-solving issues, strategies, and consequences factors proved significant, all $Fs(3,3946) > 2.60$, $p < .05$, $.016 < \omega^2 < .156$. A series of pairwise contrasts revealed a consistent profile among individuals with different smoking histories. To summarize the data reported in Table 1: With regard to issues, nonsmokers considered health matters and the opinions of others (affective issues) to be of greater relevance in decision making than did all other smoking groups, with health and affective concerns being least salient among regular smokers. Likewise, regarding perceived consequences, nonsmokers were more likely than were all other groups to view cigarette use as a violation of both their self-interest and their expectations of the reactions of others (affective consequences), thereby anticipating greater emotional upset if they smoked. Additionally, nonsmokers perceived the use of cigarettes as less likely to result in feelings of maturity and autonomy (needs consequences) and to create greater health hazards than did all other groups (health consequences). Finally, regarding strategies, nonsmokers were more likely to adopt a thoughtful decision-making mode than were any other groups, with such reflectivity being least in evidence among regular smokers. Moreover, interpersonal strategies involved in the processes of negotiation were more salient among nonsmokers, as well as a willingness to discuss such tactics with their parents (parent strategy). Conversely, regular smokers displayed a greater tendency to follow the advice of their friends and/or respond to their own desires (self/peer strategy).

One of the most striking aspects of this overall data pattern was the fact that these reliable differences in social problem solving emerge after only the briefest, casual exposure to cigarettes (NS versus ES groups). Apparently the act of smoking per se, irrespective of amount, duration or frequency of cigarette use, is associated with a subtle yet discernible shift in self and situational perceptions. This finding corroborates other research that documents the rapid onset of labeling of one's self as a smoker once cigarette use begins (D'Onofrio, 1983a). Equally interesting was the fact that self-designated ex-smokers were also reliably differentiated from continuing smokers on several dimensions. It appears that the initiation of smoking as well as its cessation is related to a powerful restructuring of one's perceptions, expectations and actions in tempting situations. The only apparent exceptions to this consistent rank-ordered differentiation (e.g., NS > ES > XS > RS) were: (1) the uniform importance assigned by all groups to the perceived instrumental value of cigarettes for enhancing feelings of autonomy, maturity and affiliation (needs issues); and (2) the fact that the ES, XS, and RS groups, all of whom had been involved to some degree with cigarettes, were largely undifferentiated in their tendency to yield to their friends' wishes (peer strategy) even when (especially for the ES and XS groups) this meant rejecting parental advice.

Causal Dynamics

Given the above evidence for consistent differences in problem-solving approaches among the various smoking status groups, we can now consider the potential causal role of these various factors in the dynamics of smoking uptake and resistance. As will be recalled, this inquiry was pursued in the context of the causal model presented in Figure 1. In essence, we asked: How substantial is the causal dependency of smoking intentions on problem-solving factors, and is this source of variance sufficiently robust to reduce the initially dominant influence of temptation on intentions?

In order to determine the most discriminating set of problem-solving factors, all ten variables listed in Table 1 were entered into a preliminary multiple regression analysis using stepwise inclusion criteria with intentions to smoke as the criterion variable. Six significant factors emerged. In descending order of importance these were: affecting consequences ($\beta = -.272$, $R^2 = .166$); needs consequences ($\beta = .136$, $R^2_i = .031$); interpersonal strategies ($\beta = -.118$, $R^2_i = .020$); self/peer strategies ($\beta = .143$, $R^2_i = .019$); health issues ($\beta = -.109$, $R^2_i = .011$) and decision-making strategies ($\beta = -.050$, $R^2_i = .002$). As a group, these factors accounted for some 24.92% of the variance in intentions to smoke, with the remaining four factors together contributing nothing additional to the prediction equation, $F(4,3816) = .559$ ($p < .05$). Next, these six problem-solving variables were entered as a block in a hierarchical regression analysis following temptation in the temporally ordered sequence portrayed in Figure 1. By employing a path-analytic interpretation, we can assess the direct effects of both the temptation-

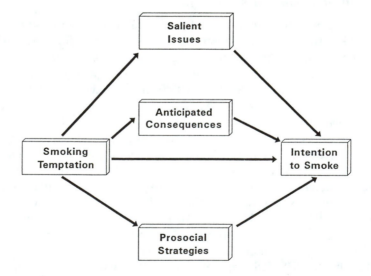

Figure 2 Path diagram of the moderating effects of problem-solving skills on the relationship between temptation and intentions to smoke. All pathways significant, $p < .05$.

intention and the problem-solving-retention linkages, as well as the moderating role of problem-solving elements in altering the temptation-intention relationship (e.g., temptation strategies intentions). The magnitude and direction of the path coefficients associated with each of the presumed causal linkages are presented in Figure 2. All pathways were significant at the $\alpha = .05$ level.

Inspection of the first column of Table 2 indicates a significant zero-order correlation between temptation and intentions to smoke of .569 ($p < .05$) that decomposes into a direct effect from temptation ($\rho = .440$, $p < .05$), and into a total indirect influence moderated through the problem-solving elements of .129. Among all the mediating problem-solving variables, affective consequences was the most substantial transmitter of temptation, accounting for approximately half (.058) of the total indirect influence on intentions.

Table 2

Decomposition of the Zero-Order Correlation of Temptation Level With the Intention to Smoke

	Effect	% Effect
Zero-order correlation (r)	.569*	
Direct (ρ)[a]	.440*	77.3%
Indirect via:		
Health issues	.019	3.3%
Decision-making strategies	.008	1.4%
Interpersonal strategies	.014	2.5%
Self/peer strategies	.019	3.3%
Affective consequences	.058	10.2%
Needs consequences	.011	1.9%
Total indirect	.129	22.75
Total causal	.569	
Noncausal	—	

Note. [a] standardized regression coefficient; *$p < .05$.

Next, consider the direct influence of problem-solving elements on intentions to smoke. Figure 2 indicates that all six components made significant contributions to variations in intentions, irrespective of temptation level, $p < .05$. Thus, for instance, to the extent that health issues were salient to an individual, intentions to smoke were correspondingly reduced ($\rho = -.089$, $p < .05$). The same inhibiting influence was seen in the presence of decision-making strategies ($\rho = -.046$), in the possession of interpersonal strategies ($\rho = -.049$), and to the degree that smoking represents a violation of affiliative bonds (affective consequences) ($\rho = .180$), $p < .05$. Contrariwise, intentions to smoke increased to the extent smoking was perceived as leading to need-fulfillment regarding autonomy and maturity ($\rho = .048$) and to the degree that subjects were likely to defy authority and comply with perceived peer group wishes ($\rho = .096$), $p < .05$.

The results of incremental F-tests (not tabled) provided an overall summary of this path analysis. As the first predictor variable entered, temptation accounted for some 79.8% ($R^2_i = .324$) of the total explained variation in intentions ($R^2_i = .406$) through all paths of influence, both direct and indirect, $F(1,4090) = 2230.91$, $p < .01$. The six combined problem-solving sources added the remaining 22.2% of the explained variance ($R^2_i = .082$), $F(6,4084) = 93.96$, $p < .01$. These results establish not only the importance of the aggregated problem-solving variables as direct sources of influence on intentions to smoke in the face of temptation, but also indicates something of their indirect role in mediating temptation. This latter causal source amounted to approximately one-fifth ($R^2_i = .059$) of the explained variance attributable to temptation ($R^2_i = .324$).

Finally, consider the evidence on whether or not the elements of problem-solving under investigation contribute equally to smoking intentions regardless of the age and smoking history of the individual. As to age level, pairwise comparisons of the seven direct effect regression slopes across the three age levels revealed essentially identical findings, all $t (\infty) < 1.96$, $p < .05$. Thus, for example, while the affective consequences of a smoking decision may be more salient to younger children (see Table 1), the causal mechanisms by which such variations in expected parental, peer and self-upset translate into intentions are no more evident among 11- to 12-year-olds among older youngsters. Nor are the above findings subject to qualification depending on the individual's smoking history. Pairwise contrasts between the regression slopes of all four smoking status categories for each direct linkage portrayed in Figure 1 revealed no differences in the causal role of any of the problem-solving components in determining smoking intentions, all $t (\infty) < 1.96$, $p < .05$. For instance, while RS individuals may have less well-developed interpersonal skills to deflect smoking temptation and express greater intentions to smoke (Table 1), we conclude from these insignificant comparisons of regression slope that such deficiencies in problem-solving approaches exert no greater causal impact on smoking intentions among smokers than among adolescents with little or no smoking experience. Several educational implications emerge from these data. First, according to the empirically confirmed linkages portrayed in Figure 1, any interventions that act to increase the saliency of health issues and the availability of skills in interpersonal, prosocial coping strategies can be expected to decrease smoking intentionality, regardless of the temptation value of a given circumstance. Likewise, any instruction that decreases the tendency toward defiance of authority and the uncritical acceptance of cigarettes as evidence of maturity will also dampen intentions. Moreover, it is possible—although no empirical demonstration is yet available—that interventions might simultaneously act to alter the magnitude of causal relationships between the various problem-solving elements and intentionality. Thus, for example, in theory, instruction might act to increase the causal importance of various problem-solving elements (e.g., interpersonal skills) for reducing the likelihood of smoking, as well as to raise the absolute level of skill proficiency. In such an instance, instruction would be doubly effective in controlling intentions to smoke.

Second, the indirect linkages by which problem-solving components mediate the influence of temptation on intentions (temptation → problem solving → intentions) is another prime source for educational interdiction. In effect, by enhancing problem-solving skills, the instructional planner can control a proportion of the variability in intentions that would otherwise be subject totally to the whims of temptation. However, in order to maximize this potential source of control, the inhibitory effects of temptation on the various problem-solving components must be offset, as reflected in Figure 2 (temptation → problem solving). For instance, consider the all-too-common human tendency to discount rational, self-interested concerns in the face of temptation and pressure, a tendency which often takes the form of denying and minimizing health risks (Covington & Omelich, in press). These dynamics are well illustrated by the behavior of the subjects regarding the health issue variable. In effect, health issues became less salient to the decision-making process as self-perceived temptation increased ($\rho = -.218$, $p < .05$). These data underscore the need to teach more than health facts alone since such information is subject to avoidance, minimization and distortion, a process thought to be caused by strong emotional needs including the denial of illness and death (DeLong, 1970). The same distorting influence of temptation can also be seen at work in the suspension of otherwise inhibitory decision-making propensities ($\rho = -.182$), interpersonal strategies ($\rho = .332$), $p < .05$.

Educationally speaking, one reasonable intervention strategy is to enhance the saliency of problem-solving considerations as a direct, inhibitory influence on intentions to smoke, and simultaneously to reduce the distorting effects of temptation on rational, problem-solving considerations. At the same time, those mechanisms associated with temptation that lead to increased perceptions of the utility of smoking (need fulfillment; $\rho = .229$, $p < .05$) and to a greater willingness to abide by perceived peer wishes (peer orientation; $\rho = .195$, $p < .05$) must also be made targets of special corrective treatment.

GENERAL DISCUSSION

The overall results of this study offer support for the view that a social problem-solving orientation represents a potentially viable approach to anti-smoking intervention. First, not only did various problem-solving elements such as perceived issues, prosocial strategies and expected consequences influence intentions to smoke in their own right, but they also acted to offset the considerable impact of temptation as a primary cause of smoking uptake. Second, this problem-solving dynamic appeared to operate in essentially the same fashion for smokers and nonsmokers alike, a parallelism that suggests the broad applicability of such an approach whether the educational goal is that of smoking prevention or cessation.

A further implication to be drawn from these data is that to be most effective, strategies for intervention must not focus solely on health issues, but must also address the need of young people to satisfy naturally occurring motives of personal/social significance. If instruction remains solely at the level of health facts, then educators will be forced to rely heavily on the child's will-power and sometimes on poorly developed cognitive controls to motivate a nonsmoking decision. Although the health issues factor in this study made a distinct impact on smoking intentions, and while smokers appeared disproportionately disposed to reject health facts, health issues nonetheless were a relatively minor causal source when compared to other factors such as anticipated affective consequences. This is not to suggest that health facts are unimportant or irrelevant, but only that they must be placed in proper perspective as only one of several promising foci for intervention.

How, then, can the role of problem solving be best conceptualized without underemphasizing the role of health facts and in ways that are suggestible of specific types of intervention activities? An overall organizing principle is strongly suggested by the present data: *informed self-interest*. Concern for the social and personal consequences of smoking emerged as a major predictor of intentionality for both smokers and nonsmokers. Inspection of the items that make up the affective consequences factor in the principal components analysis used to derive the scales in this study indicates that concern for one's self-image has the highest factor loading (.765), followed by concern for parental reactions (.643) and peer reactions (.597) to one's smoking. In this context, self-interest involves the potential violation of self-integrity by actions that are inconsistent with one's ideal self as well as the need to maintain family harmony and yet to maximize peer acceptance. These are the problem elements that must be balanced if the child is to avoid smoking. For nonsmokers these elements are compatible with the child's self-expectations, as well as with those of his or her family and peers. By comparison, most smokers suffer a sense of misalignment regarding smoking values. Their parents' advice is often at odds with prevailing peer values and with their own emerging perceptions of self. This conflict may range in emotional tone from feeling mildly frustrated to an expression of outright antagonism toward parents, if we are to judge from the data. The behavior of the peer strategy factor underscores this point. Not only do many smokers discount parental values, but for some this amounts to an outright rejection in favor of anarchistic freedom (e.g., "I'll do what I like, after all it's my life"). Such a conflict makes it all the more difficult to disentangle health issues from their emotional overlay. When intrafamily stress is combined with a greater acceptance of smoking among one's peers, and with compelling, if false, beliefs about the instrumentality of smoking, then the scales are tipped decidedly in favor of a decision to smoke.

This analysis suggests that successful anti-smoking intervention should involve at least three kinds of problem-solving training. First, it is important to enhance the capacity of youngsters to identify the essential issues of self-interest that arise in any smoking-related decision including: (a) self-consistency and valued self-image; (b) the desirability of harmonious relations with parents; (c) the need to maintain positive peer relationships; and (d) the necessity of continued health maintenance.

A second intervention focus strongly implied by the significant interpersonal strategies factor in this study is to provide youngsters with repeated practice in generating resolutions to tempting situations that balance each of these self-interest elements. Or, as young students best understand the task, "What can I do to keep my friends, feel good about myself, get along with my parents—all without smoking?" The item content of the interpersonal strategy factor suggests some of the specific skills that such dilemma resolutions might embody: "Do something so that others do not feel they have to smoke"; "Talk about my decision so that everyone will still be friends no matter what the others do"; and "Try to talk the others out of smoking." In this connection one fruitful direction for effective decision-resolution training might involve practice in establishing a cost/benefits hierarchy; in effect, helping children determine which resolutions are better or worse given all the likely consequences of each.

A third problem-solving focus implied by the present study is to dismantle health rationalizations that tend to discount the risk of smoking especially when temptation is great. Some evidence (Covington, 1981) suggests that youngsters often smoke without explicit intentions to do so and without any particular thought given to it (i.e., simply because the cigarettes are available). In cases like this, when there is no intention to smoke it seems unreasonable from the adolescent point of view that they should suffer negative health consequences. The responsibility for smoking behavior is either attributed to others (e.g., "the group made me do it") or is compartmentalized away from intentions (Covington & Omelich, in press). Needless to say, dealing with this form of denial is a complex challenge, especially among children whose sense of future is typically compressed and may be dominated by prelogical thought patterns that stress magical, unrealistic thinking. In this connection, one promising instructional approach is the use of probability games designed to simulate those real-life factors that affect the youngsters' (players') acceptance or rejection of smoking risks. Such simulations might involve a sequential series of life transitions in which the decision to smoke in an early round of play (in order to gain peer-group acceptance in the teenage years) puts the player at a handicap in future rounds (as an adult) when the objective is now to establish financial independence, a task made uncertain by increased health risks, ineligibility for certain jobs, and unexpected medical expenses. Here delayed cause-and-effect dynamics can be discovered and the implications understood by the early adolescent, all without preaching from adults and in situations that are inherently interesting.

REFERENCES

Ajzen, I., & Madden, J. T. (1986). Prediction of goal-directed behavior: Attitudes, intentions, and perceived behavioral control. *Journal of Experimental Social Psychology, 22*, 453-474.

Bandura, A. (1977). Self-efficacy: Toward a unifying theory of behavioral change. *Psychological Review, 84*, 191-215.

Bandura, A. (1989). Self-efficacy mechanism in physiological activation and health-promoting behavior. In J. Madden, S. Matthysse, & J. Barchas (Eds.), *Adaptation, learning and affect.* New York: Raven.

Best, J. A., & Hakstian, A. R. (1978). A situation-specific model for smoking behavior. *Addictive Behaviors, 3,* 79-92.

Botvin, G. J. (1983). *Life skills training: A self-improvement approach to substance abuse prevention.* Teacher's Manual. New York: Smithfield.

Botvin, G. J., & Eng, A. (1980). A comprehensive school-based smoking prevention program. *Journal of School Health, 50,* 209-213.

Botvin, G. J., & Eng, A. (1982). The efficacy of a multicomponent approach to the prevention of cigarette smoking. *Preventive Medicine, 11,* 199-211.

Botvin, G. J., Eng, A., & Williams, C. L. (1980). Preventing the onset of cigarette smoke through life skills training. *Preventive Medicine, 9,* 135-143.

Cohen, S., Lichtenstein, E., Mermelstein, R., Kingsolver, K., Bauer, J. S., & Kamarck, T. W. (1988). Social support interventions for smoking cessation. In B. H. Gottlieb (Ed.), *Marshaling social support. Formats, processes, and effects* (pp. 211-240). Beverly Hills, CA: Sage.

Covington, M. V. (1981). Strategies for smoking prevention and resistance among young adolescents. *Journal of Early Adolescence, 1,* 349-356.

Covington, M. V. (1986). Instruction in problem-solving planning. In S. L. Friedman, E. K. Scholnick, & R. R. Cocking (Eds.), *Blueprints for thinking: The role of planning in cognitive development,* (pp. 469-511). New York: Cambridge University Press.

Covington, M. V., D'Onofrio, C. N., Thier, H. D., Schnur, A. E., & Omelich, C. L. (1983). *Risk and youth: Smoking (RAY:S) prevention program.* Lawrence Hall of Science, University of California at Berkeley.

Covington, M. V., & Omelich, C. L. (1986). *Family vs. peer influences on adolescent smoking decisions: A developmental approach.* Unpublished manuscript, Department of Psychology, University of California at Berkeley.

Covington, M. V., & Omelich, C. L. (1988). I can resist anything but temptation: Adolescent expectations for smoking cigarettes. *Journal of Applied Social Psychology, 18,* 203-227.

Covington, M. V., & Omelich, C. L. (in press). The perceived costs and benefits of cigarette smoking among adolescents: Need instrumentality, self-anger and anxiety factors. In D. G. Forgays, T. Sosnowski, & K. Wrzeniewski (Eds.), *Anxiety: Recent developments in self-appraisal, psychophysiological and health research.* New York: Hemisphere.

Delong, W. R. (1970). *Individual differences in patterns of anxiety arousal, stress-relevant information and recovery from surgery.* Unpublished doctoral dissertation, University of California at Los Angeles.

De Vries, H., Dijkstra, M., & Kuhlman, P. (1988). Self-efficacy: The third factor besides attitude and subjective norm as a predictor of behavioral intentions. *Health Education Research, 3,* 273-282.

D'Onofrio, C. N. (1983a, April). *Smoking among children: The nature of the problem.* Paper presented at the Annual Convention of the Western Psychological Association, San Francisco.

D'Onofrio, C. N. (1983b). *Review of evaluated school-based anti-smoking programs.* Unpublished manuscript, University of California at Berkeley.

D'Onofrio, C. N., Thier, H. D., Schnur, A. E., Buchanan, D. R., & Omelich, C. L. (1982). The dynamics of adolescent smoking behavior. *World Smoking and Health, 7,* 18-24.

Evans, R. I., Hansen, W., & Mittlemark, M. B. (1977). Increasing the validity of self-reports of behavior in a smoking-in-children investigation. *Journal of Applied Psychology, 62,* 521-523.

Evans, R. I., Henderson, A., Hill, P., & Raines, B. (1979). Smoking in children and adolescents: Psychosocial determinants and prevention strategies. In N. A. Krasnegor (Ed.), *The behavioral aspects of smoking.* Washington, DC: NIDA Research Monograph 26.

Fishbein, M. (1977). *Consumer beliefs and behavior with respect to cigarette smoking: A critical analysis of the public literature.* A report prepared for the staff of the Federal Trade Commission.

Garcia, M. E., Schmitz, J. M., & Doerfler, L. A. (1990). A fine-grained analysis of the role of self-efficacy in self-initiated attempts to quit smoking. *Journal of Consulting and Clinical Psychology, 58*(3), 317-322.

Gilchrist, L. D., Schinke, S. P., & Blythe, B. J. (1979). Primary prevention services for children and youth. *Children and Youth Services Review, 1,* 379-391.

Herrnstein, R. J., Nickerson, R. S., Sanchez, M., & Swets, J. A. (1986). Teaching thinking skills. *American Psychologist, 41,* 1279-1289.

Jones, J., Piper, G. W., & Matthews, V. L. (1970). A student-directed program in smoking education. *Canadian Journal of Public Health, 61,* 253-256.

Kim, S. (1982). Feeder area approach: An impact evaluation of a prevention project on student drug abuse. *International Journal of the Addictions, 17,* 305-313.

Kirk, R. E. (1968). *Experimental design: Procedures for the behavioral sciences.* Belmont, CA: Brooks/Cole.

Leventhal, H., & Cleary, P. D. (1980). The smoking problem: A review of the research and theory in behavioral risk modification. *Psychological Review, 88,* 370-405.

Nickerson, P. S., Perkins, D. N., & Smith, E. E. (1985). *The teaching of thinking.* Hillsdale, NJ: Erlbaum.

Pedhazur, E. J. (1982). Multiple regression in behavioral research: Explanation and prediction (2nd ed.). New York: Holt, Rinehart & Winston.

Piper, G. W., Jones, J. A., & Matthews, V. L. (1974). *The Saskatoon smoking project—The model.* Canadian Journal of Public Health, 65, 127-129.

Schinke, S. P., Gilchrist, L. E., Snow, W. H., & Schilling, R. J. (1985). Skills building methods to prevent smoking by adolescents. *Journal of Adolescent Health Care, 6*(6), 439-444.

Sutton, S. (1989). Smoking attitudes and behavior: Applications of Fishbein and Ajzen's theory of reasoned action to predicting and understanding smoking decisions. In T. Ney & A. Gale (Eds.), *Smoking and human behavior* (pp. 289-312). Chichester: Wiley.

Williams, C. L., & Arnold, C. G. (1980). Teaching children self-care for chronic disease prevention: Obesity reduction and smoking prevention. *Parent Counseling and Health Education, 8,* 92-98.

Williams, C. L., Eng, A., Botvin, G. J., Hill, P., & Wynder, E. (1979). Validation of students' self-reported cigarette smoking status with plasma cotinine levels. *American Journal of Public Health, 69,* 1272-1274.

V

SELF-EFFICACY, PHYSICAL SYMPTOMS, AND REHABILITATION OF CHRONIC DISEASE

ROLE OF PHYSICAL SELF-EFFICACY IN RECOVERY FROM HEART ATTACK

Craig K. Ewart

Large numbers of heart attack survivors experience unnecessary distress and put themselves at significant medical risk due to excessive fear of physical activity. Self-efficacy theory has improved our ability to identify and alleviate these inappropriate fears. Research reviewed in this chapter suggests that self-efficacy appraisals influence patient involvement in exercise regimens and mediate beneficial effects of exercise participation. The development of scales to measure self-efficacy makes it possible to identify individuals who may be at risk of dangerous overexertion due to unrealistically optimistic appraisals of their physical capabilities. Research on affect and self-appraisal suggests that self-efficacy can be strengthened by mood-dependent memories of past successes, and that self-efficacy gains foster positive affect. Factors affecting self-evaluative and affective responses to rehabilitative exercise are reviewed. Behavioral interventions to modify these influences and enhance self-efficacy enable patients to cope more effectively with the many challenges posed by heart attack.

Heart attack, or acute myocardial infarction, is a frightening experience that severely disrupts the lives of patients and their families. The fact that the heart attack is sudden, unexpected, and beyond personal control leaves deep feelings of uncertainty and dread. Bodily sensations that would have gone unnoticed before the illness now cause alarm; states of fatigue that might have been ignored are anxiously scrutinized. Unsure of what these events may signify, and fearful of triggering another attack, patients refrain from work and leisure activities that formerly provided security and pleasure. Feelings of frustration and loss intermingle with worry and self-doubt. Attempts to alter diet, avoid tobacco, or reduce alcohol consumption may exacerbate these feelings, as may the behaviors of family members who try to protect the patient by discouraging physical exertion or communication about topics that could arouse strong emotion. Paradoxically, efforts like these undermine recovery by prolonging the patient's inactivity and social isolation, while placing a heavy burden on those who would be supportive (Croog & Levine, 1982). In a large proportion of acute myocardial infarction survivors, these behavioral, psychological, and social sequelae have the potential to retard recovery, impair adjustment, and even increase risk of recurrent.

Self-efficacy theory clarifies the role of self-appraisal processes in shaping behavioral and emotional responses to acute myocardial infarction and suggests ways to identify and alter them. This chapter will examine three of the theory's major contributions. These include an improved understanding of how self-appraisals determine the patient's return to normal physical activities, how they mediate the impact of physical exertion on emotional adjustment, and how they influence the ways family members react to the illness. The first part of the chapter summarizes current medical guidelines for managing the patient's physical recovery and return to normal activities after and explains the importance of routine exercise in speeding recovery. I then review self-efficacy research that I have conducted during the past decade with colleagues in the cardiology divisions of Stanford University and Johns Hopkins University. This work indicates how self-efficacy judgments guide patients' reactions to acute myocardial infarction and suggests the value of social-cognitive intervention in promoting health-protective exercise during recovery. Next, I examine ways in which self-efficacy may influence—and be influenced by—mood states and emotions patients experience as they try to resume their lives. Finally, I argue that perceptions of self-efficacy are affected by other persons in the patient's immediate interpersonal milieu, and by the patient's valued personal projects and self-strivings. Personal projects and interpersonal transactions moderate the degree to which efforts to enhance self-efficacy will lead to effective behavioral coping and lifestyle change.

Physical Recovery From Acute Myocardial Infarction

Fears evoked by acute myocardial infarction often lead to prolonged physical inactivity with adverse psychological, social, and economic consequences for patients. Moreover, lack of exercise may prove medically harmful to the large proportion of patients in whom the likelihood of recurrent acute myocardial infarction in the near future is relatively low. From 33% to 50% of patients fall into this low-risk category, as do approximately 75% of patients who have undergone coronary artery bypass graft (CABG) surgery (DeBusk, et al., 1986). Low-risk patients are those who have not developed severe exercise-induced ischemia or severe left ventricular dysfunction; their annual mortality is less than 2%. These patients need less medical intervention and can return to work sooner than those at higher risk. Functional capacity of low-risk patients increases rapidly in the first six months after acute myocardial infarction even without physical exercise training, and within three to six months after acute myocardial infarction, they enjoy a functional exercise capacity similar to that of healthy men in their 50's (DeBusk et al., 1986).

Physical training. Recovery of functional capacity is enhanced by having the patient engage in progressive exercise training (e.g., walking, jogging, cycling, swimming) beginning three weeks after acute myocardial infarction. Patients are encouraged to exercise at intensities within a range of 70% to 85% of peak heart rate (as determined by symptom-limited exercise test) for 20 to 30 minutes per day, three to five days per week. Low-risk patients can exercise safely at home (Miller, Haskell, Berra, & DeBusk, 1984). Safety is increased by having patients wear a portable monitor to help them maintain their heart rate within prescribed limits.

Coronary Artery Bypass Graft (CABG). Patients who have undergone CABG can exercise safely without disrupting the wound or the vascular anastomosis after three weeks of healing; leg discomfort (from removal of vein for grafting) rarely persists beyond four weeks. These patients are often advised to engage in walking and, later, in stationary cycling as this activity is less likely to cause nonunion of the sternum than is jogging. Exercise is particularly important during recovery from CABG because bed rest following surgery causes deconditioning that contributes to fatigue—a condition patients often inaccurately construe as a sign of cardiac illness. Even a program of moderate walking can prevent this fatigue. Patients who have undergone CABG tend to interpret chest wall pain as ischemic; they may abandon prescribed exercises unless they are counseled on how to interpret those exercise-induced sensations that are without cardiac importance.

Return to work. Low-risk patients can resume most of their pre-illness activities, including returning to work, within three to six months after acute myocardial infarction. The occupational work environment is thought to be more stressful than the home environment but acute myocardial infarction occurs no more frequently in one setting than in the other (DeBusk et al., 1986). Only 5% of patients in the United States now perform "heavy" occupational work, so only a very small percentage of patients are advised to seek assignment to less demanding jobs. By three months after acute myocardial infarction, low-risk patients are capable of exercising at intensities that are much higher than the levels they encounter at work. Considering that not working creates significant stress or hardship for many patients, after three months low-risk individuals generally are not advised to delay their return to work on medical grounds.

Exercise program. In the first few months after acute myocardial infarction, exercise helps patients feel less tired and more vigorous, enhances recovery of functional capacity, and accelerates return to normal activities. Maintenance of regular exercise over longer periods in a cardiac rehabilitation program appears to reduce risk; meta-analysis of 22 randomized trials of rehabilitation with exercise indicates that participation in rehabilitation is associated with a 20% reduction in overall mortality over the first three years after acute myocardial infarction (O'Connor et al., 1989). While the independent effects of physical exercise are difficult to determine due to the fact that rehabilitation programs usually include diet, smoking cessation, stress reduction, or other interventions, metaanalysis of all available studies suggests that patients who shun exercise after acute myocardial infarction would appear to be at somewhat greater risk of reinfarction during the first three years and of sudden death during the first year after acute myocardial infarction.

Enhancing Physical Self-Efficacy

From a social-cognitive perspective, many problematic behavioral and emotional reactions to acute myocardial infarction stem from uncertainties about one's physical capabilities. Self-efficacy theory provides methods to identify and measure these uncertainties, and to increase patient participation in healthful exercise by altering self-appraisal. The theory asserts that the most effective way to help patients overcome inappropriate fear of exertion is to have them perform feared activities in gradually increasing intensities *(mastery experiences)*, permit them to observe other patients like themselves performing the activity *(vicarious mastery)*, have physicians and nurses provide reassurance and encouragement *(persuasion)*, and prevent the "pathologizing" of innocuous bodily sensations or states by suggesting more benign interpretations *(physiologic feedback)*. These interventions are, in fact, key components of well-designed cardiac rehabilitation programs and may constitute the most important benefit these programs provide.

My own investigation of self-appraisal processes in recovery from acute myocardial infarction began with an attempt to construct and validate physical self-efficacy scales for cardiac patients. Interviews with patients and review of relevant literature revealed significant concerns about walking, climbing stairs, jogging, lifting heavy objects, and engaging in sexual activity; initial findings led to the creation of scales that asked patients to indicate their level of confidence (on a scale ranging from 0 = *not at all confident*, to 100 = *completely confident*) that they could walk or jog various distances, climb flights of stairs, lift various amounts of weight, and engage in sexual activity for various time periods (as the sample available to us consisted of heterosexual married men, sexual activity was defined as "sexual intercourse").[1] In the initial validation study, patients completed these scales before their three-week treadmill test, immediately after the test, and again after the results and implications of the test had been explained by a cardiologist and nurse.

As predicted by self-efficacy theory, results showed that the experience of mastery, persuasion, and internal feedback provided during this evaluation increased physical self-efficacy in patients tested three weeks after acute myocardial infarction. The treadmill exercise test protocol required the patient to exercise at gradually increasing intensities while a physician and nurse offered encouragement and suggested appropriate interpretations of internal physical states. After the test, the cardiologist met with patient and spouse to explain the test results and their implications for activity. Analysis of self-efficacy ratings revealed that patients tended to underestimate their physical capabilities before stepping onto the treadmill but registered impressive gains after completing the test. As self-efficacy theory predicts, self-efficacy gains were largest for activities that resemble the large muscle, dynamic exertion performed on the treadmill (e.g., walking, jogging, climbing stairs), and were smaller for dissimilar

---

[1] Self-efficacy scales derived from this work are available in Ewart (1990), in Ewart & Taylor (1985), or can be obtained from the author.

behaviors (e.g., lifting weights with one's arms, engaging in sexual intercourse). Post-treadmill interpretive counseling by a physician and a nurse helped patients generalize their exercise test experience to lifting and sexual activity (Ewart, Taylor, Reese, & DeBusk, 1983).

Self-Efficacy Mediates Physical Exertion

Self-efficacy changes observed after treadmill exercise supported the validity of the scales but did not address the hypothesis that self-efficacy mediates involvement in physical activities. To evaluate this prediction we had patients wear a portable activity monitor and complete daily exercise diaries for one week before and for one week after the treadmill test. Subsequent analyses revealed that changes in patients' jogging self-efficacy scores immediately following treadmill evaluation predicted changes in their home activity levels better than did the peak heart rate and maximal energy expenditure level achieved during the exercise test. Patients' actions conformed more closely to their self-appraisals than to their actual medical condition.

A subsequent study with colleagues at Johns Hopkins provided further evidence that self-efficacy mediates exercise involvement (Ewart, Stewart, Gillilan, & Kelemen, 1986). Patients in this study were men who had suffered acute myocardial infarction more than six months before the study began and were participating in a cardiac rehabilitation program consisting of supervised group jogging. Patients performed a maximal treadmill exercise test and completed self-efficacy scales. Several weeks later, they were monitored individually by Holter recorder during one of their regular group jogging sessions. Analysis of the Holter electrocardiogram data revealed that the number of minutes men exercised within their prescribed heart rate range was predicted by their self-efficacy for jogging but not by their performance on the treadmill test. Correlational data from these studies of recovering and recovered cardiac patients are summarized in Table 1. The correlations offer remarkably consistent evidence that self-efficacy appraisals are superior to functional exercise evaluation in predicting exercise adherence, especially when adherence is defined as the duration of exercise.

Specificity of Self-Appraisal

Self-efficacy theory holds that appraisals of personal capabilities tend to be behaviorally and situationally specific (Bandura, 1986). This implies that return to normal activity after acute myocardial infarction may be determined as much by the *variety* of exercises offered in a rehabilitation program as by exertional intensity and duration. Specificity of self-appraisal in cardiac patients is revealed by changes in self-efficacy scores occurring when untrained individuals perform a battery of strength and endurance tests. My colleagues and I examined correlations between self-efficacy, strength, and endurance in the 40 recovered patients who participated in the supervised jogging program (Ewart, Stewart, Gillilan, & Kelemen, 1986). These correlations (Table 2) show that self-appraised ability to

Table 1

Prediction of Patient Activity Levels From Leg Self-Efficacy Score (Leg SE) and Maximal Heart Rate (HR) During Treadmill Exercise (TME) in Two Separate Groups of Patients (from Ewart, 1989)

Predictor	Early Home Activity $(n = 40)$[a]		Supervised Group Exercise $(n = 40)$[b]	
	Heart Rate	Duration	Heart Rate	Compliance (minutes)
Leg SE	.53***	.34*	.44**	.39**
TME (HR max)	.30*	.08	.27	.14

Note. [a]Intensity and duration of home walking evaluated 21 days after acute myocardial infarct (Ewart, Taylor, Reese, & DeBusk, 1983).
[b]Exercise intensity and number of minutes within prescribed heart rate range during group jogging evaluated > 6 months after myocardial infarct (Ewart, Stewart, Gillilan, Kelemen, Valenti et al., 1986).
*$p < .05$; **$p < .01$; ***$p < .001$.

Table 2

Pearson Correlation Coefficients Showing Association of Self-Efficacy Scores for Arm and Leg Tasks With Measured Arm Strength and Treadmill (TM) Endurance (from Ewart, 1989)

Self-Efficacy[a]	Arm Strength	Endurance (TM)
Lift	.73****	-.16
Push-ups	.31*	.14
Climb stairs	.22	.35**
Jog	.12	.54***

Note. [a]Self-efficacy estimates were obtained prior to strength and endurance testing in cardiac patients who had previously participated in supervised group jogging but not strength training (Ewart, Stewart, Gillilan, & Kelemen, 1986).
****$p < .0001$; ***$p < .001$; **$p < .03$; *$p < .05$.

lift varying amounts of weight and do push-ups are significantly related to subsequently measured arm strength but are unrelated to self-appraised aerobic endurance as determined by treadmill exercise test. Conversely, self-perceived ability to jog and climb stairs is related to treadmill endurance but is unrelated to measured arm strength. Changes in arm (lift, push-ups) self-efficacy when patients underwent arm and leg strength tests in counterbalanced order disclosed that self-appraised arm strength increased after arm strength testing but not after the leg strength tests. Performing tests of leg strength had no effect on self-appraised ability to lift weights with one's arms or do push-ups. These findings suggest that it is important to include varied strength and flexibility enhancing exercise in addition to traditional walking and jogging protocols in rehabilitation programs designed to speed return to normal activity and promote well-being.

Self-Efficacy Mediates Physical Gains in Exercise Rehabilitation

In laboratory studies that manipulate self-efficacy appraisals experimentally by providing false performance feedback for an unfamiliar task, subjects with high induced self-efficacy for the task work longer at it on subsequent trials than do subjects in whom low or moderate self-efficacy has been induced (Bandura & Cervone, 1983). In the context of cardiac rehabilitation, these findings suggest that patients with higher self-efficacy for prescribed exercises will work harder and achieve greater training benefits than will patients with lower exercise self-efficacy. We evaluated this hypothesis in the 40 patients who participated in the study of group jogging (Ewart, Stewart, Gillilan, & Kelemen, 1986). Half of the men were randomly assigned to a circuit weight training protocol, while the other half played volleyball. Exercise sessions for both groups were of the same frequency and duration. We evaluated the predictive power of pretreatment self-efficacy by regressing posttreatment arm strength gains on pretreatment arm strength, type of training (weight versus volleyball), frequency of exercise class attendance, and pretreatment arm self-efficacy. The step-wise analysis revealed that arm strength at posttest was predicted best by pretreatment arm strength, pretreatment arm self-efficacy, and the type of exercise training (weight training was superior to volleyball). Thus even after controlling for pretreatment differences in arm strength, patients who expressed a high degree of confidence in their ability to lift various amounts of weight achieved greater benefits from training than did men who lacked confidence in their lifting potential. The pattern of findings was consistent with the hypothesis that appraisals of personal capabilities would mediate patient responses to the exercise training program.

Self-Efficacy Predicts Over-Exertion

While many patients shun physical activity after acute myocardial infarction, a few become overly active and run the risk of reinfarction. We considered the possibility that patients who overexert themselves may have excessively high levels of confidence in their physical capabilities. In laboratory experiments, subjects' responses to manipulated failure feedback on an unfamiliar task vary according to the level of self-efficacy that had been induced by performance feedback they had received on earlier trials; subjects with low induced self-efficacy become less involved in the task after "failure," whereas subjects with high induced self-efficacy redouble their efforts and work even harder than they had before (Bandura, 1986). This suggests the interesting possibility that individuals with high levels of confidence in their physical capabilities prior to acute myocardial infarction might be at somewhat greater risk of overexerting themselves physically during recovery.

We examined the relationship between self-efficacy and overexertion during supervised jogging in the 40 men who participated in the weight training study. After measuring self-efficacy for arm and leg activities, we recorded the mens' heart rates by means of the Holter monitor while they participated in one of their 20-minute jogging sessions (Holter monitoring was performed approximately four to eight weeks after self-efficacy had been assessed). Each individual's adherence to his exercise prescription was defined as the number of minutes he exercised at a heart rate that was above or below his prescribed heart rate range (Ewart, Stewart, Gillilan, Kelemen, Valenti et al., 1986). Patients with high confidence in their ability to jog—as indicated by a jogging self-efficacy score in the top third of the distribution—greatly exceeded their prescribed heart rate range, while patients with scores in the middle and bottom thirds of the distribution did not. We designated patients who exercised for more than 10 minutes (more than half the session) as "overachievers;" over half (57%) of the individuals with high pretest self-efficacy for jogging were found to belong to the overachiever group. On the other hand, patients with lower self-efficacy for jogging had an 81% chance of not being identified as overachievers.

As it was impossible to measure these patients' self-efficacy appraisals or activity levels *prior* to acute myocardial infarction, we could not determine if high levels of confidence in one's capabilities before a heart attack increases the likelihood that one will become an overachiever during recovery. Nevertheless, present findings are consistent with this assumption and suggest the importance of remaining alert for indications that patients may be feeling excessively self-efficacious. Individuals who had been accustomed to performing vigorous exercise in leisure or occupational work may be at greater risk; their self-efficacy perceptions should be monitored regularly during training to be sure that high levels of confidence do not lead to dangerous overexertion.

Self-Efficacy, Mood, and Emotion

In addition to its cardiovascular benefits, physical exercise is believed to yield important emotional benefits to recovering acute myocardial infarction patients by alleviating anxiety, enhancing self-esteem, and improving quality of life (Brown, 1991; Folkins & Sime, 1981; Taylor, Sallis, & Needle, 1985). Epidemiologic research in healthy adults indicates that higher levels of participation in sports and physical exercise are associated with greater psychological well-being (Ross & Hayes, 1988). Individuals possessing a strong sense of "instrumentalism" (belief that one is responsible for one's fate and that success or failure is a function of personal effort) reported fewer symptoms of depression, anxiety, or malaise. The positive association between exercise and well-being remained significant even after controlling for demographic characteristics, overweight, and instrumentalism.

Distinguishing self-efficacy from affect. Current cognitive theories of emotion emphasize the importance of attention and appraisal processes in determining affective responses to bodily sensations (Bandura, 1990; Cioffi, 1991; Lazarus, 1991). Physical exertion can produce a wide variety of emotional effects, depending upon how one attends to somatic information or interprets its causes and implications. Unlike "pure" cognition, emotions are comprised of physiologic changes in conjunction with interpretive cognitive activity (Lazarus, 1991). Self-efficacy estimates concerning one's physical capabilities thus are distinguished from emotional responses, such as the feeling of relief (diminished autonomic arousal accompanied by favorable self-appraisal) that low-risk patients often experience following a diagnostic treadmill test. It also is useful to distinguish between reflexive, automatic affective reactions to bodily sensations —as in pain or pleasure—and the emotions these sensations can evoke. Emotions differ from primitive pain or pleasure by including cognitive interpretations concerning the origin of painful or pleasant sensations and their implications for personal well-being. Through appraisal, even painful sensations may be transformed into positive emotion, as when the pain accompanying a valued athletic achievement evokes pride in one's ability to push oneself to new attainments. Emotional appraisals typically entail a goal or action tendency (Frijda, Kuipers, & ter Schure, 1989); a CABG patient who believes that ambiguous chest wall sensations indicate cardiac illness experiences feelings of fear that include a desire to withdraw from activities that appear to elicit the troubling sensations. On the other hand, the patient who construes the same sensations as signs of healing may experience feelings of happiness and pride that include an inclination to become more active. This action tendency helps distinguish emotions from moods, which are diffuse states of pleasure or pain that lack a specific focus (Lazarus, 1991).

Effects of mood states on self-efficacy appraisals. How then, are self-efficacy, mood, and emotion interrelated? Research suggests that the relationship is *bi-directional*; in some instances, self-efficacy influences emotion, while in other instances, emotions influence appraisals of self-efficacy. Inducing a pleasant mood by having subjects recall a pleasant romantic experience enhances self-efficacy for athletic performance, whereas inducing a sad mood by recalling unhappy romantic moments lowers athletic self-efficacy (Kavanagh & Bower, 1985). The finding that recalling a happy *non-athletic* experience increases athletic self-efficacy indicates that the pleasant mood, and not the specific memory used to evoke it, is responsible for enhancing self-efficacy. Research by Bower (1981) suggests that memory is mood-dependent; people in a given mood state can most easily recall past experiences that evoked similar feelings at the time they occurred. This implies that the emotion one experiences at the moment of self-appraisal will activate memories and judgments that are congruent with that emotion. When subjects are in a happy mood, favorable self-appraisals become more accessible in short-term memory, and thus bias self-efficacy (Kavanagh & Bower, 1985). When sad, cardiac patients are more likely to judge their capabilities by recalling their weakest physical moments, whereas when happy, they will be more inclined to base their appraisals on memories of how they have performed when at their best.

Limits of self-efficacy enhancement via mood induction. Creating a pleasant atmosphere and environment for exercise may, by inducing positive moods, cause people to appraise their capabilities more favorably and exercise more intensely. Yet the ability of mood changes to alter self-efficacy is not without limits. Affective states are less likely to bias self-appraisal when patients receive prompt and frequent feedback concerning their physical capabilities. Moreover, mood-dependence in memory implies that affect biases appraisal by directing attention to actual instances of success or failure; resulting self-efficacy appraisals therefore should not be expected to far surpass the individual's best and worst prior attainments.

Effects of self-efficacy on emotion. There also is evidence that self-efficacy appraisals influence emotion. Laboratory studies that manipulate failure feedback on an unfamiliar task reveal that subjects with low self-efficacy for the task become despondent following failures, whereas subjects with high task self-efficacy do not (Bandura, 1986). A key ingredient in the emotion of sadness is the belief that there is no way to restore the loss of a valued object or condition (Lazarus, 1991). It appears that positive appraisals of one's capabilities prevent sadness after failure by supporting the expectation that that which was lost may yet be regained. These experimental findings are in accord with epidemiologic data indicating that individuals with a strong sense of instrumentalism (a construct that includes positive appraisals of one's capabilities) exercise more often and report feeling less anxious and depressed than do individuals with low instrumentalism.

The present analysis suggests that even mild to moderate levels of exercise may enhance affect and strengthen physical self-efficacy. Exercises that do not greatly alter strength or aerobic endurance may still be effective in reducing muscle tension, promoting relaxation, increasing alertness, providing opportunities for pleasant social interaction, and generating pride in one's accomplishments. By contributing to improvements in one's mood, these changes could bias self-appraisal and strengthen physical self-efficacy. It seems likely that, in sedentary individuals, favorable mood changes induced by mild exercise play an important early role in building motivation to adhere to an exercise program. Later in the program, measurable gains in physical capabilities may play a greater role in determining self-efficacy gains that foster pursuit of more challenging exercise goals. This analysis suggests that in the initial phases of an exercise program, it is important to create a pleasant atmosphere and strive to make the exercise experience as enjoyable as possible, whereas later on, goal setting and performance feedback become more critical (Martin et al., 1984).

Using Exercise to Enhance Self-Efficacy and Affect:
Problems and Questions

At present, our ability to use exercise intervention to enhance emotional adjustment by strengthening self-efficacy is limited by insufficient data on relevant exercise effects. Existing research highlights several problems facing efforts to evaluate the impact of exercise on self-appraisal and emotion. In this section I summarize some of these problems and suggest hypotheses to guide future research efforts. Problems are indicated by data suggesting that the emotional effects of physical exercise vary according to type of affect, type of exercise, the time interval when affect is measured, individual differences in somatic attention and information processing, and the nature of the exercise environment.

Type of affect. Research on the dimensional structure of affect repeatedly has identified two independent factors, representing *positive* and *negative* affect respectively (Tellegen, 1985; Watson, Clark, & Tellegen, 1988; Watson & Pennebaker, 1989). Positive affect refers to moods and emotions characterized by high energy, full concentration and pleasurable engagement; high positive affect reflects the extent to which an individual feels enthusiastic, active, and alert, while low positive affect reflects the degree to which one feels sad and lethargic. High negative affect, on the other hand, embraces feelings of anger, nervousness, fear, and disgust; low negative affect can be characterized as a state of calmness and serenity in which these feelings are absent. Positive affect and negative affect have different correlates; negative affect (but not positive affect) is positively associated with self-reported stress, tension, physical pains and symptoms, and daily "hassles." Positive affect (but not negative affect) is related to frequency of social interaction, pleasant events, and physical exercise (Watson & Pennebaker, 1989). Research on daily fluctuations in mood reveal that positive affect and negative affect vary independently; people may experience high positive affect (e.g., pride, enthusiasm) at the same time they experience high negative affect (e.g., anxiety, tension). While physiologic changes can be observed in both negative affect and positive affect, marked increases or reductions in autonomic arousal are more typical of negative affect emotions such as anger, fear, or relief. Physiologic changes are detectable in pride, joy, or gratitude, but people are much more likely to speak of a "pounding heart," "cold hands," or "shaky knees" when referring to the anxiety they experience before performing a diagnostic exercise test than when describing the happiness they feel after learning that their treadmill performance showed them to be at low risk. Because happiness, pride, joy, and other positive emotions tend to be more evanescent and less physiologically distinct than negative emotions like anger or fear, they may prove more difficult to measure. Thus the impact of exercise on positive affect may be inherently more difficult to demonstrate than are the effects of exercise on negative affect. It is interesting to note in this respect that studies investigating the effects of exercise more often have succeeded in demonstrating that exertion alleviates feelings of depression and anxiety than that it increases joy, pride, or happiness (Ross & Hayes, 1988).

Timing of assessment. Relationships between physical exertion, affect, and self-efficacy may vary greatly according to the time interval in which these variables are measured. Beneficial emotional effects of exercise often are found in studies that measure exertion and emotion on two different occasions; when affect is measured during exercise, different patterns of association may be found. For example, in one study positive affect and negative affect were measured in fit and unfit subjects immediately after 8-minute bouts of stationary cycling at varying levels of intensity (Steptoe & Cox, 1988). Higher exertional intensities produced increases in negative affect, whereas exercising at lower intensities reduced perceived exertion and lowered negative affect. Positive affect was not increased, even when exercise was accompanied by exhilarating music. Measures of affect taken during or soon after intense exercise may reflect increased fatigue, dizziness, or discomfort (higher negative affect); measures taken at longer intervals after exertion might be expected to detect desired reductions in negative affect or increased positive affect.

Individual physical differences. Constitutional characteristics of individuals also influence the impact of exercise on emotion. Highly fit individuals have been found to experience significant reductions in state anxiety after a vigorous run, while less fit individuals failed to experience diminished state anxiety after running (Boutcher & Landers, 1988). Fit and unfit runners probably approach exercise with very different expectations and may derive different kinds of somatic information from their exercise bout.

Individual dispositional differences. Some individuals seem more inclined to report higher levels of tension and distress at all times, even in the absence of overtly visible stressors. They also voice more health complaints, despite the fact that they do not have more documentable illness, disabilities, activity restrictions, or health care use (Watson & Pennebaker, 1989). These individuals have been found to score higher on measures of introspectiveness (self-focus and awareness), suggesting they may attend more carefully to bodily sensations than do people who report fewer symptoms and complaints (and hence detect discomforts others may not notice), or that they may be more disposed than others to "pathologize" somatic information. The latter interpretation is strengthened by the finding that instructing healthy subjects to notice and remember any "unpleasant symptoms" they experience during an exercise stress test results in their reporting higher levels of distress than does instructing subjects to attend to and describe their "physical sensations" in detail (Cioffi, 1991). The former instructions presumably encourage a more "pathology-sensitive" mind set whereas the latter do not. In either case, individuals who are more disposed to report negative sensations might be expected to report more negative affect during vigorous exercise, especially when they are unfit. On the other hand, they also should register greater self-efficacy gains in response to strength or endurance building exercise, either because they are more attuned to favorable internal bodily feedback associated with exercise gains, or because physical changes are more likely to reassure those who worry excessively about the implications of aches and pains.

Exercise environment. The environment in which exercise takes place can influence affective responses to exertion. Pleasant music and social interaction are frequently provided in exercise programs as a means to enhance mood during work-outs. These environmental influences improve mood directly by evoking pleasurable associations, as well as indirectly, by distracting attention from bodily discomfort. Research with joggers discloses that increasing *self*-focus (as opposed to focusing on the external environment) during running leads to reports of increased fatigue and discomfort, and reduces running time (Pennebaker, 1982). Discouraging morbid self-focus by providing an enjoyable and stimulating environment for exercise may prevent these negative reactions.

Type of exercise. A social-cognitive analysis of emotion suggests that emotional reactions to exertion may be affected by the type, intensity, and duration of exercise. Exercises that relax tense muscles, increase alertness, and elevate arousal may suffice to induce pleasant mood states and reduce negative affect. On the other hand, emotional responses entail cognitive appraisals of the significance or implications of the exercise experience. Challenging exercises that provide evidence of mastery or resilience may be required to inspire positive emotions such as happiness, pride, or joy, or to alleviate despondancy and depression.

The above review, while not exhaustive, should suggest the complexity of the relationship between physical exertion, mood, and emotion, as well as to suggest the paucity of pertinent empirical data. In general, it appears that favorable emotional responses to exercise in cardiac patients are most likely to be detected when: (a) the investigator measures changes in negative emotions such as fear and anxiety; (b) affect is assessed after the patient has had an opportunity to recover from and to interpret the exercise experience; (c) the individual is chronically prone to notice and worry about somatic sensations; (d) a trusted authority figure encourages the patient to be aware of these sensations during exercise but not to interpret them negatively; (e) a stimulating and pleasant environment offers an alternative to pathologic selffocus; and (f) the level of physical exertion is moderately challenging (Bandura, 1990; Ewart, 1991). Research testing these hypotheses could advance our ability to use exercise training to enhance emotional adjustment to acute myocardial infarction.

Interpersonal Determinants of Physical Self-Efficacy

Up to now, I have tended to emphasize the role of intra-individual processes of attention, and appraisal in determining the activities patients choose to pursue and the extent to which they persevere. A social-contextual view of self-regulation holds, however, that processes of attention, appraisal, and self-motivation are greatly influenced by important others in one's immediate interpersonal milieu (Ewart, 1991). In close social relationships, the activity patterns or "action scripts" of the people involved are interconnected; each person to the relationship has the ability to impede or facilitate the other person's activities, including their pursuit of valued goals related to love, work, or self-care (Bersheid, 1983). After acute myocardial infarction, changes that disrupt the patient's activities also tend to disrupt the important routines and goals of significant others, leading to frustration, sadness, and even anger. A partner's emotional reactions to disrupted routines can undermine patients' determination to follow diet, activity, or other behavioral guidelines during recovery. Anticipating this, partners sometimes try to conceal their unpleasant reactions, a tactic Coyne and his associates have labeled "protective buffering" (Coyne & Smith, 1991). Such buffering is not without costs, however. Partners who hide their feelings and concerns are more likely to become depressed and to have difficulty meeting their own as well as the patient's needs.

In a recent study of wives' responses to their husband's acute myocardial infarction, Coyne and Smith (1991) found that wives who adopted a buffering strategy also tended to overprotect their husbands by discouraging involvement in routine activities. Unfortunately, this overprotectiveness was counterproductive in that it increased the wive's emotional burden while prolonging the source of distress by impeding their partner's recovery. A significant factor in the wives' overprotectiveness was an unrealistically low appraisal of their husband's physical capabilities; they perceived their partners to be more vulnerable than actually was the case. These misperceptions appeared to result from lack of opportunity to discuss their concerns with the physicians and nurses who provided cardiac care.

Misperceptions on the part of the patient's family may be prevented by means of simple and inexpensive interventions that are not difficult to implement in conventional health care settings. A patient's spouse can be given direct and convincing information about the patient's physical capabilities by having the worried spouse participate in the early diagnostic treadmill exercise evaluation. Patients underestimate their capabilities prior to diagnostic exercise, and spouses' estimates of the patient's capabilities are even less optimistic than the patients' estimates. Following the initial demonstration that self-efficacy changes after treadmill exercise predicted activity in the normal environment (Ewart et al., 1983), my colleagues and I proceeded to evaluate the effect of exercise participation on patients' wives. Male patients participating in a diagnostic study three weeks after acute myocardial infarction were randomly assigned to one of three conditions: (a) wife waits in clinic lobby during husband's exercise test and later is advised of the results; (b) wife accompanies husband to the stress lab and watches him perform the treadmill test; and (c) wife accompanies husband to the stress lab, watches him perform the test, and then performs treadmill exercise herself to a level of intensity equal to the maximum her husband had achieved, unless limited by fatigue, shortness of breath, sudden drops in blood pressure, or cardiac signs. Patients and wives separately completed the self-efficacy scales before the treadmill test, immediately after completing the test, and after learning the test results; wives rated their confidence in their husband's capabilities.

Results showed that only those wives who actually engaged in treadmill exercise changed their ratings to levels matching those of their husband. Waiting in the lobby or simply watching their husbands exercise had no appreciable effect on wive's perceptions of their husband's capabilities (Taylor, Bandura, Ewart, Miller, & DeBusk, 1985). These findings suggest a practical model for increasing family members' confidence in the patient's condition, thus reducing their emotional burden and removing psychological barriers to their providing support for health-protective exercise.

Personal Goals and Projects

If patients' appraisals of their physical self-efficacy and their expectations concerning the beneficial effects of exercising were the only factors determining their motivation to exercise after acute myocardial infarction, properly programmed mastery experiences and health information during their hospital stay might be sufficient to launch them on a rehabilitative activity program after being discharged. These activities often must compete with other preoccupations and priorities, however. Recent work by personality theorists suggests that people tend to organize their lives around valued "strivings" or "projects" that respond to fundamental tasks of living such as influencing or being accepted by others, acquiring resources, achieving intimacy, or protecting one's safety (Emmons, 1986). Projects change with changes in the normative age-graded tasks that confront people at different points of the life span. Project priorities are likely to influence the extent to which self-efficacy enhancement alters motivation to engage in regular exercise.

For example, a patient for whom an important current project involves managing a challenging but rewarding career is apt to respond differently to self-efficacy enhancement maneuvers than is a patient whose valued projects involve trying to devote more time to sedentary hobbies, to maintaining close ties with family and friends, or to reducing the stress of an unrewarding job. These priorities have implications for efforts to motivate patients by setting attractive exercise goals (Ewart, 1991). Patients who see exercise as a way to enhance personal strength, endurance, or resilience are likely to be motivated by *moderately* challenging exercise goals that are feasible to attain but are sufficiently difficult to allow a sense of self-mastery (Bandura, 1990). On the other hand, patients who view exercise as an unpleasant but necessary means to reduce discomfort or lower health risks are likely to be motivated by a succession of easy goals, as *easy* goals minimize demand while making the final attainment of desired end states more certain. Elsewhere I present a social action theory of self-change to clarify how self-efficacy appraisals, personal projects, and interpersonal action contexts operate in concert to affect patients' ability to cope with acute myocardial infarction (Ewart, 1991).

Conclusions

Every year, a very large number of heart attack survivors experience unnecessary distress and may place themselves at significant medical risk due to their excessive fears of physical activity. Self-efficacy theory has improved our ability to help these patients by identifying their inappropriate anxieties and alleviating them. Research reviewed in this chapter suggests that self-efficacy appraisals influence patient involvement in exercise regimens and mediate their beneficial effects. The development of scales to assess self-efficacy has made it possible to identify patients who could benefit from self-efficacy enhancement, or who may be at risk of dangerous overexertion due to unrealistically optimistic appraisals of their physical capabilities. Research on affect and self-appraisal discloses bi-directional effects; self-efficacy can be strengthened by mood-dependent memories of past successes, and self-efficacy gains foster positive affect. The degree to which self-efficacy changes stimulate beneficial exercise and lifestyle changes is moderated by interpersonal contexts and the patient's valued personal strivings or projects. Efforts to modify these influences, together with self-efficacy enhancing interventions, comprise a comprehensive treatment approach for increasing patients' ability to cope with the many challenges posed by acute myocardial infarction.

REFERENCES

Bandura, A. (1986). *Social foundations of thought and action.* Englewood Cliffs, NJ: Prentice-Hall.

Bandura, A. (1990). Perceived self-efficacy in the exercise of personal agency. *Applied Sport Psychology, 2*, 128-163.

Bandura, A., & Cervone, D. (1983). Self-evaluative and self-efficacy mechanisms governing the motivational effects of goal systems. *Journal of Personality and Social Psychology, 45*, 1017-1028.

Bersheid, E. (1983). Emotion. In H. Kelley, E. Bersheid, A. Christensen, J. H. Harvey, T. L. Huston, G. Levinger, E. McClintock, L. A. Peplau, & D. R. Peterson (Eds.), *Close relationships* (pp. 110-168). New York: Freeman.

Boutcher, S. H., & Landers, D. M. (1988). The effects of vigorous exercise on anxiety, heart rate, and alpha activity of runners and nonrunners. *Psychophysiology, 25*, 696-702.

Bower, G. H. (1981). Mood and memory. *American Psychologist, 36*, 129-148.

Brown, J. D. (1991). Staying fit and staying well: Physical fitness as a moderator of life stress. *Journal of Personality and Social Psychology, 60*, 555-561.

Cioffi, D. (1991). Beyond attentional strategies: A cognitive-perceptual model of somatic interpretation. *Psychological Bulletin, 109*, 25-41.

Coyne, J. C., & Smith, D. A. F. (1991). Couples coping with a myocardial infarction: A contextual perspective on wives' distress. *Journal of Personality and Social Psychology, 61*, 404-412.

Croog, S., & Levine, S. (1982). *Life after a heart attack: Social and psychological factors.* New York: Human Science Press.

DeBusk, R. F., Blomqvist, C. G., Kouchoukous, N. T., Luepker, R. V., Miller, H. S., Moss, A. J., Pollock, M. L., Reeves, T. J., Selvester, R. H., Stason, W. B., Wagner, G. S., & Willman, V. L. (1986). Identification and treatment of low-risk patients after acute myocardial infarction and coronary-artery bypass graft surgery. *New England Journal of Medicine*, *314*, 161-166.

Emmons, R. A. (1986). Personal strivings: An approach to personality and subjective well-being. *Journal of Personality and Social Psychology*, *51*, 1058-1068.

Ewart, C.K. (1989). Psychological effects of resistive weight training: Implications for cardiac patients. Medicine and Science in Sports and Exercise, 21, 683-688.

Ewart, C. K. (1990). A social problem-solving approach to behavior change in coronary heart disease. In S. Shumaker, E. Schron, & J. Ockene (Eds.), *Handbook of health behavior change* (pp. 153-190). New York: Springer.

Ewart, C. K. (1991). Social action theory for a public health psychology. *American Psychologist*, *46*, 931-946.

Ewart, C. K., Stewart, K. J., Gillilan, R. E., & Kelemen, M. H. (1986). Self-efficacy mediates strength gains during circuit weight training in men with coronary artery disease. *Medicine and Science in Sports and Exercise*, *18*, 531-540.

Ewart, C. K., Stewart, K. J., Gillilan, R. E., Kelemen, M. H., Valenti, S. A., Manley, J. D., & Kelemen, M. D. (1986). Usefulness of self-efficacy in predicting overexertion during programmed exercise in coronary artery disease. *American Journal of Cardiology*, *57*, 557-561.

Ewart, C. K., & Taylor, C. B. (1985). The effects of early postmyocardial infarction exercise testing on subsequent quality of life. *Quality of Life and Cardiovascular Care*, *1*, 162-175.

Ewart, C. K., Taylor, C. B., Reese, L. B., & DeBusk, R. F. (1983). Effects of early postmyocardial infarction exercise testing on self-perception and subsequent physical activity. *American Journal of Cardiology*, *51*, 1076- 1080.

Folkins, C. H., & Sime, W. E. (1981). Physical fitness training and mental health. *American Psychologist*, *36*, 373-389.

Frijda, N. H., Kuipers, P., & ter Schure, E. (1989). Relations among emotion, appraisal, and emotional action readiness. *Journal of Personality and Social Psychology*, *57*, 212-228.

Kavanagh, D. J., & Bower, G. H. (1985). Mood and self-efficacy: Impact of joy and sadness on perceived capabilities. *Cognitive Therapy and Research*, *9*, 507-525.

Lazarus, R. S. (1991). Progress on a cognitive-motivational-relational theory of emotion. *American Psychologist*, *46*, 819-834.

Martin, J. E., Dubbert, P. M., Katell, A. D., Thompson, J. K., Raczynski, J. R., Lake, M., Smith, P. O., Webster, J. S., Sikora, T., & Cohen, R. E. (1984). Behavioral control of exercise in sedentary adults: Studies 1 through 6. *Journal of Consulting and Clinical Psychology*, *52*, 795-811.

Miller, N. H., Haskell, W. L., Berra, K., & DeBusk, R. F. (1984). Home versus group exercise training for increasing functional capacity after myocardial infarction. *Circulation*, *70*, 645-649.

O'Connor, G. T., Buring, J. E., Yusuf, S., Goldhaber, S. Z., Olmstead, E. M., Paffenbarger, R. S., & Hennekens, C. H. (1989). An overview of randomized trials of rehabilitation with exercise after myocardial infarction. *Circulation*, *80*, 234-244.

Pennebaker, J. W. (1982). *The psychology of physical symptoms*. New York: Springer.

Ross, C. E., & Hayes, D. (1988). Exercise and psychologic well-being in the community. *American Journal of Epidemiology*, *127*, 762-761.

Steptoe, A., & Cox, S. (1988). Acute effects of aerobic exercise on mood. *Health Psychology, 7*, 329-340.

Taylor, C. B., Bandura, A., Ewart, C. K., Miller, N. H., & DeBusk, R. F. (1985). Exercise testing to enhance wives' confidence in their husband's capability soon after clinically uncomplicated myocardial infarction. *American Journal of Cardiology, 55*, 636-628.

Taylor, C. B., Sallis, J. F., & Needle, R. (1985). The relation of physical activity and exercise to mental health. *Public Health Reports, 100*, 195- 202.

Tellegen, A. (1985). Structures of mood and personality and their relevance to assessing anxiety, with an emphasis on self-report. In A. H. Tuma & J. D. Maser (Eds.), *Anxiety and the anxiety disorders* (pp. 681-706). Hillsdale, NJ: Erlbaum.

Watson, D. W., Clark, L. A., & Tellegen, A. (1988). Development and validation of brief measures of positive and negative affect: The PANAS scales. *Journal of Personality and Social Psychology, 54*, 1063-1070.

Watson, D. W., & Pennebaker, J. W. (1989). Health complaints, stress, and distress: Exploring the central role of negative affectivity. *Psychological Review, 96*, 234-254.

Author Notes

Preparation of this manuscript was supported in part by grants R01-HL36298 and R01-HL45139 from the National Heart, Lung, and Blood Institute of the National Institutes of Health, Bethesda, Maryland.

PERCEIVED SELF-EFFICACY IN SELF-MANAGEMENT OF CHRONIC DISEASE

Halsted Holman and Kate Lorig

Chronic disease, now the most prevalent form of disease in the United States, differs from acute disease in many ways. One of the most important is the potential for self-management by patients. Appropriate self-management is based upon a partnership between the patient and health professionals in which each takes responsibility for portions of the management. For patients, this requires learning new skills and assuming new responsibilities. Growing evidence indicates that perceived self-efficacy to cope with the consequences of chronic disease is an essential contributor to developing self-management capabilities, and that perceived self-efficacy can be rapidly enhanced by appropriate learning experiences. Thus perceived self-efficacy is an important personal attribute in the maintenance of health. Enhancing perceived self-efficacy should be an important ingredient of the provision of health care.

The central thesis of this chapter holds that, in the presence of a chronic disease, many types of self-management practices are both feasible and beneficial, and that perceived self-efficacy to execute those practices and to manage the consequences of the disease improves the outcomes greatly. In order to explain and substantiate the thesis, we must make clear each of the component concepts. Therefore this chapter is organized into sections which define and discuss (1) the nature of chronic disease and its management (2) characteristics of self-management and (3) the interactions among self-efficacy, self-management and chronic disease outcomes. Each section will include some pertinent references so that the reader can explore the subject more fully. However, this chapter is not a comprehensive review. It presents conceptual approaches, citing supporting empirical evidence.

The Nature of Chronic Disease and its Management

Chronic disease has become the most prevalent form of disease in the United States (Rice & Feldman, 1983; Verbrugge, 1984). It is the principal source of disability and a major cause of escalating health care expenditures (Colvez &

Blanchet, 1981). Because the prevalence of chronic disease increases with age, the aging of the population has contributed to increases in prevalence. However, in recent years, the prevalence of chronic disease has increased for virtually every age group in the population (Rice & LaPlante, 1988). While chronic disease typically arises spontaneously, it can also be created by contemporary treatment of acute illness. For example, modern treatment of an acute heart attack which previously would be fatal can now result in an individual with chronic heart disease. Usually, chronic disease cannot be cured. It must be managed over time. Treatment may correct certain biological abnormalities, can ameliorate some consequences of chronic disease, and may prevent overall deterioration, but it does not terminate the disease. Commonly it is not possible to predict accurately what effect a particular treatment or management technique will have. The effect may be beneficial, neutral or even harmful; usually only a trial of treatment will reveal the effects.

The intensity of a chronic disease typically fluctuates of its own accord. That is, the disease process is not relentless but rather has periods of greater and lesser severity. Treatment influences the fluctuations, usually for the better. However, if a treatment has an adverse effect, an additional medical problem is actually created by the management effort.

The chronicity of a disease creates problems beyond the specific consequences of the particular biological abnormality (e.g., the symptoms such as thirst and urination due to high blood sugar in diabetes or pain and reduced exercise tolerance due to reduced blood supply from hardening of the arteries in arteriosclerosis). The additional consequences are also a result of the disease and its treatment, and fall in many categories: fatigue, depression, unfavorable employment and financial circumstances, reduced social activities, family conflict. At times, these additional consequences react back on the disease process to make matters worse. Examples would be the emotional refusal of a diabetic to secure an appropriate diet with resultant worsening of the diabetes, or the financial inability of a physically handicapped person to obtain appropriate physical rehabilitation with resultant worsening of the handicap. It is common to refer to the biological abnormalities of a disease as the disease process and the composite of that disease process and all of its consequences as an illness. Thus a chronic illness has many components and these components can interact with one another to worsen or lessen the total illness effect.

Many illness attributes are common across chronic diseases. That is, while the underlying biological abnormalities of chronic diseases may be quite distinct, the illness components such as those mentioned above, and their potential interactions, have many similarities. Therefore, it is appropriate to examine chronic diseases as a group, seeking common themes in both their manifestations and their management.

A useful first step in understanding chronic diseases is recognition that they are different from acute diseases. Table 1 enumerates some of the distinctions. For example, acute diseases usually result from identifiable, abrupt and potentially reversible specific events (e.g., infection, injury, blood vessel rupture or occlusion). By contrast, initiating events for most chronic diseases are obscure. The disease processes appear to emerge over time from protracted interaction among environmental, genetic and behavioral risk factors. Once established, chronic disease may be further altered by interactions among the disease process and its consequences (see above).

Table 1
Disease Characteristics

	Acute Disease	Chronic Disease/ Illness
Onset	Abrupt	Commonly gradual
Duration	Limited	Lengthy; indefinite
Cause	Usually single cause	Multivariate causation of both disease and illness, changing over time
Diagnosis and prognosis	Commonly accurate	Diagnosis often uncertain; prognosis obscure
Technological intervention	Usually effective (laboratory testing, imaging, medication, surgery)	Commonly indecisive; adverse effects frequent
Outcome	Cure likely with return to normal health	No cure; management over time necessary
Uncertainty	Minimal	Pervasive
Knowledge	Profession knowledgeable; laity inexperienced	Profession and laity partially and reciprocally knowledgeable

For purposes of this chapter, the most relevant difference between acute and chronic disease lies in the role of the patient and family, particularly in relation to management. For acute diseases, the patients are usually inexperienced and are dependent upon health professionals for knowledge, decisions and therapy. With chronic illness, however, the patient commonly becomes the most knowledgeable person concerning both consequences of disease and effects of therapy. At times, the physician is dependent upon the patient even for decisions in changing the medical management. For instance, patients are often best equipped to sense the effect of changes in medication dose, to perceive the relevance of a particular management maneuver to the state of the illness, and to decide to persevere in the face of sub-optimal treatment outcomes. Appropriate management of chronic disease requires development of a partnership between the patient and the physician.

Patients, families and physicians come to the relationship created by chronic disease with widely different backgrounds, levels and types of understanding, and suppositions. Patients initially have almost no experience with chronic disease, are beset by fears, and conceptualize the illness through a variety of cultural and metaphorical understandings. Within these understandings, symptoms may have different individual and symbolic meanings. For example, pain may be viewed as a routine manifestation of disease, or as a symbol of worsening and reason for pessimism, or even as a punishment. Understandings of the symbolisms create explanatory models for the patient about his or her circumstances and fate. Thus patients with the same diseases may have strikingly different illness patterns and explanatory models (Lewis & Daltroy, 1990). Further, patients commonly seek certainty in explanation, prognoses and treatment. Physicians, on the other hand, generally share a biologically-based explanatory model and related treatment methods. While familiar with wide variation in illness patterns and responses to therapy, and hence with uncertainty, they tend to disregard that which is outside their explanatory model.

The views of the patient and the physician affect the mood of each, the willingness of each to act, and the types of actions taken. Effective management of chronic disease requires building a partnership based on merged understandings and actions, a process which requires inquiry, interpretation, learning and negotiation.

Gradually, as experience with the chronic disease grows, patients' understanding of their particular circumstances grows. This growth of understanding includes not only the physical effects of the disease and treatment but also the consequences in all of the affected aspects of living. Further, the patient and family learn what can be done to ameliorate undesirable consequences through such steps as modification of life styles and living routines, use of rehabilitation and assistive devices, and drawing upon community resources.

Characteristics of Self-Management

Historically, in the health field, there have been two general lineages from which contemporary self-management arose: medical therapy and public health practices. Long before the days of medical professionalism, individuals and families engaged in various forms of treatment and/or management of their health problems (Starr, 1982). Similarly, there is a long tradition of community action to protect public health such as improving water and food supplies, providing appropriate housing, and specifying behavior such as quarantine and immunization to prevent spread of disease. In the present era of predominant chronic disease, these traditions tend to modify and meld, creating new roles for both patients and health professionals. The new roles are exemplified by the goal of partnership. In our view, the patient's role is to engage in the maximum feasible self-management; the health professional's role is to develop and facilitate that self-management, teaching and providing expert knowledge.

Self-management means having, or being able to obtain, the skills and resources necessary to best accommodate to the chronic disease and its consequences (Holroyd & Creer, 1986). The skills and resources are both general across chronic diseases and specific to particular diseases. Because chronic diseases and illnesses are unpredictable and may fluctuate even on a day-to-day basis, they often must be "managed" on a daily basis. Appropriate management arises in the collaborative partnership of patients with health professionals, and collaboration distinguishes self-management from self-help and twelve-step programs which are fundamentally conducted by patients without the participation of health professionals.

Understanding self-management of chronic diseases requires knowledge of the chronic disease, the relevant self-management practices and the relationship between self-management and professional medical management. The scope of this knowledge has been only partially sketched by the foregoing discussion. It is useful to look more closely at characteristics of chronic diseases in order to specify the role of self-management.

Identifying the Illness Course and Management Effects

Chronic diseases and their resulting chronic illnesses typically fluctuate in intensity over time, both spontaneously and in response to therapies. Because there is no cure, these fluctuations continue indefinitely. Appropriate management requires appropriate responses to these fluctuations: Increased disease intensity usually requires increased treatment intensity while the opposite is true when the disease becomes less active. Figure 1 depicts this situation in a hypothetical course of fluctuating disease intensity. Points A, B and C represent the same disease intensity. However, Point A reflects a time when the disease trend is worsening and the appropriate response would usually be to intensify or change therapy. Point B represents an improving trend in the disease with a likely lesser need for therapy. Point C represents a disease activity plateau in which the minimum therapy necessary to maintain the stable situation would probably be appropriate. The central requirement in interpreting such situations is accurate identification of the disease *trend* as reflected by the arrows.

But knowing the trend alone is not sufficient. The tempo or speed along the trend is also essential. Is the disease worsening rapidly or slowly? How quickly must one react? How rapidly must the treatment take effect? In Figure 1, the tempo is depicted by the slope or steepness of the curve. In both medical emergencies and chronic disease, trend and tempo are essential in assessing a patient's state; in emergencies they are compressed into minutes or hours while in chronic disease they play out over days, weeks and months.

However, the situation is not as simple as depicted in Figure 1. Because the disease process and the various components of the resulting illness all fluctuate over time, Figure 2 is a truer representation of the clinical setting in which signs and symptoms oscillate appreciably around the true course of the disease and/or illness. Sometimes, those oscillations may be so extreme as to suggest a trend

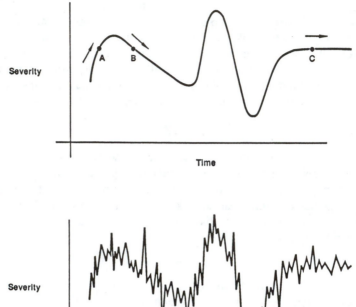

Figure 1

Figure 2

opposite to the true one. Also, the trends of the disease and the illness may not move in parallel; that is, a disease may be improving or stable but a particular illness component may worsen. An example could be pain in chronic arthritis. The intensity of pain, a major consequence of arthritis, can vary with a person's emotional state; pain can worsen with emotional distress and lessen when a person is emotionally tranquil. Thus, though the arthritis may be stable, external emotional circumstances can aggravate a primary symptom of arthritis. If the proper cause of the increased pain is not identified and addressed, treatment could be wrong. The result could be lack of benefit and adverse treatment effects. Thus it is not only essential that trends in disease and illness be identified but that oscillations around the true trend be accurately interpreted. This usually requires, in addition to diagnostic perceptiveness, *observation over time* in order to understand the meaning of trends in sign and symptoms. Sometimes the interpretation is assisted by diagnostic tests but commonly with chronic diseases and illness, appropriate use of time is all that is necessary to interpret physical signs and symptoms and thus to identify the trend and tempo. Indeed, when used wisely, time can be the most accurate, most available and least expensive tool for the management of chronic disease.

The discussion of Figures 1 and 2 reveals two of the most crucial attributes of good management of chronic disease and illness, namely, the identification of trends and tempo, and the wise use of time to accomplish that identification. These two attributes of sound management provide the conceptual base for self-management of chronic disease. While the physician and other health professionals are most knowledgeable about the biology of the disease and the principal treatment methods, the patient and the family are usually in the best position to identify the impact of the disease and treatment on the individual, and to interpret changes in the impact. Particularly if the patient develops understanding of (1) the nature of the disease, (2) the ways to interpret signs and symptoms, (3) the types of treatments and management procedures which are available, and also learns (4) to execute those aspects of management which can be done personally, a true partnership can emerge.

Basic Self-Management Skills

In addition to learning about the nature of chronic disease and illness, and about medical management, there are seven basic areas of skill which are central to those aspects of management which can be done personally. These are (1) minimizing or overcoming physical debility, (2) establishing realistic expectations and emotional responses to the vicissitudes of the illness, (3) interpreting and managing symptoms (4) learning how to judge the effects of medications and manage their use (5) becoming adept at ways to solve problems as they arise, (6) communicating with health professionals and (7) using community resources to advantage. Each will be discussed in sequence.

1. In the presence of chronic disease, physical deconditioning can result from many causes: the disease itself (as when muscles or joints are affected), reduced activity (as when bedridden, handicapped or short of breath), treatment (as when using drugs which affect muscle strength like cortisone), and poor nutrition. Furthermore, the deconditioning creates its own symptoms in that, when used, deconditioned muscles, joints and tendons can cause pain and accentuate fatigue. The latter consequences are similar to those experienced by a deconditioned athlete who resumes training. Maintaining the maximum possible physical fitness is therefore a cardinal goal in management of any chronic disease. Most people with chronic diseases are benefitted by exercise and most can establish exercise programs that are within their tolerance and which lead to maintaining or improving physical capability. Such programs are often aided by simple pain reducing mechanisms such as the use of heat, mild analgesics like aspirin and cognitive pain control methods. Physical activity and stamina are also aided by assuring appropriate nutrition and sleep, both of which can be achieved by various physical, cognitive and medical strategies.

2. Achieving appropriate expectations and new emotional adjustments can be the most important changes to be made by a patient with chronic disease. Patients with chronic illness often find themselves unable to relieve persistent symptoms and unable to participate in desired activities. Simultaneously they are

often faced with uncertainty in diagnosis and prognosis. For many, this uncertainty extends, through the fluctuations in illness intensity, to their lives from day to day. Planning becomes difficult; loss of work, of social activities and of social support systems may occur. In such a setting, patients may develop a sense of helplessness and depression.

Health professionals can help in various ways but much of an appropriate response lies within the realm of self-management. It is particularly helpful for patients to learn what is known and is not known about both the disease and its therapy. This allows the patient to place himself/herself in the context of prevailing knowledge. Understanding that context aids in accommodating to uncertainty in a variety of ways: knowing that appropriate steps are being taken; identifying other patients with similar problems whose experiences can be helpful; learning particular activities which prevent or compensate for consequences of the disease; learning how to confront most effectively a new problem from the illness or its therapy. Activities in each of these categories can be very specific, for example, minimizing pain by cognitive techniques, maximizing mobility by use of appropriate assist devices, reducing fatigue by both exercise and rectifying sleep disturbances, building new friendships with persons with similar difficulties. Such approaches can be generally summarized under the headings of learning to function effectively and pleasurefully within the limits imposed by the disease while simultaneously taking actions to expand those limits. As a patient's repertoire of skills grows the distress of uncertainty declines because of a rising capacity to confront the variations which the disease creates.

3. The most obvious effect of a chronic disease is a symptom—pain, fatigue, breathlessness, nausea. The disease may directly cause the symptom, or the symptom may be caused by a behavior such as exertion or by an emotional upset, or the symptom might arise from an error in medication dose or from an adverse effect of a drug. With chronic disease, patients often become quite adept at interpreting their symptoms. This skill is essential to identifying appropriate action and avoiding useless or harmful treatment changes. Often, when there is uncertainty about symptom interpretation, a brief observation period or a slight treatment change followed by observation will provide the answer.

4. Most management of chronic disease includes the use of medications. The medications are not intended as a cure but rather as a means of diminishing the intensity of the disease or alleviating some of its consequences. It is almost always the responsibility of the patient or the family to administer the treatment on a day to day basis. Skills involved in medication self-management include those which assist in complying with the regimen and in interpreting the effects of the medication, in particular recognizing adverse effects. When a new or unanticipated event arises, the patient must be prepared to describe and interpret the event, to seek medical advice, and potentially to alter the treatment program. Patients can readily develop these skills but, to do so, they must learn about medications and their effects, and monitor their own experiences carefully.

5. Problem solving is a major self-management skill. One cannot predict in advance the problems which an individual patient will face. These can range from the discomforts and disabilities of the illness to inability to pay for health care, to the need to change a residence, or to difficulties in a marriage. Success in dealing with new adverse situations greatly influences how a patient accommodates to and manages an illness.

Problem solving with chronic disease is similar to that of virtually any other situation. It includes defining the problem, identifying alternative solutions, choosing a solution to be tried, monitoring the results of the trial, and testing alternative solutions if desirable. While it is impossible to teach patients all potential solutions, it is possible to teach them the generic skills for finding those solutions. This involves teaching general problem solving skills rather than solving of specific problems. Though initially inexperienced at resolving medical problems, patients commonly become expert in knowledge of their disease generally. Building this knowledge into an understanding of how medical problems are solved, and providing access to appropriate consultation or supervision, allows the patient's common sense skills in problem solving to be applied in a new area.

6. Health professionals are the most common consultants used by people with chronic illness. Unfortunately, all too often, care for chronic disease is provided like care for acute disease: Health professionals solve the problems for a passive patient; patients are neither encouraged nor assisted to solve problems independently. For the partnership necessary for the best possible outcome from chronic disease, patients need at least two essential skills. First, the patient must know when to seek advice, how to describe symptoms and how to identify the trends and tempo of the disease. Second, patients must be able and willing to express concerns and to negotiate with health professionals concerning the next action. Often this means questioning the physician, and accepting or rejecting treatment options. For their part, physicians must encourage development of these skills by the patient and must be willing to enter into a partnership. When both parties develop these skills, a process emerges which is both efficient and satisfying.

7. Identification and use of resources beyond those which are personal or are provided by health professionals is the final general self-management skill. Problems caused by chronic illness are often soluble only outside the health care system. These include, but are not limited to, use of exercise facilities and programs and use of special educational opportunities such as libraries, community colleges and special education programs. Community groups may be invaluable such as senior citizen centers and organizations for people with particular diseases. At times, Meals-on-Wheels and Friendly Visitors can be particularly helpful.

Prevention

Prevention of disease is commonly perceived in terms of direct prevention such as sanitation, immunization, avoidance of substance abuse and wearing seatbelts. This is called primary prevention. There are two other types of prevention, secondary and tertiary. Secondary prevention involves avoiding a disease once a risk factor is present. Examples include modifying a diet when a blood cholesterol level is high or reducing weight and salt intake when blood pressure is elevated. Tertiary prevention involves preventing loss of independent function once a disease is present. Examples include maintaining general physical strength and stamina in the presence of disease, use of specific breathing patterns to improve oxygenation in lung disease and elimination of household obstacles over which one might fall when physically handicapped.

In the presence of chronic disease, secondary and tertiary prevention are particularly important. Some of the appropriate practices can be learned from health professionals while others entail the use of common sense in confronting the issues which arise in daily life. Prevention practices designed to minimize the consequences of chronic disease and maintain independent living illustrate the convergence of classical medical and public health principles to create the most effective management program for the patient and the family.

The afore-mentioned components of self-management—understanding and interpreting disease and illness patterns, using specific self-management practices and applying prevention principles—apply generally across chronic diseases. As well, there are disease specific aspects of self-management which must be integrated with the general skills. These include particular medications and specific activities such as pursed-lip breathing, controlled coughing and respiratory exercises for chronic lung disease, diets for heart disease and special exercise for arthritis. Such disease-specific activities are determined together with the physician or other health professionals. Once learned, they fit well with general self-management skills.

The Relevance of Perceived Self-Efficacy to Self-Management and Health Outcomes in Chronic Disease

For patients to engage in effective self-management, a number of preconditions are important. The first is an understanding of the appropriateness and value of the self-management activity. This understanding flows from recognition of the nature of chronic illness and the complementary roles of patients, families and health professionals in management over time. The second precondition is the development of skills and confidence on the part of the patient concerning the specific, useful self-management practices. This is a matter of learning, practicing and evaluating the personal benefits derived from particular self-management practices. The third precondition, highly desirable but often absent, is a health care service which encourages and coordinates with self-management, preferably together with a social network which supports and facilitates self-management behaviors.

The desired preconditions generally fall outside of the classical biomedical model of health care in which the relatively passive patient is attended by the all-knowing physician. Instead, the pre-conditions fall far better under the biopsychosocial model of health and health care in which biology, knowledge, treatment, beliefs, emotions and socioeconomic circumstances interact to determine health outcomes (Engel, 1977). For instance, cognitive and motivational factors have long been recognized as influencing the level of functioning of patients with chronic disability; witness, for example, the severely deformed person with rheumatoid arthritis who leads an independent and satisfying life compared to persons with mild forms of the same disease who remain despondent and functionally incapacitated.

Of special relevance to self-management is the impact on health status of people's beliefs in their efficacy to exercise some control over conditions that affect their lives (Bandura, 1986). A growing body of research has identified various processes—cognitive, motivational, affective and physiological—through which self-beliefs of efficacy exert their effects. Perceived self-efficacy influences what people chose to do, their motivation, their perseverance in the face of difficulty, the self-enhancing or self-hindering nature of their thought patterns, and their vulnerability to stress and depression. Indeed, people's beliefs in their personal efficacy has been found to influence outcomes in a number of acute and chronic illnesses, including the level of benefit they receive from therapeutic interventions. Thus perceived self-efficacy provides a linking mechanism between psychosocial factors and functional status.

Beliefs in personal efficacy can be strengthened in four principal ways (Bandura, 1986). The most powerful relies on *guided mastery experiences* that build coping capabilities. In essence, this involves learning and practicing the appropriate behaviors. This is best done by breaking the desired behavior into small, graded tasks which can be accomplished in a relatively short time. Feedback is important so that patients can see progress. Once a component task is accomplished, another is added until the whole behavior is achieved. Thus, a patient may start a walking program by walking one block four times a week. Gradually blocks are added until the ultimate goal of walking a mile four times weekly is achieved.

The second approach to building personal efficacy draws upon the power of *social modeling* to convey skills and a coping orientation. This is the experience of observing others exercise the skills and gain the benefits. When using models in teaching it is important that the models be as much like patients as possible. If a 60-year-old patient with osteoarthritis is attempting to learn exercise, the model should also be an older person experiencing problems with arthritis. Prominent persons and young models leading exercise programs do not serve as good examples for persons unlike them. There are two general types of models for persons suffering a handicap. Supermodels are those who have reached some great achievement in the face of much adversity. An example is the young cancer patient who walks across the country with an artificial limb. While such models are inspirational, they do little for enhancing efficacy because people don't believe they can come close to a similar achievement. Coping models are people who have a problem but cope with it on a day-to-day basis. They have good and bad days, but on the whole, are able to lead full and active lives. These models enhance efficacy because patients are able to relate realistically to them.

Social persuasion provides a third type of efficacy enhancing influence; successful efficacy builders do more than convey positive approaches, they also design and explain activities for others in ways that bring success. Effective persuasion usually involves urging learners to do just a little more than they are presently doing. For instance, instead of urging a patient to lose 40 pounds, it is better to urge them to lose a pound this week. The goal is realistic and can be seen by the patient as reasonable. In building self-efficacy, success leads to success.

The final mode of influence is aimed at reducing aversive *physiological reactions* or interpreting them in less pathological ways. An example of the former for a person with chronic lung disease would be learning how to accomplish a desired physical activity without undesirable shortness of breath, perhaps through use of assisting devices; an example of the latter for a person with arthritis or heart disease would be recognizing that the appearance of pain does not commonly mean worsening disease.

Perceived self-efficacy is specific to particular activities. That is, one can feel efficacious for walking on a level surface but not for mounting many stairs. Therefore, just as the appropriate self-management activities result from the particular consequences of the chronic illness for a given individual, so the development of perceived self-efficacy must relate to those particular self-management activities.

With this background, it is pertinent to review some recent evidence which supports a mediating role for perceived self-efficacy in the response to, and treatment of, chronic diseases. Historically, one of the first applications of self-efficacy concepts occurred in the treatment of phobias (Bandura, 1986). An example is snake phobias which prevent individuals from walking in fields or other places where they fear snakes might lurk. Rapid and successful ways of curing established phobias were devised using different combinations of the four principal ways mentioned above to modify the patient's perceived self-efficacy. Since then, measures to enhance perceived self-efficacy have been applied with very salutary effects in a number of disease settings, some which are discussed elsewhere in this book. These settings include recovery from heart attacks, improvement of lung function in chronic pulmonary disease, pain reduction in a variety of settings such as headaches and child birth, changing eating and exercise habits and reduction in drug abuse (for discussion and references see Bandura, 1991). In all these settings, patients and their families have learned new practices and behaviors which minimize or eliminate dysfunction and discomfort.

We shall illustrate the application of self-efficacy principles and practices to chronic disease through a brief recounting of their use in patients with chronic arthritis. Chronic arthritis limits the mobility of joints and ultimately the strength of muscles and tendons which move those joints. One of the principles of good medical management is exercise to retain or improve mobility and strength. Such exercise is frequently painful and it is common for patients to imagine that exercise will make the joint disease worse. Good management therefore involves not only illustrating the appropriate exercises but also aiding the patient to understand that, despite the pain, exercise is beneficial and that as strength improves pain will decline. Some years ago, we decided that a health education program about exercise and other aspects of management for chronic arthritis would be beneficial to groups of patients. A program called the Arthritis Self-Management Program (ASMP) was designed to cover, in six two-hour sessions, such subjects as: current understanding of the nature of arthritis, present therapies and how they are used, interpretation of symptoms, communication with physicians and other health professionals, self-management skills such as exercise and cognitive pain control, and marshalling of community resources. The program was tested in randomized, prospective studies, the results of which showed that, compared to control persons, participants in the ASMP experienced significant reductions in pain, less depression, increased social and physical activities and decreased use of physician services (Lorig, Lubeck, Kraines, Seleznick & Holman, 1985). The pain reductions were 15 to 20% from baseline levels which is similar to that achieved by the milder medications used for arthritis.

In order to understand the true effects of the ASMP, it was important to know whether the people who improved were those who learned the most and practiced what was taught most frequently. Because of large numbers of participants, it was possible to correlate health outcomes with knowledge gained and reported use of the self-management practices which were taught. Surprisingly, the results showed very little correlation; the best was 0.14 between exercise and pain reduction (Lorig, Seleznick, Lubeck, Ung, Chastain, & Holman, 1989). In order to understand this unexpected turn, structured and open-ended interviews were conducted with ASMP participants. The results revealed a fairly consistent pattern: Persons who did well in ASMP generally did not believe that their chronic arthritis had irretrievably damaged their lives and believed that they could do things to improve matters; persons who did not do well had opposite views (Lenker, Lorig, & Gallagher, 1984). These findings suggested that patients' perceived self-efficacy to cope with the consequences of arthritis was mediating the outcomes of ASMP. An instrument (see Appendix) was therefore designed to measure such perceived self-efficacy. In four months following start of the ASMP, perceived self-efficacy grew 10% to 15%. Further, whereas the highest correlation between health outcomes and either knowledge gain or practice of taught behaviors had been 0.14, as seen in Table 2, the correlations of perceived self-efficacy with health outcome scores were much higher (Lorig, Chastain, Ung, Shoor & Holman, 1989). As a consequence, the content of ASMP was modified to emphasize efficacy enhancing activities. Subsequent outcomes of the new ASMP were improved over those of the initial version (Table 3).

Recently, it has been possible to study two groups of persons four years after taking ASMP who had not experienced any organized educational intervention in the interim. Again surprisingly, as seen in Table 4, the beneficial effects had either persisted or increased. Pain remained reduced by approximately 20% and visits to physicians were reduced by approximately 40%. Both of the latter results occurred despite a modest increase in physical disability. During the four years, perceived self-efficacy to cope with the consequences of arthritis as measured by the final version of the instrument had grown by an average of 29% (Holman, Mazonson, & Lorig, 1989).

Table 2

Associations Between Self-Efficacy and Health Status at Four Months After Start of the Arthritis Self-Management Program (ASMP)

	Pain	Depression
Self-efficacy for pain	-0.39[a]	-0.45
Self-efficacy for other symptoms	-0.47	-0.59

Note. [a]Pearson correlations for combined data from 144 persons (49 from control group and 95 from ASMP). All correlations significantly different from zero ($p < 0.01$).

Because of the persistent decline in use of physician services over the four years, it was possible to estimate cost savings which accrued from the lesser dependence on medical care. Taking into account the costs of providing the course and discounting the dollar value at 6% annually, it was calculated that the net four-year savings per participant with osteoarthritis were approximately $190.00 and the net savings per patient with rheumatoid arthritis were almost $650.00. Multiplying these savings by 1% of individuals suffering those two diseases identifies potential savings approximating $32,000,000 in four years if only that small portion of patients participated in the ASMP (or similar program) and achieved the same results as have been found in the initial studies.

The health benefits for patients with chronic arthritis described thus far have been in the subjective (pain, depression) and behavioral (activity, visits to physicians) realms. In one controlled study of persons with moderately severe inflammatory rheumatoid arthritis participating in the ASMP, pain declined, self-efficacy grew and joint inflammation diminished over seven weeks (O'Leary, Shoor, Lorig, & Holman 1988). The latter suggested a biological effect of the ASMP on inflammation. However, measured immunological parameters did not change and the benefits were not sustained at four months. Therefore, at this time, there is no substantial evidence of a biological benefit of the ASMP. The results of ASMP and its evaluations indicate that health education for self-management, operating significantly through the vehicle of perceived self-efficacy to cope with the consequences of arthritis, results in reductions in pain, depression and dependence on medical care while improving participants' physical and social activities. These personal, social and financial benefits strongly imply that enhanced perceived self-efficacy is a vehicle through which major advantage for patients and for the health care system can be achieved simultaneously.

Table 3

Comparison of Changes Achieved by the Original and Revised Arthritis Self-Management Programs (ASMP)

	Original ASMP (N = 500)		Revised ASMP (N = 97)	
	Baseline Mean	Four Month Change	Baseline Mean	Four Month Change
Pain				
0-10 Scale	4.8	-12%	5.7	-18%*
Disability				
0-3 Scale	.7	-1%	.91	-10%**
Depression				
0-60 Scale	12.7	-8%	15.2	-16%*

Note. *p < .15; ** p < .05.

Table 4

Summary of Changes in Outcome Attributes in Two Groups of Participants at Four Months and Four Years After Start of the Arthritis Self-Management Course

	Group I (N = 224)		Group II (N = 177)	
Outcome Attribute	Four Months	Four Years	Four Months	Four Years
Pain[a]	-12%	-19%	-17%	-22%
Disability[b]	-3%	+9%	-4%	+8%
Depression[c]	-11%	-2%	-18%	-3%
Visits to physicians	-21%	-43%	-24%	-44%
Original self-efficacy measure	+7%	+17%	—	—
Final self-efficacy measure for pain	—	—	+12%	+34%
Final self-efficacy measure for other symptoms	—	—	+10%	+25%

Note. [a]Visual Analogue Scale (0-10); [b]Stanford Health Assessment Questionnaire (Scale 0-3) (Fries, Spitz, Kraines, & Holman, 1980); [c]Beck Depression Inventory (0-39) (Beck, Ward, Mendelson, Mock, & Erbaugh, 1961).

The precise mechanism whereby perceived self-efficacy exerts its effects on patients with arthritis or other chronic diseases is not known. The involved patients have been heterogenous with diverse disease and illness manifestations. Hence it is not possible to infer that a specific consequence of enhanced self-efficacy, such as handling snakes in the case of phobia, mediated the overall benefit. More likely, given the diversity of patients and manifestations, individual patients developed understandings and adopted practices which were pertinent to their particular situation. Such a general conclusion is consistent with what is known about self-efficacy from many different studies and settings. Perceived self-efficacy affects people's willingness to initiate change, the magnitude of the change achieved, and their persistence in the change. Because self-efficacy is also specific to beliefs and activities, it is reasonable that patients identify areas of self-management pertinent to them and develop a repertoire of relevant attitudes and skills. In this regard, it is very interesting that, in the ASMP studies, self-efficacy grew, pain remained improved and use of physician services remained reduced over four years while physical disability actually increased. A reasonable interpretation would hold that the successful use of self-management skills reinforced and enhanced perceived self-efficacy and sustained the benefits despite a worsening physical situation.

Summary

Chronic disease has replaced acute disease as the predominant form of disease in this country, and is the primary cause of disability. Because chronic disease can rarely be cured, its consequences extend out over time. Sound management of chronic disease and its consequences requires participation of patients and their families at most levels of health care from understanding the disease to applying management practices. Such participation, called self-management, requires a functioning partnership between the patient and the physician. To engage in effective self-management requires that the patient achieve new knowledge and master new skills. In turn, the new learning and skill development appears to be dependent upon a person's perceived self-efficacy in those realms. Perceived self-efficacy can be developed and enhanced through a variety of learning experiences. High and increasing levels of perceived self-efficacy to cope with the consequences of chronic disease are associated with improvement in symptoms, physical and emotional well-being and social activities. Thus perceived self-efficacy is an essential precondition for the appropriate management of chronic disease.

The present health care system was developed in an era when acute disease predominated, with concepts and structures adhering to the attributes of acute disease (Table 1). It can readily be argued that significant responsibility for the ineffectiveness and inefficiency in present health services arises from the discordance between a health care system designed to treat acute disease and the dominating prevalence of chronic disease. Designing health services which are more appropriate for chronic disease would be an essential element in resolving the health care crisis. The scope of such a design is beyond the limits of this chapter but, we argue, fostering and supporting self-management practices and developing the skills for them, would be an essential ingredient of any successful plan.

REFERENCES

Bandura, A. (1986). *Social foundations of thought and action: A social cognitive theory.* Englewood Cliffs, NJ: Prentice-Hall.

Bandura, A. (1991). Self-efficacy mechanism in physiological activation and health-promoting behavior. In J. Madden (Ed.), *Neurobiology of learning, emotion and affect* (pp. 229-270). New York: Raven Press.

Beck, A. T., Ward, C. H., Mendelson, M., Mock, J., & Erbaugh, J. (1961). An inventory for measuring depression. *Archives of General Psychiatry, 4,* 561-571.

Colvez, A., & Blanchet, M. (1981). Disability trends in the United States population 1966-76: Analysis of reported causes. *American Journal of Public Health, 71,* 464-471.

Engel, G. L. (1977). The need for a new medical model: A challenge for biomedicine. *Science, 196,* 129-136.

Fries, J. F., Spitz, P. W., Kraines, R. G., & Holman, H. R. (1980). Measurement of patient outcome in arthritis. *Arthritis and Rheumatism, 23,* 137-145.

Holman, H. R., Mazonson, P., & Lorig, K. (1989). Health education for self-management has significant early and sustained benefits in chronic arthritis. *Transactions Association of American Physicians, 102,* 204-208.

Holroyd, K. A., & Creer, T. L. (Eds.). (1986). *Self-management of chronic disease: Handbook of clinical interventions and research.* Athens, OH: Academic Press.

Lenker, S., Lorig, K., & Gallagher, D. (1984). Reasons for the lack of association between changes in health behavior and improved health status: An exploratory study. *Patient Education and Counseling, 6,* 69-72.

Lewis, F. M., & Daltroy, L. H. (1990). How causal explanations influence health behavior: Attribution theory. In K. Glanz, F. M. Lewis, & B. K. Rimer (Eds.), *Health behavior and health education theory research and practice* (pp. 90-114). San Francisco, CA: Jossey-Bass.

Lorig, K., Chastain, R., Ung, E., Shoor, S., & Holman, H. R. (1989). Development and evaluation of a scale to measure the perceived self-efficacy of people with arthritis. *Arthritis and Rheumatism, 32,* 37-44.

Lorig, K., Lubeck, D., Kraines, R. G., Seleznick, M., & Holman, H. R. (1985). Outcomes of self-help education for patients with arthritis. *Arthritis and Rheumatism, 28,* 680-685.

Lorig, K., Seleznick, M., Lubeck, D. H., Ung, E., Chastain, R. L., & Holman, H. R. (1989). The beneficial outcomes of the Arthritis Self-Management Course are inadequately explained by behavior change. *Arthritis and Rheumatism, 32,* 91-95.

O'Leary, A., Shoor, S., Lorig, K., Holman, H. (1988). A cognitive-behavioral treatment for rheumatoid arthritis. *Health Psychology, 7(6),* 527-544.

Rice, D. P., & Feldman, J. J. (1983). Living longer in the United States: Demographic changes and health needs of the elderly. *Milbank Quarterly, 61,* 362-395.

Rice, D. P., & LaPlante, M. P. (1988). *The economics and ethics of long-term care and disability*. Washington, DC: American Enterprise Institute for Public Policy Research.

Starr, P. (1982). *The social transformation of American medicine*. New York: Basic Books.

Verbrugge, L. M. (1984).   Longer life but worsening health?   Trends in health and mortality of middle-aged and older persons. *Milbank Quarterly, 62*, 475-519.

APPENDIX

ARTHRITIS SELF-EFFICACY SCALE

Self-Efficacy Pain Subscale

In the following questions, we'd like to know how your arthritis pain affects you. For each of the following questions, please circle the number which corresponds to your certainty that you can now perform the following tasks.

1. How certain are you that you can decrease your pain quite a bit?
2. How certain are you that you can continue most of your daily activities?
3. How certain are you that you can keep arthritis pain from interfering with your sleep?
4. How certain are you that you can make a small-to-moderate reduction in your arthritis pain by using methods other that taking extra medication?
5. How certain are you that you can make a large reduction in your arthritis pain by using methods other than taking extra medication?

Self-Efficacy Function Subscale

We would like to know how confident you are in performing certain daily activities. For each of the following questions, please circle the number which corresponds to your certainty that you can perform the tasks as of now, without assistive devices or help form another person.   Please consider what you routinely can do, not what would require a single extraordinary effort.

AS OF NOW, HOW CERTAIN ARE YOU THAT YOU CAN:

1. Walk 100 feet on flat ground in 20 seconds?
2. Walk 10 steps downstairs in 7 seconds?
3. Get out of an armless chair quickly, without using your hands for support?
4. Button and unbutton 3 medium-size buttons in a row in 12 seconds?
5. Cut 2 bite-size pieces of meat with a knife and fork in 8 seconds?
6. Turn an outdoor faucet all the way on and all the way off?
7. Scratch your upper back with both your right and left hands?
8. Get in and out of the passenger side of a car without assistance from another person and without physical aids?
9. Put on a long-sleeve front-opening shirt or blouse (without buttoning) in 8 seconds?

Self-Efficacy Other Symptoms Subscale

In the following questions, we'd like to know how you feel about your ability to control your arthritis. For each of the following questions, please circle the number which corresponds to the certainty that you can now perform the following activities or tasks.

1. How certain are you that you can control your fatigue?
2. How certain are you that you can regulate your activity so as to be active without aggravating your arthritis?
3. How certain are you that you can do something to help yourself feel better if you are feeling blue?
4. As compared with other people with arthritis like yours, how certain are you that you can manage arthritis pain during your daily activities?
5. How certain are you that you can manage your arthritis symptoms so that you can do the things you enjoy doing?
6. How certain are that you can deal with the frustration of arthritis?

Each question is followed by the scale:

10	20	30	40	50	60	70	80	90	100
very				moderately					very
uncertain				uncertain					certain

Each subscale is scored separately, by taking the mean of the subscale items. The pain and other symptoms scales can be scored separately or together. The function scale should not be combined with anything else. If one-fourth or less of the data are missing, the score is a mean of the completed data. If more than one-fourth of the data are missing, no score is calculated. (The authors invite others to use the scale and would appreciate being informed of the study results.)

SELF-EFFICACY EXPECTANCIES IN CHRONIC OBSTRUCTIVE PULMONARY DISEASE REHABILITATION

Michelle T. Toshima, Robert M. Kaplan, and Andrew L. Ries

The role of self-efficacy in the rehabilitation of adult patients with chronic obstructive pulmonary disease (COPD) was examined. One hundred and nineteen COPD patients were randomly assigned to either a comprehensive rehabilitation program or to an education control group. Each program lasted two months. Patients were evaluated on pulmonary function, exercise, treadmill endurance, and psychosocial measures. These tests were administered prior to the intervention, immediately following the intervention, and one year after the start of the program. The treadmill endurance walk and the psychosocial measures were also administered six months after the start of the program. Self-efficacy was measured using a questionnaire that evaluated expectancies to engage in specific activities that reflect the functional disabilities often associated with COPD. Validity of the self-efficacy construct was demonstrated through systematic correlations with both pulmonary function and exercise variables. Although rehabilitation patients demonstrated significant improvements in treadmill performance, a trend toward improved self-efficacy for walking was non-significant. Further, the modest improvement in self-efficacy for walking did not generalize to similar behaviors. Patients with high initial self-efficacy scores for walking demonstrated the greatest endurance on the treadmill. However self-efficacy expectancies did not predict other health status outcomes. We conclude that physiological feedback is a strong source of self-efficacy expectation. These expectancies might be modified by performance accomplishment. However, continuing physiologic feedback provides a significant obstacle for modifying self-efficacy in chronically ill patients.

Recent advances in health psychology research have demonstrated the importance of cognitive variables in explaining and predicting health behaviors. Social learning theory and value-expectancy theory form the basis for several cognitive constructs that have been useful in explaining diverse forms of health behavior such as smoking cessation, pain management, and exercise (see review O'Leary, 1985). Bandura's (1977) self-efficacy theory, in particular, has received substantial empirical support for its explanatory role in the therapeutic change process and maintenance of treatment gains in smoking cessation (Baer, Holt, & Lichtenstein, 1986; Devins & Edwards, 1988) the behavioral treatment of pain (Dolce, 1987; Reese, 1982); exercise following uncomplicated myocardial infarction (Ewart, Taylor, Reese, & DeBusk, 1983); and exercise training for patients with chronic lung diseases (Kaplan, Atkins, & Reinsch, 1984).

Self-appraisal of capabilities can be altered in a number of ways, including mastery experiences, observing models, accepting social persuasion, and alteration of physiological state (Bandura, 1977). The most effective way of influencing self-efficacy expectancies is through mastery experiences (Bandura, 1977). However, self-efficacy expectancies may develop through the other channels without direct experiences of a particular behavior. In this chapter, we consider the importance of physiological feedback on self-efficacy expectancies and subsequent task performance in patients with chronic obstructive pulmonary disease (COPD). Before proceeding, a brief overview of COPD and the role of rehabilitation in the management of patients with this disease will be presented.

CHRONIC OBSTRUCTIVE PULMONARY DISEASE AND PULMONARY REHABILITATION RESEARCH

Chronic obstructive pulmonary disease (COPD) is a disorder characterized by persistent expiratory airflow obstruction (American Thoracic Society, 1987). The diseases most often categorized as COPD include emphysema, chronic bronchitis, and irreversible asthma. Many patients exhibit features of more than one specific disease process. Although the etiology and severity of these diseases vary, the common clinical problem is impaired airflow which results in the symptom of shortness of breath.

COPD is a major health problem in the United States today; current estimates reveal that 13.5 million Americans have COPD (Higgins, 1989). This condition is the fifth leading cause of death in the U.S. and accounts for approximately 71,000 deaths per year (National Center for Health Statistics, 1988). In addition, the death rate is increasing rapidly at a rate of 1.4% per year, second only to AIDS as the most rapidly increasing common cause of death in the United States (Lenfant, 1988). Since respiratory diseases are generally considered to be of greater importance as causes of morbidity and disability than mortality, the economic consequences of COPD are great. COPD has been linked to an estimated 4.7 million hospital days per year and 32.7 million physician office visits per year, approximately 5% of total physician visits (Feinleib et al., 1989). Direct and indirect costs for COPD were estimated to be $4.5 billion in 1972, $19 billion in 1979, and $27 billion in 1982 (Lenfant, 1982). Recent reports suggest that 1.14 million years of potential life are lost to COPD each year (Kaplan, Atkins, & Ries, 1985). The total mortality rate and years of potential life lost rate are higher for men than for women and higher for whites than for other races. These findings most likely reflect previous differences in smoking patterns among these groups (Morbidity and Mortality Weekly Report, 1986).

COPD has a profound impact upon the daily lives of afflicted patients. Dyspnea, the clinical symptom of shortness of breath, interferes with daily activities, often restricting patients to their homes. One of the largest and most detailed studies on the quality of life of COPD patients was reported by McSweeney and colleagues (McSweeney, Grant, Heaton, Adams, & Timms, 1982). They studied 203 patients suffering from COPD, and concluded that these people were significantly more impaired than a matched control group in ambulation, self-care, social interaction, and recreational activities. Depression and dissatisfaction with life were also significantly more common in the COPD patient.

The progressive course of COPD is often expressed in terms of functional loss, impairment of gas exchange, and structural changes in the lungs. For example, deterioration in forced expiratory volume in one second (FEV_1) for healthy persons is estimated to be 20 to 30 mL/year. Deterioration in FEV_1 for COPD patients approximates 40 to 80 mL/year (Morbidity and Mortality Weekly Report, 1986). Lung dysfunction often causes symptoms that result in a sedentary lifestyle which further erodes the patient's functional capacity. Thus, the pulmonary patient often falls victim to a cyclical downward pattern of increasing disability and dyspnea. The patient who experiences exertional dyspnea may stop or restrict activities that produce the uncomfortable and frightening symptom of dyspnea. Prolonged restriction of activities can lead to the deconditioning of diaphragmatic muscles and inefficient oxygen utilization and ventilation. In order to interrupt this cyclical increase in dyspnea and the resulting decrease in functional ability, pulmonary rehabilitation has been promoted as an intervention strategy (Bass, Whitcomb, & Forman, 1970; Mertens, Shephard, & Kavanagh, 1978). A major component of pulmonary rehabilitation is a structured exercise program. In these programs, patients exercise on a treadmill under close medical supervision. Maximum exercise levels for COPD patients can be predicted from just a few variables (Carlson, Ries, & Kaplan, 1991) and some patients can exercise at levels close to their maximum (Punzal, Ries, Kaplan, & Prewitt, 1991). However, since exercise causes shortness of breath, many patients avoid physical activity. Rehabilitation programs encourage regular, safe exercise programs that are generalized to home settings.

Rehabilitation programs for the management of COPD have expanded substantially in recent years and continue to gain momentum. The primary goal of most programs is to restore the patient to the highest possible level of functioning. Results from previous studies suggest that participation in a pulmonary rehabilitation program offers numerous positive outcomes for COPD patients (Dudley, Glaser, Jorgenson, & Logan, 1980; Moser, Bokinsky, Savage, Archibald, & Hansen, 1980). These benefits include improved work tolerance and work efficiency, improvement in activities of daily living, reduced ventilatory demand, decreased by dyspnea, and a reduction in hospital days without any appreciable change in pulmonary function. These outcomes have been documented using various research designs and training programs.

SELF-EFFICACY IN COPD REHABILITATION

Rehabilitation programs for COPD patients emphasize a systematic increase in activity levels through a structured exercise program. A major component to many exercise programs is treadmill walking in combination with free walking. The treadmill exercise experiences in rehabilitation programs may affect self-efficacy expectancies through multiple sources of information. Many COPD patients may have low self-efficacy because of their preconceptions of pulmonary deficiencies and limitations. Years of experience with a chronic illness can result in negative symptoms such as shortness of breath, fatigue, and pain. These symptoms become more apparent when the patient attempts activities such as walking. The more prolonged or strenuous the activity, the greater the increase in distressing symptoms. A strong preconception of limitations and impairment increases the focus on negative physiological reactions to exertion. Therefore, it is likely that patients who focus on their physical capabilities as they engage in physically demanding tasks will judge their pulmonary functioning as stronger than those patients who selectively focus on the discomforting symptomatology. Providing patients with ongoing feedback about their performance as they encounter more challenging physical demands, can shift the focus away from the negative physiological feedback to the more positive aspects of their capabilities. Therefore, judgments of efficacy will vary depending on how patients interpret their symptoms during a physically demanding task.

Many patients with COPD often experience moderate to severe discomforting symptoms with even minimal exertion. For these patients, their physiological state may have an even greater impact on self-efficacy judgments, particularly for behaviors taxing the respiratory system. Self-efficacy theory assumes that people rely on inferences from their physiological state in judging their capabilities. Thus, for activities involving strength and stamina, patients with COPD may judge or interpret their shortness of breath, fatigue, and pain as signs of physical inefficacy.

This chapter considers the validity of the self-efficacy construct as well as its function in promoting and maintaining change in patients with COPD. In addition, the association between sources of self-efficacy information, in particular physiological feedback and activity levels, will be evaluated in a clinical trial of rehabilitation for patients with COPD. A test of the validity of the self-efficacy construct is provided by anchoring self-efficacy expectancies, the hypothesized mediator, to independently measurable variables of pulmonary function such as forced expiratory volume in one second (FEV_1), residual volume/total lung capacity (RV/TLC), single breath diffusing capacity (DLCO), exercise tolerance as measured by oxygen uptake at maximum exercise (VO_2max), and maximum workload which can be estimated as metabolic equivalents (METS max). Postulated mediators, in this case self-efficacy expectancies, are not directly observable. Nevertheless, theoretically self-efficacy expectancies should be associated with several observable indicators, in this case physiological parameters of lung functioning.

This chapter considers self-efficacy expectancies at two levels. We suggest that self-efficacy in untreated patients is largely determined by physiological feedback. Thus, without intervention, the primary source of information will be disease severity. However, we also expect performance accomplishment to override physiological feedback. Specifically, patients who participate in a rehabilitation program designed to enhance activity should improve in efficacy expectation despite their physiological status.

CLINICAL TRIAL OF PULMONARY REHABILITATION

Method

Subjects

Over a one-year period, 350 patients with COPD were screened for study; 129 met entry criteria and were randomized into either a comprehensive pulmonary rehabilitation program or an education control group. Ten patients dropped out prior to treatment, leaving 119 patients who received the intervention. There were no differences between those patients who dropped out prior to the intervention and those who remained in the study. The subjects were 32 female and 87 male patients. This female/male ratio approximates the distribution of COPD in females and males in the general population. In order to be included, the patient had to meet the following criteria:

1. Clinical diagnosis of COPD, mild to severe, confirmed by history, physical examination, spirometry, arterial blood gases, and chest roentgenograms. Patients with emphysema, chronic bronchitis, or asthmatic bronchitis were accepted. Patients with primarily acute, reversible airway disease (asthma) without chronic airflow obstruction were not accepted.

2. Patients were required to be stable on an acceptable medical regimen. If the treatment was considered inappropriate or the patient was unstable, the primary physician was contacted and the treatment regimen adjusted prior to inclusion in the study.

3. Patients were excluded if they had other significant disabling lung disease, serious heart problems, or other medical conditions that would interfere with their participation.

Assessment. Each patient underwent pulmonary function tests, exercise tests, treadmill endurance walks, and psychosocial measures prior to the intervention (baseline), immediately following the intervention (two months) and one year from the start of the program (twelve months). A six-month assessment was also conducted but involved only the treadmill endurance walk and the administration of the psychosocial measures. Due to the physical demands of the pulmonary function, exercise, and endurance walk tests, patients were scheduled for the tests on several occasions over a five-day period. Typically, patients were given the pulmonary function tests in the hospital laboratory on the first day, the exercise tests in the hospital laboratory on the third day, and the treadmill endurance walk and psychosocial measures in the rehabilitation building on the fifth day.

Certified cardiopulmonary respiratory technicians administered the pulmonary function tests and exercise tests in the laboratory. During the exercise test, a pulmonary physician was also present to ensure the safety of the patient. The endurance walk tests and the psychosocial measures were administered by trained psychology graduate students who had current cardio-pulmonary resuscitation certification. In some instances where the patient required continuous electrocardiogram monitoring during the endurance walk test, a pulmonary physician and registered nurse observed for arrythmias and/or premature ventricular contractions. The physicians, technicians, and graduate students were blind to the group assignment of the patients.

Physiological Measures

Descriptions of selected physiological and psychosocial variables examined in this chapter are presented below.

Pulmonary function tests. Pulmonary function tests included:

1. Spirometry to determine the following parameters: (a) Vital Capacity (VC)—the maximum volume of air that can be expelled from fully inflated lungs; (b) Forced Expiratory Volume in one second (FEV_1); and (c) FEV_1/VC ratio.

2. Plethysmographic measurements: (a) Functional Residual Capacity (FRC); (b) Airway Resistance (RAW); (c) Residual Volume (RV); (d) Total Lung Capacity (TLC); and (e) RV/TLC ratio.

3. Single-breath diffusing capacity for carbon monoxide (DLCO).

4. Maximal inspiratory and expiratory pressures to assess respiratory muscle strength. Although pulmonary rehabilitation does not typically lead to changes in standard measures of pulmonary function, it was important to monitor these parameters in order to follow the progression of the patient's disease.

Exercise tests. The laboratory exercise tests included: (a) an incremental, symptom-limited exercise test to the maximal tolerable level on a treadmill, and (b) a treadmill test to define the steady-state walking level for subsequent training sessions. In the incremental exercise test, the work load was increased at one-minute intervals by 0.5 miles per hour up to 3.0 miles per hour with further work increments made by increasing elevation by 2% to a maximum, symptom-limited level. This multiple-stage test assessed the maximal exercise tolerance. In the steady-state exercise test, the work load was maintained at a constant level for a predetermined period of time to allow the subject to reach steady-state for the variables of interest. This test was used to make measurements at defined levels for subsequent exercise training. After the incremental exercise test and an appropriate rest, patients performed the steady-state treadmill test at the highest possible level to determine a level for subsequent endurance walk testing and exercise training.

During the tests, patients breathed through a low-resistance breathing valve; expired gases were analyzed continuously for measurements of oxygen uptake (VO_2), carbon dioxide elimination (VCO_2), expired minute ventilation (V_e), and other related variables. Metabolic equivalent (METS) was estimated at the maximal treadmill speed and grade as a measure of exercise workload. During all exercise tests an electrocardiogram with a single (modified V_5) lead was used to measure heart rate and monitor for arrhythmias or ischemia. Blood pressure was measured at regular three-minute intervals. Arterial blood was sampled from an indwelling radial artery catheter for measurement of arterial oxygen pressure (P_aO_2), arterial carbon dioxide pressure (P_aCO_2), pH, and alveolar-arterial oxygen gradient ($P(A-a)O_2$) An ear oximeter was used to monitor continuous arterial oxygen saturation (S_aO_2).

Patients who demonstrated severe resting ($P_aO_2 < 55mmHg$) or exercise hypoxemia ($P_aO_2 < 50mmHg$ or $S_aO_2 < 85\%$) were given supplemental oxygen and repeated the treadmill exercise test on oxygen to define a safe level for subsequent exercise training. Ratings of perceived breathlessness and perceived exertion were assessed after each exercise test using standard scales adapted from Borg (1982). Patients were asked to rate their degree of breathlessness and fatigue on a scale from 0 to 10, with 0 representing *nothing at all* and 10 representing *the maximum ever experienced.*

Treadmill Endurance Walk Test. Based on the maximal, symptom-limited graded exercise test, each patient was given an exercise prescription which approximates maximal sustained exercise tolerance levels. The target rates for the individualized exercise prescriptions ranged from a treadmill speed of 0.6 mph at 0% grade to 3.0 mph at 16% grade. The endurance walk test was designed to assess the patient's endurance for walking, the type of exercise used in the rehabilitation program. Prior to endurance walk testing, heart rate, respiratory rate, and blood pressure were recorded with the patient seated. Those patients requiring supplemental oxygen waited for ten minutes with the oxygen prior to being tested. All patients walked at 1.0 mph for two minutes (0.6 mph for patients with that target speed). For patients whose prescribed target rate was higher than 1.0 mph, after two minutes the examiner asked the patient if they felt they could walk faster. If the patient replied yes or maybe, the treadmill speed was increased to a level 0.5 mph (or 2 to 4% grade) less than the target speed/grade. If the patient did not feel he or she could walk faster, or if the target rate was less than or equal to 1.0 mph, the initial speed was maintained. After two more minutes, if the target rate had not yet been reached, the patient was once again asked if he or she felt they could walk faster. If the response was positive, the treadmill speed was increased to the target rate. Once the individualized target rate was achieved, all patients were instructed to walk as long as possible. If the patient walked for 20 minutes at the target rate, the treadmill speed was increased another 0.5 mph (or 2 to 4% grade). A maximum endurance walk protocol was achieved if the patient walked 20 minutes at the target rate and 10 minutes at a higher rate (i.e., 30 minutes maximum test). During the entire endurance walk, the patient's blood pressure was monitored every three minutes. The test was stopped when a patient stated that he/she was unable to walk any longer. In addition, the examiner stopped the test for any of the following conditions: (a) chest pain; (b) dizziness; (c) excessive rise in blood pressure (> 250 mmHg systolic or > 130 mmHg diastolic pressure); or (d) excessive fall in blood pressure (< 20 mmHg in systolic pressure). At the completion of the test, sitting pulse rate, respiratory rate, and blood pressure were measured. Symptoms of perceived breathlessness and fatigue were rated after the first two minutes on the treadmill and at the end of the test, using a 10-point scale (Borg, 1982). The examiner then recorded the reasons for stopping the test (e.g., dyspnea, chest pain, maximum protocol).

Psychosocial Measures

All patients completed a battery of psychosocial measures at baseline, two months, six months, and twelve months. The battery included the following measures:

Self-Efficacy Questionnaire. The self-efficacy questionnaire used in this study was constructed and used in a previous study by Kaplan, Atkins, and Reinsch (1984) to demonstrate that specific rather than generalized expectancies mediate behavior changes in patients with COPD. The self-efficacy questionnaire was adapted from self-efficacy scales used to measure levels of capability to engage in activities that imposed stress on the heart for patients with uncomplicated myocardial infarction (Ewart et al., 1983). The self-efficacy questionnaire used in this study was modified to more accurately measure the functional disabilities associated with chronic obstructive pulmonary disease. The questionnaire consists of a list of seven behaviors that require physical and/or emotional stamina. The seven scales represent activities progressively more dissimilar to the target behavior of walking. Within each of the seven scales is a series of brief statements describing progressively more difficult performance requirements. For example, the scale for walking includes the following statements: walk 1 block (approximately 5 minutes), walk 2 blocks (10 minutes), walk 3 blocks (15 minutes) ... walk 3 miles (90 minutes). The scale for walking has nine items representing unequal intervals of increasing difficulty. For each item, the patient rated the degree of confidence or strength of their expectation to perform that activity on a 100-point probability scale, ranging in 10-point intervals from 0 (complete uncertainty) to 100 (complete certainty). The seven scales included in the measurement of self-efficacy expectancies are listed in the Appendix. The scale scores on the self-efficacy questionnaire reflect the highest level that the patient expressed 100% confidence they could perform or tolerate the behavior.

Quality of Well-Being Scale. The Quality of Well-Being (QWB) scale is a comprehensive measure of health-related quality of life that includes several components. First, it obtains observable levels of functioning at a point of time. The levels of functioning are obtained from three separate scales: mobility, physical activity, and social activity. Second, symptomatic complaints and disturbances are noted. Each patient is classified according to the symptom or problem that he or she finds most undesirable. Then, the observed level of function and subjective symptomatic complaint are weighted by preference or the desirability of the state on a scale ranging from 0 (for dead) to 1.0 (for optimum function). The weights are obtained from independent samples of judges who rate the desirability of the observable health status. This system has been used extensively in a variety of medical and health services research applications (Kaplan & Anderson, 1988). In addition, specific validity and reliability studies using this measure for COPD patients have been published (Kaplan, Atkins, & Timms, 1984). These studies demonstrate that the QWB scale is sensitive to relatively minor changes in health status and that it is correlated with a variety of physical and functional measures of health status.

Centers for Epidemiologic Studies Depression Scale (CES-D). Depression was measured using the CES-D scale. The CES-D scale is a general measure of depressive symptoms that has been used extensively in epidemiologic studies (Weissman, Sholomskas, Pottenger, Prusoff, & Locke, 1977). The scale includes twenty items and taps dimensions of depressed mood, feelings of guilt and worthlessness, appetite loss, sleep disturbance, and energy level. These items are assumed to represent all of the major components of depressive symptomatology. Sixteen of the symptoms are worded negatively, while the other four are worded positively to avoid the possibility of patterned responses. The patient is asked to report how often they experienced a particular "symptom" during the past week on a four-point scale: 0 (*rarely or none of the time—less than 1 day*), 1 (*some or a little of the time—1 to 2 days*), 2 (*occasionally or a moderate amount of time— 3 to 4 days*), 3 (*most or all of the time—5 to 7 days*). The responses to the four positive items are reverse scored and then the total sum of the responses is derived. Scores on the CES-D scale can range from 0 to 60 with scores greater than 18 suggestive of clinically significant levels of depression. The CES-D scale has been found to have high internal consistency and test-retest reliability (Radloff, 1977). It has also been documented to be highly correlated to other standardized depression scales (Weissman et al., 1977). Eaton and Kessler (1981) have presented evidence for the reliability and validity of this measure.

Group Comparisons of Baseline Measures

As described in the previous section, the patients were randomly assigned to either a rehabilitation or an education contro group. Patients in the rehabilitation group participated in an outpatient rehabilitation program consisting of education about their disease, physical and respiratory care instruction, psychosocial support, and supervised exercise training, while patients in the education control group received information about their disease through a series of videotape and lecture presentations.

There were no significant differences between patients in the rehabilitation or education control group on baseline measures of self-efficacy ratings, treadmill performance, and other psychosocial measures including Quality of Well-Being score, number of illness symptoms endorsed, depression, and subjective ratings of fatigue and dyspnea during the treadmill endurance walk. These group comparisons are presented in Table 1.

Table 1

Group Comparisons of Variables at Initial Evaluation

Variable	Rehabilitation Mean	SD	Education Mean	SD	F
FEV_1	1.39	0.66	1.44	0.62	1.12
RV/TLC	60.01	10.80	61.22	10.44	1.07
DLCO	14.17	7.45	14.01	6.83	1.19
VO_2max	1.24	0.51	1.24	0.54	1.12
Treadmill endurance	12.37	8.36	11.79	7.97	1.10
QWB	0.6656	0.0960	0.6523	0.067	2.08
CES-D	14.02	8.74	15.34	10.03	1.32
Perceived dyspnea	0.49	2.19	4.52	2.09	1.10
Perceived fatigue	4.28	2.23	4.25	2.17	1.06
SE-Walk	3.70	3.22	4.11	3.32	1.06
SE-Climb	2.11	1.40	2.08	1.51	1.16
SE-Lift	4.07	2.93	3.85	2.96	1.02
SE-Exert	2.30	1.16	1.94	1.25	1.16
SE-Push	2.81	1.14	2.55	1.33	1.35
SE-Stress	2.52	1.80	2.35	1.84	1.04
SE-Anger7	2.51	1.88	2.08	1.80	1.10

Note. SE = self-efficacy.

Results

Part 1: Efficacy and Physiological Feedback in Untreated Patients

In order to evaluate the relationship of baseline self-efficacy judgments with baseline physiological and psychosocial parameters, the self-efficacy scores of all patients were partitioned into tertiles, reflecting those patients with the lowest, middle and highest scores. A series of analyses of variance tests were then conducted. In these analyses, the efficacy tertiles for walking, climbing, lifting, pushing, exertion, stress, and anger served as independent variables. A selected group of pulmonary function, exercise, and psychosocial assessment variables were the dependent variables. The pulmonary function test variables (including FEV_1, RV/TLC, and DLCO) and the exercise test variables (including METSmax, VO_2max, and treadmill endurance) were selected as representative measures of lung disease severity and exercise tolerance, respectively. Quality of Well-Being and depression scores were the psychosocial variables selected.

The analyses suggest that self-efficacy expectancies are significantly influenced by physiological state, particularly if the patient has had little or no mastery experiences with the task. The univariate F values for the associations between the pulmonary function test, exercise test, and psychosocial variables and self-efficacy expectancies for each category are shown in Table 2. Figure 1 summarizes the relationship between pulmonary function test variables, FEV_1, RV/TLC, and DLCO, and self-efficacy expectancies for patients by lowest, middle, and highest tertiles for each efficacy category. As predicted, the self-efficacy measures reflecting a physical demand or task (e.g., walk, climb, lift, push, exert) were significantly related to the pulmonary function variables. The only exception was the non-significant relationship between RV/TLC and self-efficacy expectancies for the push category, though the trend was in the expected direction. Similarly, Figure 2 summarizes the relationship between exercise test variables, VO_2max and treadmill endurance, and tertiles of self-efficacy expectancies for each efficacy category. As demonstrated with the pulmonary function measures, the exercise variables were also significantly related to the self-efficacy measures reflecting a physical demand or task. Thus, there was a highly significant linear relationship between the physical self-efficacy measures (e.g., walk, climb, lift, exert, push) and the pulmonary function and exercise test variables. The relationship between the pulmonary function and exercise test measures and the self-efficacy judgments for stress and anger, on the other hand, were not systematically related.

In contrast to the systematic relationships observed with the pulmonary function and exercise test variables, the relationships between the psychosocial variables, QWB, CES-D, and Treadmill, and tertiles of self-efficacy expectancies for each efficacy category were not as systematic. Figure 3 summarizes the relationship between psychosocial variables and self-efficacy tertiles for each efficacy category. The Quality of Well-Being scale much like the psychological and exercise test variables was significantly related to tertiles of self-efficacy involving a physical demand. The CES-D scale, a scale in which higher scores indicate more depression, had significant linear relationships with self-efficacy categories measuring both a physical and emotional demand. It was not significantly related to self-efficacy for lifting, pushing, or tolerating stress. Interestingly, the self-efficacy measures reflecting an emotional demand, in this case, stress and anger, were not systematically related to any of the pulmonary function or exercise test variables, nor to most of the psychosocial variables.

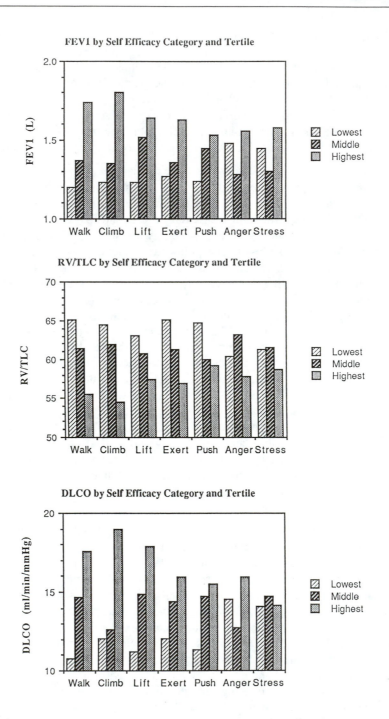

Figure 1 Relationship between pulmonary function measures (FEV$_1$, RV/TLC, & DLCO) and self-efficacy.

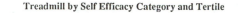

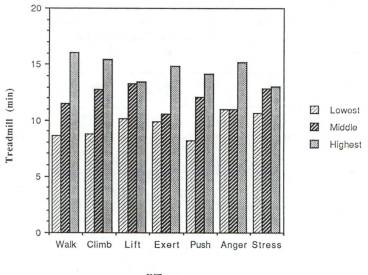

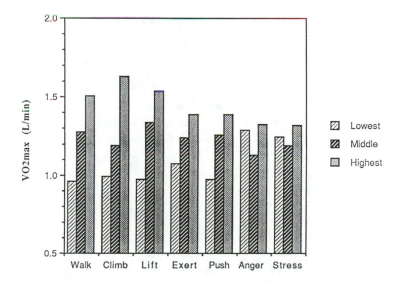

Figure 2 Relationship between exercise test variables (treadmill endurance & VO₂MAX) with self-efficacy tertiles for each efficacy category.

Table 2

Analysis of Variance Values for Pulmonary Function Test, Exercise Test, and
Psychosocial Variables by Self-Efficacy Tertiles for Each Efficacy Category

Efficacy	Pulmonary Function Test Variables					
	RV/TLC		FEV_1		DLCO	
	F	p	F	p	F	p
Walk	9.96	0.01	8.13	0.01	10.80	0.01
Climb	10.72	0.01	9.19	0.01	13.20	0.01
Lift	3.02	0.05	4.90	0.01	10.73	0.01
Exert	6.55	0.01	3.38	0.04	2.94	0.06
Push	2.32	n.s.	1.54	n.s.	2.83	n.s.
Anger	2.32	n.s.	1.73	n.s.	1.78	n.s.
Stress	1.59	n.s.	1.63	n.s.	.10	n.s.

Efficacy	Exercise Test Variables			
	VO_2max		Treadmill	
	F	p	F	p
Walk	13.11	0.01	10.11	0.01
Climb	18.74	0.01	7.99	0.01
Lift	15.99	0.01	2.29	n.s.
Exert	3.64	0.03	5.08	0.01
Push	5.25	0.01	4.47	0.01
Anger	1.52	n.s.	3.12	0.05
Stress	0.57	n.s.	1.13	n.s.

Efficacy	Psychosocial Variables			
	QWB		CES-D	
	F	p	F	p
Walk	4.59	0.01	2.67	0.07
Climb	7.61	0.01	3.36	0.04
Lift	3.14	0.05	1.94	n.s.
Exert	0.29	0.01	4.97	0.01
Push	11.78	0.01	0.15	n.s.
Anger	0.46	n.s.	7.40	0.01
Stress	1.59	n.s.	1.54	n.s.

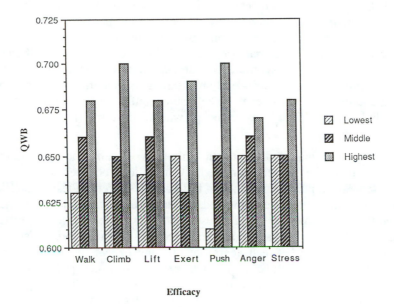

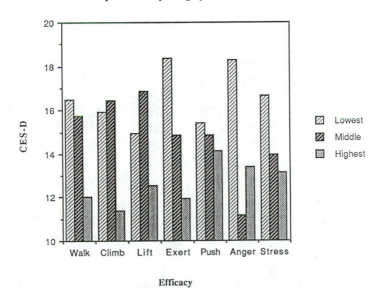

Figure 3 Relationship between psychosocial variables (QWB, CES-D) and self-efficacy for each efficacy category.

Although self-efficacy expectancies are not directly observable, the results suggest that the efficacy expectancies are anchored to physiological variables which, in turn, are associated with observable levels of behavior. Thus, the self-efficacy expectancies have observable correlates other than the behaviors they presumably govern. These data provide evidence for the validity of the self-efficacy construct. Validity inferences are supported by the anchoring of self-efficacy expectancies to independently measurable indicators, in this case, physiological and exercise parameters. The results confirm that external factors are indeed linked to efficacy expectancies which, in turn, may be linked to observable behaviors.

The degree and nature of the relationship between self-efficacy expectancies and behavior can be further quantified. Correlations between aggregate self-efficacy scores and pulmonary function test variables, exercise test variables, and psychosocial variables were computed. Results of the correlational analyses revealed that the pulmonary function test, and the exercise test were significantly correlated with most of the aggregate perceived self-efficacy scores. Table 3 displays the relationship between aggregate efficacy expectation scores for each category and pulmonary function test and exercise test, and psychosocial variables respectively. High scores on RV/TLC and CES-D reflect diagnostically poorer status. Thus, negative relationships of these variables and efficacy expectancies were expected.

Table 3
Correlation Among Mean Pulmonary Function Test, Exercise Test, and Psychosocial Variables and Aggregate Self-Efficacy Scores for Each Efficacy Category

	Self-Efficacy Category						
	Walk	Climb	Lift	Exert	Push	Stress	Anger
FEV1	.42**	.35**	.17*	.18*	.11	.04	.04
RV/TLC	-.44**	-.39**	-.28**	-.17*	-.15*	-.08	-.08
DLCO	.46**	.37**	.18**	.34**	.17*	.05	.06
VO2max	.50**	.41**	.15**	.45**	.28**	.02	.03
Treadmill Endurance	.42**	.35**	.27**	.19**	.27**	.17*	.18*
QWB	.31**	.42**	.31**	.18*	.42**	.09	.09
CES-D	-.24**	-.19*	-.27**	-.07	-.10	-.20*	-.24**

Note. *$p < .05$; **$p < .01$.

Although the magnitude of many of the associations are significant, of most interest is the nature of the relationships between the variables and the efficacy categories. For all physiological variables, the efficacy category for walking was most highly correlated, closely followed by climbing and/or lifting. Moreover, stress and anger efficacy categories were consistently least correlated with the physiological measures. In contrast, the pattern of associations between the psychosocial variables and efficacy expectancies for the various efficacy categories did not follow the pattern of association found between physiological variables and efficacy expectancies. Self-efficacy for walking, climbing, and lifting were not necessarily the most highly correlated with the psychosocial measures. In addition, self-efficacy ratings for stress and anger were not consistently the least correlated with the psychosocial measures.

Part 2: The Effects of Performance Accomplishment Upon Efficacy Expectations.

Numerous studies in the health behavior change literature suggest that self-efficacy expectancies play a crucial role in the initiation and maintenance of behavior change. Uniformly across studies of change in health-related behavior, including smoking cessation, pain management, and exercise compliance, post-treatment self-efficacy judgments have been found to be associated with outcome. In general, enhanced self-efficacy perceptions have been associated with greater behavior change and maintenance of gains over time. Despite the substantial literature base supporting this general finding, only a select few have examined self-efficacy expectancies across groups receiving different health behavior change interventions (Blittner, Goldberg, & Merbaum, 1978; Chambliss & Murray, 1979; Kaplan, Atkins, & Reinsch, 1984; Nicki, Remington, & MacDonald, 1985; Reese, 1982). This investigation not only addresses the role of self-efficacy expectancies on outcome, but addresses changes in self-efficacy judgments as a result of participation in a rehabilitation program.

Efficacy expectancies are based on four major sources of information: mastery experiences, observing models, accepting social persuasion, and alteration of physiological state (Bandura, 1977). Successful experiences performing a behavior (performance accomplishment) are the most potent influence on self-efficacy expectancies. In this investigation, it was hypothesized that the rehabilitation patients would have successful experiences walking on the treadmill, as well as, free walking on their own; thus, raising their efficacy expectancies for walking. Once efficacy expectancies for walking are established, it was predicted that enhanced efficacy for walking would generalize to other similar behaviors as demonstrated in a study by Kaplan, Atkins, and Reinsch (1984). Thus, it was predicted that improvements in walking behavior, and subsequent increases in self-efficacy expectancies for walking, transfer to similar behaviors, and, to a lesser degree, to behaviors dissimilar to those on which the intervention was based.

The effect of the rehabilitation program on efficacy expectancies was evaluated in several ways. First, it was predicted that for patients in the rehabilitation group, self-efficacy expectancies for walking would significantly improve following participation in the rehabilitation program, while no increases were expected for the education control group. Secondly, for patients in the rehabilitation group, it was proposed that improvements in self-efficacy expectancies for walking would generalize to efficacy expectancies for other behaviors, with tasks most similar to walking expected to have greater increases in self-efficacy expectancies than tasks dissimilar to walking. This gradient of generalizability was not expected to emerge in the education control group. Self-efficacy expectancies were also predicted to be associated with health status outcome measures.

For both groups, strict attendance records were kept to ensure that all patients completed their respective programs. All patients were required to make up any sessions they had missed. Table 4 shows the status of patient participation at the various assessment periods. Two months after enrollment, 104 patients had complete follow-ups, 4 patients had partial follow-ups, and 11 patients were unavailable for testing. There was a 91% follow-up rate at two months, 89% at six months, and 79% at twelve months. Attrition rates for the two groups were not significantly different, but by the twelve-month assessment, twice as many education control patients than rehabilitation patients were unavailable for follow-up.

Table 4

Patient Follow-Up Status by Group at Baseline, Two-Month, Six-Month, and Twelve-Month Evaluations

	Number of Patients							
	Baseline		2 Months		6 Months		12 Months	
Status	R	E	R	E	R	E	R	E
Complete follow-up	57	62	48	56	50	53	46	42
Partial follow-up	0	0	3	1	1	2	3	3
No follow-up (totals)	0	0	6	5	6	7	8	17
Deaths	0	0	0	0	1	0	2	2
Drop	0	0	1	1	2	4	2	5
Other	0	0	5	4	3	3	4	10
% of patients tested	100		91		89		79	

Note. R = rehabilitation, E = education control.

At both two-month and six-month post-intervention assessments, patients in the rehabilitation group performed significantly better on the treadmill endurance walk than education control patients as reported by Toshima, Kaplan, and Ries (1990). Furthermore, analysis of twelve-month follow-up data demonstrate continued superior performance on the endurance walk by the rehabilitation patients, though the effect was not significant. These effects are shown graphically in Figure 4.

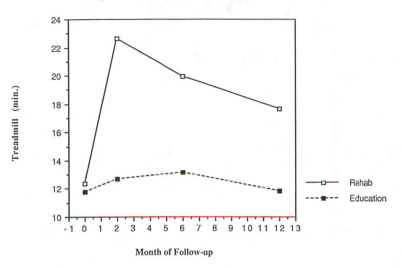

Figure 4 Comparison of treadmill endurance for rehabilitation and education patients over 12 months.

Despite significantly improved treadmill performance by the rehabilitation patients at two-, six-, and twelve-month follow-up visits, self-efficacy rating scores for walking were not statistically significant between the patient groups at any of the three post-intervention assessments. Figure 5 shows self-efficacy rating scores for both groups from baseline through twelve-month assessments. Although the self-efficacy ratings between groups were not statistically significant, the pattern of scores was in the predicted direction.

There were significant differences between groups for subjective ratings of fatigue and dyspnea that were measured during the treadmill endurance walk. Not only did the patients in the rehabilitation group walk longer and report somewhat increased self-efficacy in their ability to do so, they also reported less fatigue and dyspnea at the end of the endurance walk test. Repeated measures analysis of variance for ratings of fatigue revealed significant main effects for group $[F(1,67) = 5.21, p < .05]$ and time $[F(1,67) = 5.73, p < .01]$ and a significant group by time interaction $[F(3,201) = 3.15, p < .05]$. For ratings of dyspnea, repeated measures analysis of variance revealed a significant main effect for time $[F(1,67) = 7.05, p < .01]$ and a significant group by time interaction $[F(3,201) = 6.77, p < .01]$. These differences in subjective symptom ratings were statistically significant at two-month follow-up for dyspnea $[F(1,104) = 10.69, p < .01]$ and for fatigue $[F(1,104) = 10.05, p < .01]$. At the six-month follow-up, the differences were still significant for dyspnea $[F(1,103) = 7.34, p < .01]$ and for fatigue

$F(1,103) = 9.61$, $p < .01$]. By the twelve-month assessment, the differences had diminished somewhat, though still present. These results are shown in Figure 6.

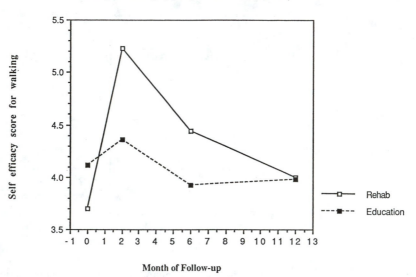

Self efficacy for walking by group and follow-up period

Figure 5 Comparison of walking efficacy expectations for rehabilitation and education patients over 12 months.

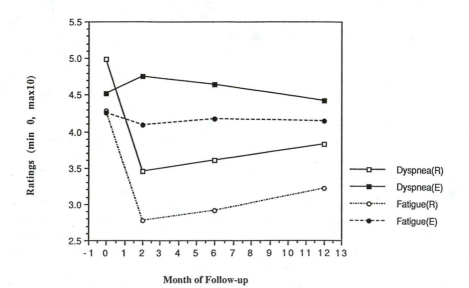

Post-treadmill dyspnea and fatigue ratings by group and follow-up period

Figure 6 Comparison of rating of perceived fatigue and dyspnea for rehabilitation and education patients over 12 months.

Correlations between self-efficacy for walking and treadmill performance for both rehabilitation and education control patients were also assessed. For the rehabilitation patients, correlations between the two variables at each assessment period are as follows: baseline ($r = .42$, $p < .01$), two month ($r = .23$, n.s.), six month ($r = .39$, $p < .01$), twelve month ($r = .40$, $p < .01$). For the education control patients, correlations between the two variables are as follows: baseline ($r = .43$, $p < .01$), two month ($r = .30$, $p < .05$), six month ($r = .32$, $p < .05$), twelve month ($r = .30$, n.s.). These findings provide further support that patients in both groups were fairly accurate in judging efficacy expectancies for walking in relation to actual treadmill performance.

It had been predicted there would be a systematic gradient for changes in efficacy expectancies for the rehabilitation but not for the control group. Specifically, the rehabilitation patients were expected to show the largest change in expectancies to perform the target behavior, walking, with changes in expectancies for other behaviors changing as a function of their similarity to walking. However, the proposed gradient of generalizability did not emerge and no significant differences between the rehabilitation and education control group were noted for self-efficacy ratings of climbing, lifting, exertion, pushing, anger tolerance, or stress tolerance at any follow-up period.

To determine whether health status outcomes as measured by Quality of Well-Being and CES-D could be predicted from self-efficacy expectancies and other variables, multiple regression analysis was employed. Both baseline and post-intervention self-efficacy expectancies did not account for a significant amount of the variance in predicting Quality of Well-Being or depression scores at any of the assessment periods.

Part 3: Microanalyses of Self-efficacy and Behavior Change

In a series of experiments, Bandura, Reese, and Adams (1982) sought to clarify the causal link between self-efficacy and behavior through a method they called microanalysis. This method examines the relationship between differential levels of efficacy expectancies and behavioral change. Their first series of analyses demonstrated that performance varies systematically as a function of perceived self-efficacy. Increasing levels of perceived self-efficacy both across experimental groups and within experimental subjects resulted in progressively higher performance accomplishments. Thus, groups whose efficacy expectancies were raised to either low, medium, or high levels had correspondingly low, medium, or high performance attainment.

Although there appears to be a correspondence between enhanced self-efficacy expectancies and subsequent performance, efficacy expectancies may exceed, match, or remain below performance attainments, depending on how they are cognitively appraised. The following example illustrates that self-efficacy expectancies are not merely a reflection of past performance. Data from several case study experiments (Bandura et al., 1982) show how similar mastery experiences have variable effects on perceived self-efficacy over the course of treatment. In one comparison, two moderately phobic patients had very similar performance attainment curves. In one case, self-efficacy increased substantially during initial successes but rapidly leveled off, even though progressively more demanding tasks were mastered, while the other patient continued to exhibit a steady increase in self-efficacy with each successive mastery experience. Because individuals are influenced more by how they interpret their performance successes than by the successes per se, perceived self-efficacy is often a better predictor of subsequent behavior than is past performance attainments.

Several analyses were conducted to evaluate the role of differential levels of initial perceived self-efficacy ratings on future performance attainment. To facilitate the analyses, baseline self-efficacy rating scores for walking were categorized into tertiles with rating scores through one comprising the low efficacy group ($n = 41$), scores two through five comprising the medium efficacy group ($n = 37$); scores greater than five comprised the high efficacy group ($n = 41$).

To assess the relationship between differential levels of initial self-efficacy for walking and subsequent treadmill performance, an analysis of variance across groups for tertiles of efficacy for walking was conducted. Rehabilitation and education control patients were grouped together since there were no initial differences between the groups on treadmill performance or self-efficacy for walking scores prior to the intervention. The results, as displayed in Figure 7, revealed a strong linear relationship between initial perceived self-efficacy expectancies for walking and treadmill performance [$F(1,119) = 10.11, p < .01$].

Initial treadmill performance by initial self efficacy for walking

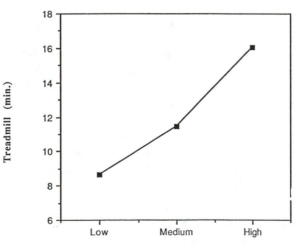

Figure 7 Treadmill endurance performance by initial efficacy expectation for both groups combined.

A 2 x 3 (Group x Efficacy tertiles) analysis of variance was conducted to examine the role of differential levels of initial self-efficacy expectations on improvements in treadmill performance following the intervention for both the rehabilitation and education control patients. The results, shown in Figure 8, demonstrates significant main effects for group [$F(1,108) = 26.98$, $p < .001$] and self-efficacy for walking [$F(2,106) = 2.86$, $p < .05$], but no significant inter-actions. The figure shows that for the rehabilitation patients, those initially high in self-efficacy for walking had less improvement in treadmill performance, while those initially low in self-efficacy for walking demonstrated the greatest improvements. For the education control patients, there was little change in treadmill performance regardless of initial self-efficacy expectancies for walking.

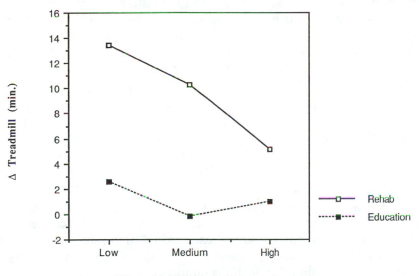

Δ Treadmill performance by baseline efficacy for walking

Figure 8 Initial efficacy expectations and subsequent improvements in treadmill performance for rehabilitation and education patients.

DISCUSSION

Patients with COPD experience significant limitation in daily activities. However, evidence from the pulmonary rehabilitation literature suggests that most of these patients can safely increase their levels of exercise and activity. Considering sources of information about self-efficacy, we observed that psychological indicators of disease severity were significantly correlated with efficacy expectations. In other words, disease severity was significantly associated with the expectation that patients could perform various activities. Results from Part 1 of the study suggest that without intervention, physiological state appears to dominate self-efficacy beliefs. Thus physiological feedback, in the form of symptoms, helps form expectations about performance. These findings help define the validity of the self-efficacy construct and suggest that it indeed has meaning in the context of understanding function in COPD patients.

One of the problems in this line of research is that physiological feedback may not always be accurate. Although patients with COPD may experience discomforting symptoms when active, most evidence suggests that they can perform more exercise without endangering their health. In fact, exercise is typically advocated as part of treatment.

The intervention in this investigation demonstrated that, despite these physiological limitations, significant increases in exercise performance were attainable. Self-efficacy theory contends that mastery or performance-based success experiences are the most potent influence on self-efficacy expectancies. Thus, it was predicted that patients in the rehabilitation program would show increased self-efficacy expectancies for walking as a function of demonstrated improvements in actual treadmill performance. Results from Part 2 of the study showed improvements in exercise performance.

There are several possible explanations for these findings. One explanation for the non-significant results is that there was insufficient statistical power to detect a meaningful difference. With low power, true differences might not be detected. This study, however, was designed to have a .80 probability to detect differences of .7 Z units. This might be classified as a moderate effect size. Thus, although moderate effects should have been detected, small effect sizes could have been missed.

Another possible explanation is that performance accomplishment in this group of COPD patients may not be as strong a source of self-efficacy expectancies as might be predicted from self-efficacy theory. It may be important to distinguish between information available to the individual from the environment and the individual's interpretation of the information. The impact of information on efficacy expectancies is dependent on how it is cognitively appraised. Thus, even success experiences do not necessarily create strong generalized expectancies of personal efficacy. Success experiences are more likely to produce positive changes in efficacy expectancies if performances are perceived as resulting from within the individual rather than from some external source. The attribution of increased performance capabilities to external factors such as the efforts of the staff, rather than to the patients' own capabilities may account for these findings.

Numerous investigations of health behavior change, have demonstrated increased self-efficacy ratings for individuals who participated in a variety of intervention programs including smoking reduction and cessation, pain management, and exercise maintenance. A majority of the studies, however, made no comparisons to a control group. In this study, the rehabilitation patients certainly gained in their ability to walk, but did not show an equally strong increase in self-efficacy expectancies for walking, while the education control patients did poorly on the treadmill exercise and showed little change in efficacy expectancies.

Previous investigations have shown that self-efficacy expectancies derived from successful performance with a particular task generalized along dimensions of task similarity to other behaviors (Kaplan, Atkins, & Reinsch, 1984). In this investigation, the hypothesized gradient of generalizability of self-efficacy expectancies did not emerge. This finding was unexpected because the study used the same measure and a similar patient group. One possible explanation for the divergent finding is that the previous study used a fairly specific, cognitive behavioral intervention rather than a medical model rehabilitation intervention as employed in this investigation. The critical difference being the cognitive behavioral intervention stressed internal attributions for behavior change.

Various studies have also shown self-efficacy ratings to be predictive of successful performance with many responses including phobias (Bandura, Adams, Hardy, & Howells, 1980), physical stamina (Ewart et al., 1983; Kaplan, Atkins, & Reinsch, 1984; Weinberg, Gould, & Jackson, 1979) and self-regulation of addictive behaviors (Coelho, 1984; Condiotte & Lichtenstein, 1981; Godding & Glasgow, 1985). The findings from this investigation suggest that self-efficacy expectancies for walking predict actual treadmill performance. However, self-efficacy judgments did not predict other health status outcomes. This supports self-efficacy theory and suggests that self-efficacy expectancies are task specific and do not necessarily reflect more general outcomes.

The finding that the rehabilitation patients reported significantly decreased dyspnea and fatigue following the treadmill endurance walk is important. Dyspnea is recognized in the literature as one of the most disabling symptoms of COPD. The literature addresses at length the fear/dyspnea cycle. Basically, the fear/dyspnea cycle refers to the downward cyclical process whereby patients are limited in their functional capabilities because of their fear of dyspnea. This fear of dyspnea often produces increased anxiety and leads to greater feelings of shortness of breath, further limiting the patients ability to engage in activities. At the present time, the interaction of environmental stimuli, psychological variables, physical capacity, and physiological mechanisms on the perception of dyspnea is not well understood. Attempts to reduce the symptom of dyspnea through pharmacological and medical interventions have produced mixed and often conflicting results. The finding from this study suggests that rehabilitation may be an effective method to break the cycle by decreasing the fear associated with dyspnea, ultimately leading to greater functioning.

The findings from Part 3 of the study suggest that initial beliefs about abilities to perform a certain behavior are important predictors of subsequent performance capabilities. Prior to the intervention, there was a clear and direct relationship between self-efficacy ratings for walking and actual treadmill performance, with patients high in self-efficacy for walking demonstrating the longest duration on the treadmill. Conversely, those patients low in self-efficacy had the poorest performance on the treadmill. These results are consistent with previous investigations of health behavior change, and indicate that self-efficacy is a good predictor of performance.

Although initial self-efficacy expectancies for walking predicted treadmill performance before the intervention, following the intervention, initial self-efficacy expectancies had differential effects on improvements in treadmill performance. It was predicted that higher efficacy expectancies would predict higher performance capabilities. An unexpected finding was that patients in the rehabilitation group with initially low self-efficacy expectancies showed the greatest gains in treadmill performance, while those patients with initially high self-efficacy expectancies had the smallest performance gains. One possible explanation is that patients with initially low self-efficacy had the greatest improvement, since a performance ceiling may have prevented those highest in efficacy at baseline from achieving even higher performance accomplishments. In other words, the patients who started out at initially low levels of efficacy for walking had the greatest opportunity for making improvements because they started out at lower levels of performance. Another possible explanation is that the rehabilitation program may have produced some increases in efficacy expectancies, and again those with initially low levels had the most to gain. It it also possible that self-efficacy expectancies have less value for those who are already performing at a high level.

CONCLUSIONS

Contributions to Self-Efficacy Theory

Measurement of self-efficacy. According to self-efficacy theory, self-efficacy expectancies are established through both physiological and psychological feedback. The theory suggests that feedback from physiological indicators has a more central role in establishing efficacy expectancies when there has been little or no exposure to the task or behavior. The results from this investigation lend support to this assertion and suggest that, indeed, physiological variables, as measured by pulmonary function and exercise tests, are associated more strongly with self-efficacy judgments than psychosocial variables. These results demonstrate that self-efficacy expectancies are associated with observable correlates other than the behaviors they presumably govern; thus, providing evidence for the validity of the self-efficacy construct. This is one of a handful of experimental investigations that has systematically evaluated the validity of the construct.

Self-efficacy enhancement through success experiences. Self-efficacy theory maintains that efficacy expectancies can be influenced by various sources of incoming information, the most influential being performance attainment. In this investigation, rehabilitation resulted in significant increases in performance attainment without similar significant increases in self-efficacy. In comparison, the control group experienced no improvements in treadmill performance accomplishment or self-efficacy expectancies. Although self-efficacy theory maintains that performance accomplishment is the most influential factor in enhancing self-efficacy expectancies, the data from this study suggest that self-appraisals of performance accomplishment may be attenuated by a number of contextual factors. For example, in this patient population, efficacy changes derived from performance accomplishment may be attenuated by strong physiological feedback. For this reason, even success experiences do not necessarily create strong expectancies of self-efficacy. Therefore, although performance accomplishment is an important factor in building efficacy, the information from successful performance can be attenuated, leading to smaller changes in self-efficacy expectancies than might be expected.

The present research findings do not provide unanimous support for principles of self-efficacy theory (Bandura, 1977, 1982, 1986). Self-efficacy theory suggests that while specific procedures for achieving change may differ for different clinic populations, the general strategy of assessing and enhancing self-efficacy expectancies by providing performance mastery experiences has substantial utility. The results from this investigation raise some questions about the functional relationship between successful performance experiences and enhancement of efficacy expectancies. Although the value of self-efficacy expectancies in health promotion and maintenance has been demonstrated in numerous studies, the present results provide mixed support for the usefulness of the self-efficacy construct in understanding health behavior change in COPD patients. Further investigations into self-efficacy expectancies in more seriously ill patients is needed in elucidating the role self-efficacy expectancies play in promoting and maintaining positive health behaviors.

REFERENCES

American Thoracic Society. (1987). Standards for the diagnosis and care of patients with Chronic Obstructive Pulmonary Disease (COPD) and asthma. *American Review of Respiratory Disease, 136(1)*, 225-244.

Baer, J. S., Holt, C. S., & Lichtenstein, E. (1986). Self-efficacy and smoking reexamined: Construct validity and clinical utility. *Journal of Consulting and Clinical Psychology, 54*, 846-852.

Bandura, A. (1977). Self-efficacy: Toward a unifying theory of behavioral change. *Psychological Review, 84*, 191-215.

Bandura, A. (1982). Self-efficacy mechanism in human agency. *American Psychologist, 37*, 122-147.

Bandura, A. (1986). Scope of self-efficacy theory. *Journal of Social and Clinical Psychology, 4*, 359-373.

Bandura, A., Adams, N. E., Hardy, A. B., & Howells, G. N. (1980). Tests of the generality of self-efficacy theory. *Cognitive Therapy and Research, 4*, 39-66.

Bandura, A., Reese, L., & Adams, N. E. (1982). Microanalysis of action and fear arousal as a function of differential levels of perceived self-efficacy. *Journal of Personality and Social Psychology, 7*, 111-116.

Bass, H., Whitcomb, J. F., & Forman, R. (1970). Exercise training: Therapy for patients with chronic obstructive pulmonary disease. *Chest, 57*, 116-121.

Blittner, M., Goldberg, J., & Merbaum, M. (1978). Cognitive self-control factors in the reduction of smoking behavior. *Behavior Therapy, 9*, 553-561.

Borg, G. A. V. (1982). Psychophysical bases of perceived exertion. *Medical Science Sports Exercise, 14*, 377-381.

Carlson, D.J., Ries, A.L., & Kaplan, R. M., (in press). Prediction of maximum excersise tolerance in patients with chronic obstructive pulmonary disease. *Chest.*

Chambliss, C. A., & Murray, E. J. (1979). Cognitive procedures for smoking reduction: Symptom attributions versus efficacy attribution. *Cognitive Therapy and Research, 3*, 91-95.

Coelho, J. E. (1984). Self-efficacy and cessation of smoking. *Psychological Reports, 54*, 309-310.

Condiotte, M. M., & Lichtenstein, E. (1981). Self-efficacy and relapse in smoking cessation programs. *Journal of Consulting and Clinical Psychology, 49*, 648-658.

Devins, G. M., & Edwards, P. J. (1988). Self-efficacy and smoking reduction in chronic obstructive pulmonary disease. *Behavior Research and Therapy, 26*, 127-135.

Dolce, J. J. (1987). Self-efficacy and disability beliefs in behavioral treatment of pain. *Behavior Research and Therapy, 25*, 289-299.

Dudley, D. L., Glaser, E. M., Jorgenson, B. N., & Logan, D. L. (1980). Psychosocial concomitants to rehabilitation in chronic obstructive pulmonary disease: Part 1. Psychosocial and psychological considerations; Part 2. Psychosocial treatment; Part 3. Dealing with psychiatric disease. *Chest, 77*, 413-420; 544-551; 677-684.

Eaton, W. W., & Kessler, L. G. (1981). Rates of symptoms of depression in a national sample. *American Journal of Epidemiology, 114*, 528-538.

Ewart, C. K., Taylor, C. B., Reese, L. B., & Debusk, R. F. (1983). Effects of early post-myocardial infarction exercise testing on self-perception and subsequent physical activity. *American Journal of Cardiology, 51*, 1076-1080.

Feinleib, M., Rosenberg, H. M., Collins, J. G., Delozier, J. E., Pokras, R., & Chevarley, F. M. (1989). Trends in COPD morbidity and mortality in the United States. In: The rise in chronic obstructive pulmonary disease mortality. *American Review of Respiratory Diseases, 140* (suppl 3 pt 2), S9-S18.

Godding, P. R., & Glasgow, R. E. (1985). Self-efficacy and outcome expectancy as predictors of controlled smoking status. *Cognitive Therapy and Research, 9*, 583-590.

Higgins, M. W. (1989) Chronic airways disease in the United States: Trends and determinants. *Chest, 96* (suppl), 328s-334s.

Kaplan, R. M., & Anderson, J. P. (1988). A general health policy model: Update and applications. *Health Services Research, 23*, 203-235.

Kaplan, R. M., Atkins, C. J., & Reinsch, S. (1984). Specific efficacy expectancies mediate exercise compliance in patients with COPD. *Health Psychology, 3*, 223-242.

Kaplan, R. M., Atkins, C. J., & Ries, A. L. (1985). Behavioral issues in the management of chronic obstructive pulmonary disease. *Annals of Behavioral Medicine, 7*, 5-10.

Kaplan, R. M., Atkins, C. J., & Timms, R. M. (1984). Validity of a quality of well-being scale as an outcome measure in chronic obstructive pulmonary disease. *Journal of Chronic Diseases, 37*, 85-95.

Lenfant, C. (1982). Government and Community. *American Review of Respiratory Disease, 126(15)*, 753-757.

Lenfant, C. (1988). Introduction. In A. J. McSweeney & I. Grant (Eds.), *Chronic Obstructive Pulmonary Disease: A behavioral perspective* (pp. iii-iv). New York: Marcel Dekker.

McSweeney, A. J., Grant, I., Heaton, R. K., Adams, K. M., & Timms, R. M. (1982). Life quality of patients with chronic obstructive pulmonary disease. *Archives of Internal Medicine, 142*, 473-478.

Mertens, D. J., Shephard, R. J., & Kavanagh, T. (1978). Long-term exercise therapy for chronic obstructive pulmonary disease. *Respiration, 35*, 96-107.

Morbidity and Mortality Weekly Report (1986). Deaths due to Chronic Obstructive Pulmonary Disease and Allied Conditions. *MMWR, 35(32)*, 507-510.

Moser, K. M., Bokinsky, G. E., Savage, R. T., Archibald, C. J., & Hansen, P. R. (1980). Results of a comprehensive rehabilitation program: Physiologic and functional effects on patients with Chronic Obstructive Pulmonary Disease. *Archives of Internal Medicine, 140*, 1596-1601.

National Center for Health Statistics. (1988).Current estimates from the National Health Interview Survey, United States. *Vital and Health Statistics.* Series 10, No. 173, DHHS Pub. No. (PHS)90-1232. Washington, DC: US Department of Health and Human Services, 1990.

Nicki, R. M., Remington, R. E., & MacDonald, G. A. (1985). Self-efficacy, nicotine-fading/self-efficacy monitoring and cigarette smoking behavior. *Behavior Research and Therapy, 22*, 477-485.

O'Leary, A. (1985). Self-efficacy and health. Behavior Research and Therapy, 23, 437-451.

Punzal, P. A., Ries, A. L., Kaplan, R. M., & Prewitt, L. M. (in press). Maximum intensity exercise training in patients with chronic obstructive pulmonary disease. *Chest.*

Radloff, L. S. (1977). The CES-D Scale: A self-report depression scale for research in the general population. *Applied Psychological Measurement, 1*, 385.

Reese, L. B. (1982). *Pain reduction through cognitive, self-relaxative and placebo means: A self-efficacy analysis.* Unpublished doctoral dissertation, Stanford University, Stanford, California.

Toshima, M. T., Kaplan, R. M., & Ries, A. L. (1990). Experimental evaluation of rehabilitation in chronic obstructive pulmonary disease: Short-term effects on exercise endurance and health status. *Health Psychology, 9*, 237-252.

Weinberg, R. S., Gould, D., & Jackson, A. (1979). Expectancies and performance—An empirical test of Bandura's self-efficacy theory. *Journal of Sports Psychology, 1*, 320-331.

Weissman, M. M., Sholomskas, D., Pottenger, M., Prusoff, B. A., & Locke, B. Z. (1977). Assessing depressive symptoms in five psychiatric populations: A validation study. *American Journal of Epidemiology*, 106, 203-214.

Author Notes

Supported by Grant RO1 HL 34732 from the National Heart, Lung, and Blood Institute. Address requests for reprints to the second author, Robert M. Kaplan.

APPENDIX

SELF-EFFICACY EXPECTANCIES MEASURE

Instructions: The following measure describes various tasks and activities. Under the column marked <u>Can Do</u>, put a check mark next to the tasks or activities you expect you could do now. For each of the tasks you checked under <u>Can Do</u>, indicate in the column marked <u>Conf.</u>, how confident you are that you could do that task now. Rate the degree of your confidence using a number from 0 to 100 on the scale below:

0	10	20	30	40	50	60	70	80	90	100
Uncertain					Moderately Certain				Certain	

<u>LIFTING OBJECTS</u>	Can Do	Conf.		<u>WALKING</u>	Can Do	Conf.
Lift a 10 lb. object	___	___		Walk 1 block (5 min.)	___	___
Lift a 20 lb. object	___	___		Walk 2 blocks (10 min.)	___	___
Lift a 30 lb. object	___	___		Walk 3 blocks (15 min.)	___	___
Lift a 40 lb. object	___	___		Walk 4 blocks (20 min.)	___	___
Lift a 50 lb. object	___	___		Walk 5 blocks (25 min.)	___	___
Lift a 60 lb. object	___	___		Walk 1 mile (30 min.)	___	___
Lift a 80 lb. object	___	___		Walk 1.5 miles (45 min.)	___	___
Lift a 100 lb. object	___	___		Walk 2 miles (60 min.)	___	___
Lift a 120 lb. object	___	___		Walk 3 miles (90 min.)	___	___
Lift a 150 lb. object	___	___				
Lift a 175 lb. object	___	___		<u>GENERAL EXERTION</u>		
				Capable of very light exertion	___	___
				Capable of light exertion	___	___
				Capable of moderate exertion	___	___
<u>CLIMBING</u> (without rest)	___	___		Capable of hard exertion	___	___
Walk up several stairs	___	___		Capable of very hard exertion	___	___
Walk up 1 flight of stairs	___	___		Capable of extremely hard		
Walk up 2 flight of stairs	___	___		exertion	___	___
Walk up 3 flight of stairs	___	___				
Walk up 4 flight of stairs	___	___		<u>TOLERANCE OF EMOTIONAL</u>		
				<u>TENSION/STRESS</u>		
				Tolerate mild tension/stress	___	___
				Tolerate some tension/stress	___	___
				Tolerate moderate tension/stress	___	___
<u>PUSHING/MOVING OBJECTS</u>				Tolerate substantial tension/stress	___	___
Move a light weight object				Tolerate a great deal of tension/		
(Kitchen chair)	___	___		stress	___	___
Move a medium weight						
object (Coffee table)	___	___		<u>TOLERANCE OF ANGER AROUSAL</u>		
Move a fairly heavy object				Tolerate mild anger arousal	___	___
(Armchair)	___	___		Tolerate some anger arousal	___	___
Move a heavy object				Tolerate moderate anger arousal	___	___
(Sofa or Bed)	___	___		Tolerate substantial anger arousal	___	___
				Tolerate a great deal of anger arousal	___	___

SELF-EFFICACY MECHANISM IN PSYCHOBIOLOGIC FUNCTIONING

Albert Bandura

Perceived self-efficacy operates as an important psychological mechanism linking psychosocial influences to health functioning. Perceived self-efficacy affects a wide range of biological processes that mediate human health and disease. Many of these biological effects arise in the context of coping with acute and chronic stressors. Exposure to stressors with a sense of efficacy to control them has no adverse effects. But exposure to the same stressors with perceived inefficacy to control them activates autonomic, catecholamine, and opioid systems and impairs the functioning of the immune system. Depending on their nature, lifestyle habits enhance or impair health status. This enables people to exercise some control over their vitality, quality of health, and rate of aging. Self-efficacy beliefs affect every phase of personal change—whether people even consider changing their health habits; whether they can enlist the motivation and perserverance needed to succeed should they choose to do so; and how well they maintain the changes they have achieved. Health outcomes are related to predictive factors in complex, multidetermined and probabilistic ways. Prognostic judgments, therefore, involve some degree of uncertainty. Because prognostications can alter self-efficacy beliefs, such judgments have a self-validating potential by influencing the course of health outcomes.

The recent years have witnessed a major change in the conception of human health and illness. The traditional approaches relied on a biomedical model which places heavy emphasis on infectious agents, ameliorative medications, and repair of physical impairments. The newer conceptions adopt a broader biopsychosocial model (Engel, 1977). Viewed from this perspective, health and disease are products of interactions among psychosocial and biological factors. Health is not merely the absence of physical impairment and disease. The biopsychosocial perspective emphasizes health enhancement as well as disease prevention. It is just as meaningful to speak of degrees of wellness as of degrees of impairment. Thus, for example, there are degrees of immunocompetence, cardiovascular robustness, physical strength and stamina, movement flexibility and cognitive functioning. Health enhancement seeks to raise the level of psychobiological competencies.

It is now widely acknowledged that people's health rests partly in their own hands. In analyzing mortality rates within and between countries, Fuchs (1974) has shown that expenditures for medical care have only a small impact on life expectancy. The quality of health of a nation is largely determined by lifestyle habits, and environmental conditions. People often suffer physical impairments, and die prematurely of preventable health-impairing habits. Industrial and agricultural practices are injecting carcinogens and harmful pollutants into the air we breathe, the food we eat, and the water we drink, all of which take a heavy toll on the body. Changing health habits, and environmental practices yields the large health benefits.

Psychosocial determinants of health status operate largely through the exercise of personal agency. Among the mechanisms of personal agency, none is more central or pervasive than people's beliefs in their capability to exercise control over their own motivation and behavior and over environmental demands. Evidence from diverse lines of research shows that perceived efficacy operates as an important psychological mechanism linking psychosocial influences to health functioning. One can distinguish two levels of research on the psychosocial determinants of health functioning in which perceived self-efficacy plays an influential role. The more basic level examines how perceived coping self-efficacy affects biological systems that mediate health and disease. The second level is concerned with the exercise of direct control over the modifiable aspects of health and the rate of aging.

BIOLOGICAL EFFECTS OF PERCEIVED SELF-EFFICACY

Perceived self-efficacy can activate a wide range of biological processes that mediate human health and disease. Many of these biological effects arise in the context of coping with acute or chronic stressors in the many transactions of everyday life. Stress has been implicated as an important contributing factor to many physical dysfunctions (Goldberger & Breznitz, 1982; Krantz, Grunberg, & Baum, 1985). Recent investigations with animals have identified controllability as a key organizing principle regarding the nature of stress effects. Exposure to stressors with a concomitant ability to control them has no adverse effects. However, exposure to the same stressors without the ability to control them activates neuroendocrine, catecholamine, and opioid systems and impairs the functioning of the immune system (Bandura, 1991; Coe & Levine, 1991; Maier, Laudenslager, & Ryan, 1985; Shavit & Martin, 1987).

Biochemical Effects of Self-Efficacy in
Coping With Stressors

Social cognitive theory views stress reactions in terms of perceived self-inefficacy to exercise control over aversive threats and taxing environmental demands. If people believe they can deal effectively with potential environmental stressors they are not perturbed by them. But if they believe they cannot control aversive events they distress themselves and impair their level of functioning. Our understanding of the biological effects of uncontrollable stressors is based mainly on experimentation with animals involving uncontrollable physical stressors. Stressors take diverse forms and can produce different patterns of physiological activation. This places certain limitations on extrapolation of conclusions across different species, stressors, and patterns of controllability. Uncontrollable physical stressors are not only stressful but also inflict some physical trauma that can activate a variety of complicating physiological processes. Most of the important stressors with which humans have to cope involve psychological threats (Lazarus & Folkman, 1984). Moreover, stress reactions are governed largely by perception of coping self-efficacy rather than being triggered directly by the objective properties of threats and environmental demands (Bandura, 1988a). It is the perception of environmental threats as exceeding one's coping capabilities that becomes the stressful reality.

Efforts to verify the effects of controlling efficacy on biological stress reactions in humans have relied extensively on correlational or quasi-experimental studies in which occurrences of life stressors are related to indices of biological functioning or infectious illnesses. Such studies leave some ambiguity about the direction of causality and even whether the biological effects are due to the stressor or other unsuspected factors operating at the time. To overcome these problems, we devised a research paradigm combining strong phobic stressors with mastery efficacy induction procedures that enables us to examine causal relationships under laboratory conditions with a high degree of experimental control over confounding sources of influence. Participants cope with a uniform stressor that can be varied in intensity. Because a high sense of controlling efficacy can be quickly instilled through guided mastery experiences, we can create conditions combining exposure to chronic stressors with, and without, perceived controlling self-efficacy. By the end of each study, the phobia is eradicated in all participants so they all gain lasting relief from chronic phobic stressors while contributing to knowledge.

Autonomic Activation

In studies of autonomic activation, elevation in blood pressure and cardiac acceleration were measured in phobics during anticipation and performance of intimidating tasks corresponding to strong, medium, and weak strength of perceived self-efficacy. Following the test for autonomic reactions, subjects received guided mastery experiences until they perceived themselves to be maximally self-efficacious on all of the previous coping activities. Then their autonomic reactions were again measured.

Figure 1 shows the mean change from the baseline level of heart rate and blood pressure as a function of differential strength of perceived self-efficacy. Subjects were viscerally unperturbed by coping tasks they regarded with utmost

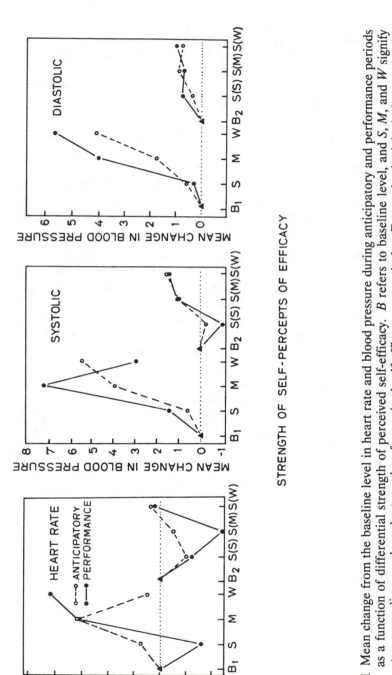

Figure 1 Mean change from the baseline level in heart rate and blood pressure during anticipatory and performance periods as a function of differential strength of perceived self-efficacy. *B* refers to baseline level, and *S*, *M*, and *W* signify strong, medium, and weak strengths of perceived self-efficacy, respectively. For each physiological measure the figure on the left in each panel shows the autonomic reactions related to self-efficacy beliefs of differing strengths (performance arousal at perceived weak self-efficacy is based on only a few subjects who were able to execute only partial performances). The figure on the right of the same panel shows the autonomic reactions to the same set of tasks after self-beliefs of efficacy were strengthened to the maximal level (Bandura, Reese, & Adams, 1982).

self-efficacy. However, on tasks about which they had moderate doubts about their coping efficacy, their heart rate accelerated and their blood pressure rose during anticipation and performance of the activities. When presented with tasks in their weak self-efficacy range, most subjects promptly rejected them as too far beyond their coping capabilities to even attempt. Indeed, only a few subjects were able to do any of them. Although lack of coping action precluded a meaningful analysis of performance arousal, data from the anticipatory phase shed light on how autonomic reactions change when people withdraw from transactions with threats they judge will overwhelm their coping capabilities. Cardiac reactivity promptly declined but blood pressure continued to climb. After perceived self-efficacy was strengthened to the maximal level, everyone performed these previously intimidating tasks without any autonomic activation.

Heart rate is affected more quickly than blood pressure by personal restructuring of intimidating task demands, which may explain the different pattern of autonomic reactivity at the extreme level of perceived self-inefficacy. Catecholamines, which govern autonomic activity, are released in different temporal patterns during encounters with external stressors (Mefford et al., 1981). Heart rate is especially sensitive to momentary changes in catecholamine patterns, with epinephrine, which is rapidly released, having a more pronounced effect on cardiac activity than on arterial pressure.

Catecholamine Activation

Investigation of the biochemical effects of perceived coping efficacy was further extended by linking strength of perceived self-efficacy to plasma catecholamine secretion (Bandura, Taylor, Williams, Mefford, & Barchas, 1985). The range of perceived coping efficacy in severe phobics was broadened by modeling which conveyed predictive information about the phobic threat and demonstrated effective ways of exercising control over it. They were then presented with coping tasks they had previously judged to be in their low, medium, and high self-efficacy range, during which continuous blood samples were obtained through a catheter.

Figure 2 presents graphically the microrelation between self-efficacy beliefs and plasma catecholamine secretion. Levels of epinephrine, norepinephrine, and dopac, a dopamine metabolite, were low when phobics coped with tasks in their strong efficacy range. Self-doubts in coping efficacy produced substantial increases in these catecholamines. When presented with tasks that exceeded their perceived coping capabilities the phobics instantly rejected them. Catecholamines dropped sharply.

The dopac response differs markedly from the other catecholamines. Whereas epinephrine and norepinephrine dropped upon rejection of the threatening task, dopac rose to its highest level, even though the phobics had no intention of coping with the task. Dopac seems to be triggered by the mere apperception of environmental demands overwhelming one's perceived coping capabilities. These

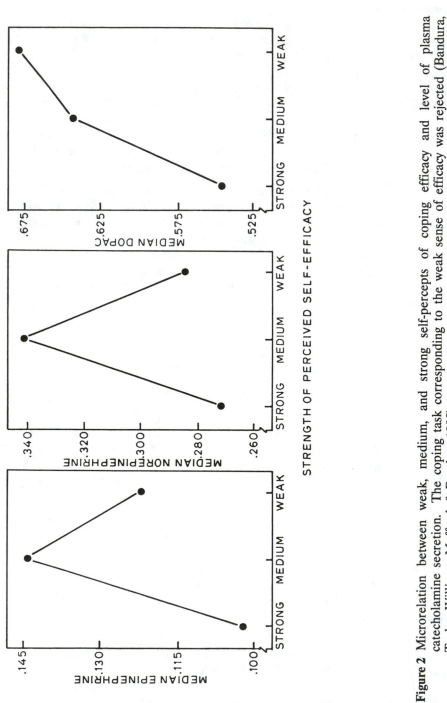

Figure 2 Microrelation between weak, medium, and strong self-percepts of coping efficacy and level of plasma catecholamine secretion. The coping task corresponding to the weak sense of efficacy was rejected (Bandura, Taylor, Williams, Mefford, & Barchas, 1985).

data suggest that under some conditions plasma dopac could reflect activity of brain dopamine neurons. Such a central contribution would be consistent with the enhanced dopac concentrations observed with perceived inefficacy to cope with a task, as shown in Figure 2.

After perceived coping efficacy was strengthened to the maximal level by guided mastery, performance of the previously intimidating tasks no longer elicited differential catecholamine reactivity. Thus, the elevated catecholamine secretions observed in the initial test resulted from a perceived mismatch between coping capabilities and task demands, rather than from properties inherent in the tasks themselves. The evidence across a variety of biological indices is consistent in showing that biological stress reactions to coping activities differ when perceived self-efficacy differs, but biological reactions are the same when perceived self-efficacy is raised to the maximal level.

The crucial role of controllability in biological activation is further shown in microanalysis of changes in catecholamine secretion as phobics gain mastery over phobic threats through guided mastery treatment (Bandura et al., 1985). In this approach, phobics quickly gain mastery over threats through aided guided mastery. As treatment progresses, the mastery aids are discontinued to verify that coping attainments stem from the exercise of personal efficacy rather than from mastery aids. Self-directed mastery experiences are then arranged to strengthen and generalize the sense of coping efficacy. Figure 3 presents the plasma catecholamine levels at five demarcated stages in treatment. During the initial phases of treatment, when phobics lacked a sense of coping efficacy, even the mere sight or minimal contact with phobic threat activated catecholamine responses. After participants gained controlling efficacy, their catecholamine level dropped and remained relatively low during the most intimidating interactions with the phobic threat. When they were asked to relinquish all control, which left them completely vulnerable, catecholamine reactivity promptly rose. This pattern of results is in accord with a mechanism involving controllability rather than simple extinction or adaptation over time.

Autonomic arousal to stressors is reduced by self-knowledge that one can wield control over them at any time even though that controlling capability is unexercised (Glass, Reim, & Singer, 1971). Choosing not to exercise control at a particular time, but being able to do so whenever one wants to, should be distinguished from relinquished control in which one is deprived of all means of control while subjected to stressors. Relinquished control leaves one completely vulnerable, whereas freely usable control, though unexercised at a particular occasion, leaves one in full command.

Opioid Activation

Endogenous opioids play a paramount role in the regulation of pain (Fanselow, 1986) and as mediators of the effects of uncontrollable stressors on immunocompetence (Shavit & Martin, 1987). Studies with animals subjected to painful stimulation show that stress can activate endogenous opioids that block pain transmission (Fanselow, 1986). Opioid involvement is indicated by evidence that stress-induced analgesia is reduced by opiate antagonists, is blocked by adrenalectomy, and is reinstated by administering corticosterone to adrenalectomized animals (Grau, Hyson, Maier, Madden, & Barchas, 1981; MacLennan et al., 1982). It is not the physically painful stimulation, per se, but the psychological stress over its uncontrollability that seems to be a key factor in opioid activation (Maier, 1986). Animals who can turn off shock stimulation show no opioid activation, whereas yoked animals who experience the same shock stimulation without being able to control its offset give evidence of stress-activated opioids.

Another line of research on biological mediators examined the impact of perceived coping efficacy on endogenous opioid activation (Bandura, Cioffi, Taylor, Brouillard, 1988). Differential levels of perceived cognitive self-efficacy were induced by having subjects exercise control over the pace of cognitive demands or by having the same demands controlled externally at a pace that strained cognitive capabilities. Strong perceived self-efficacy was accompanied by low stress, whereas subjects who judged themselves inefficacious to cope with the cognitive demands experienced high subjective stress and autonomic arousal. Stress can activate endogenous opioids that block pain transmission (Kelley, 1986). Opioid involvement is indicated by evidence that stress-induced analgesia is reduced by opiate antagonists, such as naloxone, which blocks opiate receptors. To test for opioid activation, subjects were therefore administered either naloxone or an inert saline solution, whereupon their pain tolerance was measured at periodic intervals by cold pressor tests. Efficacious subjects, whose high sense of control kept stress low, gave no evidence of opioid activation in that their pain tolerance was unaffected by naloxone (Figure 3). In contrast, the perceived self-inefficacious subjects, who experienced high stress, gave evidence of opiate-mediated analgesia. They displayed high pain tolerance under saline, but found pain difficult to bear under naloxone opioid blockage. The greater the decline in perceived cognitive efficacy, the greater was the opioid activation.

Opioid and Cognitive Mechanisms in Pain Control

Pain is a complex psychobiological phenomenon, influenced by psychosocial factors, rather than simply a sensory experience arising directly from stimulation of pain receptors. The same intensity of pain stimulation can give rise to different levels of conscious pain depending on how attention is deployed, how the experience is cognitively appraised, the coping strategies used to modulate pain, and on modeled reactions to nociceptive stimulation (Cioffi, 1991; Craig, 1986; Turk, Meichenbaum, & Genest, 1983). Pain can be regulated through different mechanisms. We have already examined how pain sensations can be counteracted at the locus of pain receptors by opioid blockage. Pain can also be regulated by central processes involving attentional and other cognitive activities that reduce consciousness of pain sensations.

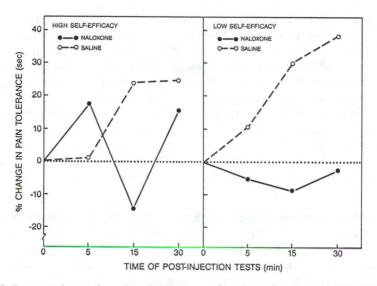

Figure 3 Percent change in pain tolerance as a function of perceived self-efficacy to exercise control over cognitive demands and whether people received saline or the opiate antagonist, naloxone (Bandura, Cioffi, Taylor, & Brouillard, 1988).

There are several ways by which perceived coping efficacy can bring relief from pain by cognitive means. People who believe they can alleviate pain enlist whatever ameliorative skills they have learned and will persevere in their efforts to reduce the level of experienced pain. Those who judge themselves as inefficacious give up readily in the absence of quick relief. Consciousness has a very limited capacity (Kahneman, 1973). It is hard to keep more than one thing in mind at the same time. If pain sensations are supplanted in consciousness, they are felt less. Dwelling on pain sensations only makes them more noticeable and, thus, more difficult to bear. Perceived self-efficacy can lessen the extent to which painful stimulation is experienced as conscious pain by diverting attention from pain sensations to competing engrossments. Thus, for example, attentional diversion enables long-distance runners to press on even though their body is wracked in pain. Were they to focus on their mounting pain sensations they could not continue for long. During deep engrossment in activities people can become oblivious to chronic pain sensations. Finally, people who believe they can exercise some pain control are likely to interpret unpleasant bodily sensations and states more benignly than those who believe there is nothing they can do to alleviate pain (Cioffi, 1991). Construals that highlight the sensory rather than the aversive aspects of pain reduce distress and raise pain tolerance (Ahles, Blanchard, & Leventhal, 1983).

Results of several lines of research indicate that perceived self-efficacy can mediate the analgesic potency of different psychological procedures. Reese (1983) found that cognitive pain control techniques, self-relaxation, and placebos all increase perceived self-efficacy to cope with and ameliorate pain. The more self-efficacious the people judged themselves to be, the less pain they experienced in later cold pressor tests, and the higher was their pain threshold and pain tolerance. Arbitrary persuasory influences, in the form of bogus feedback that one's pain tolerance is high or low compared to that of others, similarly alters people's beliefs in their efficacy to manage pain which, in turn, raises and lowers their actual pain tolerance, respectively (Litt, 1988). Change in self-efficacy belief is a better predictor of pain tolerance than is past level of pain tolerance. Arbitrarily instilled perceived inefficacy restricts pain coping behavior even when the opportunity to exercise personal control exists, whereas heightened perceived self-efficacy largely overrides ostensible external constraints on personal control of pain.

Biofeedback is widely used as a muscle relaxation procedure to ameliorate pain. Holroyd and his colleagues have shown that the benefits of biofeedback training stem more from boosts in perceived coping efficacy than from the muscular exercises themselves (Holroyd et al., 1984). Perceived self-efficacy, created by false feedback that one is a skilled relaxer for controlling pain, predicted reduction in tension headaches, whereas the actual amount of change in muscle activity achieved in treatment was unrelated to the incidence of subsequent headaches. Studies of alternative cognitive mechanisms of pain tolerance reveal that perceived self-efficacy to manage pain predicts pain tolerance, whereas outcome expectations of the amount of pain anticipated for engaging in aversive activities do not independently affect how much pain people endure when variations in perceived self-efficacy were controlled (Williams, Kinney, & Falbo, 1989). That perceived self-efficacy makes pain easier to manage is further corroborated by studies of acute and chronic clinical pain (Council, Ahern, Follick & Kline, 1988; Dolce, 1987; Lorig, Chastain, Ung, Shoor, & Holman, 1989; Manning & Wright, 1983; O'Leary, Shoor, Lorig, & Holman, 1988).

At first sight, helplessness theory and self-efficacy theory appear to be at odds on how controlling efficacy relates to pain tolerance and the mechanisms mediating it. Endurance of pain is associated with deficient control over stressors in helplessness theory, but with controlling efficacy in self-efficacy theory. There are several possible explanations for this seeming contradiction. It might be reasoned, from research on stress-induced analgesia, that coping efficacy may enhance pain control mainly through nonopioid mechanisms. Because a high sense of coping efficacy renders aversive situations less stressful, it would reduce stress activation of opioids. Although there may be less opioid blockage of pain, exercise of personal efficacy that occupies consciousness with engrossing matters can block awareness of pain sensations by a nonopioid cognitive mechanism.

A second plausible explanation for the paradoxical findings is in terms of the markedly different consequences of control in the types of coping situations used. The exercise of control produces fundamentally different conditions of pain stimulation in the situations commonly used in animal and human studies of pain that would argue for some opioid involvement with high self-efficacy. In the usual animal experimentation, behavioral control promptly terminates pain stimulation. By contrast, in the human situation, efficacious exercise of cognitive control over pain sensations enables people to tolerate high levels of pain stimulation but, in so doing, it promotes even more active engagement in activities that can heighten the level and duration of pain stimulation. A strong sense of coping efficacy often increases engagement in pain-generating activities to the point where it can create stressful predicaments. Thus, for example, self-efficacious people suffering from arthritis generate pain and discomfort when they first take on more vigorous activities. Activity eventually improves function and reduces pain but in the short term it increases pain and distress. Similarly, people experience mounting pain the longer they keep their hand immersed in icy water in the cold pressor task. Indeed, in the latter situation, continued exercise of controlling efficacy through cognitive means eventually heightens pain to the point where it begins to overwhelm people's coping capabilities and they begin to experience the intense pain stimulation as unbearable. The stress of failing control with mounting pain in later stages of coping would activate opioid systems.

In this conception of the human coping process, both opioid and nonopioid mechanisms operate in the regulation of pain, but their relative contribution varies with degree of controlling efficacy and phases of coping. A nonopioid mechanism would subserve pain tolerance while cognitive control effectively shuts out pain sensations from consciousness or renders then less aversive by benign construal. But an opioid mechanism would come into play in later phases of coping when control techniques become insufficient to attenuate mounting pain or to block it from consciousness. Thus, opioid activation would remain low during successful phases, but high during the more stressful failing phases of cognitive control. Research in which exercise of personal efficacy lowers stress rather than fosters activities of mounting aversiveness that eventually overwhelms coping capabilities yields findings similar to those from studies of uncontrollable physical stressors (Bandura et al., 1988). Perceived self-inefficacy raises pain tolerance through opioid activation.

Evidence for pain control through the dual mechanisms is provided by a study in which individuals were either taught cognitive methods of pain control, administered a placebo presented as a medicinal analgesic, or they received no intervention (Bandura, O'Leary, Taylor, Gauthier, & Gossard, 1987). Following the treatment phase, their perceived efficacy to control pain, and to reduce it, and their tolerance of cold pressor pain were measured. Participants in all conditions were then administered either naloxone, an opiate antagonist, or an inert saline solution, and thereafter their pain tolerance was measured at periodic intervals.

Training in cognitive control heightened perceived self-efficacy to endure and reduce pain (Figure 4). Placebo medication had a differential impact on perceived efficacy to endure pain and perceived efficacy to reduce its intensity. People believed they were better able to withstand pain with the aid of a supposedly pain-relieving medication. However, success in reducing experienced pain depends on effective exercise of pain ameliorating skills, which medication alone does not provide. Placebo medication did not persuade people that they became more capable of reducing the intensity of pain. These findings underscore the value of measuring different aspects of perceived self-efficacy in research designed to elucidate the exercise of control over pain. Perceived self-efficacy predicted how well people managed pain. The stronger their beliefs in their ability to withstand pain, the longer they endured mounting pain, regardless of whether their perceived self-efficacy was enhanced by cognitive means or by placebo medication or varied preexistantly without any intervention. A strong sense of efficacy to endure pain predicts tolerance of mounting pain when initial differences in pain tolerance are controlled.

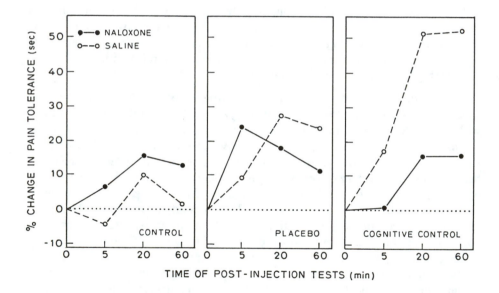

Figure 4 Percent change from pretest level in perceived self-efficacy and pain tolerance achieved by people who were taught cognitive pain control techniques, administered a placebo, or received no intervention (Bandura, O'Leary, Taylor, Gauthier, & Gossard, 1987).

The findings provide evidence for both an opioid-mediated component and a nonopioid component for attenuating the impact of pain stimulation by cognitive means. As can be seen in Figure 4, cognitive copers who were administered saline displayed a sizable increase in pain tolerance. In contrast, when pain-reducing opioids are blocked by naloxone, cognitive copers found it more difficult to manage pain. However, cognitive copers were able to increase their pain tolerance even under opioid blockage, which lends support for a nonopioid component as well in the exercise of cognitive control. For cognitive copers administered saline the combined action of both opioid and cognitive control contributed to their ability to achieve a sizable increase in pain tolerance.

The correlational findings shed some light on how different forms of self-efficacy relate to opioid activation under different modes of coping. Coping with heightened pain under opioid blockage requires active exercise of strategies for alleviating pain rather than mere forbearance. People who judge themselves to be good pain copers would be especially distressed by their eventual ineffectiveness to manage their pain. Thus, the degree of opioid activation is best predicted by perceived capability to reduce pain. The stronger the subjects' perceived self-efficacy to reduce pain, the greater was the opioid activation. The strength of this relationship is further increased when initial ability to tolerate pain is controlled by partial correlation.

The findings also provide some evidence that placebo medication may activate some opioid involvement. After the full time had elapsed for naloxone to exert its antagonistic effect, people in the naloxone condition were less able to tolerate pain than those who had been given saline. These findings are in accord with those of Levine and his associates showing that endogenous opioids can be activated by placebo medication to reduce postoperative dental pain (Levine, Gordon, & Fields, 1978; Levine, Gordon, Jones, & Fields, 1978). A socially administered placebo produces analgesia, whereas unsignaled mechanical infusion of the placebo that goes undetected by patients has no analgesic effect (Levine & Gordon, 1984). Placebo-induced analgesia may involve both a nonopioid cognitive component and a stress analgetic component that is antagonizable by naloxone (Gracely, Dubner, Wolskee & Deeter, 1983). In the study under discussion, placebo medication had its major impact on perceived self-efficacy to withstand pain. Therefore, it was this expression of efficacy that predicted degree of opioid involvement. The strength of the placebo response is predictable from how the placebo affects perceived self-efficacy to endure pain (Bandura et al., 1987). People who judge themselves efficacious to withstand pain given a supposed medicinal aid are good pain endurers, whereas those who continue to distrust their efficacy to manage pain despite receiving the placebo medication are less able to bear pain. For people who lack assurance in their efficacy, the evident failure to achieve relief from pain, even with the help of a medicinal analgesic, is only further testimony for their coping inefficacy.

So far the discussion has focused on self-efficacy regulation of pain through cognitive supplanting or construal of pain sensations and stress-induced opioid activation. There is a third possible mechanism that merits serious consideration as well. Self-efficacy expectations may directly activate the central nervous system to release pain-blocking opioids independently of stress. Animals can learn to activate their endogenous opioid systems anticipatorily in the presence of cues formerly predictive of painful experiences (Watkins & Mayer, 1982). Such findings add some credence to the possibility of direct central activation of opioid systems.

Perceived Coping Self-Efficacy and Immunocompetence

Several lines of evidence suggest that psychosocial factors modulate the immune system in ways that can influence susceptibility to illness (Coe & Levine, 1991; Kiecolt-Glaser & Glaser, 1987; Locke et al., 1985; O'Leary, 1990). The types of biological reactions that have been shown to accompany perceived coping efficacy, such as autonomic activation, catecholamines, and endogenous opioids, are involved in the regulation of the immune system. There are three major pathways through which perceived self-efficacy can affect immune function. They include mediation through stress, depression and expectancy learning.

Stress mediation. The ability to exercise control over potential stressors can have significant impact on the cellular components of the immune system. Exposure to intermittent stressors without the ability to control them causes impairment in various facets of immune function, whereas exposure to the same stressful events, but with efficacy to control them, has no adverse effects on immune function (Coe & Levine, 1991; Maier et al., 1985). There is evidence that some of the immunosuppressive effects of inefficacy in controlling stressors, such as reduced natural killer cell cytotoxicity, are mediated by release of endogenous opioids (Shavit & Martin, 1987). When opioid mechanisms are blocked by opiate antagonists, the stress of coping inefficacy loses its immunosuppressive power. These findings are based on experimentation with animals involving uncontrollable physical stressors.

Human coping involves an important feature that is rarely examined in either animal laboratory paradigms or human field studies. In animal experimentation, controllability is usually studied as a fixed dichotomous property in which animals either exercise complete control over physical stressors or they have no control whatsoever. In contrast, human coping usually entails an ongoing process of developing one's coping efficacy rather than unalterable self-inefficacy in the face of unremitting bombardment by stressors. Most human stress is activated in the course of learning how to exercise control over environmental demands and while developing and expanding competencies. Stress activated in the process of acquiring coping self-efficacy may have very different effects than stress experienced in aversive situations with no prospect in sight of ever gaining any self-protective efficacy. There are substantial evolutionary benefits to experiencing enhanced immunocompetence during development of coping capabilities vital for effective adaptation. It would not be evolutionarily advantageous if acute stressors invariably impaired immune function, because of their prevalence in everyday life. If this were the case, people would experience high vulnerability to infective agents that would quickly do them in.

Efforts to determine the immunologic effects of psychological stressors in humans have relied extensively on correlational or quasi-experimental studies in which occurrences of life stressors are related to the incidence of infectious illnesses or to indices of immunologic functioning (Jemmott & Locke, 1984; O'Leary, 1990; Palmblad, 1981). Exposure to stressors is usually accompanied by impairment of the immune system. These lines of research have clarified some aspects of inefficacious control of stressors, but experimental studies are needed to verify the direction of causality.

That stress aroused while gaining coping mastery over acute stressors can enhance different components of the immune system is revealed in a study of exposure to a chronic stressor with experimentally varied perceived coping self-efficacy (Wiedenfeld et al., 1990). In this experiment, we measured in severe phobics their strength of perceived coping self-efficacy, autonomic and neuroendocrine activation and different aspects of their immune system at three

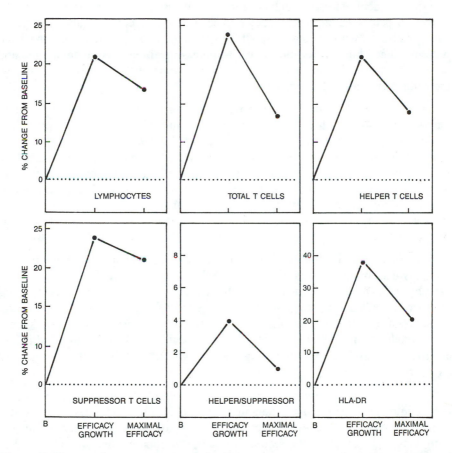

Figure 5 Changes in components of the immune system experienced as percent of baseline values during exposure to the phobic stressor while acquiring perceived coping self-efficacy *(Efficacy Growth)* and after perceived coping self-efficacy had been developed to the maximal level *(Maximal Efficacy)*. The baseline mean values for the different immune functions were as follows: Total lymphocytes = 1572; T lymphocytes = 1124; Helper T-cells = 721; Suppressor T-cells = 370; Helper/Suppressor ratio = 2.22; HLD-DR = 216 (Wiedenfeld, O'Leary, Bandura, Brown, Levine, & Raska, 1990).

phases—during a baseline control phase involving no exposure to the phobic stressor; a perceived self-efficacy acquisition phase in which they gained an increasing sense of coping efficacy over the stressor through guided mastery; and a perceived maximal self-efficacy phase during which they coped with the same stressor after they had developed a complete sense of coping efficacy.

As may be seen in Figure 5, development of strong perceived self-efficacy to control stressors had an immunoenhancing effect. However, a small subgroup of individuals exhibited a decrease in immune system status during the efficacy acquisition phase. The rate of efficacy acquisition is a good predictor of whether exposure to acute stressors enhances or attenuates the immune system. Rapid growth of perceived coping efficacy reduces stress with concomitant immunoenhancing effects, whereas slow growth of perceived coping efficacy is associated with prolonged high stress and immunosuppressing effects. High autonomic and neuroendocrine activation also attenuate components of the immune system, but their impact is somewhat weaker.

Acquisition of perceived self-efficacy to control stressors produced more than simply transient changes in immunity. The increase in immunologic competence was generally sustained over time as evident in the significantly higher immune system status in the maximal perceived self-efficacy phase than in the baseline phase. Rapid growth of perceived self-efficacy also predicted maintenance of immunocompetence during the maximal perceived self-efficacy phase. These findings indicate that vigorous mastery of chronic stressors not only instills a strong sense of self-efficacy but leaves lasting changes that can serve as protective factors against adverse immunologic effects of psychological stressors.

The field of health functioning has been heavily preoccupied with the physiologically debilitating effects of stressors. Self-efficacy theory also acknowledges the physiologically strengthening effects of mastery over stressors. A growing number of studies are providing empirical support for physiological toughening by successful coping (Dienstbier, 1989). Any comprehensive theory of psychosocial modulation of health functioning must specify the determinants and mechanisms governing both debilitating and toughening effects of coping with stressors.

Depression mediation. Bereavement and depression have been shown to reduce immune function and to heighten susceptibility to disease (Ader & Cohen, 1985; Coe & Levine, 1991). Depressive states are, therefore, often associated with increased incidence of infectious disease, development and spread of malignant neoplasms and accelerated rate of tumor cell growth. These findings suggest that another possible path of influence of coping inefficacy on immunocompetence operates through the mediating effects of depression. A sense of inefficacy to fulfill desired goals that affect evaluation of self-worth and to secure things that bring satisfaction to one's life creates depression (Bandura, 1988b; Kanfer & Zeiss, 1983). Moreover, a low sense of cognitive efficacy to turn off perturbing ruminations contributes to the depth, duration and recurrence of bouts of depression (Kavanagh & Wilson, 1989).

Supportive relationships help to lessen the aversive impact of adverse life events that can give rise to depression. When the self-doubts concern one's social capabilities, they induce depression both directly and indirectly by curtailing social relationships that can provide satisfactions and buffer the effects of chronic daily stressors (Cutrona & Troutman, 1986; Holahan & Holahan, 1987a, 1987b). O'Leary and her associates report findings that are in accord with depression mediation of immunity (O'Leary et al., 1988). A low sense of efficacy to exercise control over one's health functioning was accompanied by high levels of stress and depression, each of which was, in turn, associated with lowered functioning of several facets of the immune system.

Central mediation. The central nervous system can exert regulatory influence on immune function. Thus, a third possible path of influence of perceived self-efficacy is through central expectancy modulation of immunologic reactivity. Ader and Cohen (1981) have shown in animal experimentation that immune function is influenceable by expectancy learning. In studies with humans, induced expectations have been shown to affect physical reactions to allergens and antigens (Fry, Mason, & Pearson, 1964; Smith & McDaniel, 1983).

Experiences involving successful or failed efforts to manage environmental demands produce cognitive changes in beliefs about personal efficacy that have significant physiological consequences when the environmental stressor is no longer present (Bandura et al., 1988). Thereafter, mere thoughts about one's coping efficacy lower autonomic activation in those whose perceived self-efficacy had been enhanced, but heighten autonomic reactions in those whose sense of coping efficacy was diminished. Such findings raise the possibility that situationally aroused self-expectations of coping efficacy may produce anticipatory immunosuppressive or immunoenhancing effects.

PERCEIVED SELF-EFFICACY AND ADOPTION OF HEALTH PRACTICES

Lifestyle habits can enhance or impair health status. This enables people to exercise some control over their vitality and quality of health. Fries and Crapo (1981) have marshalled a large body of evidence that the upper limit of the human life span is fixed biologically. Figure 6 shows the mortality curves for a society at different periods of time. People are now living longer. Psychosocial factors partly determine how much of the potential lifespan is realized and the quality of life that is lived. The ideal outcome can be approximated by exercising control over modifiable factors that slow the process of aging and forestall the development of chronic diseases and infirmities. The goal is to enable people to live their expanded lifespan productively with minimum dysfunction, pain and dependence. The physical problems of "old age" get compressed into a short period at the very end of the lifespan. One makes a rapid, dignified exit when a vital system finally gives out.

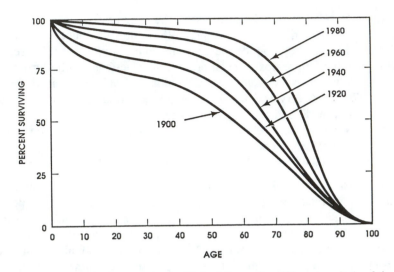

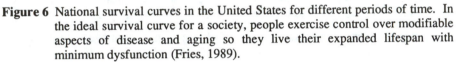

Figure 6 National survival curves in the United States for different periods of time. In the ideal survival curve for a society, people exercise control over modifiable aspects of disease and aging so they live their expanded lifespan with minimum dysfunction (Fries, 1989).

The impact of efficacy beliefs on the modifiable aspects of health and aging constitutes the second major level of research. Perceived self-efficacy affects every phase of personal change—whether people even consider changing their health habits; whether they can enlist the motivation and perseverance needed to succeed should they choose to do so; and how well they maintain the changes they have achieved.

Initiation of Personal Change

People's beliefs that they can motivate themselves and regulate their own behavior plays a crucial role in whether they even consider changing detrimental health habits or pursuing rehabilitative activities (Beck & Lund, 1981; Brod & Hall, 1984). The perceived inefficacy barrier to preventive health is all too familiar in people's resignation concerning health risks, such as smoking or obesity, over which they can exercise control. They see little point to even trying if they believe they do not have what it takes to succeed. If they make an attempt, they give up easily in the absence of quick results or setbacks.

Efforts to get people to adopt health practices that prevent disease rely heavily on persuasive communications in health education campaigns. Meyerowitz and Chaiken (1987) examined four alternative mechanisms through which health communications could alter health habits—by transmission of factual information; fear arousal; change in risk perception; and enhancement of perceived self-efficacy. They found that health communications fostered adoption of preventive health practices primarily by their effects on perceived self-efficacy.

Analyses of how community-wide media campaigns change health habits similarly reveal that both the preexisting and induced level of perceived self-efficacy play an influential role in the adoption and social diffusion of health practices (Maibach, Flora, & Nass, 1991; Slater, 1989). The stronger the preexisting perceived self-efficacy, and the more the media campaigns enhance people's self-regulative efficacy, the more they are to adopt the recommended practices (Figure 7). To help people change health-impairing habits clearly requires a shift in emphasis from trying to scare people into health, to empowering them with the tools and self-beliefs of efficacy to exercise control over their health habits.

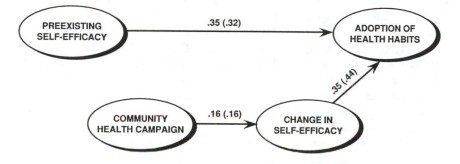

Figure 7 Path analysis of the influence of perceived self-efficacy on health habits in community-wide programs to reduce risk of cardiovascular disease. The initial numbers on the paths of influence are the significant path coefficients for adoption of healthy eating patterns; the numbers in parentheses are the path coefficients for regular exercise (Maibach, Flora, & Nass, 1991).

Achievement of Personal Change

Effective self-regulation of health behavior is not achieved through an act of will. It requires development of self-regulative skills. To build people's sense of controlling efficacy, they must develop skills on how to influence their own motivation and behavior. In such programs, they learn how to monitor the behavior they seek to change, how to set short-range attainable subgoals to motivate and direct their efforts, and how to enlist incentives and social supports to sustain the effort needed to succeed (Bandura, 1986). Once empowered with skills and self-belief in their capabilities, people are better able to adopt behaviors that promote health and to eliminate those that impair it. They benefit more from treatments for physical disabilities and their psychological well-being is less adversely affected by chronic impairments.

A growing body of evidence reveals that the impact of different therapeutic interventions on health behavior is partly mediated through their effects on perceived self-efficacy. The stronger the perceived self-efficacy they instill, the more likely are people to enlist the personal resources and sustain the level of effort needed to adopt and maintain health-promoting behavior. This has been shown in studies conducted in such diverse areas of health as enhancement of pulmonary function in patients suffering from chronic obstructive pulmonary disease (Kaplan, Atkins, & Reinsch, 1984); recovery of cardiovascular function in postcoronary patients and activity level following cardiac surgery (Gortner & Jenkins, 1990; Taylor, Bandura, Ewart, Miller, & DeBusk, 1985); reduction in pain and dysfunction in rheumatoid arthritis (Lorig, Chastain, et al., 1989; O'Leary et al., 1988); amelioration of tension headaches (Holroyd et al., 1984); control of labor and childbirth pain (Manning & Wright, 1983); management of chronic low back, neck and leg pain and impairment (Council et al., 1988); stress reduction (Bandura, Reese, & Adams, 1982; Bandura et al, 1985); adjustment to abortion (Major et al., 1990); weight reduction (Bernier & Avard, 1986; Glynn & Ruderman, 1986; Jeffrey et al., 1984; Stotland, Zuroff, & Roy, 1991); exercise of control over bulimic behavior (Love, Ollendick, Johnson, & Schlezinger, 1985; Schneider, O'Leary, & Agras, 1987; Wilson, Rossiter, Kleifield, & Lindholm, 1986); reduction of cholesterol through dietary means (McCann, Follette, Driver, Brief, & Knopp, 1988); adherence to prescribed remedial activities (Ewart, Stewart, Gillilan, & Kelemen, 1986; McCaul, Glasgow, & Schafer, 1987); adoption and long-term adherence to a regular program of physical exercise (Desharnais, Bouillon, & Godin, 1986; McAuley, 1991; Sallis et al., 1986; Sallis, Pinski, Grossman, Patterson, & Nader, 1988); maintenance of diabetic self-care (Crabtree, 1986); effective management of sexual coercions and contraceptive use to avoid unwanted pregnancies (Levinson, 1986); control of sexual practices that pose high risk for transmission of AIDS (McKusick, Coates, Morin, Pollack, & Hoff, 1990; O'Leary, Goodhart, Jemmott, & Boccher-Lattimore, 1991); and exercise of control over drug use (Gossop, Green, Phillips, & Bradley, 1990), alcohol abuse (Sitharthan & Kavanagh, 1991; Solomon & Annis, 1990), and cigarette smoking (Coletti, Supnick, & Payne, 1985; DiClemente et al., 1991; McIntyre, Lichtenstein, & Mermelstein, 1983).

Maintenance of Personal Change

Habit changes are of little consequence unless they endure. Maintenance of habit change relies heavily on self-regulatory capabilities and the functional value of the behavior. Development of self-regulatory capabilities requires instilling a resilient sense of efficacy as well as imparting skills. Experiences in exercising control over troublesome situations serve as self-efficacy builders. This is an important aspect of self-management because if people are not fully convinced of their personal efficacy they rapidly abandon the skills they have been taught when they fail to get quick results or suffer reverses. Studies of behavior that is amenable to change, but which is difficult to sustain over an extended period, show that perceived self-inefficacy increases vulnerability to relapse (Bandura, 1991). Moreover, perceived efficacy predicts how participants are likely to respond to subsequent relapse, should it occur. Those who have a strong belief in their efficacy tend to regard a slip as a temporary setback and reinstate control. In contrast, those who distrust their self-regulative capabilities display a marked decrease in perceived self-efficacy after a slip and relapse completely.

People's beliefs about their efficacy can be altered in four principal ways (Bandura, 1986). The most effective way of instilling a strong sense of efficacy is through mastery experiences. Successes build a robust sense of efficacy. Failures undermine it, especially if failures occur early in the course of events. The second method is through modeling. The models in people's lives serve as sources of competencies and motivation. People partly judge their capabilities in comparison with others. Seeing people similar to oneself succeed by perseverant effort, raises observers' beliefs about their own capabilities. The failures of others, instill self-doubts about one's own ability to master similar tasks. Social persuasion is the third mode of influence. Realistic boosts in efficacy can lead people to exert greater effort, which increases their chances of success. People also rely partly on their physiological state in judging their capabilities. They read their anxiety arousal and tension as signs of vulnerability to dysfunction. In activities involving strength and stamina, people interpret their fatigue, aches, and pains as indicants of physical inefficacy. The fourth way of modifying efficacy beliefs is to reduce people's physiological overreactions or change how they interpret their somatic sensations.

Each of these modes for enhancing self-efficacy can be put to the service of developing the resilient sense of perceived efficacy needed to override difficulties that inevitably arise from time to time. With regard to the enactive mastery mode, a resilient sense of personal efficacy is built through structured demonstration trails in the exercise of control over progressively more challenging tasks. For example, as part of instruction in cognitive control strategies, arthritic patients were given efficacy demonstration trials in which they performed selected pain-producing activities with, and without, cognitive control and rated their pain level (O'Leary et al., 1988). Explicit evidence that they achieved substantial reduction in experienced pain with cognitive control provided the patients with persuasive demonstrations that they could exercise some control over pain by enlisting cognitive strategies. Self-efficacy confirming trials not only serve as efficacy builders, but put to trial the value of the techniques being taught.

Modeling influences, in which other patients demonstrate how to cope with difficult situations, reinstate control should a setback occur and show that success usually requires tenacious effort, can further strengthen perceived self-efficacy. Moreover, modeled perseverant success can alter the diagnosticity of failure experiences as partly reflecting difficult situational predicaments rather than solely inherent personal limitations. Difficulties and setbacks prompt redoubling of efforts rather than provoke self-discouraging doubts about one's coping capabilities.

Persuasory influences that instill self-beliefs conducive to optimal utilization of skills can also contribute to staying power. As a result, people who are persuaded they have what it takes to succeed and are told that the gains achieved in treatment verify their capability are more successful in sustaining their altered health habits over a long time than those who undergo the same treatment without the efficacy-enhancing component (Blittner, Goldberg, & Merbaum, 1978).

Successful persuasory efficacy enhancers do more than convey positive appraisals. In addition to raising people's beliefs in their capabilities, they structure situations for them in ways that bring success and avoid placing them prematurely in
situations where they are likely to fail. By maintaining an efficacious attitude that
gains are attainable when clients are beset with self-doubts, they can be helped to
sustain their coping efforts in the face of reverses and discouraging obstacles.

Self-Efficacy in the Causal Structure of
Social Cognitive Theory

Perceived self-efficacy operates within social cognitive theory as one of
many determinants that regulate human motivation, emotional activation and
behavior (Bandura, 1986). In addition to the regulative function of self-efficacy
beliefs, outcome expectations concerning the effects that may flow from different
forms of behavior contribute to health behavior. These outcome expectations
take the form of detrimental or beneficial physical effects, favorable or adverse
social consequences, and positive or negative self-reactions. Cognized goals and
internal standards rooted in value systems also create self-incentives and guides
for health behavior. Cognitive and behavioral strategies aid in the translation of
self-beliefs, outcome expectations and personal goals to successful action.

Dzewaltowski and his colleagues tested the predictiveness of a subset of
sociocognitive determinants that included perceived self-efficacy to adhere to
health-promoting behavior, outcome expectations of physical benefits, and self-
evaluative reactions to one's behavioral attainments (Dzewaltowski, 1989;
Dzewaltowski, Noble, & Shaw, 1990). These three factors accounted for a
substantial amount of variance in health-promoting behavior.

A number of conceptual models, founded largely on expectancy-value
theory, have been devised to predict adoption of preventive health practices
(Becker & Maiman, 1983; Rosenstock, Strecher, & Becker, 1988; Schwarzer,
1992). They include such variables as the perceived severity of, and susceptibility to, a health threat, the perceived effectiveness and costs of the protective
action, and the anticipated outcomes for different courses of action. Recent
efforts to increase the predictiveness of such models have added the self-efficacy
determinant to the usual set of predictors. Self-efficacy beliefs make a significant
independent contribution to health behavior within the expanded models (Ajzen
& Madden, 1986; De Vries, Dijkstra, & Kuhlman, 1988; McCaul et al., 1987;
McCaul, O'Neill, & Glasgow, 1988; O'Leary et al., 1991; Schifter & Ajzen,
1985; Schwarzer, 1992).

The development of a comprehensive conceptual model of health behavior
should be guided by the principle of parsimony. The extant conceptual models
multiply predictive factors in two ways: through redundancy by including essentially the same determinant under different names; and by fractionating a higher-
order construct into facets and labeling them with dissimilar names as though
they represented fundamentally different classes of determinants. These points

can be illustrated by comparing the causal structure of social cognitive theory and the Ajzen and Fishbein (1980) theory of reasoned action.

According to the theory of reasoned action, the intention to engage in a behavior is governed by attitudes toward the behavior and by subjective norms. Attitude is measured in terms of perceived outcomes and the value placed on those outcomes. Norms are measured by perceived social pressures by significant others and one's motivation to comply with their expectations. The latter factor corresponds to expectations of social outcomes for a given behavior. In social cognitive theory normative influences regulate actions through two regulatory processes—social sanctions and instated self-sanctions. Norms influence behavior anticipatorily by the social consequences they provide. Behavior that fulfills social norms gains positive social reactions; behavior that violates social norms brings social censure. People do not act like weathervanes, constantly shifting their behavior to conform to whatever others might want. Rather, they adopt certain standards of behavior for themselves and regulate their behavior anticipatorily through self-evaluative consequences. They do things that give them self-satisfaction, they refrain from behaving in ways that violate their standards because it will bring self-censure. Social norms convey behavioral standards. Adoptions of modeled standards creates a self-regulatory system that operates through internalized self sanctions.

If one looks beyond the divergent terminology, the determinants singled out by Fishbein and Ajzen overlap with a subset of the determinants encompassed by social cognitive theory. Attitudes and subjective norms represent different classes of outcome expectations. Intentions are essentially goal representations. The overlap in determinants is confirmed empirically by Dzewaltowski and his colleagues (Dzewaltowski, 1989; Dzewaltowski et al., 1990). After establishing the contribution to health behavior of three sociocognitive determinants (i.e., perceived self-efficacy, outcome expectations of physical benefits, and self-evaluative consequences), the investigators added attitudes and norms from the Fishbein and Ajzen model to the multiple regression equation. Attitudes and norms did not account for any unique variance in health behavior over and above the social cognitive determinants.

Many of the constructs of different conceptual models of health behavior measure similar classes of determinants. But the theories differ in how well they are grounded in knowledge of regulatory mechanisms and in principles for constructing effective interventions. Health belief models seem to be concerned mainly with predicting health behavior, but they say little about how to design programs to change it. Indeed, some of the determinants tend to be conceptualized in ways that do not lend themselves easily to feasible guidelines for personal change. For example, consider the intention determinant in the model of reasoned action. Intentions presumably control actions. But one is left with considerable prescriptive ambiguity on how to change attitudes and social norms that are said to create intentions. In contrast, research conducted within the sociocognitive framework has given us a large body of knowledge on how to develop self-regulatory capabilities, structure goals and feedback systems, and mobilize social supports to foster and maintain changes in health practices (Bandura, 1986; Holroyd & Creer, 1986; Maccoby & Solomon, 1981; Puska, Nissinen, Salonen, & Toumilehto, 1983; Winett, King, & Altman, 1989).

Self-Regulatory Model of Health Promotion and Risk Reduction

Health care expenditures are soaring at a rapid rate (Fuchs, 1990). Despite the huge outlays for health services people are often poorly served by traditional health delivery systems. With people living longer and the need for health care services rising with age, societies are confronted with major challenges on how to keep people healthy throughout their lifespan, otherwise they will be swamped with burgeoning health costs. This requires intensifying health promotion efforts and restructuring health delivery systems to make them more productive.

Health promotion and risk reduction programs are often structured in ways that are costly, cumbersome and minimally effective. If services are funneled through physicians, it often creates a bottleneck in the system. Many of them do not know how to change high risk behavior. Even if they did, they cannot spare much time for any individual or make much money doing it. The net result is minimal prevention and costly remediation.

Self-management programs based on the self-efficacy model improve the quality of health and greatly reduce utilization of medical services. DeBusk and his colleagues devised an efficacy-based model combining self-regulatory principles with computerized implementation that promotes habits conducive to health and reduces those that impair it. This computerized self-regulatory system equips participants with the skills and personal efficacy to exercise self-directed change. It includes exercise programs to build cardiovascular capacity; dietary programs to reduce risk of heart disease and cancer; weight reduction programs; smoking cessation programs; and stress management programs to reduce the wear and tear on the body.

For each risk factor, individuals are provided with detailed guides on how to alter their habits, along with a self-monitoring, goal setting, and feedback system to facilitate their efforts at self-directed change. A single program implementor, assisted by the computerized system, oversees the behavioral changes of large numbers of participants. Figure 8 portrays the structure of the self-regulatory system. At selected intervals, the computer generates and mails to participants individually-tailored guides for self-directed change that specify subgoals and portray graphically the progress patients are making toward their subgoals and their month-to-month changes. Self-efficacy ratings identify areas of vulnerability and difficulty. The participants, in turn, send data to the implementor on the changes they have achieved and their level of personal efficacy in the various domains for the next cycle of self-directed change. The program implementor maintains telephone contact with the participants and is available to provide them extra guidance and support should they encounter difficulties. The implementor also serves as the liaison to medical personnel, who are called upon when their expertise is needed.

SELF-REGULATORY DELIVERY SYSTEM

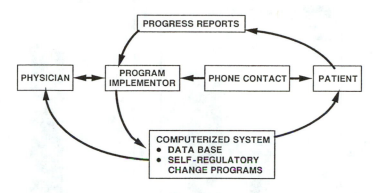

Figure 8 Computer-assisted self-regulatory system for altering health habits.

Evidence for the effectiveness of this self-regulatory system is available from a cholesterol reduction program conducted with employees with elevated cholesterol levels drawn from work sites. Each 1% reduction in serum cholesterol achieves about a 2% reduction in risk of heart attack. The program, which sought to reduce consumption of cholesterol and saturated fat, required a total of two hours per employee. The participants lowered their intake of saturated fat and achieved significant reductions in serum cholesterol by this means (Figure 9). They realized an even larger risk reduction if their spouses took part in the dietary change program as well. Some individuals have a genetic metabolic deficiency for processing saturated fats and cholesterol so their body produces high levels of cholesterol even though they do not consume much fat. Among patients with elevated plasma cholesterol, the more room for dietary reduction of saturated fats the more substantial the reductions they achieve by self-regulative means in plasma cholesterol. The success of this system to reduce morbidity and mortality in post-coronary patients is currently being compared against the usual medical post-coronary care. In this effort to reduce the likelihood of future heart attacks, a number of risk factors, including obesity, elevated cholesterol, smoking, sedentariness, and stress proneness, are selected for change.

The self-regulatory system is well received by participants because it is individually tailored to their needs; it provides them with continuing personalized guidance and informative feedback that enables them to exercise considerable control over their own change; it is a home-based program that does not require any special facilities, equipment, or attendance at group meetings that usually have high drop-out rates; and it can serve large numbers of people simultaneously. The substantial productivity gains are achieved by process innovations combining self-regulatory and computer technologies that provide effective health-promoting services in ways that are individualized, intensive, highly convenient and inexpensive.

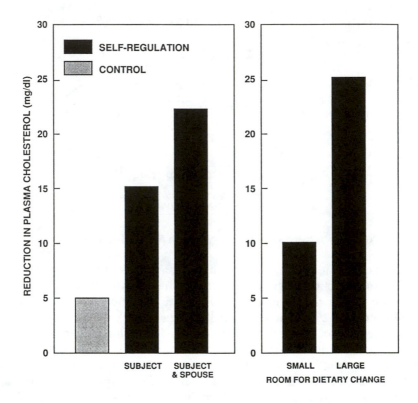

Figure 9 Levels of reduction in plasma cholesterol achieved with the computerized self-regulation system. The panel on the left summarizes the mean cholesterol reductions achieved in applications in the workplace by participants who used the system either by themselves, along with their spouses, or did not receive the system to provide a control baseline. The right panel presents the mean cholesterol reductions achieved with the self-regulative system by patients whose daily cholesterol and fat intake was high or relatively low at the outset of the program.

Self-Management of Chronic Diseases

Chronic disease has become the dominant form of illness and the major cause of disability. Such diseases do not lend themselves well to biomedical approaches devised primarily to treat acute illness. The treatment of chronic disease must focus on self-management of physical conditions over time rather than on cure. This requires, among other things, pain amelioration, enhancement and maintenance of functioning with growing physical disability and development of self-regulative compensatory skills. Lorig and her colleagues have devised a prototypic model for the self-management of different types of chronic diseases

(Lorig, Seleznick, et al., 1989). The self-management skills include cognitive pain control techniques, self-relaxation, proximal goal setting to increase level of activity and use of self-incentives as motivators, problem solving and self-diagnostic skills for monitoring and interpreting one's health status and skills in locating community resources, managing medication programs, and effective ways of dealing with physicians and other aspects of health care systems to optimize health benefits. Participants are taught how to exercise some control over their physical condition through modeling of self-management skills, guided mastery practice, informative feedback and efficacy demonstration trials.

The effectiveness of this self-regulative approach has been tested extensively for ameliorating the debility and chronic pain of arthritis (Lorig, Seleznick, et al., 1989). Patients suffering from rheumatoid arthritis, substantially improve their psychophysical functioning following treatment compared to matched controls who received an arthritis helpbook describing self-management techniques and were encouraged to be more active (O'Leary et al., 1988). The self-management program increased patients perceived self-efficacy to reduce pain and other debilitating aspects of arthritis, and to pursue potentially painful activities (Figure 10). The treated patients reduced their pain and inflammation in their joints, and were less debilitated by their arthritic condition. The higher their perceived coping efficacy, the less pain they experienced, the less they were disabled by their arthritis, and the greater the reduction they achieved in joint impairment. The more efficacious were also less depressed, less stressed, and they slept better.

The treatment did not alter immunologic function, but significant relationships were found between perceived coping efficacy and immunologic indices. There is some evidence that in the arthritic disorder the suppressor T-cell function of the immune system is depressed. This results in proliferation of antibodies, which is aided by helper T-cells. Arthritis is an autoimmune disorder in which the immune system produces antibodies that destroy normal tissues of the body. Increases in suppressor T-cells, which tend to inhibit production of antibodies, suggest improvement in the immune system for this disorder. Perceived coping efficacy was associated with increases in the number of suppressor T-cells and with a decrease in the ratio of helper to suppressor T-cells.

In a follow-up assessment conducted four years later, arthritis patients who have had the benefit of self-management training displayed increased self-efficacy, reduced pain, much lower utilization of medical services (43%), and slower biological progression of their disease over the four-year period (Holman, Mazonson, & Lorig, 1989; Lorig, 1990). These changes are shown in Figure 11. Enhancement of functioning despite some biological progression of the disease provides further testimony that functional limitations may be governed more by self-beliefs of capability than by degree of actual physical impairment (Baron, Dutil, Berkson, Lander, & Becker, 1987). Tests of alternative mediating mechanisms reveal that neither increases in knowledge nor degree of change in health behaviors are appreciable predictors of health functioning (Lorig, Chastain, et al., 1989; Lorig, Seleznick, et al., 1989). However, both baseline perceived self-

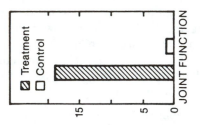

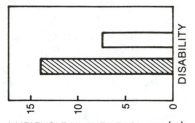

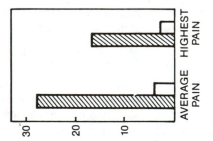

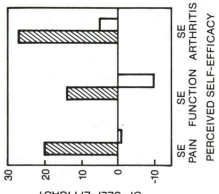

Figure 10 Changes exhibited by arthritic patients in perceived self-efficacy and reduction in pain and impairment of joints as a function of training in self-regulatory techniques (O'Leary, Shoor, Lorig, & Holman, 1988).

efficacy and changes in perceived self-efficacy to exercise some control over one's arthritic condition instilled by treatment explain more than 40% of the variance in pain four years later (Lorig, 1990). When patients are equated for degree of physical debility, those who believe they can exercise some influence over how much their arthritic condition affects them lead more active lives and experience less pain (Shoor & Holman, 1984). This self-management model lends itself well to other types of chronic diseases.

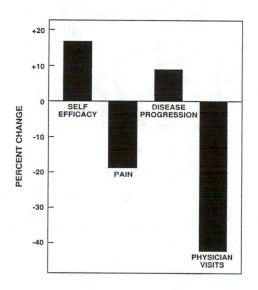

Figure 11 Enduring healthful changes achieved by training in self-management of arthiritis as revealed in a follow-up assessment four years later. The 9% biological progression of the disease is much less than the 20% disease progression one would normally expect over four years for this age group. Plotted from data of Lorig, 1990.

IMPACT OF PROGNOSTIC JUDGMENTS ON SELF-EFFICACY AND HEALTH OUTCOMES

Much of the work in the health field is concerned with diagnosing maladies, forecasting the likely course of different physical disorders and prescribing remedies. Medical prognostic judgments involve probabilistic inferences from knowledge of varying quality and inclusiveness about the multiple factors governing the course of a given disorder. Because psychosocial factors account for some of the variability in the course of health functioning their inclusion in prognostic schemes will enhance their predictive power. Prognostic judgments can alter perceived self-efficacy in ways that affect health outcomes rather than simply serve as nonreactive forecastings of things to come (Bandura, 1992).

Scope of Prognostic Schemes

One important issue regarding prognosis concerns the range of factors included in a prognostic scheme. As previously noted, level of health functioning is determined not only by biologically-rooted factors but also by patients' self-beliefs and a system of social influences that can enhance or impede the progress they make. If one takes no notice of psychosocial determinants one is left with puzzling variability in the courses that health changes take and unexplained differential functional attainments of people who are equally physically impaired. Thus, arthritics with deformed hands may lead fulfilling productive lives, whereas others with minimal arthritic impairment become despondent and abandon activities. Neither biochemical laboratory tests nor measures of degree of actual physical impairment predicts functional attainments (Baron et al., 1987). Results of a program of research on enhancement of perceived self-efficacy for post-coronary recovery indicate that strength of perceived self-efficacy is a psychological prognostic indicator of the course that health outcomes are likely to take.

About half the patients who experience myocardial infarctions have uncomplicated ones (DeBusk, Kraemer, & Nash, 1983). Their heart heals rapidly, and they are physically capable of resuming an active life. However, the psychological and physical recovery is slow for patients who believe they have an impaired heart. They avoid physical exertion. They fear that they cannot handle the strains in their vocational and social life. They give up recreational activities. They fear that sexual activities will do them in. The recovery problems stem more from patients' beliefs that their cardiac system has been impaired than from physical debility. The rehabilitative task is to convince patients that they have a sufficiently robust cardiovascular system to lead productive lives.

Psychological recovery from a heart attack is a social, rather than solely an individual matter. Virtually all of the patients are males. The wives' judgments of their husbands' physical and cardiac capabilities can aid or retard the recovery process. The direction that social support takes is partly determined by perceptions of efficacy. Spousal support is likely to be expressed in curtailment of activity if the husband's heart function is regarded as impaired, but as encouragement of activity if his heart function is judged to be robust. In the program designed to enhance postcoronary recovery (Taylor et al., 1985), the treadmill was used to raise and strengthen spousal and patients' beliefs in their cardiac capabilities.

Several weeks after patients have had a heart attack we measured their beliefs about how much strain their heart could withstand. They then performed a symptom-limited treadmill, mastering increasing workloads with three levels of spouse involvement in the treadmill activity. The wife was either uninvolved in the treadmill activity; she was present to observe her husband's stamina as he performed the treadmill under increasing workloads; or she observed her husband's performance, whereupon she performed the treadmill exercises herself to gain firsthand information of the physical stamina it requires. We reasoned that having the wives personally experience the strenuousness of the task, and seeing their husbands match or surpass them, should convince them that their husband has a robust heart.

After the treadmill activities, couples were fully informed by the cardiologist about the patients' level of cardiac functioning and their capacity to resume activities in their daily life. If the treadmill is interpreted as an isolated task, its impact on perceived cardiac and physical capability may be limited. In order to achieve a generalized impact of enhanced self-efficacy on diverse domains of functioning, the stamina on the treadmill was presented as a generic indicant of cardiovascular capability—that the patients' level of exertion exceeded whatever strain everyday activities might place on their cardiac system. This would encourage them to resume activities in their everyday life that place weaker demands on their cardiac system than did the heavy workloads on the treadmill. The patient's and spouse's beliefs concerning his physical and cardiac capabilities were measured before and after the treadmill activity, and again after the medical counseling.

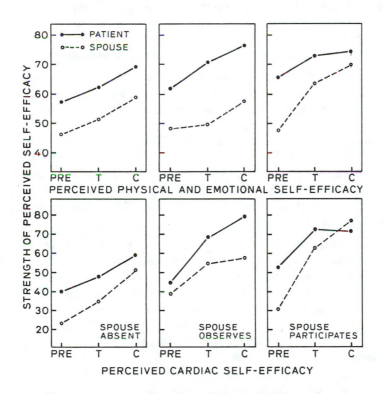

Figure 12 Changes in perceived physical and cardiac efficacy as a function of level of spouse involvement, patients' treadmill exercises, and the combined influence of treadmill exercises and medical counseling. Perceived efficacy was measured before the treadmill *(Pre)*, after the treadmill *(T)*, and after the medical counseling *(C)* (Taylor, Bandura, Ewart, Miller, & DeBusk, 1985).

Figure 12 shows the patterns of changes in beliefs concerning the patients' physical and cardiac capabilities at different phases of the experiment under different levels of spousal involvement in the treadmill activity. Treadmill performances increased patients' beliefs in their physical and cardiac capabilities. Initially the beliefs of wives and their husbands were highly discrepant—husbands judged themselves moderately hearty, whereas wives judged their husbands' cardiac capability as severely impaired and incapable of withstanding physical and emotional strain. Spouses who were either uninvolved in, or merely observers of, the treadmill activity, did not change their considerable doubts about their husbands' physical and cardiac capabilities. Even the detailed medical counseling by the cardiology staff did not alter their preexisting beliefs of cardiac debility. However, wives who had personally experienced the strenuousness of the treadmill were persuaded that their husbands had a sufficiently robust heart to withstand the normal strains of everyday activities. The participant experience apparently altered spousal cognitive processing of treadmill information, giving greater weight to indicants of cardiac robustness than to symptomatic signs of cardiac debility. Efficacy beliefs affect receptivity to prognostic information. Thus, the change in perceived efficacy made the wives more accepting of the medical counseling. Following the medical counseling, couples in the participant spouse condition had congruently high perceptions of the patients' cardiac capabilities.

The findings further show that beliefs of cardiac capabilities can affect the course of recovery from myocardial infarction. The higher the patients' and the wives' beliefs in the patients' cardiac capabilities, the greater was the patients' cardiovascular functioning as measured by peak heart rate and maximal workload achieved on the treadmill six months later. The joint belief in the patients' cardiac efficacy proved to be the best predictor of cardiac functional level. Initial treadmill performance did not predict level of cardiovascular functioning in the follow-up assessment when perceived efficacy is partialled out. But perceived cardiac efficacy predicted level of cardiovascular functioning when initial treadmill performance was partialled out.

Wives who believe that their husbands have a robust heart are more likely to encourage them to resume an active life than those who believe their husband's heart is impaired and vulnerable to further damage. The positive relation between the wife's perceptions of her husband's cardiac capability and his treadmill accomplishments months later is, in all likelihood, partly mediated by spousal encouragement of activities during the interim period. Pursuit of an active life improves the patient's physical capability to engage in activities without overtaxing their cardiovascular system.

Self-Validating Potential of Prognostic Judgments

Health outcomes are related to predictive factors in complex, multidetermined and probabilistic ways. Prognostic judgments, therefore, involve some degree of uncertainty. The predictiveness of a given prognostic scheme will depend on the number of relevant predictors it encompasses, the relative validities and inter-relations of the predictors, and the adequacy with which they are measured. There is always leeway for expectancy effects to operate because prognostic schemes rarely include all of the relevant biological and psychosocial predictors and even the predictors that are singled out usually have less than perfect validity. Based on selected sources of information, diagnosticians form expectations about the probable course of a disease. The more confident they are in the validity of their prognostic scheme, the stronger are their prognostic expectations.

Prognostic judgments are not simply nonreactive forecasts of a natural course of a disease. Because prognostic information can affect patients' beliefs in their physical efficacy, diagnosticians not only foretell but may partly influence the course of recovery from disease. Prognostic expectations are conveyed to patients by attitude, word, or the type and level of care provided them. Prognostic judgments have a self-confirming potential. Expectations can alter patients' self-beliefs and behavior in ways that confirm the original expectations. Evidence indicates that the self-efficacy mechanism operates as one important mediator of self-confirming effects (Bandura, 1992; Litt, 1988). Analysis of self-confirming processes has focused mainly on how people's self-beliefs of efficacy and behavior are affected by what they are told about their capabilities. Other evidence suggests that prognostic judgments may bias how people are treated as well as what they are told. Individuals treat others differently under high than under low expectations in ways that tend to confirm the original expectations (Jones, 1977; Jussim, 1986). Under induced high expectations individuals generally pay more attention to those in their charge, provide them with more emotional support, create greater opportunities for them to build their competences and give them more positive feedback than under induced low expectations.

Differential care that promotes in patients different levels of self-efficaciousness and skill in managing health-related behavior can exert stronger impact on the trajectories of health functioning than simply conveying prognostic information. The effects of verbal prognostications alone may be short-lived if they are repeatedly disconfirmed by personal experiences. But a sense of personal efficacy rooted in enhanced competencies fosters functional attainments that create their own experiential validation. Clinical transactions operate bidirectionally to shape the course of change. The functional improvements fostered by positive expectancy influences further strengthen clinicians' beneficial expectations and their sense of efficacy to aid progress. In contrast, negative expectations that breed functional declines can set in motion a downward course of mutual discouragement.

Medical conditions that produce severe permanent impairments can be devastatingly demoralizing to patients and their families. Patients have to reorganize their perspective to learn alternative ways of regaining as much control as possible over their life activities. Goals need to be restructured in functional terms that capitalize on remaining capacities (Ozer, 1988). Focus on achievement of functional improvements rather than on degree of organic impairments helps to counteract self-demoralization. Making difficult activities easier by breaking them down into graduated subtasks of attainable steps helps to prevent self-discouragement of rehabilitative efforts and enhances functional attainments.

CONCLUDING REMARKS

The converging lines of evidence reported in this chapter indicate that the self-efficacy mechanism plays an influential role in mediating the impact of psychosocial factors both on biological systems that interrelatedly alter physical functioning and on health habits that prevent or mitigate pathogenic conditions. The value of a psychological theory is judged not only by its explanatory and predictive power, but also by its operational power to effect change in human functioning. Social cognitive theory provides prescriptive specificity on how to enhance people's sense of personal efficacy in ways that promote their health and psychological well-being.

REFERENCES

Ader, R., & Cohen, N. (1981). Conditioned immunopharmacologic responses. In R. Ader (Ed.), *Psychoneuroimmunology* (pp. 281-319). New York: Academic Press.

Ader, R., & Cohen, N. (1985). CNS-immune system interactions: Conditioning phenomena. *The Behavioral and Brain Sciences, 8,* 379-394.

Ahles, T. A., Blanchard, E. B., & Leventhal, H. (1983). Cognitive control of pain: Attention to the sensory aspects of the cold pressor stimulus. *Cognitive Therapy and Research, 7,* 159-178.

Ajzen, I., & Fishbein, M. (1980). *Understanding attitudes and predicting social behavior.* Englewood Cliffs, NJ: Prentice-Hall.

Ajzen, I., & Madden, T. J. (1986). Prediction of goal-directed behavior: Attitudes, intentions, and perceived behavioral control. *Journal of Experimental Social Psychology, 22,* 453-474.

Bandura, A. (1986). *Social foundations of thought and action: A social cognitive theory.* Englewood Cliffs, NJ: Prentice-Hall.

Bandura, A. (1988a). Self-efficacy conception of anxiety. *Anxiety Research, 1,* 77-98.

Bandura, A. (1988b). Self-regulation of motivation and action through goal systems. In V. Hamilton, G. H. Bower, & N. H. Frijda (Eds.), *Cognitive perspectives on emotion and motivation* (pp. 37-61). Dordrecht: Kluwer Academic Publishers.

Bandura, A. (1991). Self-efficacy mechanism in physiological activation and health-promoting behavior. In J. Madden, IV, (Ed.), *Neurobiology of learning, emotion and affect* (pp. 229-270). New York: Raven.

Bandura, A. (1992). Psychological aspects of prognostic judgments. In R. W. Evans, D. S. Baskin, & F. M. Yatsu (Eds.), *Prognosis in neurological disease.* New York: Oxford University Press (in press).

Bandura, A., Cioffi, D., Taylor, C. B., & Brouillard, M. E. (1988). Perceived self-efficacy in coping with cognitive stressors and opioid activation. *Journal of Personality and Social Psychology, 55,* 479-488.

Bandura, A., O'Leary, A., Taylor, C. B., Gauthier, J., & Gossard, D. (1987). Perceived self-efficacy and pain control: Opioid and nonopioid mechanisms. *Journal of Personality and Social Psychology, 63*, 563-571.

Bandura, A., Reese, L., & Adams, N. E. (1982). Microanalysis of action and fear arousal as a function of differential levels of perceived self-efficacy. *Journal of Personality and Social Psychology, 43*, 5-21.

Bandura, A., Taylor, C. B., Williams, S. L, Mefford, I. N., & Barchas, J. D. (1985). Catecholamine secretion as a function of perceived coping self-efficacy. *Journal of Consulting and Clinical Psychology, 53*, 406-414.

Baron, M., Dutil, E., Berkson, L., Lander, P., & Becker, R. (1987). Hand function in the elderly: Relation to osteoarthritis. *Journal of Rheumatology, 14*, 815-819.

Beck, K. H., & Lund, A. K. (1981). The effects of health threat seriousness and personal efficacy upon intentions and behavior. *Journal of Applied Social Psychology, 11*, 401-415.

Becker, M. H., & Maiman, L. A. (1983). Models of health-related behavior. In D. Mechanic (Ed.), *Handbook of health, health care, and the health professions* (pp. 539-568). New York: The Free Press.

Bernier, M., & Avard, J. (1986). Self-efficacy, outcome and attrition in a weight reduction program. *Cognitive Therapy and Research, 10*, 319-338.

Blittner, M., Goldberg, J., & Merbaum, M. (1978). Cognitive self-control factors in the reduction of smoking behavior. *Behavior Therapy, 9*, 553-561.

Brod, M. I., & Hall, S. M. (1984). Joiners and non-joiners in smoking treatment: A comparison of psychosocial variables. *Addictive Behaviors, 9*, 217-221.

Cioffi, D. (1991). Beyond attentional strategies: Advancing the study of somatic interpretation. *Psychological Bulletin, 109*, 25-41.

Coe, C. L., & Levine, S. (1991). Psychoimmunology: An old idea whose time has come. In P. R. Barchas (Ed.), *Social physiology of social relations*. Oxford: Oxford University Press (in press).

Coletti, G., Supnick, J. A., & Payne, T. J. (1985). The smoking self-efficacy questionnaire (SSEQ): Preliminary scale development and validation. *Behavioral Assessment, 7*, 249-260.

Council, J. R., Ahern, D. K., Follick, M. J., & Kline, C. L. (1988). Expectancies and functional impairment in chronic low back pain. *Pain, 33*, 323-331.

Crabtree, M. K. (1986). *Self-efficacy beliefs and social support as predictors of diabetic self-care*. Unpublished doctoral dissertation, University of California, San Francisco.

Craig, K. D. (1986). Social modeling influences: Pain in context. In R. A. Sternbach (Ed.), *The psychology of pain* (2nd ed., pp. 67-95). New York: Raven Press.

Cutrona, C. E., & Troutman, B. R. (1986). Social support, infant temperament, and parenting self-efficacy: A mediational model of postpartum depression. *Child Development, 57*, 1507-1518.

DeBusk, R. F., Kraemer, H. C., & Nash, E. (1983). Stepwise risk stratification soon after acute myocardial infarction. *The American Journal of Cardiology, 12*, 1161-1166.

Desharnais, R., Bouillon, J., & Godin, G. (1986). Self-efficacy and outcome expectations as determinants of exercise adherence. *Psychological Reports, 59*, 1155-1159.

De Vries, H., Dijkstra, M., & Kuhlman, P. (1988). Self-efficacy: The third factor besides attitude and subjective norm as a predictor of behavioural intentions. *Health Education Research, 3*, 273-282.

DiClemente, C. C., Fairhurst, S. K., Velasquez, M. M., Prochaska, J. O., Velicer, W. F., & Rossi, J. S. (1991, in press). The process of smoking cessation: An analysis of precontemplation, contemplation and preparation stages of change. *Journal of Consulting and Clinical Psychology.*

Dienstbier, R. A. (1989). Arousal and physiological toughness: Implications for mental and physical health. *Psychological Review, 96,* 84-100.

Dolce, J. J. (1987). Self-efficacy and disability beliefs in behavioral treatment of pain. *Behaviour Research and Therapy, 25,* 289-300.

Dzewaltowski, D. A. (1989). Towards a model of exercise motivation. *Journal of Sport and Exercise Psychology, 11,* 251-269.

Dzewaltowski, D. A., Noble, J. M., & Shaw, J. M. (1990). Physical activity participation: Social cognitive theory versus the theories of reasoned action and planned behavior. *Journal of Sport and Exercise Psychology, 12,* 388-405.

Engel, G. L. (1977). The need for a new medical model: A challenge for biomedicine. *Science, 196,* 129-136.

Ewart, C. K., Stewart, K. J., Gillilan, R. E., & Kelemen, M. H. (1986). Self-efficacy mediates strength gains during circuit weight training in men with coronary artery disease. *Medicine and Science in Sports and Exercise, 18,* 531-540.

Fanselow, M. S. (1986). Conditioned fear-induced opiate analgesia: A competing motivational state theory of stress analgesia. In D. D. Kelly (Ed.), *Stress-induced analgesia. Annals of the New York Academy of Sciences* (Vol. 467, pp. 40-54). New York: New York Academy of Sciences.

Fries, J. F. (1989). *Aging well.* Reading, MA: Addison-Wesley.

Fries, J. F., & Crapo, L. M. (1981). *Vitality and aging: Implications of the rectangular curve.* San Francisco: Freeman.

Fry, L., Mason, A. A., & Pearson, R. S. B. (1964). Effect of hypnosis on allergic skin responses in asthma and hay fever. *British Medical Journal, 5391,* 1145-1148.

Fuchs, V. R. (1974). *Who shall live? Health, economics, and social choice.* New York: Basic Books.

Fuchs, V. R. (1990). The health sector's share of the gross national product. *Science, 247,* 534-538.

Glass, D. C., Reim, B., & Singer, J. (1971). Behavioral consequences of adaptation to controllable and uncontrollable noise. *Journal of Experimental Social Psychology, 7,* 244-257.

Glynn, S. M., & Ruderman, A. J. (1986). The development and validation of an eating self-efficacy scale. *Cognitive Therapy and Research, 10,* 403-420.

Goldberger, L., & Breznitz, S. (Eds.).(1982). *Handbook of stress: Theoretical and clinical aspects.* New York: Free Press.

Gortner, S. R., & Jenkins, L. S. (1990). Self-efficacy and activity level following cardiac surgery. *Journal of Advanced Nursing, 15,* 1132-1138.

Gossop, M., Green, L., Phillips, G., & Bradley, B. (1990). Factors predicting outcome among opiate addicts after treatment. *British Journal of Clinical Psychology, 29,* 209-216.

Gracely, R. H., Dubner, R., Wolskee, P. J., & Deeter, W. R. (1983). Placebo and naloxone can alter post-surgical pain by separate mechanisms. *Nature, 306,* 264-265.

Grau, J. W., Hyson, R. L., Maier, S. F., Madden, J., IV, & Barchas, J. D. (1981). Long-term stress-induced analgesia and activation of the opiate system. *Science, 213,* 1409-1411.

Holahan, C. K., & Holahan, C. J. (1987a). Self-efficacy, social support, and depression in aging: A longitudinal analysis. *Journal of Gerontology, 42*, 65-68.

Holahan, C. K., & Holahan, C. J. (1987b). Life stress, hassles, and self-efficacy in aging: A replication and extension. *Journal of Applied Social Psychology, 17*, 574-592.

Holman, H., Mazonson, P., & Lorig, K. (1989). Health education for self-management has significant early and sustained benefits in chronic arthritis. *Transactions of the Association of American Physicians, 102*, 204-208.

Holroyd, K. A., & Creer, T. L. (1986). *Self-management of chronic disease.* New York: Academic Press.

Holroyd, K. A., Penzien, D. B., Hursey, K. G., Tobin, D. L., Rogers, L., Holm, J. E., Marcille, P. J., Hall, J. R., & Chila, A. G. (1984). Change mechanisms in EMG biofeedback training: Cognitive changes underlying improvements in tension headache. *Journal of Consulting and Clinical Psychology, 52*, 1039-1053.

Jeffrey, R. W., Bjornson-Benson, W. M., Rosenthal, B. S., Lindquist, R. A., Kurth, C. L., & Johnson, S. L. (1984). Correlates of weight loss and its maintenance over two years of follow-up among middle-aged men. *Preventive Medicine, 13*, 155-168.

Jemmott, J. B., III, & Locke, S. E. (1984). Psychosocial factors, immunological mediation, and human susceptibility to infectious diseases: How much do we know? *Psychological Bulletin, 95*, 78-108.

Jones, R. A. (1977). *Self-fulfilling prophesies: Social, psychological, and physiological effects of experiences.* Hillsdale, NJ: Erlbaum.

Jussim, L. (1986). Self-fulfilling prophecies: A theoretical and integrative review. *Psychological Review, 93*, 429-445.

Kahneman, E. (1973). *Attention and effort.* Englewood Cliffs, NJ: Prentice-Hall.

Kanfer, R., & Zeiss, A. M. (1983). Depression, interpersonal standard-setting, and judgments of self-efficacy. *Journal of Abnormal Psychology, 92*, 319-329.

Kaplan, R. M., Atkins, C. J., & Reinsch, S. (1984). Specific efficacy expectations mediate exercise compliance in patients with COPD. *Health Psychology, 3*, 223-242.

Kavanagh, D. J., & Wilson, P. H. (1989). Prediction of outcome with a group version of cognitive therapy for depression. *Behaviour Research and Therapy, 27*, 333-347.

Kelley, D. D. (Ed.).(1986). *Stress-induced analgesia. Annals of the New York Academy of Sciences* (Vol. 467). New York: New York Academy of Sciences.

Kiecolt-Glaser, J. K., & Glaser, R. (1987). Behavioral influences on immune function: Evidence for the interplay between stress and health. In T. Field, P. M. McCabe, & N. Schneiderman (Eds.), *Stress and coping across development* (Vol. 2, pp. 189-206). Hillsdale, NJ: Erlbaum.

Krantz, D. S., Grunberg, N. E., & Baum, A. (1985). Health psychology. *Annual Reviews in Psychology, 36*, 349-383.

Lazarus, R. S., & Folkman, S. (1984). . New York: Springer.

Levine, J. D., & Gordon, N. C. (1984). Influence of the method of drug administration on analgesic response. Stress, appraisal, and coping. *Nature, 312*, 755-756.

Levine, J. D., Gordon, N. C., & Fields, H. L. (1978, September 23). The mechanism of placebo analgesia. *The Lancet*, 654-657.

Levine, J. D., Gordon, N. C., Jones, R. T., & Fields, H. L. (1978). The narcotic antagonist naloxone enhances clinical pain. *Nature, 272*, 826-827.

Levinson, R. A. (1986). Contraceptive self-efficacy: A perspective on teenage girls' contraceptive behavior. *Journal of Sex Research, 22*, 347-369.

Litt, M. D. (1988). Self-efficacy and perceived control: Cognitive mediators of pain tolerance. *Journal of Personality and Social Psychology, 54*, 149-160.

Locke, S., Ader, R., Besedovsky, H., Hall, N., Solomon, G., & Strom, T. (Eds.). (1985). *Foundations of psychoneuroimmunology*. Hawthorne, NY: Aldine.

Lorig, K., (1990, April). *Self-efficacy: Its contributions to the four year beneficial outcome of the arthritis self-management course*. Paper presented at the meeting of the Society for Behavioral Medicine, Chicago, IL.

Lorig, K., Chastain, R. L., Ung, E., Shoor, S., & Holman, H. (1989). Development and evaluation of a scale to measure perceived self-efficacy in people with arthritis. *Arthritis and Rheumatism, 32*, 37-44.

Lorig, K., Seleznick, M., Lubeck, D., Ung, E., Chastain, R. L., & Holman, H. R. (1989). The beneficial outcomes of the arthritis self-management course are not adequately explained by behavior change. *Arthritis and Rheumatism, 32*, 91-95.

Love, S. Q., Ollendick, T. H., Johnson, C., & Schlezinger, S. E. (1985). A preliminary report of the prediction of bulimic behavior: A social learning analysis. *Bulletin of the Society of Psychologists in Addictive Behavior, 4*, 93-101.

Maccoby, N., & Solomon, D. S. (1981). Heart disease prevention: Community studies. In R. E. Rice & W. J. Paisley (Eds.), *Public communication campaigns* (pp. 105-125). Beverly Hills, CA: Sage Publications.

MacLennan, A. J., Drugan, R. C., Hyson, R. L., Maier, S. F., Madden, J., IV, & Barchas, J. D. (1982). Corticosterone: A critical factor in an opioid form of stress-induced analgesia. *Science, 215*, 1530-1532.

Maibach, E., Flora, J., & Nass, C. (1991). Changes in self-efficacy and health behavior in response to a minimal contact community health campaign. *Health Communication, 3*, 1-15.

Maier, S. F. (1986). Stressor controllability and stress-induced analgesia. In D. D. Kelly (Ed.), *Stress-induced analgesia. Annals of the New York Academy of Sciences* (Vol. 467, pp. 55-72). New York: New York Academy of Sciences.

Maier, S. F., Laudenslager, M. L., & Ryan, S. M. (1985). Stressor controllability, immune function, and endogenous opiates. In F. R. Brush & J. B. Overmier (Eds.), *Affect, conditioning, and cognition: Essays on the determinants of behavior* (pp. 183-201). Hillsdale, NJ: Erlbaum.

Major, B., Cozzarelli, C., Sciacchitano, A. M., Cooper, M. L., Testa, M., & Mueller, P. M. (1990). Perceived social support, self-efficacy, and adjustment to abortion. *Journal of Personality and Social Psychology, 59*, 452-463.

Manning, M. M., & Wright, T. L. (1983). Self-efficacy expectancies, outcome expectancies, and the persistence of pain control in childbirth. *Journal of Personality and Social Psychology, 45*, 421-431.

McAuley, E. (1991, in press). Understanding exercise behavior: A self-efficacy perspective. In G. C. Roberts (Ed.), *Understanding motivation in exercise and sport*. Champaign, IL: Human Kinetics.

McCann, B. S., Follette, W. C., Driver, J. L., Brief, D. J., & Knopp, R. H. (1988, August). *Self-efficacy and adherence in the dietary treatment of hyperlipidemia*. Paper presented at the 96th Annual Convention of the American Psychological Association, Atlanta, Georgia.

McCaul, K. D., Glasgow, R. E., & Schafer, L. C. (1987). Diabetes regimen behaviors: Predicting adherence. *Medical Care, 25*, 868-881.

McCaul, K. D., O'Neill, K., & Glasgow, R. E. (1988). Predicting the performance of dental hygiene behaviors: An examination of the Fishbein and Ajzen model and self-efficacy expectations. *Journal of Applied Social Psychology, 18,* 114-128.

McIntyre, K. O., Lichtenstein, E., & Mermelstein, R. J. (1983). Self-efficacy and relapse in smoking cessation: A replication and extension. *Journal of Consulting and Clinical Psychology, 51,* 632-633.

McKusick, L., Coates, T. J., Morin, S. F., Pollack, L., & Hoff, C. (1990). Longitudinal predictors of reductions in high risk sexual behaviors among gay men in San Francisco: The AIDS behavioral research project. *American Journal of Public Health, 80,* 978-983.

Mefford, I. N., Ward, M. M., Miles, L., Taylor, B., Chesney, M. A., Keegan, D. L., & Barchas, J. D. (1981). Determination of plasma catecholamines and free 3,4-dihy-droxyphenylacetic acid in continuously collected human plasma by high performance liquid chromatography with electrochemical detection. *Life Sciences, 28,* 447-483.

Meyerowitz, B. E., & Chaiken, S. (1987). The effect of message framing on breast self-examination attitudes, intentions, and behavior. *Journal of Personality and Social Psychology, 52,* 500-510.

O'Leary, A. (1990). Stress, emotion, and human immune function. *Psychological Bulletin, 108,* 363-382.

O'Leary, A., Goodhart, F., Jemmott, L. S., & Boccher-Lattimore, D. (1991). Predictors of safer sexual behavior on the college campus: A social cognitive analysis. *Journal of American College Health* (in press).

O'Leary, A., Shoor, S., Lorig, K., & Holman, H. R. (1988). A cognitive-behavioral treatment for rheumatoid arthritis. *Health Psychology, 7,* 527-544.

Ozer, M. N. (1988). *The management of persons with spinal cord injury.* New York: Demos.

Palmblad, J. (1981). Stress and immunologic competence: Studies in man. In R. Ader (Ed.) *Psychoneuroimmunology* (pp. 229-257). New York: Academic Press.

Puska, P., Nissinen, A., Salonen, J. T., & Toumilehto, J. (1983). Ten years of the North Karelia project: Results with community-based prevention of coronary heart disease. *Scandinavian Journal of Social Medicine, 11,* 65-68.

Reese, L. (1983). *Coping with pain: The role of perceived self-efficacy.* Unpublished doctoral dissertation, Stanford University, Stanford, CA.

Rosenstock, I. M., Strecher, V. J., & Becker, M. H. (1988). Social learning theory and the health belief model. *Health Education Quarterly, 15,* 175-183.

Sallis, J. F., Haskell, W. L., Fortmann, S. P., Vranizan, M. S., Taylor, C. B., & Solomon, D. S. (1986). Predictors of adoption and maintenance of physical activity in a community sample. *Preventive Medicine, 15,* 331-341.

Sallis, J. F., Pinski, R. B., Grossman, R. M., Patterson, T. L., & Nader, P. R. (1988). The development of self-efficacy scales for health-related diet and exercise behaviors. *Health Education Research, 3,* 283-292.

Schifter, D. E., & Ajzen, I. (1985). Intention, perceived control, and weight loss: An application of the theory of planned behavior. *Journal of Personality and Social Psychology, 49,* 843-851.

Schneider, J. A., O'Leary, A., & Agras, W. S. (1987). The role of perceived self-efficacy in recovery from bulimia: A preliminary examination. *Behaviour Research and Therapy, 25,* 429-432.

Schwarzer, R. (1992). Self-efficacy in the adoption and maintenance of health behaviors: Theoretical approaches and a new model. In Schwarzer, R. (Ed.), *Self-efficacy: Thought control of action*. Washington, DC: Hemisphere (this volume).

Shavit, Y., & Martin, F. C. (1987). Opiates, stress, and immunity: Animal studies. *Annals of Behavioral Medicine, 9*, 11-20.

Shoor, S. M., & Holman, H. R. (1984). Development of an instrument to explore psychological mediators of outcome in chronic arthritis. *Transactions of the Association of American Physicians, 97*, 325-331.

Sitharthan, T., & Kavanagh, D. J. (1991). *Role of self-efficacy in predicting outcomes from a programme for controlled drinking*. Unpublished manuscript, Drug and Alcohol Department, Royal Prince Alfred Hospital, Camperdown, Australia.

Slater, M. D. (1989). Social influences and cognitive control as predictors of self-efficacy and eating behavior. *Cognitive Therapy and Research, 13*, 231-245.

Smith, G. R., & McDaniel, S. M. (1983). Psychologically mediated effect on the delayed hypersensitivity reaction to tuberculin in humans. *Psychosomatic Medicine, 45*, 65-70.

Solomon, K. E., & Annis, H. M. (1990). Outcome and efficacy expectancy in the prediction of post-treatment drinking behaviour. *British Journal of Addiction, 85*, 659-666.

Stotland, S., Zuroff, D. C., Roy, M. (1991). *Situational dieting self-efficacy and short-term regulation of eating*. Unpublished manuscript, McGill University, Montreal, Quebec, Canada.

Taylor, C. B., Bandura, A., Ewart, C. K., Miller, N. H., & DeBusk, R. F. (1985). Exercise testing to enhance wives' confidence in their husbands' cardiac capabilities soon after clinically uncomplicated acute myocardial infarction. *American Journal of Cardiology, 55*, 635-638.

Turk, D., Meichenbaum, D., & Genest, M. (1983). *Cognitive therapy of pain*. New York: Guilford.

Watkins, L. R., & Mayer, D. J. (1982). Organization of endogenous opiate and nonopiate pain control systems. *Science, 216*, 1185-1192.

Wiedenfeld, S. A., O'Leary, A., Bandura, A., Brown, S., Levine, S., & Raska, K. (1990). Impact of perceived self-efficacy in coping with stressors on components of the immune system. *Journal of Personality and Social Psychology, 59*, 1082-1094.

Williams, S. L., Kinney, P. J., & Falbo, J. (1989). Generalization of therapeutic changes in agoraphobia: The role of perceived self-efficacy. *Journal of Consulting and Clinical Psychology, 57*, 436-442.

Wilson, G. T., Rossiter, E., Kleifield, E. I., & Lindholm, L. (1986). Cognitive-behavioral treatment of bulimia nervosa: A controlled evaluation. *Behavior Research and Therapy, 24*, 277-288.

Winett, R. A., King, A. C., & Altman, D. G. (1989). *Health psychology and public health: An integrative approach*. Elmsford, NY: Pergamon.

AUTHOR INDEX

SUBJECT INDEX